Different Views

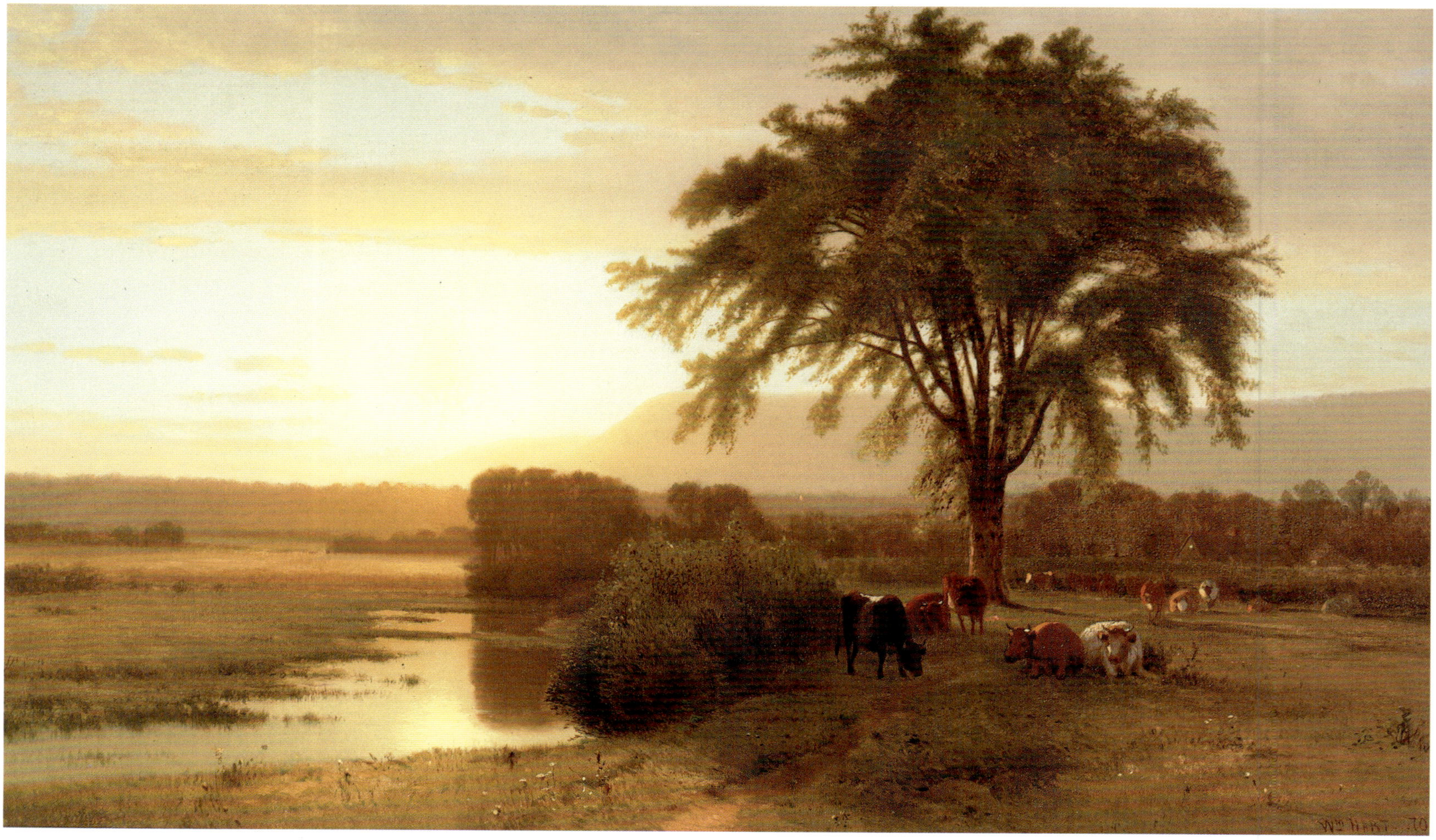
Wm HART 70

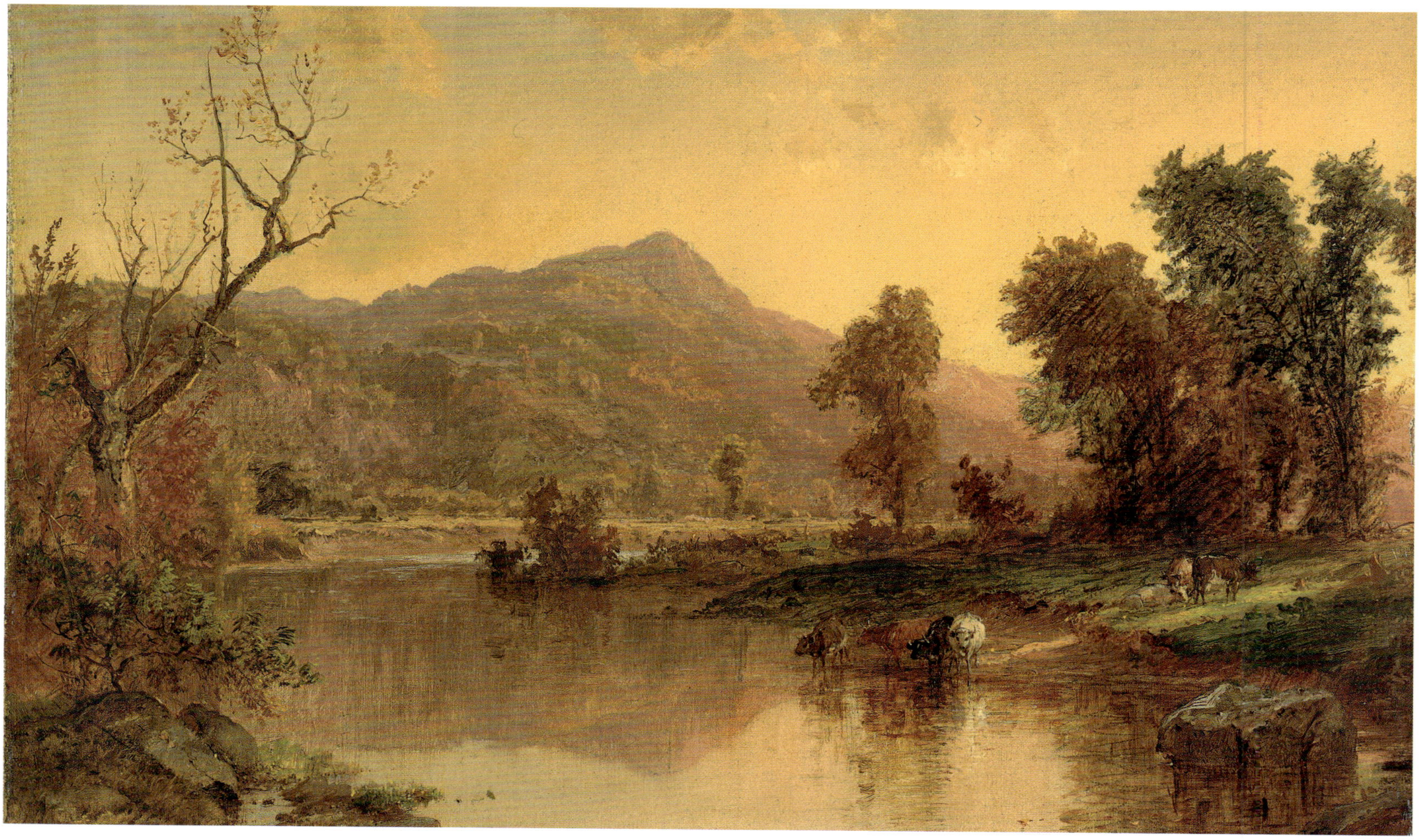

Different Views
in Hudson River School Painting

Judith Hansen O'Toole

Columbia University Press — New York
in association with
Westmoreland Museum of American Art

Columbia University Press
Publishers Since 1893
New York Chichester, West Sussex

Published by Columbia University Press
61 West 62nd Street
New York, NY 10023

in association with

Westmoreland Museum of American Art
221 N. Main Street
Greensburg, PA 15601
www.wmuseumaa.org

Produced by Chameleon Books
31 Smith Road, Chesterfield, MA 01012

Production Director/Designer: Arnold Skolnick
Production Assistant: KC Scott
Copy Editor: Jamie Nan Thaman

Library of Congress Cataloging-in-Publication Data

O'Toole, Judith H.
Different views in Hudson River School painting / Judith Hanson O'Toole.
p. cm.
Includes bibliographical references.
ISBN 978-0-231-13820-8 (cloth : alk. paper)—ISBN 978-0-231-13821-5 (pbk. : alk. paper)—ISBN 978-0-231-51094-3 (e-book)
1. Hudson River school of landscape painting—Exhibitions. 2. Landscape painting, American—Hudson River Valley (N.Y. and N.J.)—19th century—Exhibitions. 3. Art, American—New York (State)—19th century—Exhibitions. I. Title.

ND1351.5.O77 2005

2006283081

Columbia University Press books are printed on
permanent and durable acid-free paper.
Printed in China

c 10 9 8 7 6 5 4 3 2
p 10 9 8 7 6 5 4 3 2

THE HEINZ ENDOWMENTS PROVIDED GENEROUS SUPPORT FOR THIS BOOK.

(frontispiece, details)

William McDougal Hart, *Sunset in the Valley*, 1870
Oil on canvas, 14 x 23 1/2 inches

Jasper Francis Cropsey, *On the Susquehanna*, 1877
Oil on canvas, 12 x 17 1/2 inches

Contents

Foreword

CELEBRATIONS COMMEMORATING THE BICENTENNIAL of the July 4, 1776, signing by John Hancock and Charles Thomson of the amended Declaration of Independence refocused a broader public attention on the nation's cultural achievements. Landscape painting—the first native style of painting in the United States—is among the achievements that have witnessed, during the past thirty years, an increasing appreciation among the community of scholars and the public alike. The names and careers of such important figures as Thomas Cole, Asher B. Durand, John F. Kensett, Sanford Gifford, and Frederic Church have become better known—almost as rediscoveries—and their works comprise the core of any consideration of the period. Indeed, one could hardly call complete a collection of American landscape paintings of the era without the inclusion of these figures, along with such other noteworthy exponents as Albert Bierstadt, Worthington Whittredge, Martin Johnson Heade, Jasper Cropsey, Alfred T. Bricher, Thomas Moran, and George Inness. Most collectors and collections, past and present, focus mainly on the works of these named worthies. And yet, as any glance at Henry Tuckerman's landmark *Book of the Artists: American Artist Life* (1867) or a quick review of the published exhibition records of the National Academy of Design will indicate, there were many more artists contributing in important ways to the fabric of our visual culture. Yet it remains virtually impossible to find a collection that explores the broad visual culture of American landscape painting in the middle years of the nineteenth century.

The exception is a unique and diverse private collection, assembled by one brilliant and knowledgeable person over the past fifty years and composed of more than three hundred landscape paintings of the Hudson River School style. No other similar collection combining both masterworks and exemplary paintings so thoroughly and comprehensively explores the moment and history of American visual culture of the Hudson River School era. Given its scope and quality, it is a treasure trove that recommends itself as a national treasure.

In 1978, William Hull, then director of the Museum of Art at the Pennsylvania State University (now the Palmer Museum), suggested that the museum do an exhibition drawn entirely from this private collection. The collector stipulated only one important condition: that he be allowed to remain anonymous. That agreed to, I was privileged to curate the show; I selected forty or so artists for inclusion and wrote the accompanying catalogue, entitled *All That Is Glorious Around Us.* The catalogue surveyed the Hudson River School landscape movement and contained brief biographical statements about each of the artists, many of whom had barely been written about by modern scholars. Even though the catalogue soon went out of print, it seemed to have a life of its own. Eighteen years later, Judith Hansen O'Toole—the director of the Westmoreland Museum of American Art, who had also worked on the first exhibition—suggested a reprise of the catalogue, this time in book form to be published by Cornell University Press, as well as an expansion of the original exhibition to include subsequent acquisitions in the collection. This idea met with universal enthusiasm and the updated exhibition, this time with more than sixty artists and originally scheduled for four venues, circulated to fourteen museums across the nation. While this exhibition was a great success, O'Toole perspicaciously realized that the collection had much more to offer and began speaking with the collector about other ways to probe more deeply the rich resource that the collection represented. From those discussions emerged new insights, and O'Toole has sensitively selected the current exhibition and elucidated a range of comparisons and contrasts that enhance understanding of the achievements of thought and art implicit in Hudson River School landscape paintings.

The collection's vast array of representative paintings tantalize and suggest associations of mind and eye between the paintings and the artists who created them, between ideas and concepts that might not otherwise surface from a smaller selection of pictures, between images and themes that are ever renewed in the experience of generations of scholars and viewers. O'Toole surveyed the collection's available works for specific pairs, or works that might be seen in pairs, series, or groups of thematically related images. By doing so, she introduces viewers in clear and sometimes provocative ways to elements of time, weather, and season, and to a variety of other points of view central to the artists' thinking, beliefs, and experiences. The era explored in this exhibition, roughly 1825 to 1875, was the prescient moment when American landscape painting was most thoroughly explored and formalized with personal, artistic, cultural, and national identifications. It was the time when the scope of the continent was fully embraced by a populace enraptured with manifest destiny; when the crisis of our civil war lacerated the nation with wounds yet to fully heal; when government, business, and industry began forging their tenuous and still unresolved relationship with nature; and when individual citizens defined their own visions of "the land," just as we still do today. It was the era when the European concept of the Founding Fathers went through a metamorphosis to create the body of culture now conceived of as "American." It was the era when the aspiration and assertion of independence became the sure fact and manifestation of independence. The development of the American landscape tradition, so well represented in this collection and so cogently presented here, transcended place and embraced the fundamental and sometimes contradictory meanings our forebears experienced and memorialized in both the culture they defined and the visual images they employed. In O'Toole's exhibition and thoughtful text, we gain a special insight into the complexities inherent in the era and imagery of our first native style of art.

John Driscoll
New York, 2005

I have known [North Conway and Intervale] so long, and so intimately, that every corner and every stretch of view is dear to me, and I am proud to consider myself a native and part owner of the whole. A large slice of my life has been spent there, and I shall always do battle in its praise.

—Benjamin Champney
Sixty Year's of Memories of Art and Artists, 1899

Introduction

CHAMPNEY'S WORDS ATTEST TO THE PREDILECTION on the part of Hudson River School artists to observe repeatedly over time specific landscape subjects that were particularly dear to them. Often painting the same views on multiple occasions throughout a lifetime, the Hudson River School artists rarely tired of this practice because their subjects were never actually identical. Changed by seasons, weather, time of day, passages of light and dark, and seemingly infinite variations of the above, the land always revealed a refreshed surface from which to derive inspiration.

The idea for this exhibition and book began through casual discussions with a private collector who had amassed, over nearly half a century, one of the most comprehensive and extensive collections of paintings by artists of the Hudson River School. Beginning in the late 1950s and continuing through to today, he has brought together over three hundred paintings, parting with only three or four since the beginning. The breadth and depth of the artists and works represented here are unique among collections of the Hudson River School. The initial selection process was driven by the collector's sheer passion and great appetite for the works of these artists, fueled by the large selection available at that time in galleries and auction houses due to the then prevalent lack of recognition of their significance and therefore lack of competition in pursuing them. Choices were made based on the highest quality available and an interest in certain artists, including Casilear, Cropsey, Kensett, and their students. Today, choices are often limited by scarcity, price, and a comparison to what is already represented in the collection.

Visits to the collection generally began with a tour of new acquisitions, which quickly evolved into an animated review of the entire group of works, because the new paintings always led back to themes and artists already represented. Discussions touched on the name of the artist and some small amount of biographical information, but were primarily passionate observations about the capacity of each artist to render skillfully and subtly a combination of such natural effects as light, weather, time of day, and season on the three basic elements of landscape painting—land, water, and sky.

When pondering why this collector, who has always chosen to remain anonymous, collected this particular school of landscape painters so singularly, a visitor once posited that it was because he was seeking the perfect representation of these three elements. But the response is that no one such single, perfect, and entirely representative example existed. Thus, the quest was endless, since nature itself is so variable and multifaceted. Accordingly, the raison d'etre of the collection became to assemble as great a variety of outstanding and diverse representations as possible. The idea was to bring together paintings that captured the natural effects expressed through the vast landscape of America, thereby recalling the underlying spiritual, philosophical, and nationalistic significance of the land, which was fundamental to and universally understood by this group of nineteenth-century artists. It is, therefore, in recognition of the diversity of landscape subject matter rather than the similarity of it that the collection reveals its most authentic connection to the artists themselves. They were absorbed in the constant observation of the same three elements of land, water, and sky, spending lifetimes engaged in transcribing on canvas fleeting effects, both natural and man-made. Such effects varied from the dramatic to the subtle and contained everything in between.

A principal purpose of this study, just like the practice of collecting and assessing art, consists of allowing viewers to sharpen their skills of observation and participate in the visual process of comparing and contrasting paintings. By comparing and contrasting works, we can evaluate an individual artist's oeuvre or that of an entire movement. In building a collection, the collection as a whole must also be taken into consideration. What would this new addition bring to the collection? Will it help illuminate, define, complement, or further develop other pieces? Is there a similar example? a better one? Eventually every painting in the collection has been held up against others, both those that entered the collection and those that failed—for one reason or another—to do so. In this way, the paintings themselves become more distinct for their individual qualities, and the viewer—whether the collector or a visitor—hones his or her powers of observation and becomes, like the artist, keenly attuned to themes and variations.

Some of the pairs and contrasts depicted in this catalogue and exhibition were intended by the artist; others were arranged by the collector and this author in collaboration. Readers may want to make their own associations and groupings: we encourage them to do so. In fact, at one point, we had even considered designing small cards, like playing cards, with images of the paintings on the front to facilitate their movement into new couplings and groups to encourage observation on the part of our readers.

Readers will further note that we have purposely not provided much biographical or art-historical analysis of the artists represented here. Those discussions are plentiful in numerous books and studies on the school,[1] particularly in a previous exhibition and book on this collection, *All That Is Glorious Around Us*, by John Driscoll.[2] Rather, we have concentrated, as has the collector, on the visual offerings of the paintings themselves in order to enhance appreciation of them as both pictorial reflections of the natural world and vehicles for communicating timeless messages that relate to nature, including preservation of the environment; spirituality; cycles of life, death, and rebirth; and man's eternal search for meaning on earth.

Benjamin Champney (1817–1907)
Bathers at Saco River Near North Conway, NH, Summer, 1890
Oil on board, 6 x 13½ inches

Autumn View of the Intervale, Mt. Chocorua & Moat Mountain, White Mountains, 1859
Oil on canvas, 5½ x 9 ¼ inches

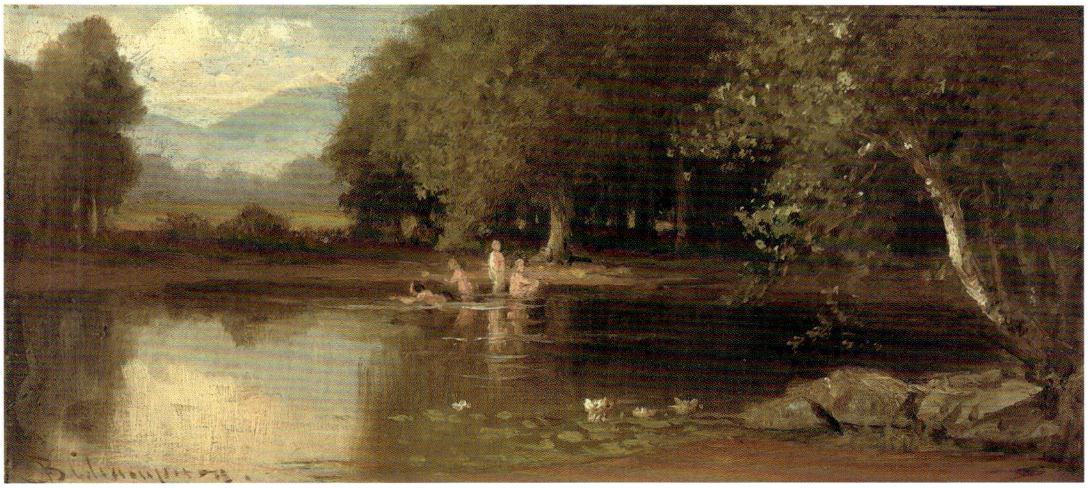

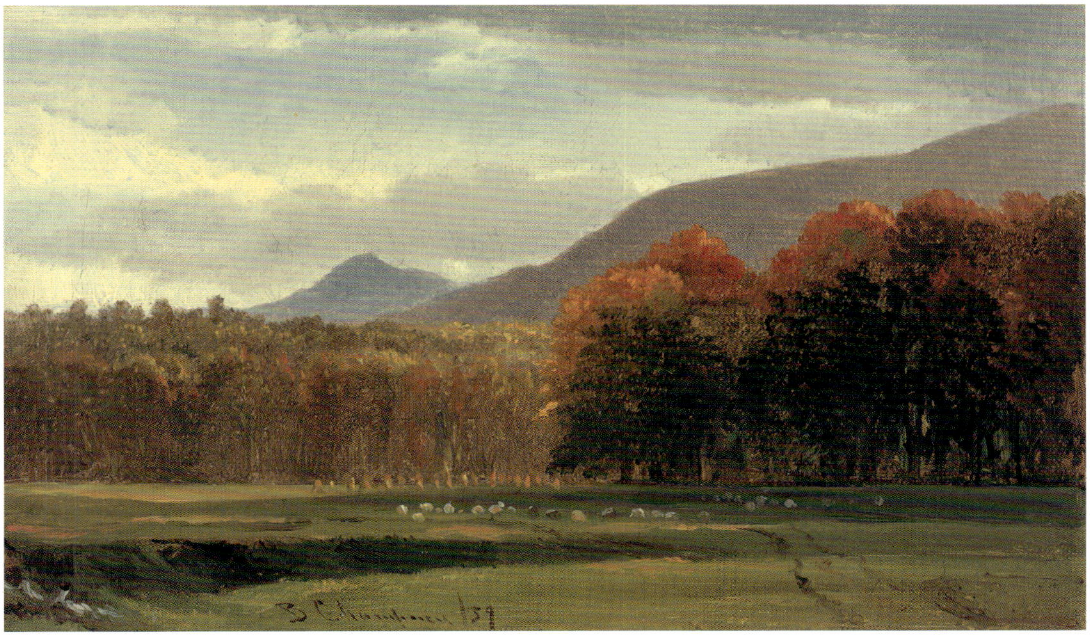

American Scenery: Themes, Symbols and Pairings in Hudson River School Painting

Poetry and Painting sublime [sic] and purify thought, by grasping the past, the present, and the future—they give the mind a foretaste of its immortality, and thus prepare it for performing an exalted part amid the realities of life. And rural nature is full of the same quickening spirit—it is, in fact, the exhaustless mine from which the poet and the painter have brought such wondrous treasures—an unfailing fountain of intellectual enjoyment, where all may drink, and be awakened to a deeper feeling of the roots of genius, and a keener perception of the beauty of our existence.

—Thomas Cole, *Essay on American Scenery*, 1836

THIS EXHIBITION OF HUDSON RIVER SCHOOL ARTISTS focuses on their frequent creation of and reliance on pairs and series of paintings to express central or recurrent themes of great significance to the movement. The underlying purpose of grouping paintings this way is to enable contemporary viewers to appreciate more readily the nineteenth-century artist's ideas and objectives through active engagement in the comparisons and contrasts delineated in these pairings. Our work is intended to reveal to a modern audience the underlying artistic theories, philosophies, and practices of a majority of Hudson River School painters.

The ideas developed in this essay emerged from close observation of the paintings themselves; study of the writings of Hudson River School artists; contemporaneous commentary by critics, patrons, and others in the nineteenth century; and insights from the published works of modern art historians. These aside, this is the first study to concentrate on illuminating the particular practice of Hudson River School artists to create pairs, series, and groups of paintings that are thematically related. Because this was a common practice in the mid-nineteenth century, it is surprising that it has not been recognized in any previous exhibition or book on Hudson River School painting

The concept of examining multiple picture groupings is further encouraged by exploring the methods by which collectors, both in the nineteenth century and today, assembled their collections—a process that relies on the practice of comparison and contrast as each new piece is considered for its role as an individual work of art and within the context of a group. In this particular instance, we have the advantage of examining paintings from one collection with a singular focus on painters of the Hudson River School, artists who had a fundamental interest in and dedication to investigating the comparisons inherent in nature.[1]

Writers including Barbara Novak, Elwood C. Perry III, and Franklin Kelly[2] have noted the persistence of pairs, series, and related groups of paintings among certain artists of the Hudson River School, most notably Thomas Cole (1801–1848). They have also documented the communal iconographical language underlying the paintings of Hudson River School artists—a common symbolism that provided both an intellectual and an aesthetic foundation for creating pairs.[3]

Franklin Kelly was the first to write an article devoted solely to describing the phenomenon of paired paintings by Hudson River School artists, and to suggest the extent to which this practice penetrated the school despite the rarity of extant documentation.[4] The father of Hudson River School painting, Thomas Cole often worked in pairs and series, as will be discussed in more detail later. Kelly noted that Cole's influence in creating paired paintings and using allegory through landscapes was "most palpable in the years immediately following his untimely death in 1848," but that it persisted through the last generation of painters, who "increasingly attempted to achieve allegorical meanings solely with landscape elements."[5] Moreover, Kelly postulated that many more pairs by artists of the school are probably now lost, due to original pairs being exhibited and sold separately. It is also likely that the passage of time caused various pairs and groups of paintings to be broken up through sale, division of inheritance, or loss.[6]

It seems likely that Thomas Cole saw and studied paired paintings by Thomas Doughty (1793–1856)—one of the earliest American painters dedicated to landscape painting—between 1818 and 1825, when Cole visited the annual exhibitions of the Pennsylvania Academy of the Fine Arts as a young man, just beginning his artistic career.[7] In time, Cole, Jasper Francis Cropsey, Sanford Robinson Gifford, Asher B. Durand, Frederic Edwin Church, Albert Bierstadt, John Frederic Kensett, and John William Casilear were among those who produced paintings intended as pairs. Later, artists including William Mason Brown, Regis Gignoux, Clinton Loveridge, Alvin Fisher, Homer Dodge Martin, D. C. Grose, Joseph Antonio Hekking, William Sonntag, William and James Hart, Benjamin Champney, and Alfred Bricher, continued to work in this manner. Many other artists of the school painted discrete pairs—that is, related paintings intended to be placed and seen together. Themes treated as pairs by these artists included times of day, seasons, different weather conditions and atmosphere, contrasting types of terrain, and various stages of man's intrusion on the wilderness. Interestingly, this practice of painting related series extended to still-life painters of the period, such as Severin Roesen; genre painters, including David Gilmore Blythe; and history painters, such as Thomas Rossiter and Peter Frederick Rothermel.[8]

The individual paintings constituting pairs and series can be viewed as intimately dependent on one another. Complete narratives, themes, and concepts might be told in sequence, as in chapters of a novel. The subjects may have all been conceived within a short period of time or could refer to earlier works as responses, reaffirmations, or reinterpretations. When conditions beyond the artist's or collector's control separated paintings created in such a manner, the subject of their exposition was completely lost. What has virtually escaped modern critical attention is that widespread production of paired paintings by artists of the Hudson River School indicated a response by these artists not only to their own impulses but also to public demand. Paired paintings became very popular and were much sought after, which helps explain why so many individual artists painted pairs on more than one occasion.

The Hudson River School—considered the first truly American or native school of painting—flourished between 1825 and 1875,[9] a time of great nationalist sentiment related to the bountiful natural resources of the New World, when expansionism was rife in American thought and policy. Founded by Thomas Cole, who emigrated from England to a fresh new America in 1818, the movement declined during the last decades of the nineteenth century when artists and their patrons became enamored of different aesthetic ideas and styles imported from Europe. Artists in America had witnessed, in these same five decades, the tumultuous results of growing pains within their young country. Among these were the tremendous addition of territory through expansion; the near dissolution of the country during the Civil War; and the subsequent revitalization through industrialization, which positioned the nation to become a leading world power in the next century.

The following arrangements of works by Hudson River School painters include actual pairs of paintings intended as such by the artist, demonstrating the popularity of this method of working among the Hudson River School painters. Also included are comparisons of individual works not conceived of as part of a pair by the artist, as well as groupings by multiple artists brought together by the author to illustrate two principles: (1) that the artists painted landscapes under different conditions in order to reveal communal, recurrent themes within the school; and (2) that the language of landscape kept three generations of painters eagerly returning to the same subjects. These groupings draw central focus and rationale from the fact that Hudson River School artists, despite individual differences in style, shared certain aesthetic and philosophical principles uniting them as a school. Primary among these unifying concepts was a belief in natural religion; the magnificence of nature; and, specifically, the significance of the fresh, untamed American scenery reflecting our national character, as opposed to the civilized European landscape.[10]

An ongoing dialogue relating to these principles is evident in the paintings, which have been arranged in groups and pairs to encourage viewers to observe the same themes as the artists and to compare and contrast different artists' interpretations.

By virtue of the fact that three generations of Hudson River School artists persisted in painting landscapes, often in the same physical location and observing the same landmarks, they were constantly engaged in making comparisons and contrasts. These artists had a seemingly unlimited appetite for direct examination of the landscape around them, fed by a belief in both the beauty and the spirituality of nature, and the desire to capture it on canvas in all its myriad effects. They were inspired by an awareness that in nature, things change continually, and that therefore nothing is ever stationary. Observing their subjects under nearly endless variables related to time of day, season, weather conditions, and lighting, they worked to capture on individual canvases the visual effects of these continual changes.

It follows that their interest in achieving fidelity to nature almost demanded the making of pairs and series to create opportunities to realize nature's specific, individual features and their vast capacity to change under different conditions. Not that they were slavishly devoted to mere transcription of nature; indeed, while close observation of nature was indispensable, so too was artistic license to alter nature judiciously in order to render it more expressive. Cole discussed the necessity of allocating time after a sketching trip out-of-doors for a "veil to be drawn over the common details, the unessential parts, which shall leave the great features, whether the beautiful or sublime, dominant in the mind."[11] Accordingly, the artist functions ideally as a conduit through which natural images are transformed into something transcending simple transcription in order to impart an idea or emotion. Cole rejected being a mere "leaf painter," by which he meant simply a transcriber of literal facts. Rather, he strove to edify—to impart a philosophical or spiritual concept or principle.

Several European theorists generally agreed with these notions, including the English writer and landscapist William Gilpin (1724–1804). Gilpin expounded on the infinite variables in nature created by different conditions of light and shade, urging artists to study these firsthand. He also recognized that nature was sometimes imperfect, requiring the painter's assistance to improve on it when needed.[12] These "necessary improvements" were permitted, even encouraged, not only for the purposes of conveying or even improving the picturesque elements inherent in a scene, but to enable the illustration of other underlying ideas and principles. In 1792, Gilpin wrote the influential book *Three Essays: On Picturesque Beauty; on Picturesque Travel; and on Sketching Landscape*, which clearly delineated how to achieve these objectives and included many illustrated examples. Two years later, Uvedale Price (1747–1829) published his *Essay on the Picturesque*, further intensifying the discussion. Price placed the picturesque as an equally important and worthy category, somewhere between the sublime and the beautiful. He urged that the artist not be satisfied with generalities alone, as Gilpin's work seemed to imply, but include as many of the multiple layers and specific details of nature as possible.

It was in America, however, that artists fully exploited the use of pairings and groupings of paintings to enhance the language of landscape by comparing emotive responses between several views. By changing the conditions of light, weather, season, or other natural phenomena, strong emotions such as angst or dread evoked in one painting could be compared in a companion piece with gentler sensations, including harmony and tranquillity. In this manner, the artist's absorption with the language of nature to create mood and communicate underlying themes—including the sublime versus the beautiful versus the picturesque; man's intrusion in or harmony with the land; the overarching power of a higher, universal spirit; and the cyclical rhythms and phases of life—became a consuming preoccupation. Thus, landscape developed into a vehicle for expressing philosophical concepts, thereby elevating itself to an art form deserving respect in its own right. The American poet William Cullen Bryant (1794–1878)—close friend and associate of Thomas Cole—and the English poet William Wordsworth (1770–1850) both found in nature an endless resource that not only demanded direct, personal confrontation but also richly rewarded such study with vital truths as well as philosophical insights. Nature had much to teach us if we would only pay attention. Man needed not just to observe and heed nature's sublime manifestations but to attend to its still, small voice, which could reveal equally profound principles. Like Cole, Wordsworth urged time to elapse after direct experiences in nature to draw important lessons, defining poetry in the preface to his second edition of *Lyrical Ballads* (1800) as emotion recollected in tranquillity. Ralph Waldo Emerson (1803–1882), the father of transcendentalism in America, also urged in his essay *Nature* (1836) devotion to and immersion in nature to achieve spiritual regeneration and union with God.

* * *

OF RELEVANCE to this study are comparisons and contrasts based on many differences between European and American landscape. These differences contained profound philosophical implications that became a continuing preoccupation for the Hudson River School. European visitors, including the French writer Jean de Crèvecoeur (1735–1813), were often the first to expound on the expansive countryside and seemingly limitless frontiers of the New World compared to scenery from the Old World.[13] Crèvecoeur's *Letters from an American Farmer*, published in London in 1782, were of such interest to Europeans that they were published the following year in Paris. Crèvecoeur's countryman Viscount Francois Rene de Chateaubriand (1768–1848) also traveled widely through America in the latter part of the eighteenth century and wrote about his experiences. Living among the Native Americans in the Great Lakes region, Chateaubriand observed that the pure wilderness of America inspired direct communication with God, interpreting nature as God's physical representation to man. Accordingly, the more virgin the natural state, the closer it approached God's original creation.

Meanwhile, Europe bore the marks of centuries of civilization dotted—even littered, as some have suggested—throughout the countryside, primarily in the form of ruins, leaving few areas free from the imprint of man's presence and habitation. European landscapes had many appealing natural characteristics in the sharply pointed peaks of its mountains and the softly diffused light of its plains. The poignancy of its aging castles, aqueducts, peristyle temples, and other architectural remains alluded not only to the presence of man but also to the rise and fall of nations; natural cycles of birth and death; and, indeed, the cyclical, changing qualities of all things.

In comparison, the wild, untamed American landscapes presented to the first European immigrants appeared primal, fresh, and even intimidating to the eyes of white men. These vistas were seemingly untouched by the Native Americans who had peopled the country. The virginity of the forests and plains, gauged by how little they had been marked by man's presence, was to European settlers symbolic of America's youth, thereby evoking in physical terms their hope for a New World abundant with opportunity, far better than the one they had left behind. Yet the rounded mountaintops of our eastern ranges were criticized for their lack of drama compared to the Alps, which had set the European standard; and to some first-generation artists and naturalists, our lakes and rivers appeared less picturesque than the Rhine.[14] Early writers lamented the lack of splendor in our topography and could make no sense of the undomesticated tangle of our wilderness.

Eventually, artists and the general public alike came to regard the wildness of the American landscape as a symbol of the independence of the American spirit. They celebrated the fact that whereas Europe was marred by the successes and failures of man, America offered purity and freshness consecrated by God's beneficence—a new Eden, as it were. As Nathaniel Parker Willis wrote in his *American Scenery:* "It strikes the European traveler, at the first burst of America on his eye, that the New World of Columbus is also a new world from the hand of the Creator. In comparison with the old countries of Europe, the vegetation is so wondrously lavish, the outlines and minor features struck out with so bold a freshness, and the lakes and rivers so even in their fulness (sic) and flow, yet so vast and powerful, that he may well imagine it an Eden newly sprung from the ocean."[15]

Nearly all the Hudson River School artists under discussion here traveled to Europe for study and edification; however, by the second generation, few went there in search of subject matter. Instead, they were traversing the American continent and painting primarily American scenes. In the second of his "Letters on Landscape Painting," Asher B. Durand—acknowledged heir to Cole as leader of the school—urged young painters to "Go not abroad then in search of material for the exercise of your pencil, while the virgin charms of our native land have claims on your deepest affections."[16]

The contrast between civilized landscapes and wilderness penetrated to the heart of the developing American spirit, affecting those who came to live in the new land with conflicting reactions: the desire to preserve its untouched beauty and a simultaneous impulse to tame and conquer it.[17] These opposing views of the American landscape—preservation versus manifest destiny—were to evolve and mature through three generations of Hudson River School artists, just as they did generally in American values and debates throughout the nineteenth century. Beginning with the school's English-born founder, Thomas Cole, who imposed civilization and allegory onto his landscapes, and continuing through the final generation of Hudson River School artists, who, just before the end of the nineteenth century, worked to preserve in paint what was disappearing quickly in nature, this dichotomy and ambiguity were deeply felt and expressed. Cole himself at once celebrated the purity of the unmarked American landscape while envisioning with rapture the imposing structures that would soon be built there.[18] He wrote, "Where the wolf roams, the plough shall glisten; on the gray crag shall rise temple and tower—mighty deeds shall be done in the now pathless wilderness; and poets yet unborn shall sanctify the soil."[19]

* * *

THOMAS COLE, clearly a key figure in this discussion, exerted a tremendous influence both during his lifetime and for several decades following his death in 1848. Cole's commitment to communicating ideas through his art, to creating pairs and series, and to using landscape subjects as "backdrops" for his literary themes set the stage for the Hudson River School artists who followed him.[20]

Having come to the United States with his parents on July 3, 1818, Cole lived in Pennsylvania, working in Philadelphia as an engraver's assistant, and then moved to Ohio. Sketchbook in hand, he walked across the state of Pennsylvania, from Philadelphia through Pittsburgh, to join his parents in Steubenville, Ohio. Nevertheless, he returned to Europe twice, from 1829 to 1832 and later from 1841 to 1842, traveling extensively in England, France, and Italy. He made his permanent home—named Cedar Grove, near Catskill, New York—at the base of the mountain range of the same name, which runs along the broad Hudson River valley.[21]

The Oxbow (1836)—his famous painting of the Connecticut River near Northampton, Massachusetts—shows in one canvas the contrast between civilization and wilderness, as well as the tension between man and nature in the style and tradition of "the sublime."[22] In the right half of the composition, the peaceful Connecticut River valley is depicted as a rich, agricultural landscape dotted with villages and farms. Bathed in the soft, benign light of the midday sun, the scene is one of bucolic domesticity. The left half is dominated by raw, dense mountainous terrain, undomesticated and menacing in its tangle of wilderness, over which dark and fast-moving storm clouds threaten the peace and harmony of the valley, still untouched by the storm. The tension between man's efforts to tame and cultivate nature and nature's resistance and power to eradicate such efforts is the subject of Cole's canvas. The passing storm holds both the threat of devastation and the promise of clearing, representing a cycle in nature that Cole implicitly compares to the human cycle of life and death or the rise and fall of civilizations.

Cole's interest in and application of allegory through which to convey moral and religious lessons lent themselves to expedition through pairs and series of paintings, which he created frequently throughout his career. His complicated programs often assumed epic proportions, requiring more than one canvas for their denouement. Cole's first-known ambitious pair of paintings, *The Garden of Eden* (1827–1828) and *The Expulsion from the Garden of Eden* (1828),[23] shows imaginary virgin landscapes under different weather conditions and at different times of day. Illuminated by the suffused light of morning, the first painting depicts an expansive landscape, lush with exotic flora and fauna. In a clearing, some deer appear across from Adam and Eve, as if greeting them. The prominent use of deer in this representation from the Old Testament is important, since for Cole and subsequent artists of the Hudson River School, deer represented solitude, innocence, wildness, and other unfettered aspects of the American wilderness as it existed in its pure state before European intrusion. Like nature itself, deer were both beautiful and vulnerable, especially to the incursion of man, his axe, and his gun.[24] In this painting, deer also seem to embody the idyllic innocence and purity of biblical Eden, the name and characteristics of which were, both before and after Cole's generation, applied to America.[25] In the second canvas, the ragged terrain, fierce weather conditions, and darkness of nightfall underscore the drama of the expulsion and provoke emotional responses in the viewer associated with a hostile, evil world.

Two other paintings by Cole were dubbed an "unofficial pair" by Ellwood C. Parry III, by which he meant two paintings having the same dimensions and connected in subject matter but conceived by the artist to stand alone.[26] *View of Schroon Mountain* and *Dream of Arcadia*, both measuring 39 1/2 x 63 inches and dating from 1838, were exhibited together at the National Academy of Design in that same year. The first canvas shows a specific place in the New World (Schroon Mountain in the Adirondacks of New York State)—a wilderness without any indication of man's intrusion, be it his physical presence, that of any structure, or any other human imprint on the land. Its pair reveals a fantasy landscape representative of the Old World, with an ancient temple set in a dramatic yet tamed countryside, peopled with children and adults enjoying nature. Reference to fundamental contrasts and distinctions between American and European landscapes is clear. The first painting represents a carefully observed, actual place in nature, precise in time and locale, rather than an imagined reconstruction of an ancient civilization (*Dream of Arcadia*). Another important distinction is the two different points along the continuum of time that are represented: the European scene refers to the past and lessons learned, whereas the American subject, in its untouched wilderness state, represents opportunity and aspirations for the future.

The many paintings conceived in serial form by Thomas Cole (*The Course of Empire, The Voyage of Life, Departure and Return, Past and Present, The Cross and the World*)[27] demonstrate that Cole set a precedent for subsequent Hudson River School painters to follow and to exploit in the use of multiple paintings or images—both "official" and "unofficial"—with which to develop and convey their themes. These series also became generally well known to the public through prints made after them, such as James Smilie's engraving of *The Voyage of Life* commissioned in 1849 by the American Art-Union. These and others like them introduced Cole's paintings to large numbers of people and further popularized the notion of painting in series.

The Hudson River School artists who followed Cole were generally subtler in their use of pairings and groupings, just as they were less overt in their efforts to edify by communicating high moral and religious principles through their paintings. Rather than relying on the human story, these artists employed the iconography[28] of trees, rocks, light, weather, and time of day to convey underlying philosophical and religious ideas that they shared about man and nature. Whereas Cole used landscape to reinforce his philosophical visions and religious themes, in the hands of later artists—such as Durand, Kensett, Casilear, and Gifford—landscape itself became the emblem.

* * *

THE HISTORICAL roots of painting pairs and series are enormously complex and far ranging, yet they deserve some mention here since there were strong antecedents to this practice among Hudson River School artists. In particular, the work of two seventeenth-century European landscape painters who worked in pairs and series, Nicholas Poussin and Claude Lorrain, interested and inspired artists of the Hudson River School.

Nicholas Poussin (1594–1665) and Claude Lorrain (1600–1682) were the two leaders of the French Baroque era whose work became the model for and foundation of modern landscape painting. Previous to their work, landscapes were primarily used only to provide the setting for religious, mythological, and historical subject matter in art—themes highly revered because of their apparently singular ability to communicate noble moral and ethical messages through their imagery. Landscape by itself was considered devoid of intellectual content and therefore unacceptable as the sole subject for a work of art.

Both Poussin and Claude, as Claude Lorrain was known, eventually became interested in landscape painting for its own sake—that is, they began to imbue individual components of nature, such as earth, trees, water, and sky, with allegorical and theological meanings intended to be conveyed to the viewer for the purpose of edification.[29] Poussin's paintings of Arcadian subjects made famous the theme of people benevolently reposing in nature. Although the term "arcadian landscape" has come to connote a pastoral simplicity and harmony, even a paradise or utopia, it was not always so. The classical Arcadia was a region in which gods and men both frolicked and battled. It was a land often fraught with danger, albeit frequently hidden from sight, exposing the duality of the world of gods and men and the potential for changeable, unpredictable nature to show a tempestuous, malevolent side as well as a benign, assuring one.

Poussin and Claude both created purposeful pairs and series of paintings. These pairs were explicitly used to illustrate such fundamental dualities as good versus evil or the temporal versus the spiritual. Also depicted were natural cycles, such as the changing seasons or different times of day, especially the sun's rising and setting. An example is Poussin's pair of paintings *Stormy Landscape* and *Calm Landscape*, two scenes that together contrast earthly dangers with its pleasures. Poussin also did a series entitled Four Seasons, a subject long established as symbolic of the ages of man, the inevitable passage of time, the transience of life, and the cyclical nature of worldly things.

Claude created many pairs and series (up to four paintings in one set) but never a formal series of the four seasons.

His groupings were extremely subtle in their use of symbolism, existing more purely as landscape paintings that emerged from Claude's protracted, intensive study of light and its effects on land and water. For example, H. Diane Russel notes: "In creating pairs of paintings representing different hours, especially pendants with strongly contrasting morning and evening light, and with the sun explicitly present in at least one of the works, Claude emphasized the linear passage of time. Cyclical time is suggested as well, owing to the viewer's knowledge that the sun will rise and set again, and that this rhythm is continuous."[30] Russel's allusions to the viewer's understanding and further extrapolation of the painter's message are important in assuming that a dialogue between artist and audience could be prompted by landscape elements seen under different light conditions. For the viewer, there was much comfort in this reassurance of nature's continuum, just as belief in life after death gives comfort to the faithful. Interestingly, another pair of paintings by Lorrain couples a landscape with a seascape, thereby creating what Russel referred to as a "complete world in itself."[31]

* * *

HAVING DESCRIBED some historical precedents for interest in pairs and series among Hudson River School painters, we turn to a discussion of intellectual and aesthetic antecedents of these artists as well as contemporaneous investigations by nineteenth-century landscape painters into the development of a visual language with which to transcribe nature. In Germany in particular, but also in France, Italy, and England, writers and painters were exploring landscape as a vehicle through which to communicate universal truths. Previously considered subordinate and unworthy of serious attention by itself, landscape was now being elevated to a much higher status. Philipp Otto Runge (1777–1810), a German painter, was one of the first to postulate that landscape paintings could serve to illustrate ideas and provide insights into understanding the divine. This meant that there needed to be a shared iconography of natural symbols with which to organize thoughts and ideas. Indeed, he developed such a language in his own paintings using flower and color symbols. Similarly, the English statesman Edmund Burke (1729–1797) wrote about the emotive powers of landscape to awaken opposing yet related human passions, such as pain and pleasure. His treatise *A Philosophical Inquiry into the Origins of Our Ideas of the Sublime and Beautiful*, published in 1756, established what became mutually agreed on attributes necessary to create sublime or beautiful elements in a landscape. Thus, all educated viewers could readily interpret a particular painting with respect to how well or poorly it fulfilled these criteria, thereby facilitating development of fixed, codified principles of taste. The price paid for the simplification of these ideas was, of course, a certain rigidity and inflexibility of thought, but it succeeded in widely disseminating to an appreciative public a method of seeing nature and judging paintings.

In his book on landscape painting, *Elements de Perspective Practique* (1799–1800), the French painter and theorist Pierre Henri de Valenciennes (1750–1819) emphasized the central role of studying light. He noted its changing effects on nature and, in particular, those that occurred throughout different times of day, from morning until night, affecting atmosphere, mood, and emotion. Valenciennes also attempted to pair subjects from classical mythology with what he believed to be times of day appropriate to their stories. This stopped short of enabling natural elements, including effects of light, to speak apart from man's activities—something landscape painters of the nineteenth century would address, especially American painters.

Claude Lorrain studied light and its effects more successfully than landscape painters who preceded him and explored effects and subtleties of daylight far beyond the limits of others.[32] He became a master of its evocation, known for his refined ability to render light effects identifiable with specific times of day, season, and climate. In fact, for this reason, his work inspired later artists, including such masters of light as J.M.W. Turner; Caspar David Friedrich; and a number of the Hudson River School artists, including Asher B. Durand, John Kensett, and John William Casilear.

As an element in landscape painting that required mastery, light passionately absorbed Hudson River School artists, up to and including the final "movement" of the school, named luminism for the painters' ability to depict serene, fleeting effects of sun and moonlight. Luminists used light and its effects to elevate the ordinary to the sublime. For them, light was the great revealer, comparable to a godlike force without which there would be little worth conveying in the visual or spiritual world. In fact, among Hudson River School painters, light often functioned as a manifestation of the divine. Cole's poetry is filled with allusions to light, especially sunlight, as representing the presence of the divine.[33] Asher B. Durand wrote that he had "more respect for the devout heathen who worships the sun as the visible Divinity, than for the artist whose pictures betray insensibility to the charm of sunlight."[34]

Light—and its effect on the natural world—is key to the conceptual comparison, contrast, and appreciation of paintings grouped together in pairs or series. Durand wrote of light, or sunshine, as "so changing and adorning all it rests upon as to seem itself creative." Later in the same letter he noted, "it [light] develops the full power of color, and evolves the interminable variety of light and shade which constitutes the magic of chiaroscuro—that controlling element of effect which theorists have in vain endeavored to portion and systemize."[35] Light is nearly always the feature that creates the most dramatic changes in weather, time of day, and season. It is also the painter's greatest and most eloquent device in the evocation of sensations such as emotion, mood, and atmosphere. The ability to render light reliably and persuasively severely tests a painter's skill and merit, separating those who could learn the technique of accurately rendering things in the natural world from those who could go beyond this important initial but incomplete phase to infuse their work with the intangible. Cole, Church, Casilear, Kensett, Cropsey, Bierstadt, the Harts, and Gifford were especially admired for their extraordinary ability to express qualities of light through oil paint. This entailed mastery of various subtleties, including the use of glazes.

Although many nineteenth-century landscape painters associated light with the divine and the mystical, other modes of natural symbolism, both religious and secular, were under investigation both in Europe and in the United States. In Germany, a stimulating interchange occurred among such theorists as Wilhelm Wackenroder (1773–1798), who believed that artists had divine inspiration, and Ludwig Tieck (1773–1853), who extended Wackenroder's theories to maintain that nature provided a view into the divine. Runge, mentioned earlier, created a complicated iconographical system by assigning nearly every individual flower and plant a specific symbolism. Friedrich Schelling (1775–1854), a transcendentalist poet, held that the true value of art lay in its ability to reveal the universal spirit through nature.[36]

A century after Claude and Poussin, and almost contemporary to the first generation of the Hudson River School, the great German painter and proponent of the Romantic landscape movement Caspar David Friedrich (1774–1840) created symbol-laden compositions overtly connecting landscape to spirituality. For example, Friedrich felt so strongly that the sky contained religious significance that he declined Goethe's invitation to paint specific cloud formations for a scientific study, feeling that this process would attempt to impose reason in a region that could not be defined or organized by the intellect. He also felt that light was "the divine foundation of visual imagery."[37]

Barbara Novak noted, "Friedrich is surely the single European landscapist whose sensibility most closely matches those of the Americans."[38] Like Cole, Friedrich defined the making of art as not only observing and rendering the natural world without, but, just as importantly, painting the world that lies within each person—that is, the world of both the intellect and the spirit. He wrote that the artist "should paint not only what he sees before him, but also what he sees within him. If, however, he sees nothing within him, then he should also refrain from painting that which he sees before him."[39]

Friedrich was also cognizant of the constantly changing character of the world and explicitly equated the inexorable turning of the seasons and the progressive times of day with the different stages of human life. His biographer wrote: "This idea stems from the desire to see man's birth and death as a cosmically regulated cyclical process on which to base the hope of a resurrection."[40] The steadfast rotation of nature's constantly evolving cycles—ever renewing, ever following one upon the other, day to night, spring to winter—brought comfort and assurance to man as he contemplated life, death, and his own hope for renewal and rebirth.

Like the Hudson River School painters, Friedrich was keenly aware of the myriad variations that the pictorial world of landscape presented to an artist. He spent his life exploring and developing as many of these as possible, observing nature under different conditions of light, weather, and season. He further converted the basic components of landscape into symbols that he arranged and rearranged in seemingly infinite variations in order to communicate important universal concerns. In his paintings, trees serve to traverse earthly and heavenly realms. Their foliage, in its young and old growth, represents life's force: fresh blooms of spring symbolize new life; withered branches or blasted trunks suggest mortality. Rocks symbolize faith; mountains, because they lead to the beyond, represent life after death; rivers harbor death, whereas their shores lead to paradise;

and so on.[41] These symbols enabled him to establish a language of nature through which he could communicate without the anecdotal presence of man.

Landscape painting became for Friedrich, and for other painters of this subject in the nineteenth century, a means of universal communication and thereby a unifying factor in an increasingly complicated, fragmented world. Whereas themes underlying historical, genre, and portrait painting could present particular political or religious points of view difficult for many viewers to appreciate, the ideas and emotions expressed through landscape imagery could be embraced by Everyman.

Friedrich was also one of the first European landscape painters to introduce into his paintings a lone observer, often with his back to the viewer. The presence of such an unidentified figure within the context of a landscape painting further asserts the communicative relationship between man and nature, establishing an understanding of universal dialogue between mortals and the immortal.

* * *

Artists of the Hudson River School had an abiding and deep passion for rendering one particular subject: landscape. Repeated examination of a single subject, as noted earlier, is itself a process of comparing and contrasting. A scholar wrote the following about artists who were preoccupied with one subject: "[W]hen creative artists observed, rethought, and observed again, and with utter devotion and intensity, small wonder that they should penetrate ever more deeply into the look and nature of those everyday objects and bring out hidden qualities, small wonder too that they should light upon unsuspected aspects in the things observed and win [aspire] to new inspirations."[42] Although Herwig Guratzsch was discussing still-life painting in these remarks, they apply as well to landscape.

A deep commitment to and fascination with landscape painting, together with similar aesthetic, religious, and political aspirations concerning nature, formed the rationale for designating these artists a "school," rather than their acceptance of a single prescribed style or method of painting. In fact, the latter varied even within the style of a single artist over time and among artists of the same generation; certainly styles had changed markedly by the time the final generation of Hudson River School painters emerged.

It is also true that members of the Hudson River School communicated closely with one another both formally and informally, solidifying their association as a school. Artists accompanied one another on excursions, where they sketched and painted together. They wrote to one another and shared their ideas with a larger community of writers, poets, critics, collectors, and even the general public. They often occupied close or adjoining studios, including the Tenth Street Studio in New York City, where they mixed freely—observing, discussing, comparing, and exhibiting one another's paintings.[43] They were familiar with and conversant in contemporary theories regarding the then popular aesthetic modes of expression, especially "the picturesque," "the beautiful," and "the sublime" in landscape painting.

Primary among the shared principles of Hudson River School artists was belief in natural religion—or, in short, the idea that celebrating and closely observing nature were spiritual acts akin to prayer, through which an individual could both acknowledge and commune with the power of a creator. These convictions went hand in hand with an appreciation of nature's beauty, tempered by a general willingness to alter nature on rare occasions to render it more picturesque.[44] Hudson River School artists had a virtually unlimited appetite for close observation of the landscape around them, an instinct fed by these unilaterally accepted principles of belief in both the magnificence and the spirituality of nature. They were inspired by their constant awareness of and sensitivity to the fact that in nature, things change continuously; that nothing remains stationary but is always in motion and evolution. Seasons, times of day, weather conditions, and various effects of light are just some features of nature observed and painted in order to create mood and depict underlying themes. Such themes include "the sublime" versus "the picturesque," man's intrusion on or harmony with the land, the overarching power of a higher and universal spirit, and the cyclical changes and rhythms of life.

What may at first seem paradoxical to the continually changing conditions of nature is the relative constancy of individual elements that together constitute her features: trees, mountains, lakes, rivers, sky, clouds, and so on. These elements had been witnessed, observed, and documented by artists for centuries. Though the contemporary reader is surely aware of this continuum, we are less likely than our nineteenth-century counterparts to consider its symbolic meaning and to recognize constants represented by allegorical interpretations of nature. In part, this is an effect of our concept of time, which is linear and focused primarily on the present.

The Hudson River School painters emerged from and embraced, both passionately and eloquently, the long and distinguished tradition of landscape painting that had preceded them. They were fully cognizant of the historical use of certain symbols in nature to express underlying, pivotal ideas.[45] These iconographical codes, some established as far back as the sixteenth century, created a well-recognized and observed practice of transferring meaning through landscape painting. Artists of the Hudson River School added new symbols to this historical language, including some that were considered specific to American landscape: the deer as a symbol of wilderness and innocence before the arrival of man; the cow as a symbol of cultivated land and man's harmonic coexistence in nature.[46] In the nineteenth century, Hudson River School artists and their audiences were keenly aware of the tradition of using natural symbols in this way and were fully able to "read" and incorporate these codes into their work.[47]

In fact, by the early half of the nineteenth century, the use of symbolism in landscape painting prevailed so that artists, critics, and audiences understood it as they would a form of language. This commonly held information allowed painters to paint, writers to write, critics to discuss, and the appreciative buying art public to understand and "read" the meaning of paintings. This was so much the case that pictorial aids for beginning artists were produced and sold—including, in 1824, a packaged set of eighteen separate cards, each depicting an individual iconographic or picturesque element of traditional landscape painting. The cards could be assembled and reassembled in any sequence, using only a few or several, in order to create a continuous panorama that could form the basis for a painting.[48]

Audiences for painters of the early decades of the Hudson River School were generally a privileged group. They were predominantly educated and well-read men with the economic means to travel to the wilderness landscapes depicted by the artists and fully appreciate them. After midcentury, however, the buying art public had grown broader and included a less sophisticated, less well-read, and less traveled group of middle-class entrepreneurs, whose interests had shifted somewhat from the intellectual appreciation of sublime messages revealed through art to the desire to own important paintings with which to decorate their new homes.[49] The refined historic moment of synchrony between American landscape artist, patron, and literary community was passing. The subsequent generation of painters, along with the older artists who lived into the twentieth century, would strive to keep the impetus of Cole, Church, and Durand alive, but the nation, as well as the art world, was changing too quickly.

Our purpose here is to revive the public's ability to appreciate nineteenth-century American landscape painting and to provide insight into the iconological base that gives it greater meaning so that viewers can fully comprehend its achievement. This will also bring about a deeper understanding of the profound reaction our forefathers experienced when encountering the extraordinary natural bounty of America and how it was attuned to the buoyant hopes they held for their lives in this new country.

We believe the Hudson River School artists painted pairs and series of paintings as a natural outgrowth of their fundamental interest in the close observation and insightful interpretation of nature. Accordingly, we offer the following pairs and groupings of paintings, both "official" and "unofficial," in the hope that our readers and viewers will develop a deeper understanding of the motivations propelling the artists of the Hudson River School.

Judith H. O'Toole
Greensburg, 2005

I. Introductory Pair: Cole and Church

We are not impotent—we pallid stones;
Not all our power is gone; not all our Fame;
Not all the magic of our high renown;
Not all the wonder that encircles us;
Not all the mysteries that in us lie;
Not all the memories that hang upon,
And cling around about us now and ever,
Clothing us in a robe of more than glory.

—*The Coliseum*, Edgar Allan Poe, 1833

THIS DISCUSSION BEGINS FITTINGLY WITH THOMAS Cole and Frederic Church—Cole, the revered father of the Hudson River School; Church, his student, the dominant figure of the second and third generations. Their houses were situated across the Hudson River from one another, Cole with an expansive view of the Catskill mountain range; Church, a dramatic view of the Hudson River Valley. The contrast in their living circumstances was substantial. Cole's home was modest, shared not only with his wife and their three children but also with his wife's three unmarried sisters and their father. Church, who initially had come there as a teenager to study with Cole, later built a spacious Middle Eastern inspired mansion, Olana, high above the Hudson. He planted thousands of trees on what had been farmland and constructed a lake on the property to echo the curve of the river. Where Cole more often manipulated or "enhanced" nature in his paintings, Church actually rearranged the landscape around him at Olana to create the natural environment in which he desired to live.

The two paintings by Cole and Church provide a striking contrast and hence introduction to our study. Deference to European precedents in both landscape painting techniques and subject matter is apparent in each work. Both depict sunset scenes with the last golden beams of light raking across the picture plane, leaving some areas steeped in dark shadow and others bathed in contrasting bright, suffused illumination. Divided in halves compositionally, both give equal space to land and sky, differentiating the two by color and light. Light is imbued with specific symbolic significance, not only representing the benign ebb of day as part of nature's diurnal cycle, but analogous to the rise and fall of civilizations throughout history. Thus, through masterful evocations of light and atmosphere at sunset, Cole and Church have produced compelling landscapes as well as profound philosophical statements comparing the different cycles of nature and man.

Cole's time in Italy during his first European trip (1829–1832) was one of the most influential experiences of his life. He spent nearly a year in Florence, where his studio afforded him a view of this beloved scene: the Arno at sunset gently flowing toward the distant Alps. Though shown at close of day and imbued with the insinuation of the parallel close of an era, the scene is active, populated with a lively, affluent society, gaily dressed, as if for a festival in boats and on land. The romantic river Arno weaves its way under the reflected glow of sunset from the horizon line to a broadening in the foreground, all under the veiled colors of Cole's palette. This composition was so popular with Americans, whose travels abroad evoked the mysteries of past civilizations, that Cole completed at least six versions of this particular scene, writing to Asher B. Durand on January 31, 1838: "I am afraid the Arno will create a deluge in Boston."[1] Cole had successfully captured the romantic vision many American travelers had of Italy, to them a land of romance and poetry.

Church, on the other hand, shows a classical ruin of a temple with only four Corinthian columns remaining upright. They stand resolutely against the light signals, as in Cole's painting, both the end of day and the end of a civilization. At the base of the columns and in the shadow to the left lie broken pieces of stone, some of which, moss encrusted, are already beginning the process of returning to the earth. This canvas by Church reflects the influence of the final painting in Cole's great series *The Course of Empire* (1836), called *Desolation*, when civilization has run its course. Among the ruins, however, there is the suggested anticipation of rebirth in the presence of the young goats tended by their goatherd and the numerous poppies in blossom. The rise and fall of civilizations is linked to the cycle of days and to the rhythmic movement of the earth around the sun. The progression of night turning to day will continue, despite the acts of man, and just as there is sunrise after sunset, there is a promise of rebirth after death. There is in this scene an inherent spirituality suggesting a greater hand at play.[2]

Church's use of Corinthian columns provides another reference to Cole's *Desolation*, which also contains a single standing column. The reference to Cole is further reinforced by the presence of the single figure in Church's composition—a goatherd, dwarfed and encompassed by both nature and the ruins, shrouded by darkness in the lower right corner. Easily overlooked at first glance, he nevertheless represents the presence of man in nature. Two types of pipes relate this figure to Cole and Church, the first being the musical pipe that rests behind the figure. The pipes were played both by Pan of ancient myth and by Cole, who loved the flute and other instruments, incorporating them often in his paintings. The other pipe, this one of the smoking kind, the figure holds to his mouth. Church smoked opium to ease the painful arthritis that eventually caused him to cease painting. The goatherd is the lone "observer," so often depicted in landscape paintings of the Hudson River School: he sits somewhat apart to witness the sunset, the close of civilization, and to serve as a reminder of the survival of man in a state much different from that of his deceased ancestors, who built the glorious empire now lying in ruins. Cole's own words, speaking from the perspective of a tree in his poem *The Lament of the Forest* (1838), resonate throughout Church's painting:

Seasons there were, when man, at war with man,
Left us [Nature] to raze proud cities, desolate
Old empires, and pour out his blood on soil
That once was all our own. When death has made
All silent, all secure, we have returned,
Twisted our roots around the prostrate shafts
And broken capitals, or struck them deep.
Into the mould made richer by man's blood.
Such seasons were but brief: so soon as earth
Was sanctified again by shade and art,
Again resolved to nature, man came back,
And once more swept our feeble hosts away.

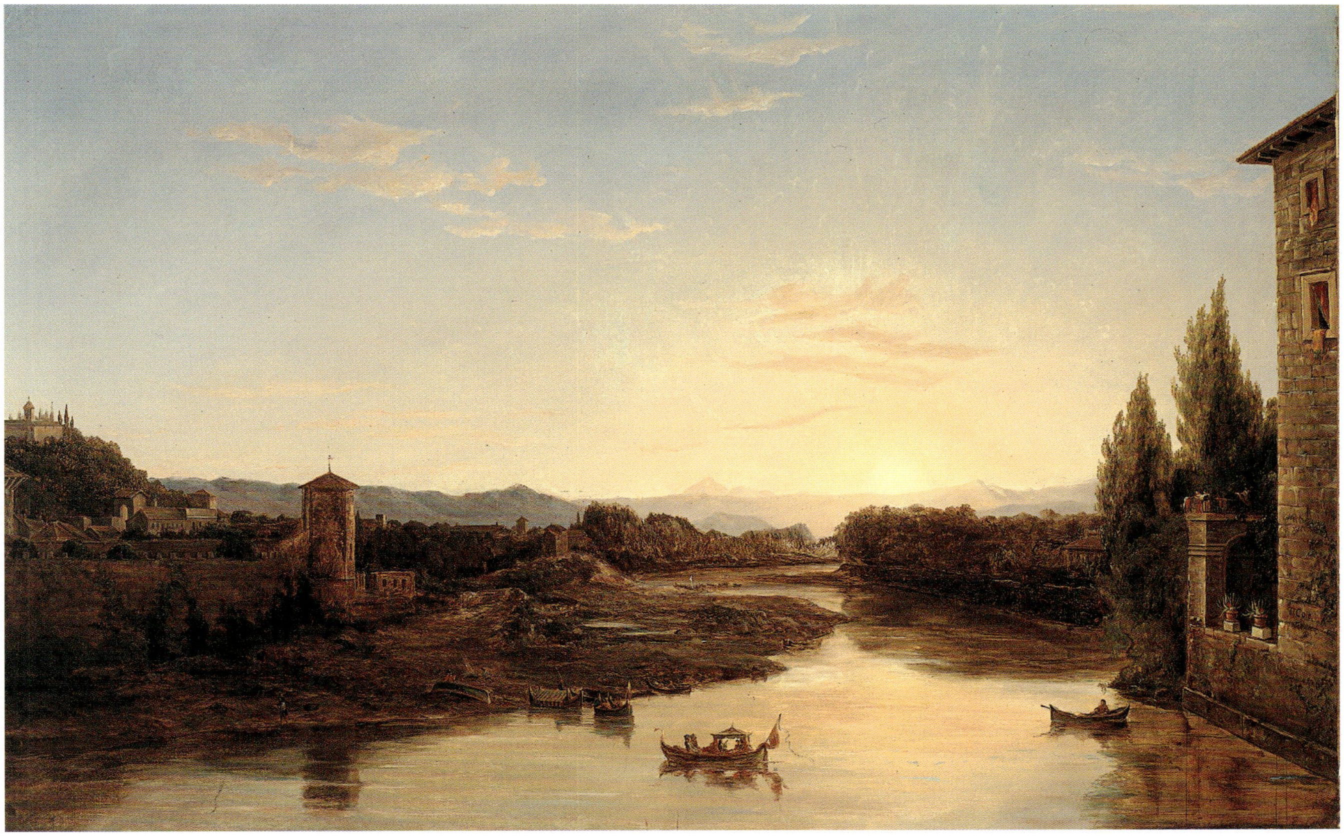

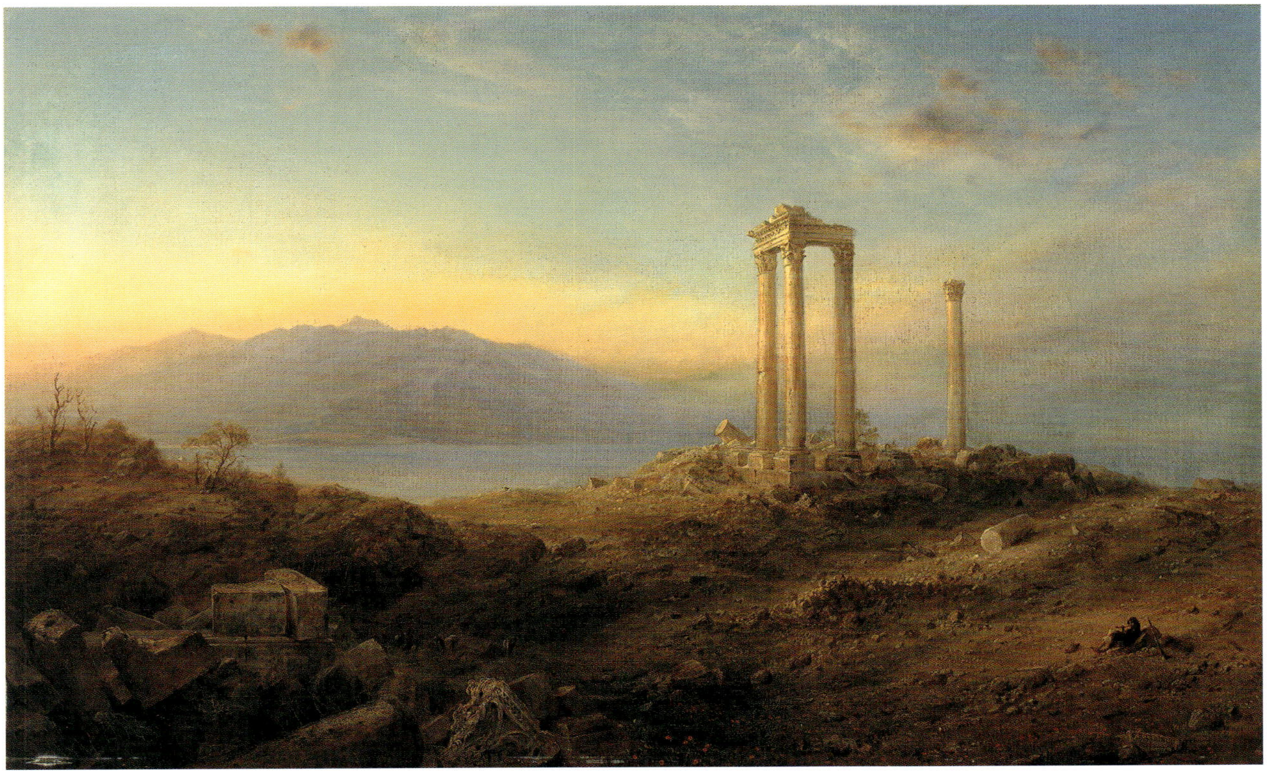

Thomas Cole (1801–1848)
Sunset on the Arno, 1837
Oil on canvas, 35 x 51 1/4 inches

Frederic Church (1826–1900)
Ruins at Baalbek, 1868
Oil on canvas, 21 3/4 x 36 1/4 inches

II. Times of Day

Youth, large, lusty, loving—youth full of grace, force, fascination
Do you know that Old Age may come after you with equal grace, force, fascination?

Day full-blown and splendid—day of the immense sun, action, ambition, laughter,
The Night follows close with millions of suns, and sleep and restoring darkness.

—Walt Whitman, "Youth, Day, Old Age and Night," *Leaves of Grass*, 1881

ONE OF THE SHORTEST CYCLES OF NATURE IS THAT of the day—dawn, morning, noon, afternoon, twilight, and finally nightfall, before the cycle repeats. The certainty of this sequence assures that regardless of daily events or man's activities, the passage of time through the cycle of days is constant and incontrovertible. As in Whitman's poem, the progression of time throughout a single day becomes a metaphor for the life cycle of man. Birth is equated to sunrise; death, to sunset and night; rebirth, to the inevitable recurrence of dawn. Hudson River School artists were very much aware of this symbolism. Cole used it to describe his series *The Voyage of Life* (1840–1841), and extending the metaphor from the birth and death of man to that of civilizations, his series *Course of Empire* (1836) unfolded in the passage of one day. Earth's cycles, both on its rotational axis, creating day and night, and in its rotation around the sun, creating the seasons, served as analogies to the stages of human life. These cycles could be used to illustrate the Christian promise of rebirth, further connecting nature to religion—an important concept to Hudson River School painters. As Caspar David Friedrich's biographer noted: "[most Romantic painters] compared the stages of human life with the times of day and the changing seasons. This idea stems from the desire to see man's birth and death as a cosmically regulated cyclical process on which to base the hope of a resurrection."[3]

This section of groupings begins with what might appear to be the unusual choice of a single painting. The idea is to demonstrate the concept that even within a single canvas, artists of the Hudson River School emphasized comparisons and contrasts through the close observation and recording of numerous variables possible in the ever-changing face of nature. In the simplest, most basic terms, nature can be considered to consist of just two components: earth and sky. James Augustus Suydam has juxtaposed these two elements in this small oval composition to create a dramatic vision at the specific moment when earth has fallen into darkness and sky retains the brilliant afterglow of the setting sun.

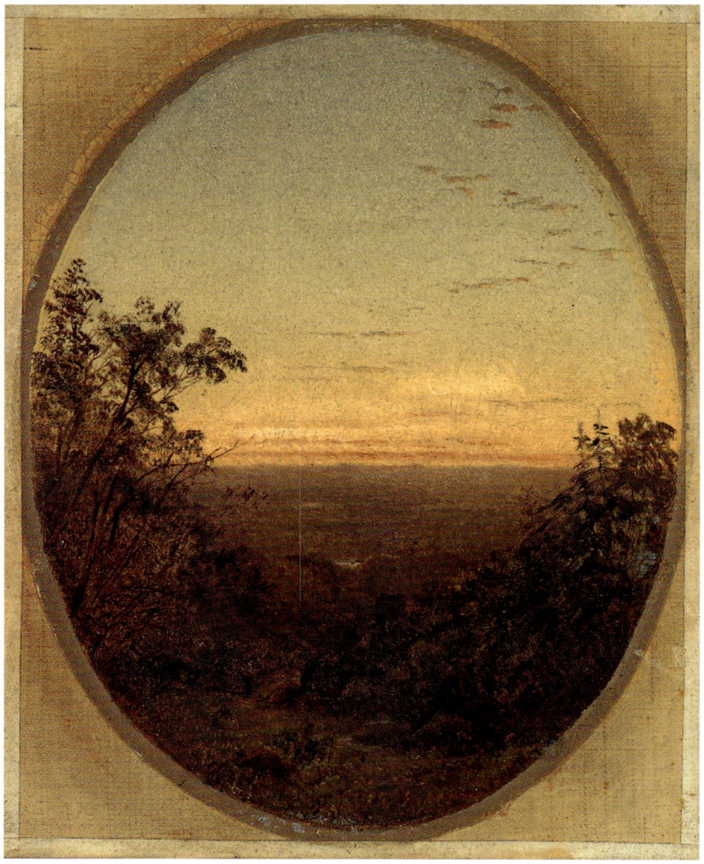

A SECOND-GENERATION HUDSON RIVER SCHOOL PAINTER, James Augustus Suydam was a quiet, sensitive man whose small landscapes seem to reflect his unassuming personality. Often painted on a small scale, his best-known subjects are peaceful panoramic views that belie their modest size by effectively evoking the vastness of nature. This is certainly the case in *Sunset Landscape*, whose oval shape also serves to expand, rather than limit, the landscape view. Split in half compositionally by the horizon line, the painting, a dramatic and arresting comparison and contrast within one single work, is divided into equal parts of earth and sky, darkness and light. Notable is the absence of the conventional tree that often served in Hudson River School landscapes to unite earth and sky as well as draw the observer's eye into the scene. A distant waterfall enlivens dense forests where a single observer stands witness to the magnificent sunset. Trailing across the sky, dark clouds stand out against the bright afterglow of sunset, suggesting hope and the promise of another day. Majestic in its ability to communicate the poetry of light, the sweetness of day's end, and the beauty of nature, this diminutive canvas succeeds in conveying the grandest of Hudson River School philosophies and visions.

In two evocative canvases, one of morning and one of evening along the shore of Saranac Lake, Homer Dodge Martin demonstrates his remarkable ability to render in paint the elusive, intangible effects of light. Martin assimilated the Hudson River School aesthetic through his contact with John Kensett, from whom he learned to be a close, accurate observer of nature. Painted when Martin was just twenty-one years old, these canvases already show the strength of his mature work in the effective marriage of naturalistic detail and atmospheric illusion. Shying away from the more dramatic effects of color and light that could be associated with dawn and dusk, Martin chooses moments of serenity and quiet introspection, revealed through subtle modulations of tone. In neither painting is the direct source of light—the sun—seen, but its effects are obliquely observed.

Morning is presented in cool blue-and-violet-colored mountains and sky which are reflected in the water. The dense greens and rich browns of the shoreline also mingle as reflections in the lake, providing a counterpoint that alludes to the hard reality of earth against the clear, amorphous atmosphere. Evening is shown in the spreading warmth of a golden yellow light with a rich glow suggesting the gentle close of day. This "intentional" pair is matched not only in subject matter but also in similarity of mood—one of contemplative reverence for nature without man's presence.

This pairing reveals greatly different qualities of morning and evening light that would hardly be appreciated if the paintings were separated from each other. The contrasting renderings of light and atmosphere are inescapably witnessed when the paintings appear side by side and demonstrate the painter's extraordinary sensitivity to the quieter moods of nature, along with his consummate skill in rendering them convincingly.

James Augustus Suydam (1819–1865)
Sunset Landscape, n.d.
Oil on canvas, 7 5/8 x 6 1/4 inches

Homer Dodge Martin (1836–1897)
Saranac Lake [Morning], 1857
Oil on canvas, 18 x 32 inches

Homer Dodge Martin (1836–1897)
Saranac Lake [Evening], 1857
Oil on canvas, 18 x 32 inches

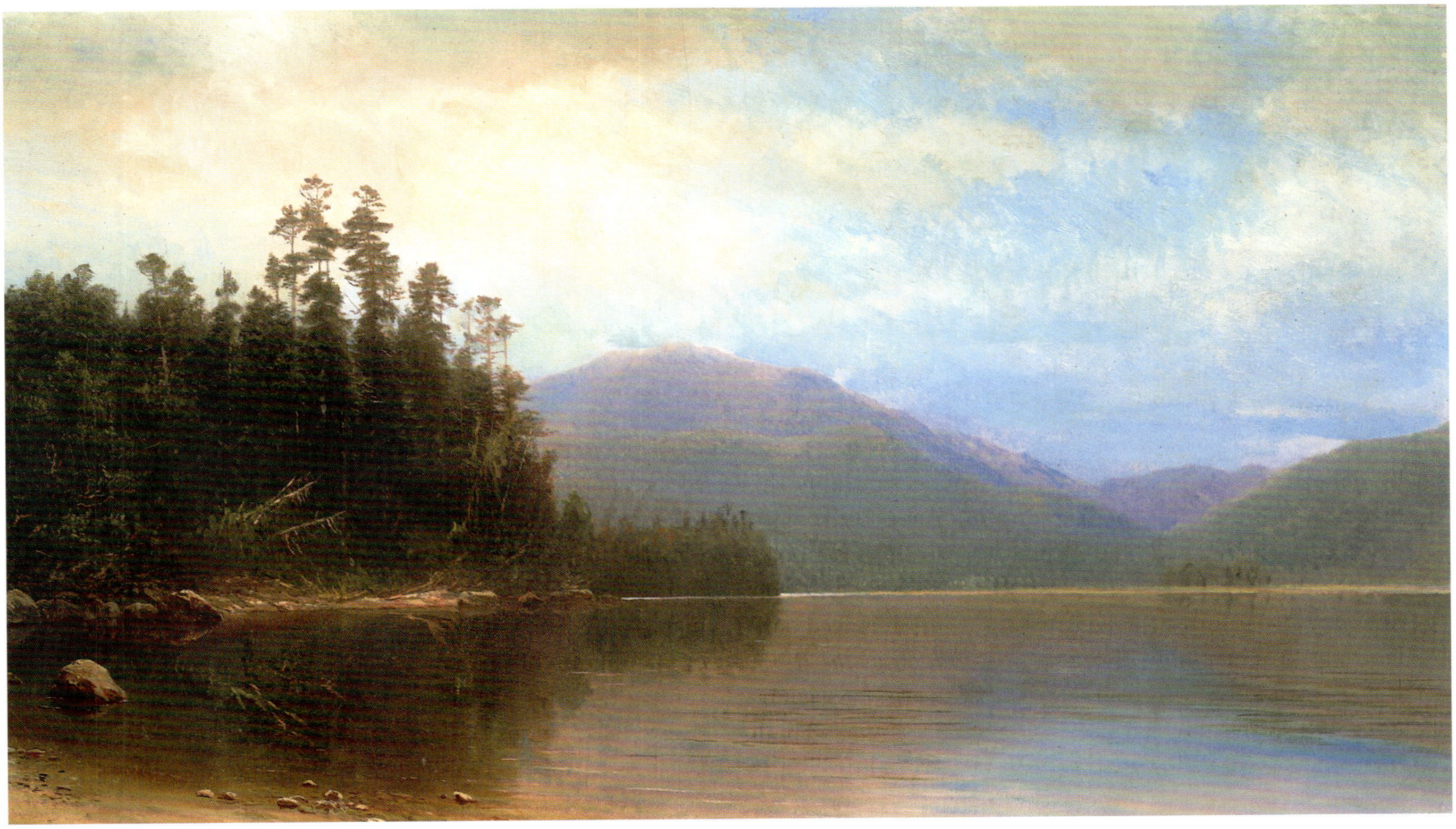

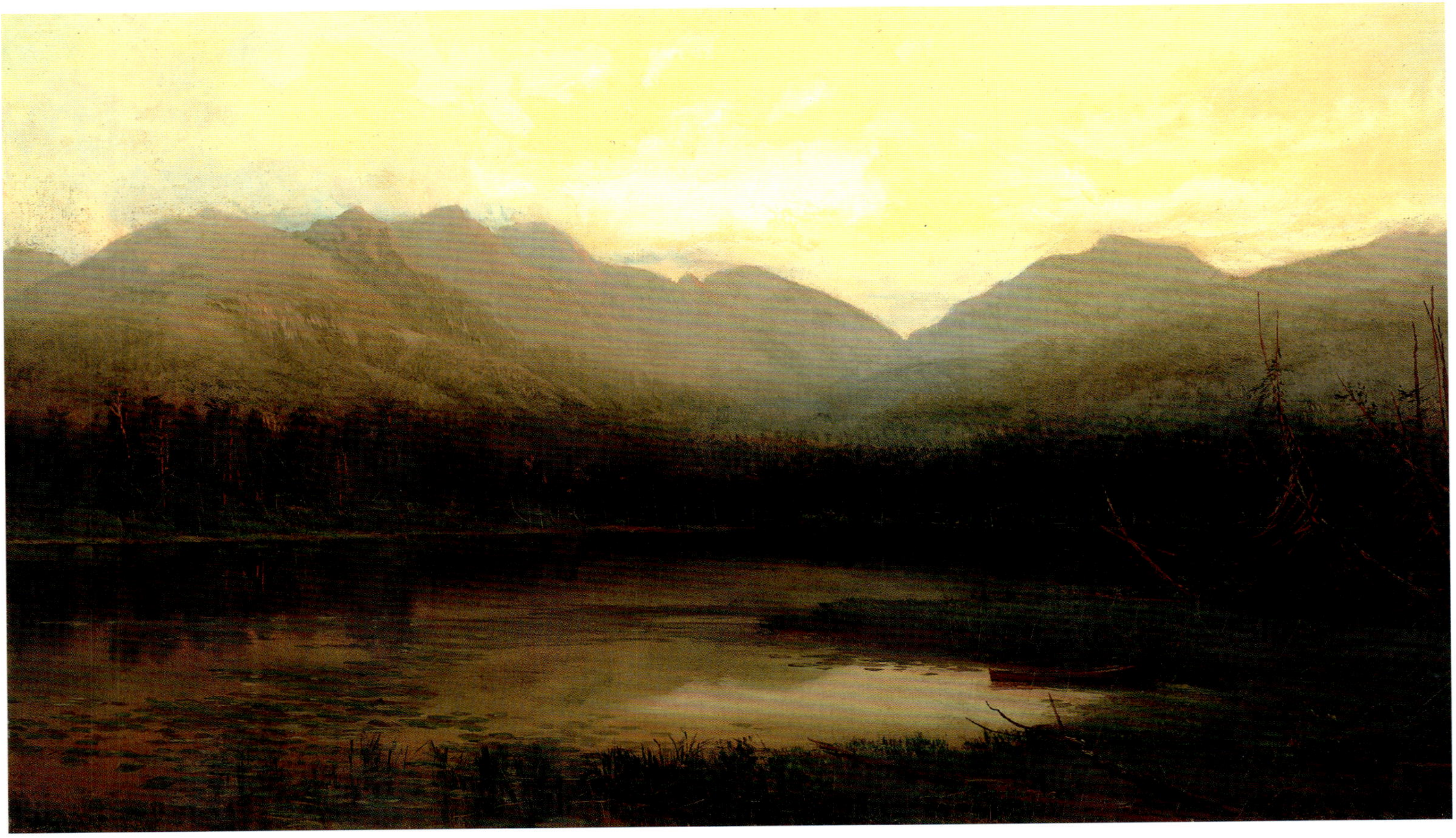

THIS PAIR OF PAINTINGS BY JAMES MCDOUGAL HART realizes the potential sought by artists who created pairs and series in order to communicate themes and ideas. Although each on its own is complete and remarkable, together they resonate, enriching one another thematically in a lively dialogue replete with comparisons and contrasts. In a modestly sized pair of paintings, Hart has produced a purposeful juxtaposition of a sublime theme with a beautiful landscape to achieve the full impact of such a comparison.

Mountain Falls portrays a turbulent, wild view of a rugged mountain waterfall. In a gesture more threatening than benign, a single scraggly pine on the left bends its skeletal branches toward the water. Mountains, made pale by the distance, rise into a fresh early-morning sky with white clouds drifting against blue. When the paintings are positioned side by side, the rushing falls in this composition flow directly to meet the contrasting calm, mirrored surface of a river running through *Conversation by the River.* Energy and movement characteristic of the first are countered and balanced by harmony and quietude in the second. A tranquil river valley, with rooftops of several dwellings jutting out from the tree line, leads into the background, consisting of a long ridge of purple-blue mountains above which a late afternoon sky mellows with color. Four women of different ages, possibly all members of the same family, are enjoying rest under the shelter of a tree, having walked along a path high above the valley. Rising in the manner of Claude Lorrain high into the yellow, pink, and blue-tinged sky, its feathery branches gesture beneficently, echoing and mirroring the curve of the scraggly pine in the companion painting. Recession of space into distance in this composition also reflects the elaborate system of winding, horizontal lines developed in many landscapes by Poussin. One woman dressed in blue and another in white face away from the landscape toward the viewer. A third, dressed in red, reclines against a fallen log, appearing to address the others. A fourth, her face hidden by the hood of her black garment, kneels beside the group. The grouping of these figures suggests some allegorical reference—perhaps inspired by Thomas Cole, whose figures were often seated or standing to observe or quietly enjoy their outdoor environment. In this particular scene, the women seem to represent harmonious coexistence with nature, as opposed to the fierce, uninhabitable, unaccommodating wilderness delineated in the companion view.

James McDougal Hart (1828–1901)
Mountain Falls, n.d.
Oil on canvas, 15 x 10 inches

James McDougal Hart (1828–1901)
Conversation by the River, n.d.
Oil on canvas, 15 x 10 inches

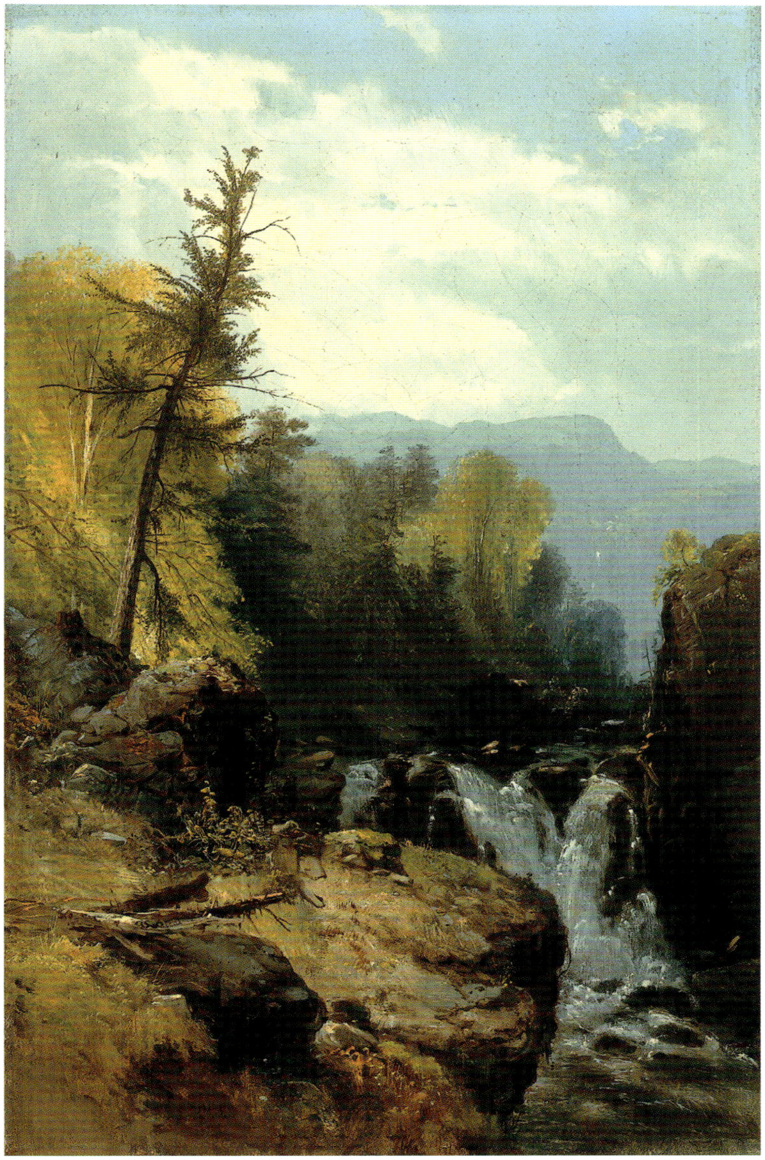

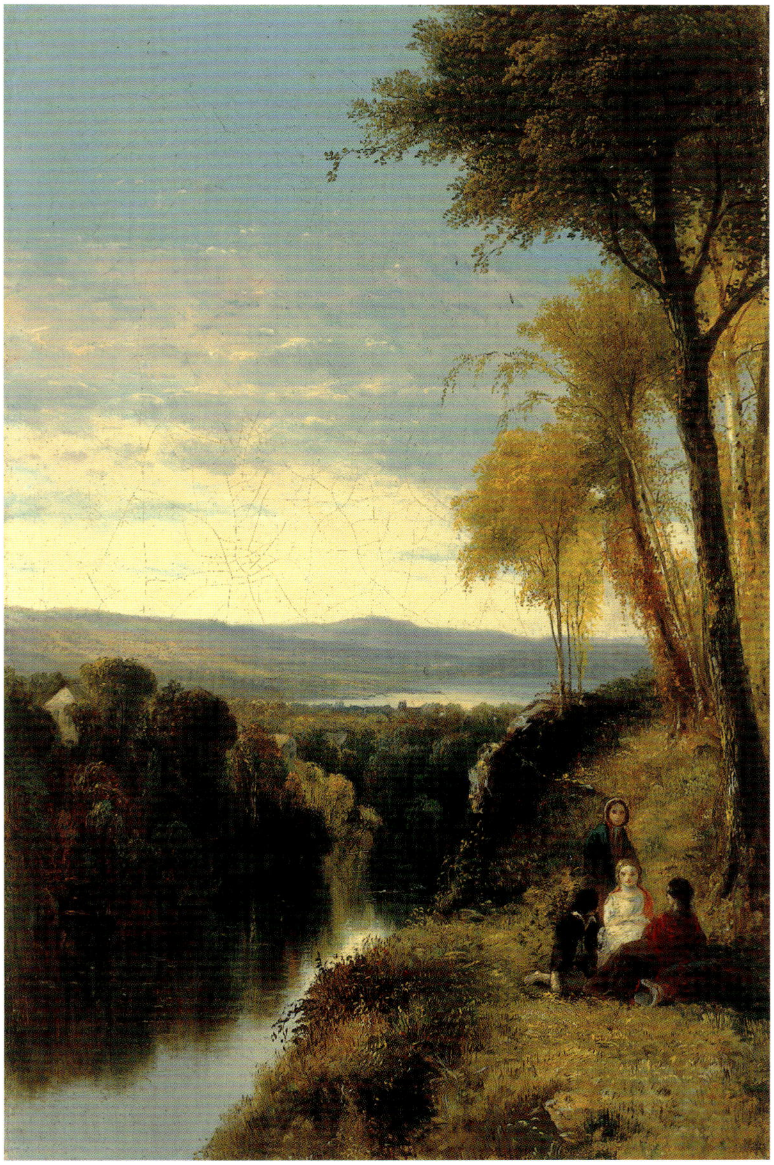

THESE THREE PAINTINGS BY JOHN FREDERICK KENSETT indicate a fascination with specific light effects created by different times of day, as well as changing weather conditions and mood. Kensett's early training as an engraver and his studies with Asher B. Durand are revealed through an interest in detail and faithfulness to nature. In each painting, Kensett engages all our senses by evoking the mood of the landscape primarily through the type of light that characterizes the specific time of day.

A chaste, diffuse light unfolds across the valley of Mt. Chocorua in New Hampshire's White Mountains at sunrise, sending cool mists rising with the nascent warmth of dawn. Dense undergrowth covering the mountainside is drenched in night's shadow, untouched as yet by the still low rays of the rising sun. Kensett uses light in its role as revealer of truth: two Native Americans watch expectantly from their position on the shadowy slopes, nearly indistinguishable in the darkness of their earthly moorings, as if to see what the dawn will bring. We, as observers, know what the figures do not: that the new day will belong to the white man and that Native Americans will be eclipsed from the scene. Correspondingly, the cultivation of nature by Europeans will supplant the wilderness home of the Native Americans.

Brooding clouds hang in dense clusters in Kensett's *Reminiscences of the Catskill Mountains*, where the sky and land share equal halves of the composition, and mountains, forests, and fields roil, echoing the turbulent atmosphere. Tops of buildings and towns peek through the green, as if just beginning to make their mark on the landscape. Light breaks through the clouds to illuminate a man and woman resting on an outcropping of rock to observe the valley below, their clothing of bright red, blue, and white contrasting sharply with the greens, browns, and grays with which they are surrounded. The dark, tangled mass of undergrowth covering the mountainside on the left suggests that not all of nature will be tamed. The overall mood is one of promise tinged with uncertainty.

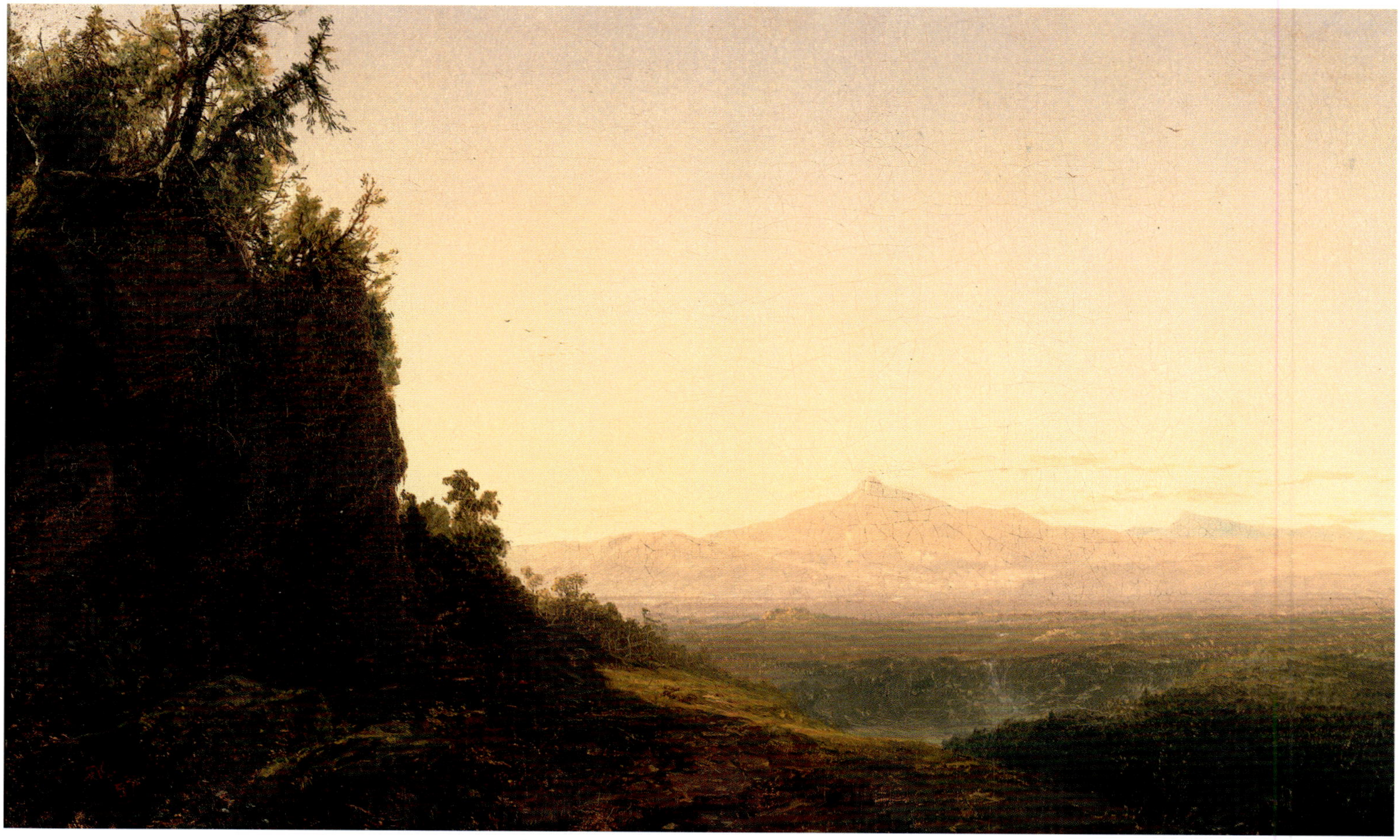

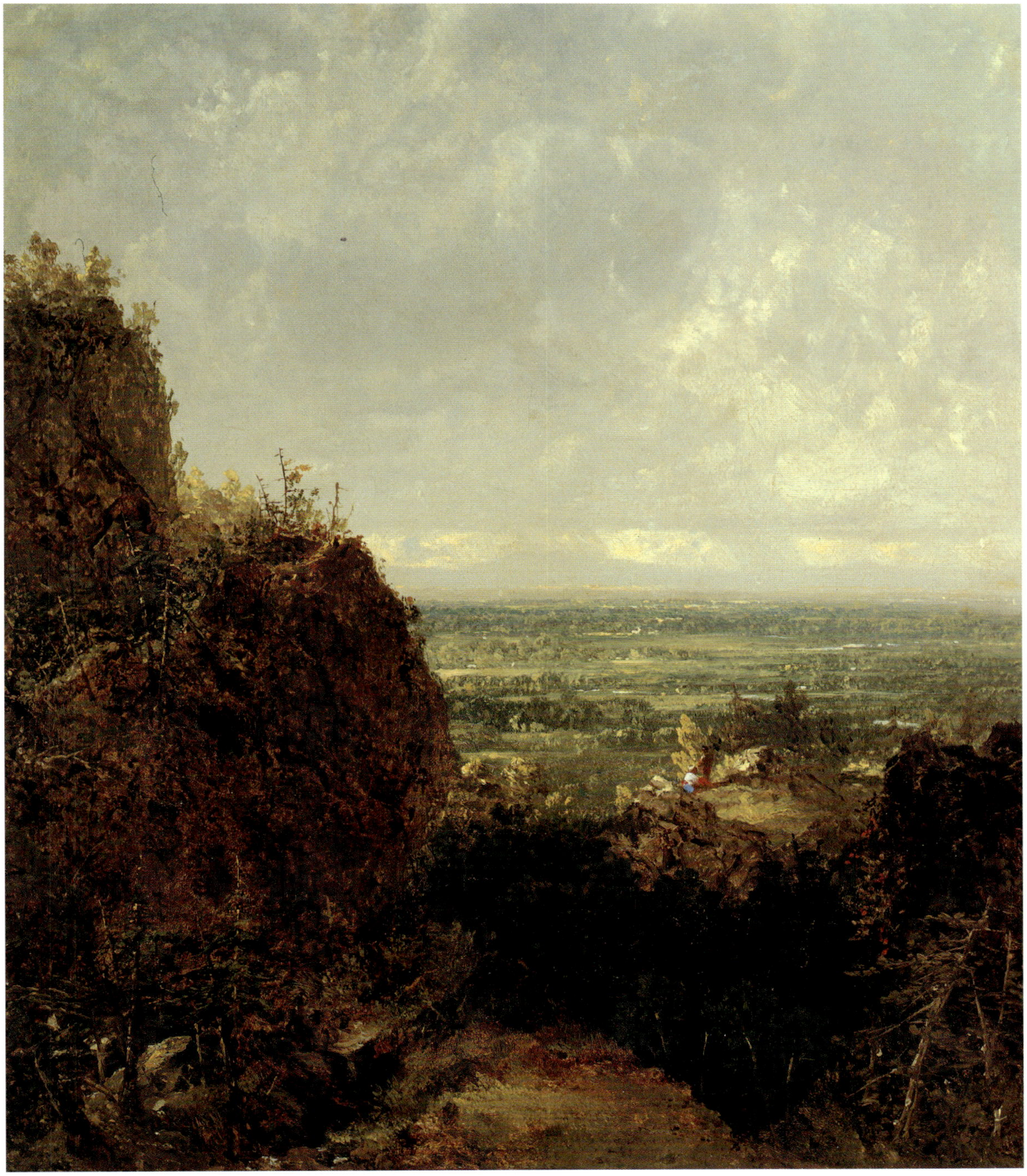

John Frederick Kensett (1818–1872)
Mount Chocorua, 1857
Oil on canvas, 14 1/2 x 24 inches

John Frederick Kensett (1818–1872)
Reminiscences of the Catskill Mountains, 1853
Oil on canvas, 22 1/2 x 18 1/4 inches

Rich atmospheric effects of light pervade Kensett's *Sunset over the Catskills* of 1855. The composition is again divided in half by sky and land. Glorious shades of orange gild the underside of clouds, drifting above a slip of lavender mountains at close of day. Light spills from the setting sun to reflect in the water—possibly Kaaterskill Creek, where Cole and Church painted. Shorelines on either side are dark. Both the creek and a path running parallel to it are intersected by a low horizontal band of trees and bushes as the creek bends to the right. A solitary figure, whose red shirt makes him stand out in the darkness, reinforces the painting's contemplative mood; his back to us, he walks toward the sunset into the landscape. We seem to follow his progress down the path. Geese, not bound to earth like man, fly in formation in the left portion of the sky. Contentment tinged with resignation distinguishes this poetic statement of day's magnificent close.

John Frederick Kensett (1818–1872)
Sunset over the Catskills, 1855
Oil on canvas, 18 x 25 inches

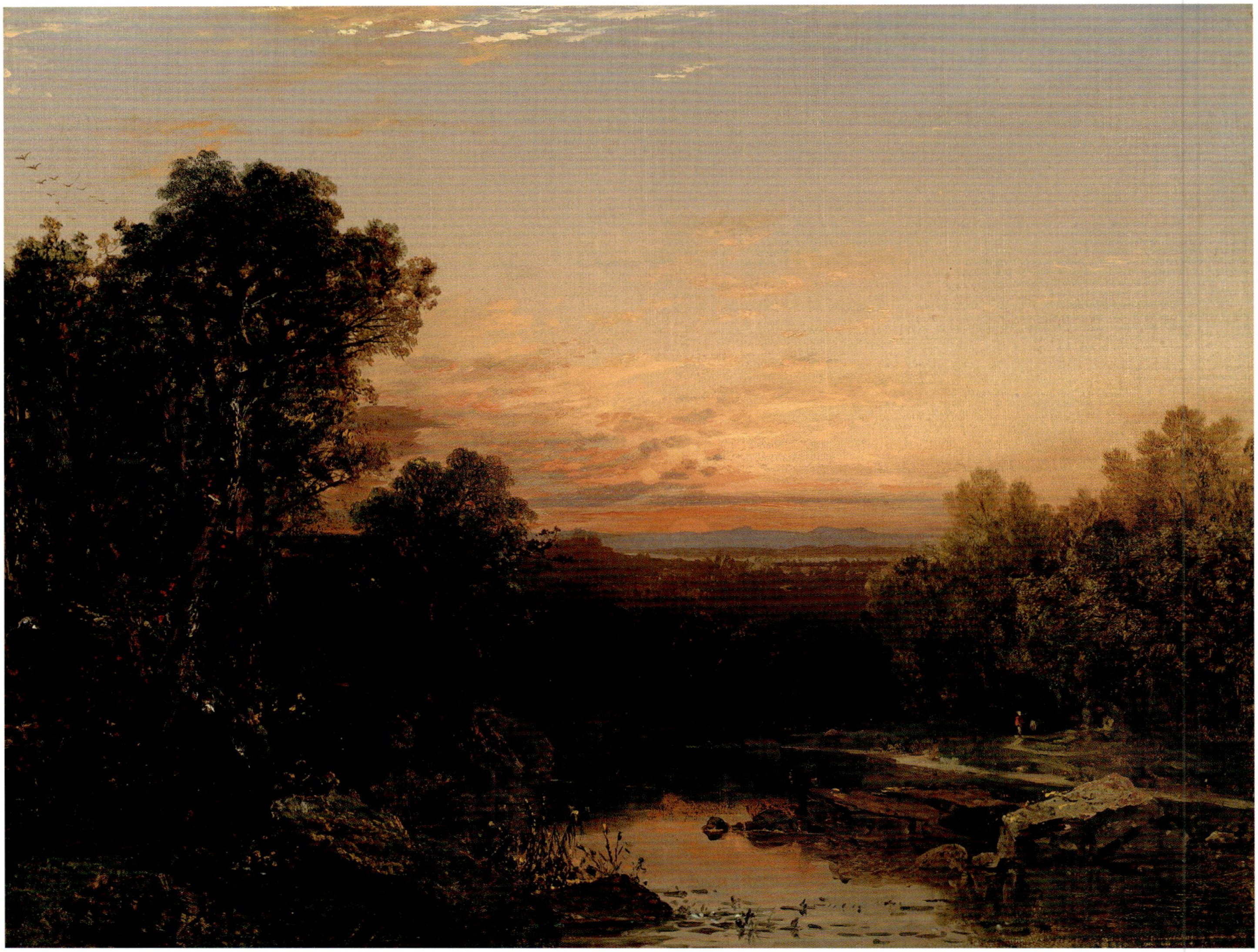

Passages: Chronicle of a Day in the Routine of Cows

In nineteenth-century America, the daily routine of tending domesticated animals was directly tied to changing times of day and therefore depicted in accord with progressive scenes of morning, afternoon, evening, and night. Later chapters will describe how Cole and other Hudson River School artists used deer to represent the virgin wildness of nature. By contrast, cows served as a symbol of man's presence and prosperity. Barbara Novak refers to the transition from "sublime," or wild, to "bovine," or domesticated, American landscapes.[4] Cows are controlled by man, who herds them through their day, bringing them from barns in the morning into fields to be fed, down to streams to drink, and back to their barns at night. Repetition of these sequences is comforting and reassuring. Second-generation Hudson River School painters relied on the iconography of the cow to show that man and his activities were in fundamental harmony with nature and nature's cycles.

Morning

VERDANT GREEN IS THE PREDOMINANT COLOR IN ALFRED Fitch Bellows's peaceful scene, presided over by a centrally placed immense oak bathed in pure morning light and dressed in delicate new leaves of spring. Spring flowers also appear in the foreground. Cows have begun their daily passage from barn to pasture, pausing along a dirt road and over a short bridge to water at the banks of a stream. Brightly dressed children guide the cows and play in the tangle of fresh growth along the nearby shore. All the activity presented to the observer is harmonious both in our immediate response to the subject and in our recognition of three synchronized cycles of nature and man: the fresh season of renewal and growth, the early hour of day, and the youthful age of man.

Gunther Hartwick's (d. 1899) orderly, highly detailed landscape reveals his early training as an artist in Germany. Drenched in golden light, the painting evokes a mood of serene domesticity. Man and animals still close to home have not yet begun their daily routines. The artist has carefully observed and transcribed details of the landscape, including two large mullein plants flanking the farmhouse gate. The mullein, brought to the New World by Europeans, was painted by Cole, Durand, Heade, and many others of the Hudson River School who considered it to symbolize good luck, hardiness, and prosperity. It has also been interpreted to represent the introduction of the white man to the New World, and the consequences to that land that were to follow.[5]

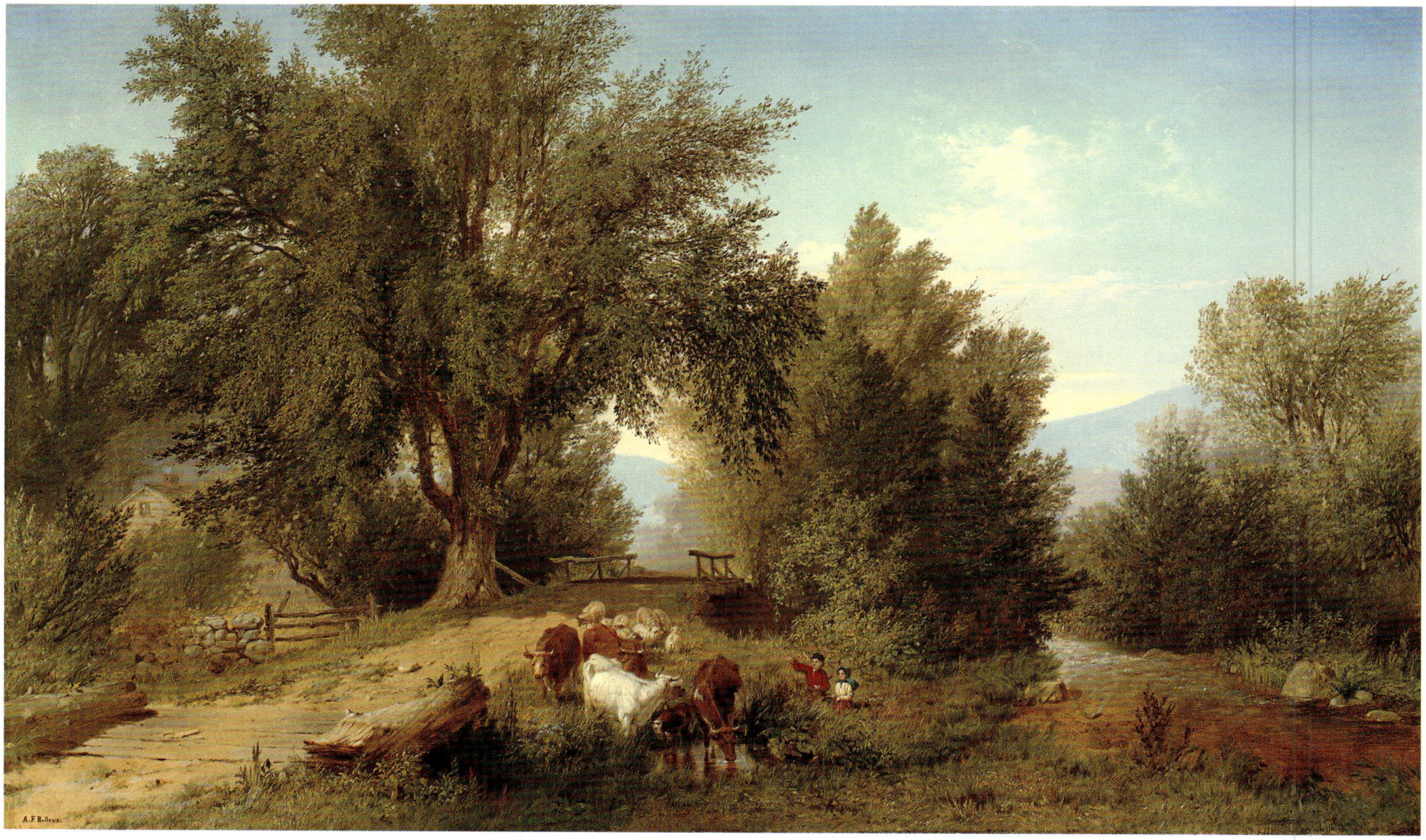

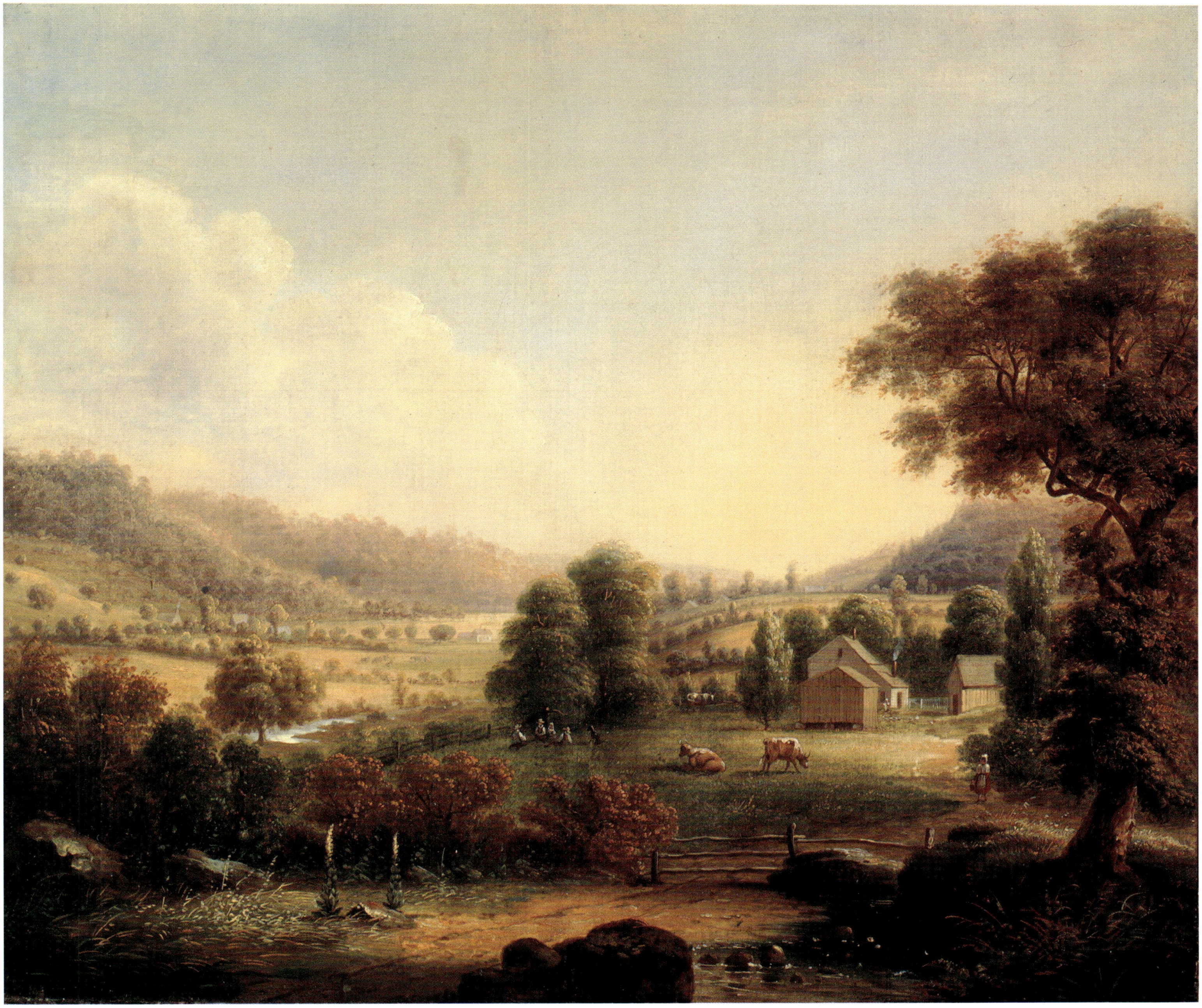

Alfred Fitch Bellows (1829–1883)
Down to the Brook, 1863
Oil on canvas, 28 x 47 1/2 inches

Gunther Hartwick (active 1847-1857)
Landscape with Farm, 1854
Oil on canvas, 25 x 30 inches

Late Morning

Born and schooled in Germany, Hermann Fuechsel met American painters Albert Bierstadt and Worthington Whittredge while studying at the Düsseldorf Academy. Later, after moving to New York, he occupied a studio in the Tenth Street Studio Building, where these three, along with Sanford Gifford and other Hudson River School painters, also worked. A narrow range of color and crisp draftsmanship reveal Fuechsel's training and skill as an engraver. Here, a strip of land along the Hudson River serves to contrast the warm, solid colors of autumn against the cool, soft hues of sky and water. Reflections of rust and yellow fall from the land into the river's surface. Autumnal colors tint the otherwise pastel-hued mountainside. Two cows stand in shadow at the water's edge, integrated by color and position into their surroundings. They act as man's surrogates in the wilderness, the symbol of nature's domestication yet, at least in this composition, not a threat to its balance or harmony. Two tall trees, their intricate foliage darkly silhouetted against the lighter sky, mimic the pair of cows; the intricate branches reach heavenward whereas the animals remain earthbound.

Late morning shifts toward early afternoon in Hekking's peaceful, richly colored, Dutch-inspired composition. In the left foreground near the stream, an elm tree links heaven and earth, providing a vertical anchor to the predominantly horizontal composition. Full-bodied clouds cast contrasting light and dark patterns across the land; three cows water in the stream. Surrounded by meadows dotted with wildflowers, the stream meanders diagonally, leading our eye to the violet-tinged mountains in the distance. Another strong diagonal is established from the watering cows situated in a wild region (left foreground) to the hay wain in the cultivated field of the middle ground. The only element of disharmony, an isolated suggestion of man's impact, can be found in the symbolism of the tree stump in the left foreground, warning of the continued and more aggressive presence of man in nature.

Hermann Fuechsel (1833–1915)
Cows in the Hudson River, c. 1875
Oil on canvas, 10 x 20 inches

Joseph Antonio Hekking (1830–1903)
Cows Watering in a Summer Landscape, c. 1870
Oil on canvas, 20 x 36 inches

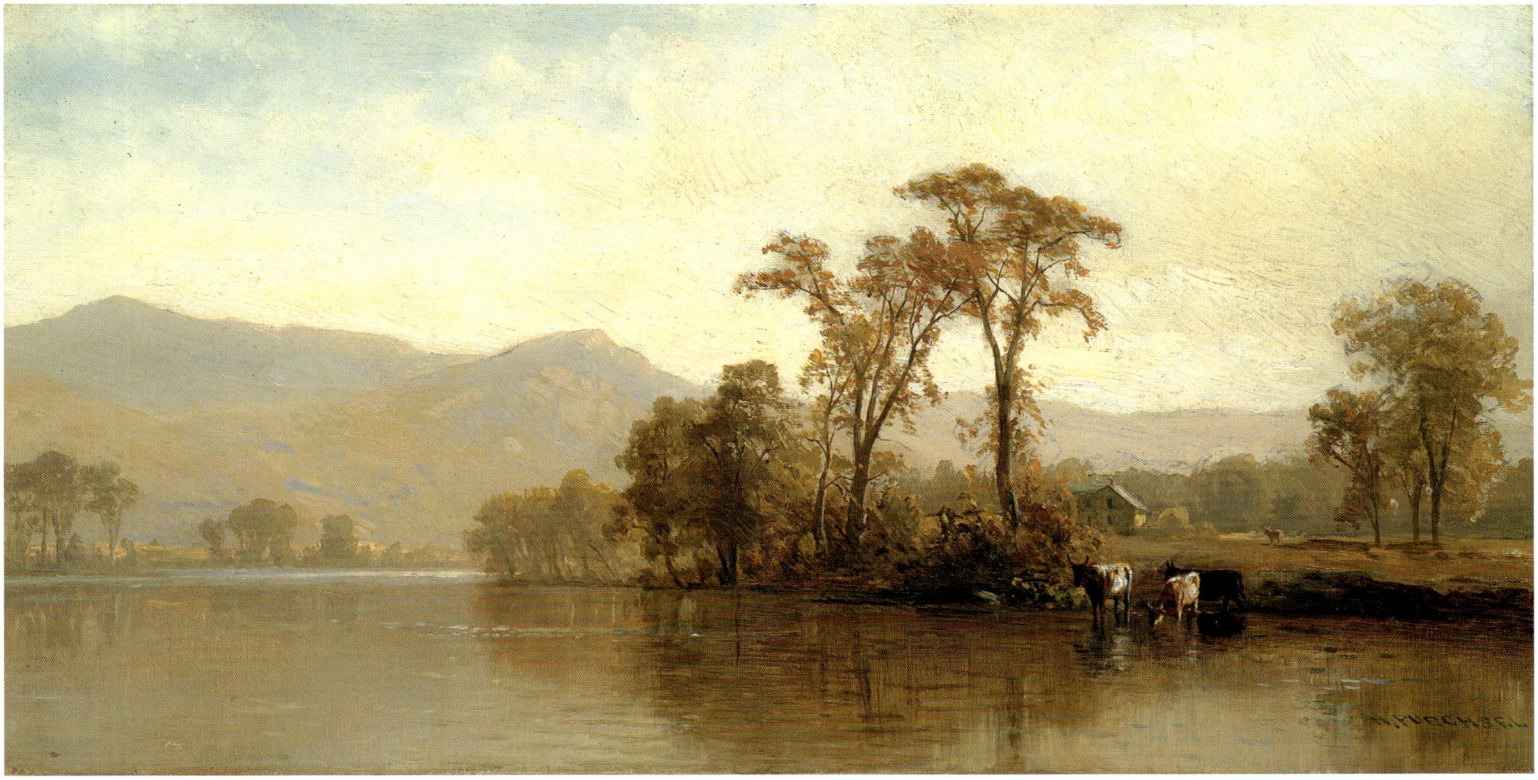

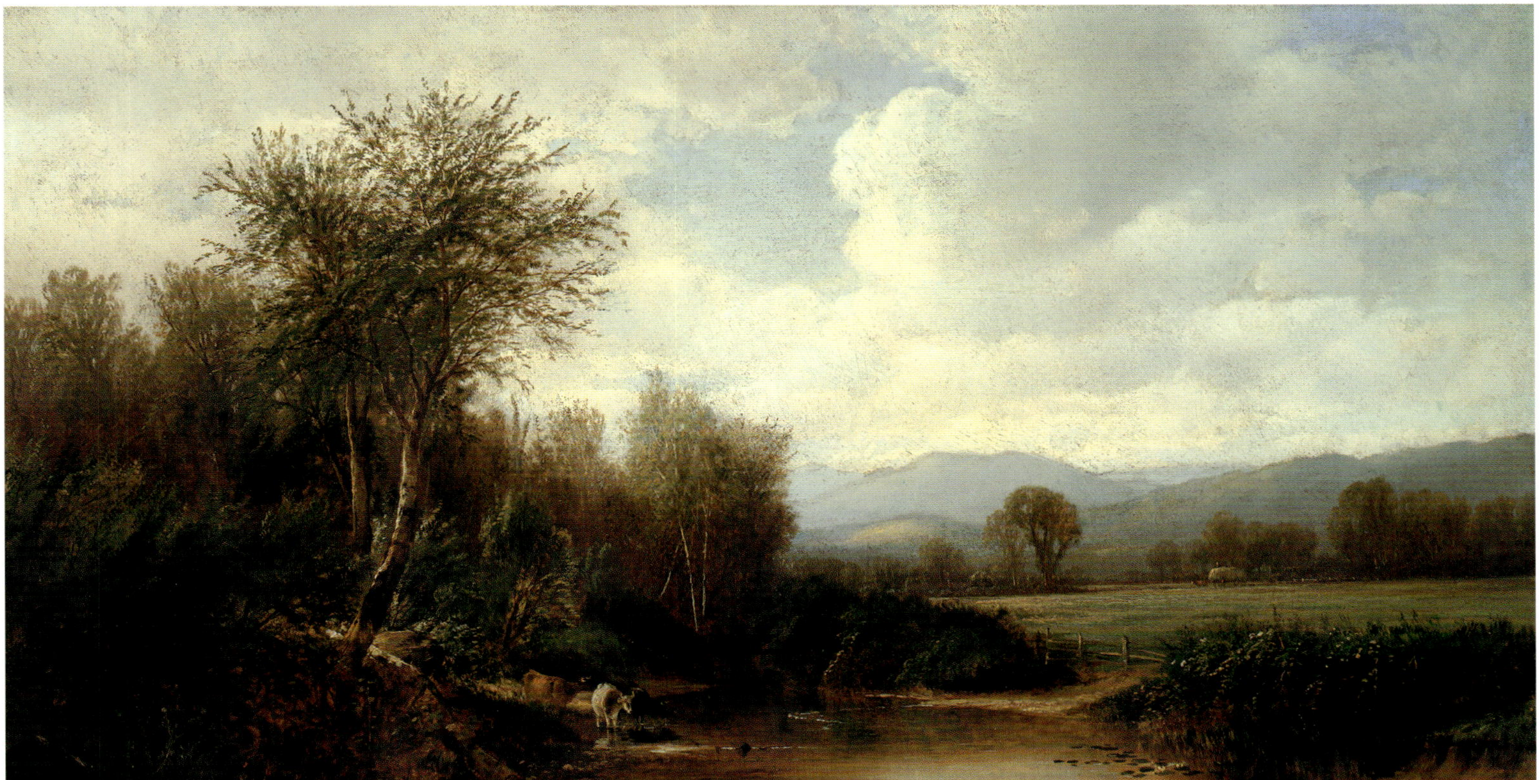

Early Afternoon

Eliza Greatorex's *Landscape Near Cragsmoor, NY*, 1863, provides little evidence of the turmoil of the times or of the artist's own personal circumstances, having been widowed and left with two young daughters five years earlier by her musician husband. An artist of great achievement, including being the first woman elected an associate member of the National Academy of Design, her work shows a sophisticated romanticism with effortless, confident brushwork. The influence of her teacher, James Hart, is apparent. Unfurling across her painting of Cragsmoor is the tranquillity associated with safe harbor. The low skyline is broken only by the boughs of a tall and broad tree, opening its foliage like a fan to shelter a group of cows reposing in the alternating sun and shade of a rough meadow. The roof of a cottage barely breaks the horizon line, resting low, as does the earth, in Greatorex's peaceful scene.

The Scottish born painter James McDougal Hart was especially fond of painting farm scenes with cows and oxen, where his sensitive, accurate renderings of both landscape and animals are clearly evidenced. The long horizontal format in this 1862 view on the Farmington River permits a panoramic vision of the peaceful river valley under the calm of a balmy summer afternoon. Cows are judiciously positioned throughout the composition, moving along the course of their routine from the homestead, nestled under the protection of a group of trees on the left of the composition, across the river to a lush, flowering meadow that consumes most of the lower half of the painting. The carefully contrasted cows of varying color and position have paired off, two still in the distance at the water's edge; four in groups of two, standing in the field as if in companionable conversation; and two others lying on the ground. Earth and sky are balanced in equal halves of the painting. The sky contains magnificent clouds varying in size, shape, and color, which contrast with many open, blue areas. The mood is also one of a delicate, harmonious balance between man, his farm animals, and nature in this scene of peaceful domesticity.

Eliza Greatorex (1820–1897)
Landscape Near Cragsmoor, NY, 1863
Oil on canvas, 15 x 25 inches

James McDougal Hart (1828–1901)
On the Farmington River, 1862
Oil on canvas, 19 x 32 inches

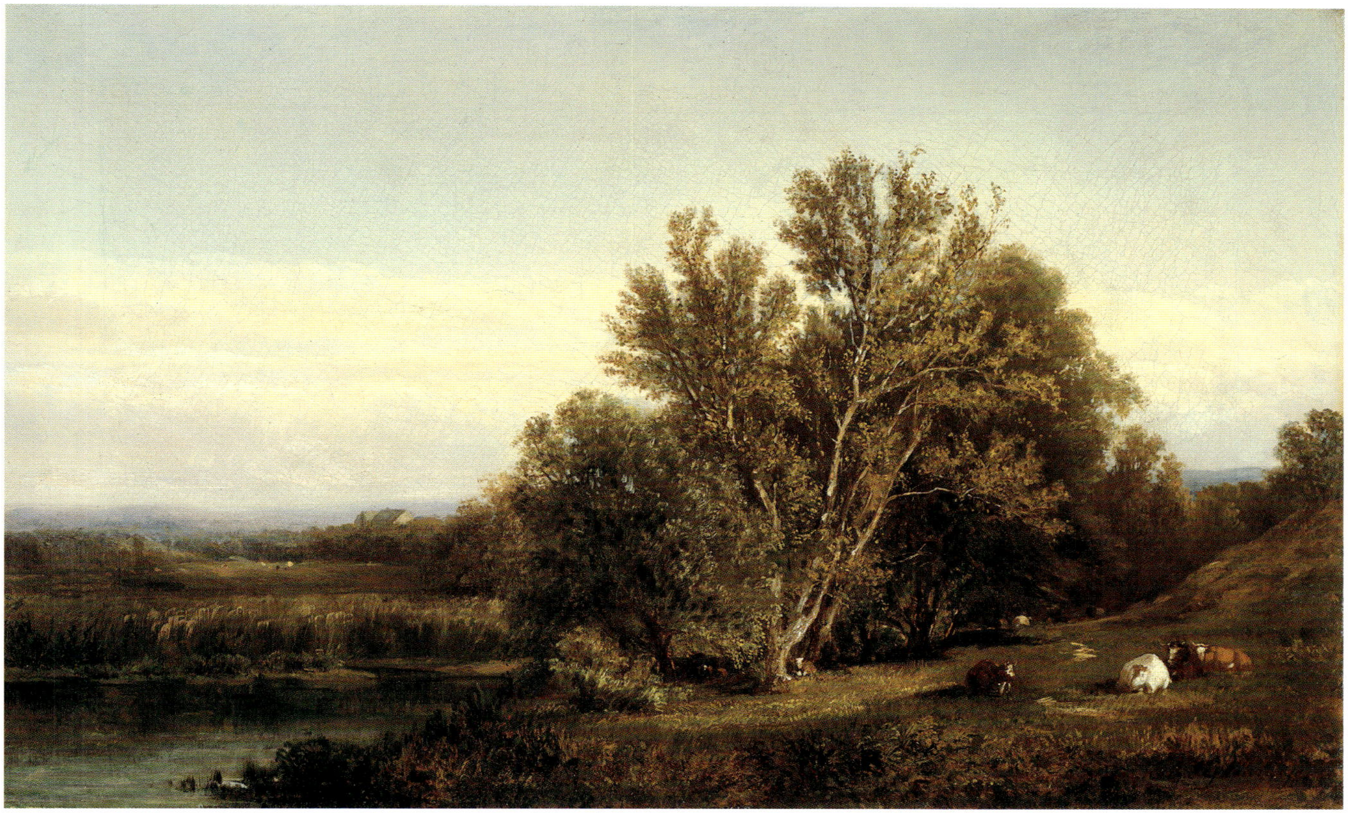

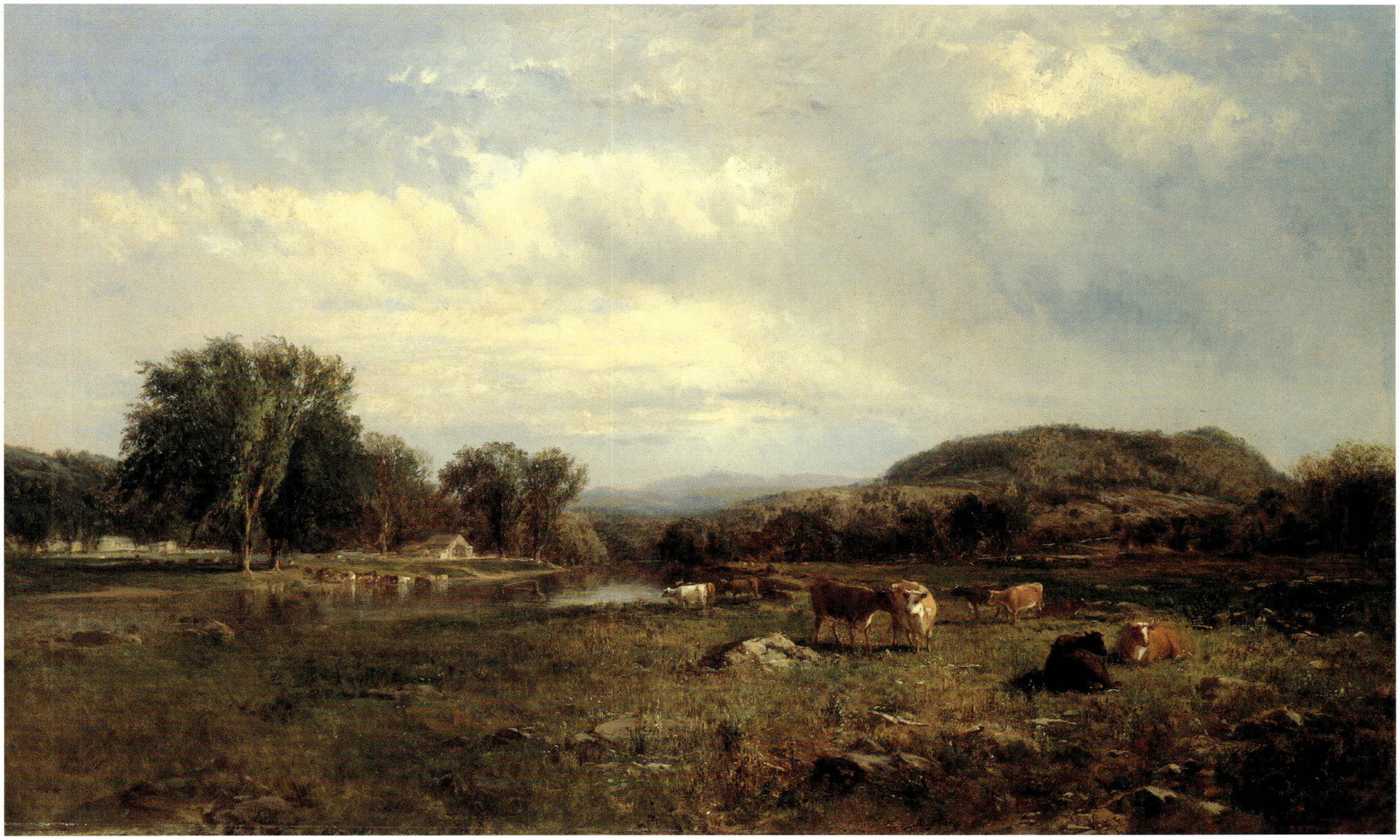

Late Afternoon

Brother of James McDougal Hart, William was also a prolific landscape painter whose canvases were in great demand by nineteenth-century audiences. His *Sunset in the Valley* is an exquisite evocation of atmosphere and light, pervading both land and sky in the warm brilliance of late afternoon. Everything is touched with gold in the strong light of sunset: reflections of sky and trees are mirrored in the glassy calm of marsh water, the backs of the cows are struck with rays of sunlight, and bark glows on a grand tree under which the animals have settled. Backlit in the radiant light, branches shimmer against the sky in a gesture of convocation to earth. The roofs of house and barn can barely be seen beyond a distant field on the right, signaling that man's impact on nature is minute. Hart's limited palette of yellow, rust, and green creates a pleasing melody, a song of nature's harmony with man and animal.

Jasper Francis Cropsey's painterly brush is contrasted to the smooth, glassy surface of William Hart in this sunset scene along the Susquehanna River. Alive with light and color, the canvas is energized by brusque traces of the artist's brush flickering across its surface. Cows have found their way down a path to the river's edge, their brown, red, black, and white shapes reflected in the water. The sun's rays have also found a path through the valley, creating a strong surge of light from right to left across the composition. Autumn has settled into the countryside with colors made more vivid by the setting sun. A mountain peak, drenched in reddish light, is silhouetted against the yellow-gold sky that dissolves into soft blue at the uppermost edge of the canvas. A nearly defoliated tree on the left reaches its bare branches in salutation to a group of trees still clad in rust and green leaves on the opposite shore. No sign of man, with the exception of his bovine surrogates, disturbs the tranquil accord of late afternoon in the wilderness.

William McDougal Hart (1823–1894)
Sunset in the Valley, 1870
Oil on canvas, 14 x 23 1/2 inches

Jasper Francis Cropsey (1823–1900)
On the Susquehanna, 1877
Oil on canvas, 12 x 17 1/2 inches

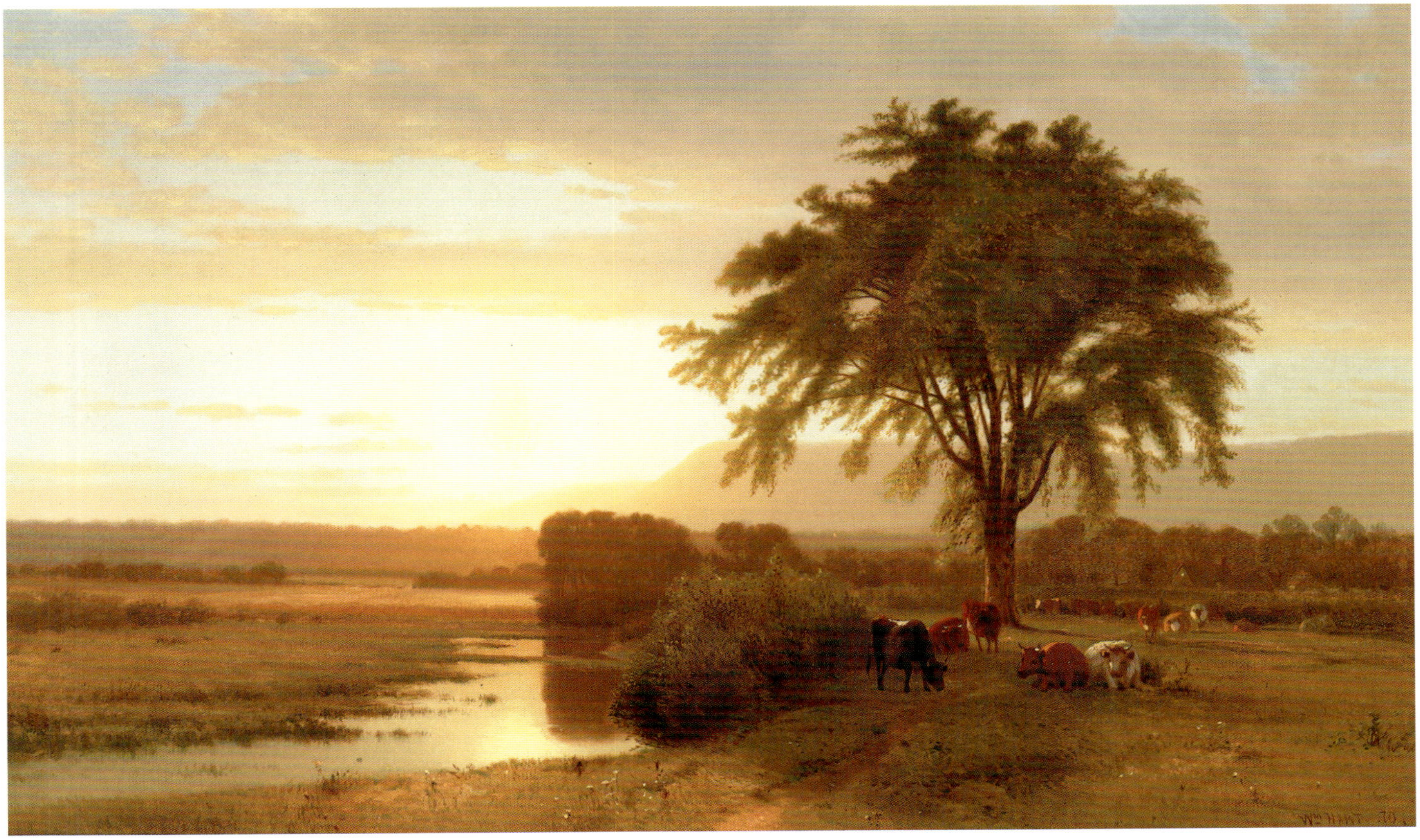

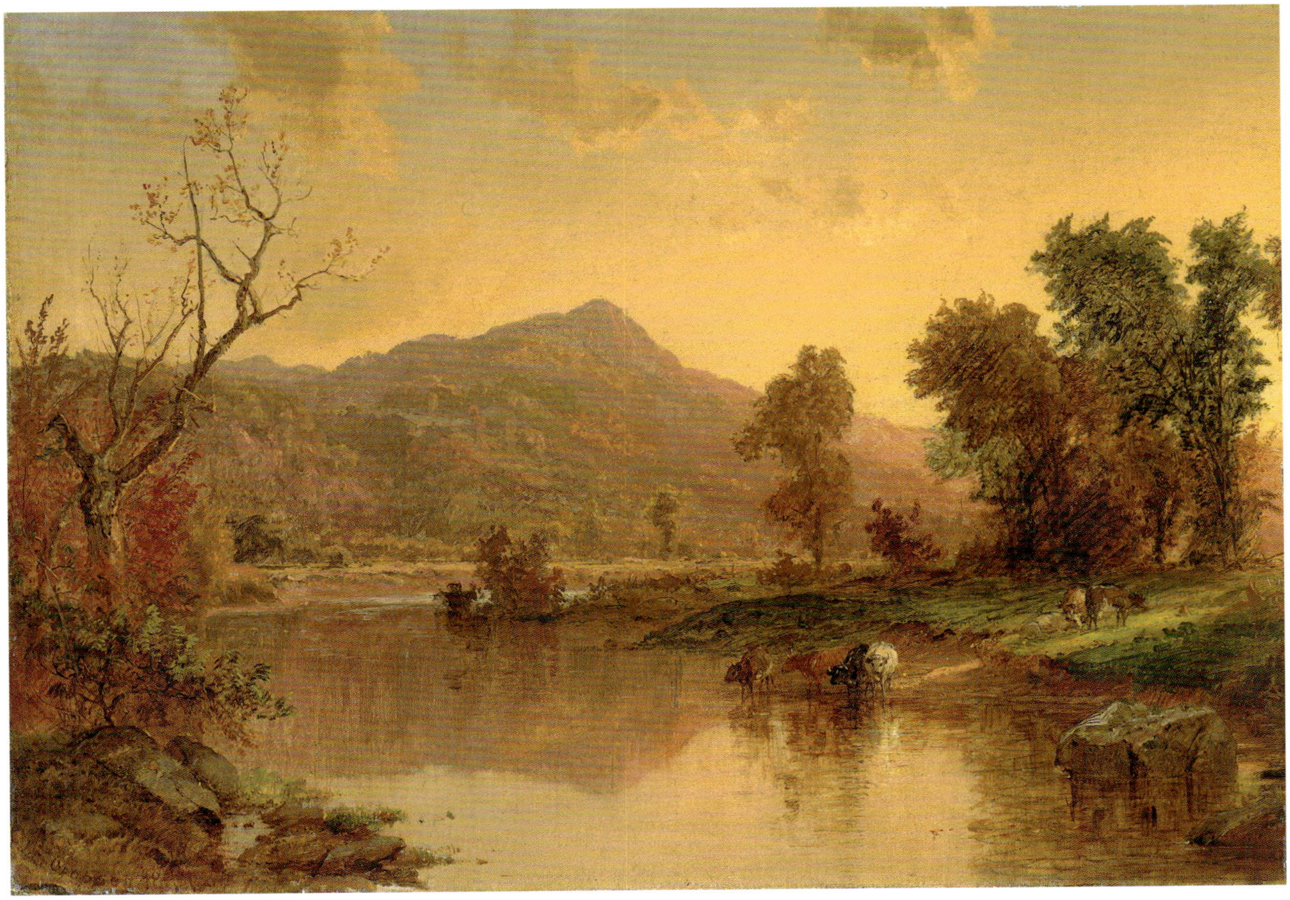

Evening

Regis Francois Gignoux—a Frenchman well trained in various Parisian studios, including that of Delaroche—and DeWitt Clinton Boutelle, a self-schooled American of French descent, are compared in these two paintings of cows returning to the barn at close of day. Gignoux has divided his composition between land and sky, using a great tree near the center foreground to unite the two. A further division suggests the theme of man encroaching on nature by contrasting a wilder landscape on the left with a more domesticated one on the right. The sun has set, coloring the sky brilliantly with its afterglow and sending long, final rays of light across the meadow to illuminate a homestead. A boy guides the herd home, nearly concluding their daily cycle just as autumn colors suggest the penultimate season. Boutelle also depicts the fall colors conjoined with close of day. Framed by an archway of trees, the slip of a new moon rises in a turquoise sky above the brightness of the sun's afterglow. Night and day are both present in the twilight hour, which is the most fleeting. Darkness has begun to settle; the day has progressed just moments after the time of Gignoux's painting, showing how quickly light can transform the landscape. A stream reflecting the dying sun provides the only earthbound light as a young boy dressed in patriotic red, white, and blue herds several cows across a bridge back to their barn. The end of day is here conveyed in as comforting a way as in the preceding scenes, all showing the steady rhythm and inevitable progression of the day to its close.

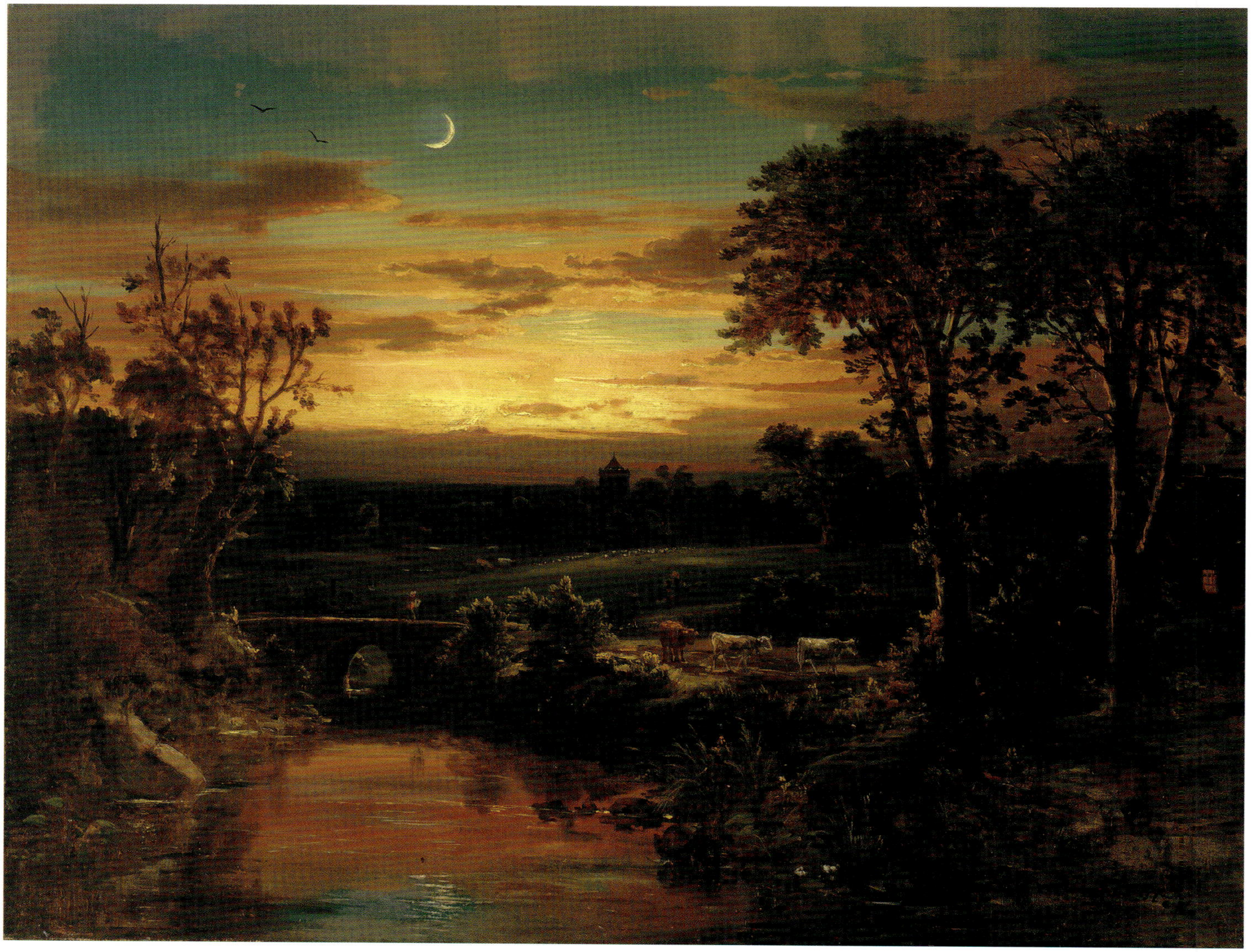

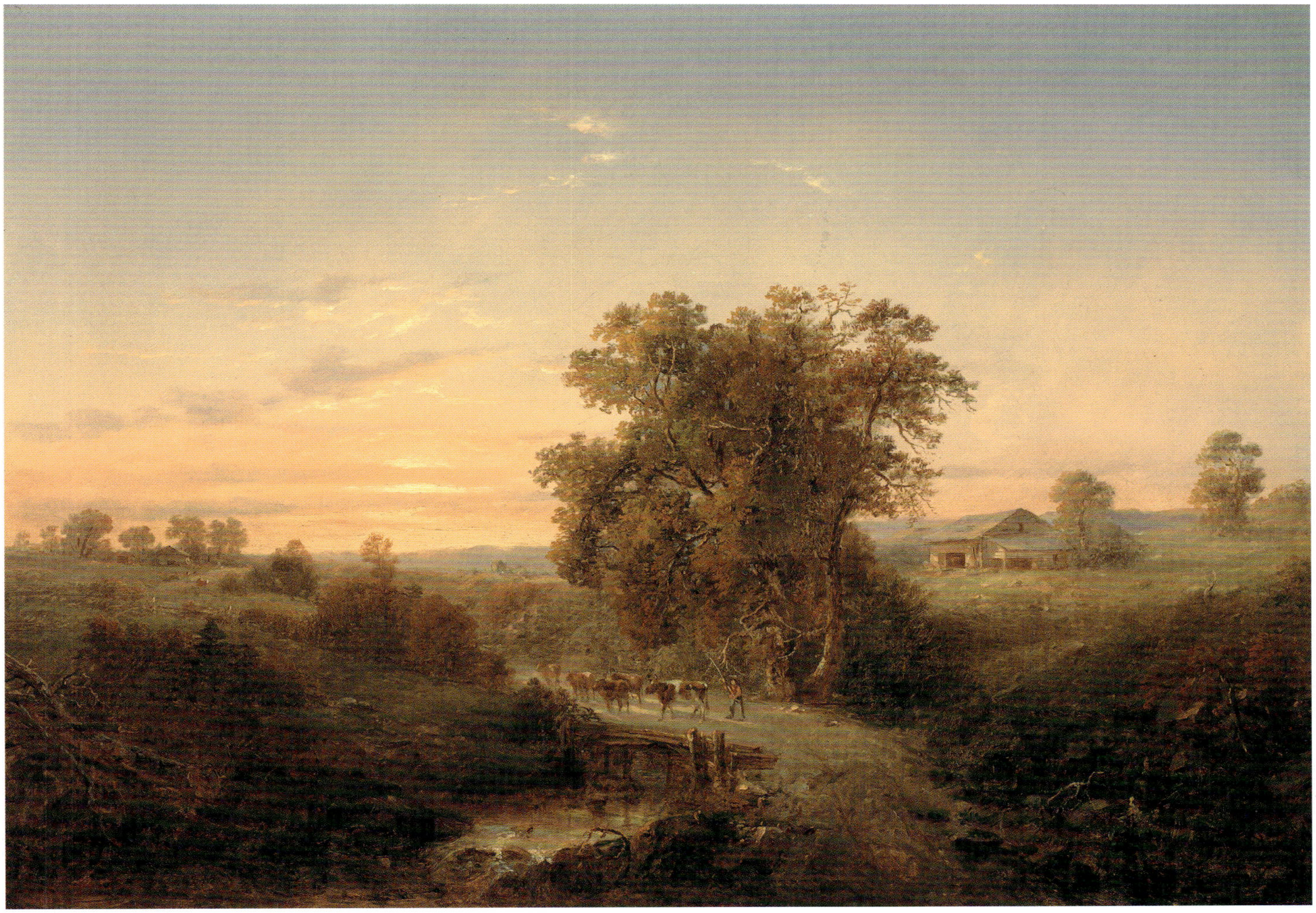

DeWitt Clinton Boutelle (1820–1884)
Sunset, n.d.
Oil on canvas board, 26 x 36 inches

Regis Francois Gignoux (1816–1882)
Heading Home, n.d.
Oil on canvas, 24½ x 35 inches

III. Weather Conditions, Atmosphere, and Mood

In these mountains he [an Indian trader] told me, according to Indian belief, was kept the great treasury of storm and sunshine, for the region of the Hudson. An old squaw spirit had charge of it, who dwelt on the highest peak of the mountain. . . . The great Manitou, or master spirit, employed her to manufacture clouds; sometimes she wove them out of cob webs, gossamers, and the morning dew, and sent them off flake after flake, to float in the air and give light summer showers—sometimes she would brew up black thunder-storms, and send down drenching rains, to swell the streams and sweep everything away.

—Washington Irving, "The Catskill Mountains," *A Landscape Book*, 1868

. . . your next step should be the study of the influence of atmosphere—the power of which defines and measures space—an intangible agent, visible, yet without that material substance which belongs to imitable objects, in fact, an absolute nothing, yet of mighty influence.

—Asher B. Durand, "Letters on Landscape Painting," V, *Crayon*

WEATHER, A SIGNIFICANT TOOL WITH WHICH TO create mood in a painting, originates from the sky by way of the combined elements of air, water, clouds, and light. As Thomas Cole wrote in his *Essay on American Scenery*:[6] "The [sky is] the soul of all scenery, in it are the fountains of light, and shade, and color. Whatever expression the sky takes, the features of the landscape are affected in unison, whether it be the serenity of the summer's blue, or the dark tumult of the storm." Cole went on to describe the "vicissitudes" of the American climate as being both a trial and a blessing—the blessing being the wonderment that comes with the observation of changing skies and weather. The mystery and power of weather, the suddenness of a punishing summer storm versus the pastoral quiet of a gentle summer day, also symbolized the power of a force greater than man: nature and God. The sky as a region of the sublime in art was not a concept originated by the Hudson River School. Caspar David Friedrich refused Goethe's commission to paint scientifically accurate studies of clouds because the artist believed that the sky possessed religious significance. Applying the reasoned study of science to any element of the sky would dispel its mystery, Friedrich believed.

Moody and atmospheric, Parton's view on the Hudson reveals the hardness of life and the challenging conditions nature can present for man to overcome. Menacing clouds darken not only the sky but also the turbulent water and shoreline dotted with scraggly, weather-worn trees. A single ray of light breaks free to fall at the water's edge on jagged rocks, themselves a threat to man. Whitecaps form across the Hudson River's surface, where a boat laden with hay—the product of man's agricultural labors—is guided on rough water away from shore by a tugboat. This activity seems to be a metaphor for man himself being guided through the challenges of nature's perils and his persistence in working to tame them. The dramatic sky, with many clouds of contrasting shapes and colors, seems to symbolize further man's struggles and conflicts with nature. The long line of steam from the tugboat parallels diagonal cloud formations, as though offering a path to safety.

A different view by Alexander Lawrie along the Hudson, this time under sunny weather conditions, provides a stark contrast in mood to Parton's painting. Lawrie's scene is lighthearted under a blue sky, with cottony clouds offering no threat of rain. The Hudson's distant mirror-smooth surface is dotted with white sails, indicating pleasure boats, as opposed to the heavy working vessels shown in Parton's composition. Changing both the visual prospect and the emotional one, this painting projects an expansive panoramic view rather than Parton's close-up and threatening one. Distant cliffs are lit with a glow from the late afternoon sun, the promise of a similarly bright and optimistic future. Small pioneer cottages nestled under the shelter of trees are barely visible and completely integrated with the landscape around them, as is the small church spire, nearly hidden by the forest surrounding it. Whereas man is at odds with nature in Parton's view on the Hudson, here man and nature seem to coexist harmoniously.

Arthur Parton (1842–1914)
On the Hudson, 1879
Oil on canvas, 12 1/4 x 20 inches

Alexander Lawrie (1828–1917)
Cold Springs on Hudson, 1871
Oil on canvas, 10 1/4 x 20 1/4 inches

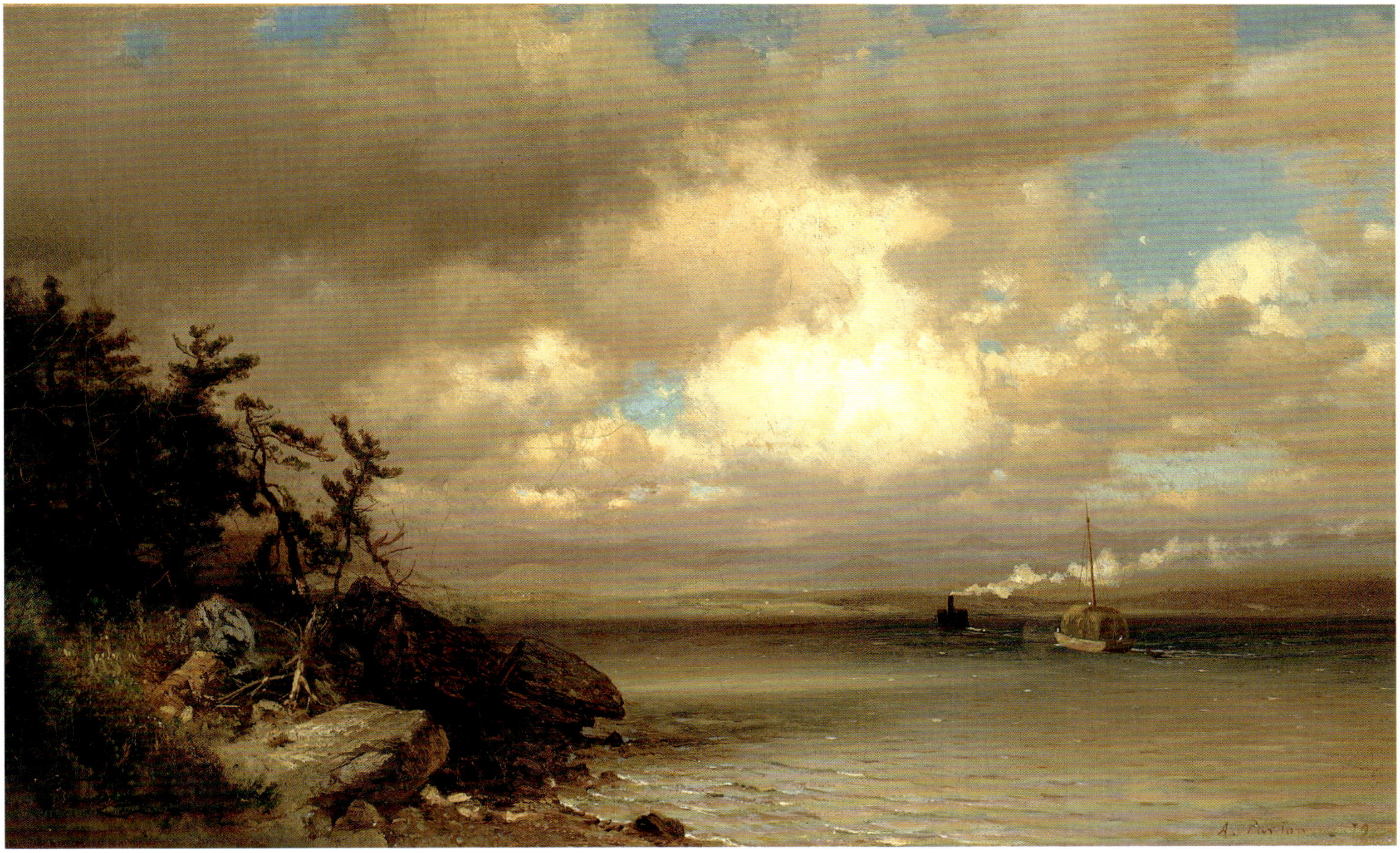

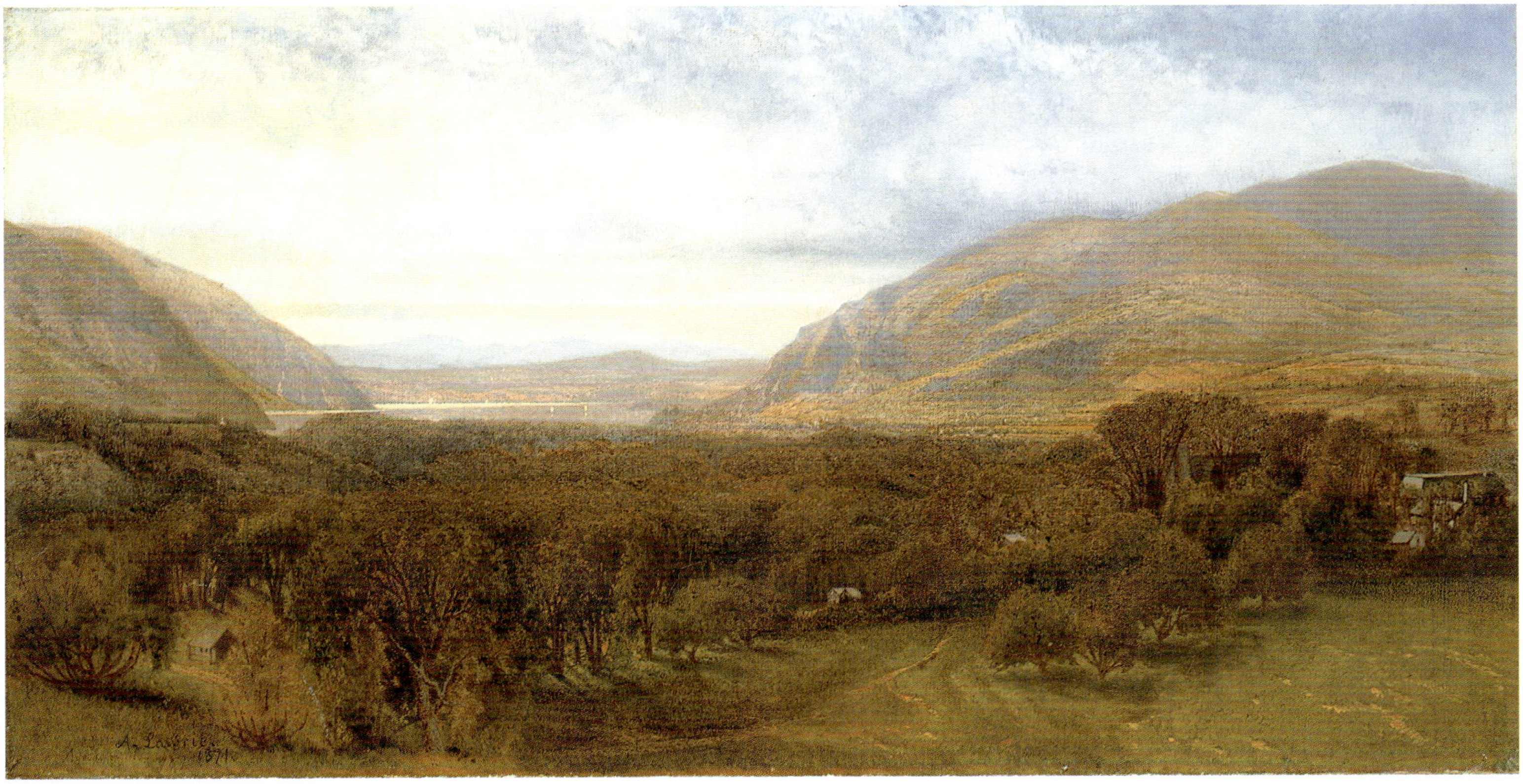

These two paintings by Gottlieb Daniel Paul Weber, an accomplished master trained in Germany, show how a single artist can observe the same landscape elements during the same season and at the same time of day, but see markedly different effects due to changed weather conditions.

In both paintings, Weber depicts a similar meadow and stream, observing them during very different atmospheric conditions. His Pre-Raphaelite-inspired, close observation of shrubs and wildflowers is careful and exact. Combined with his Germanic attention to solid draftsmanship, the result is clarity of detail. Yet in each scene, he manages to create very different nearly palpable moods that enable the viewer to experience the particular weather conditions of the day. The mood in Weber's earlier painting (1861) is languid and humid, the atmosphere heavy and oppressive with moisture from a storm that has just passed through. A dead tree fallen across the stream, a casualty of the turbulent weather, intensifies the anxious mood of this painting. By not showing the actual storm, Weber achieves the more difficult feat of capturing and conveying the sensation of humidity and warmth.

In his later work (1863), the air is translucent and buoyant with the calm sweetness of a summer day, revealing the distinct shapes, forms, and colors of the scene in midday's bright even light. The composition is harmonious and deliberate; a large tree on the left rises across the landscape to complete the arch of clouds moving up from the horizon to meet the tree's outstretched branches. Shapes echo one another in a pleasing, rhythmic repetition that further accentuates the mood of pleasant summer relaxation: golden hay harvested and mounded on a cart repeats rounded mountain tops tinted with the hues of late summer.

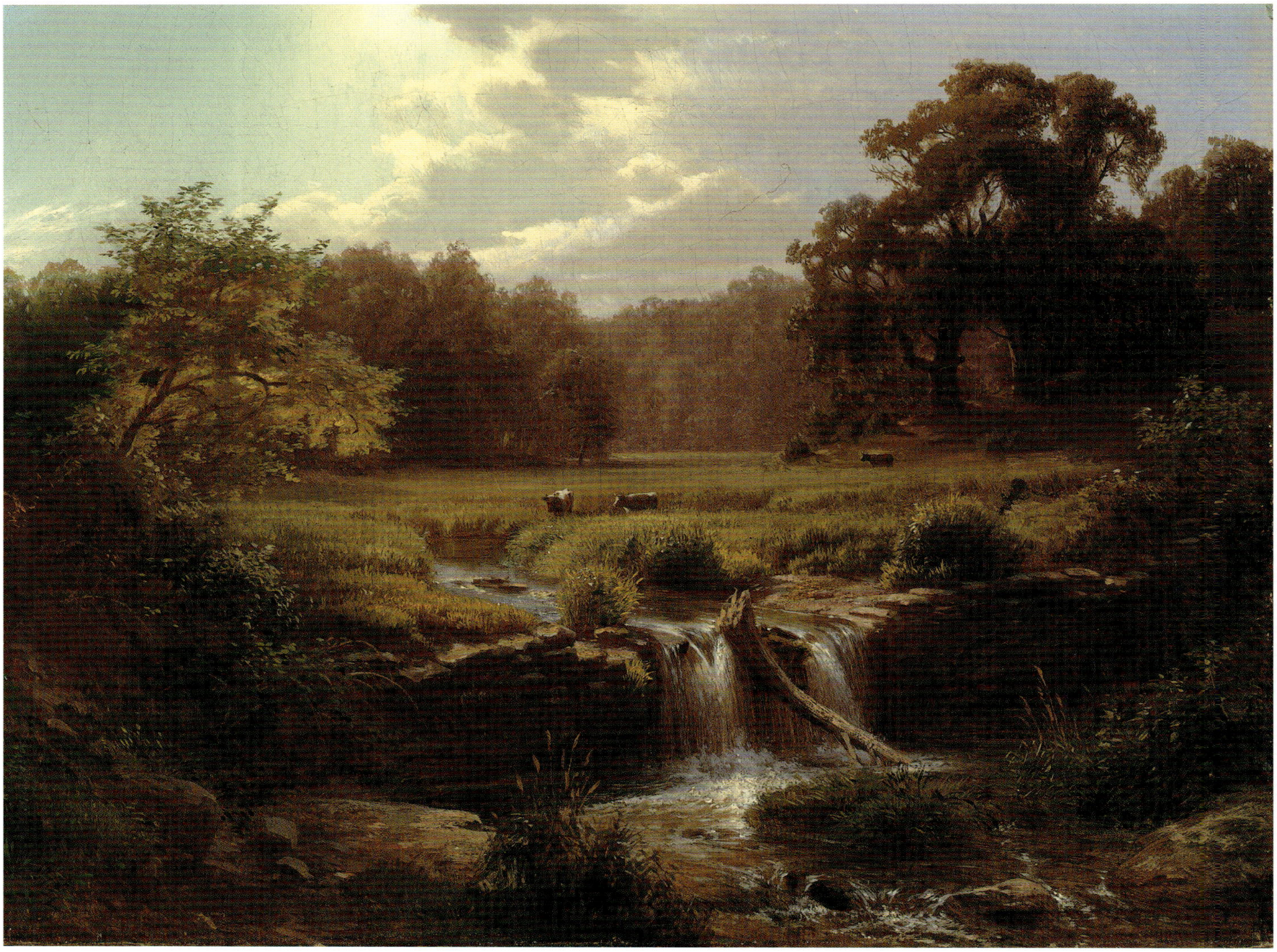

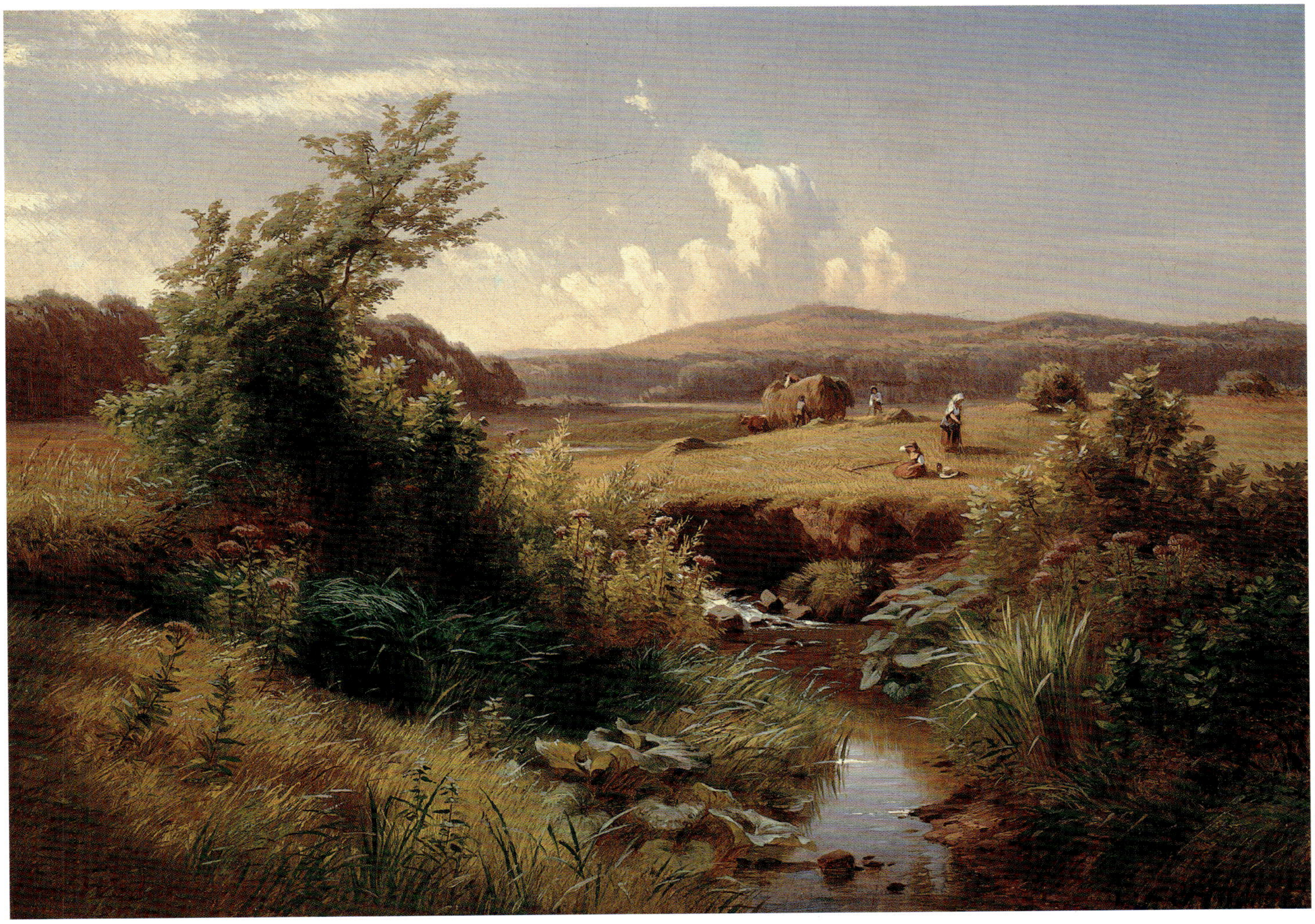

Shown apart, the subtle differences in light and atmosphere, so apparent when the paintings are paired, would be much more difficult to perceive and appreciate. Together, they demonstrate that changes in nature are not always dramatic (i.e., night versus day or winter versus summer) but can be as slight as a shift from hazy to clear on a day in late summer.

Gottlieb Daniel Paul Weber (1823–1916)
Summer Landscape, 1861
Oil on canvas, 14 x 19 inches

Gottlieb Daniel Paul Weber (1823–1916)
Haying Scene, 1863
Oil on canvas, 14 x 20 inches

John William Casilear has also selected a single scene, that of meadows along the Genesee River in upstate New York, and painted it under different weather conditions. Both canvases are typical, peaceful, and calming landscapes by the artist, who was a close friend of Durand and Kensett and traveled with them in 1840–1841 to Europe. Casilear's earlier training as an engraver is recalled through his use of a narrow color range, close observation, and careful rendering of natural detail. The special quality of pleasing, gentle light that was his hallmark has a Claudian stillness to it.

A master of nuance in color and light, Casilear's canvas of 1874 radiates peace and harmony as the serenity of a summer afternoon stretches across the canvas under the soft, languid light of midday. Cows watering at the river's edge lend an air of domesticity to the mood while serving to establish a diagonal echoed by the placement of the receding woods. Water and sky, executed in pastel shades of blue and yellow, are key motifs in this painting. A single Claudian tree rises gracefully on the left, linking land and sky and bridging the bright greens of the shore with the dark foliage of the trees across the river. Lit by the sun, this tree, the only vertical in an otherwise diagonally organized composition, serves to relieve the monotony of both pictorial structure and subject; it is the protagonist in a script with few other characters.

The same scene (1873), with cows watering in a small stream that cuts through a meadow, is slightly different in mood and composition. A dark stand of trees marches horizontally across the landscape from the left edge and breaks where the brook meanders back to meet the horizon line. Again, placement and contrast in the coloring of the cows reinforce the horizontal in this piece with very little contrast otherwise. The light is even and subdued, with nothing to break its course across the landscape. A cattle herder dressed in white shirt and blue trousers stands in the field—so small as to not clash with his natural surroundings but blend into them. No single protagonist emerges from this completely pastoral, balanced, and placid painting where time seems to be suspended. Casilear loved Genesee scenery and painted it frequently, searching for subtle differences in light, atmosphere, and mood in a manner resembling Claude Monet's (1840–1926) series of paintings, including those of haystacks, water lilies, and the cliffs at Belle Ile in the varying light of different times of day.

John William Casilear (1811–1893)
Quiet River (Genesee), 1874
Oil on canvas, 14 x 23 inches

John William Casilear (1811–1893)
Genesee River Scenery, 1873
Oil on canvas, 9 1/2 x 20 inches

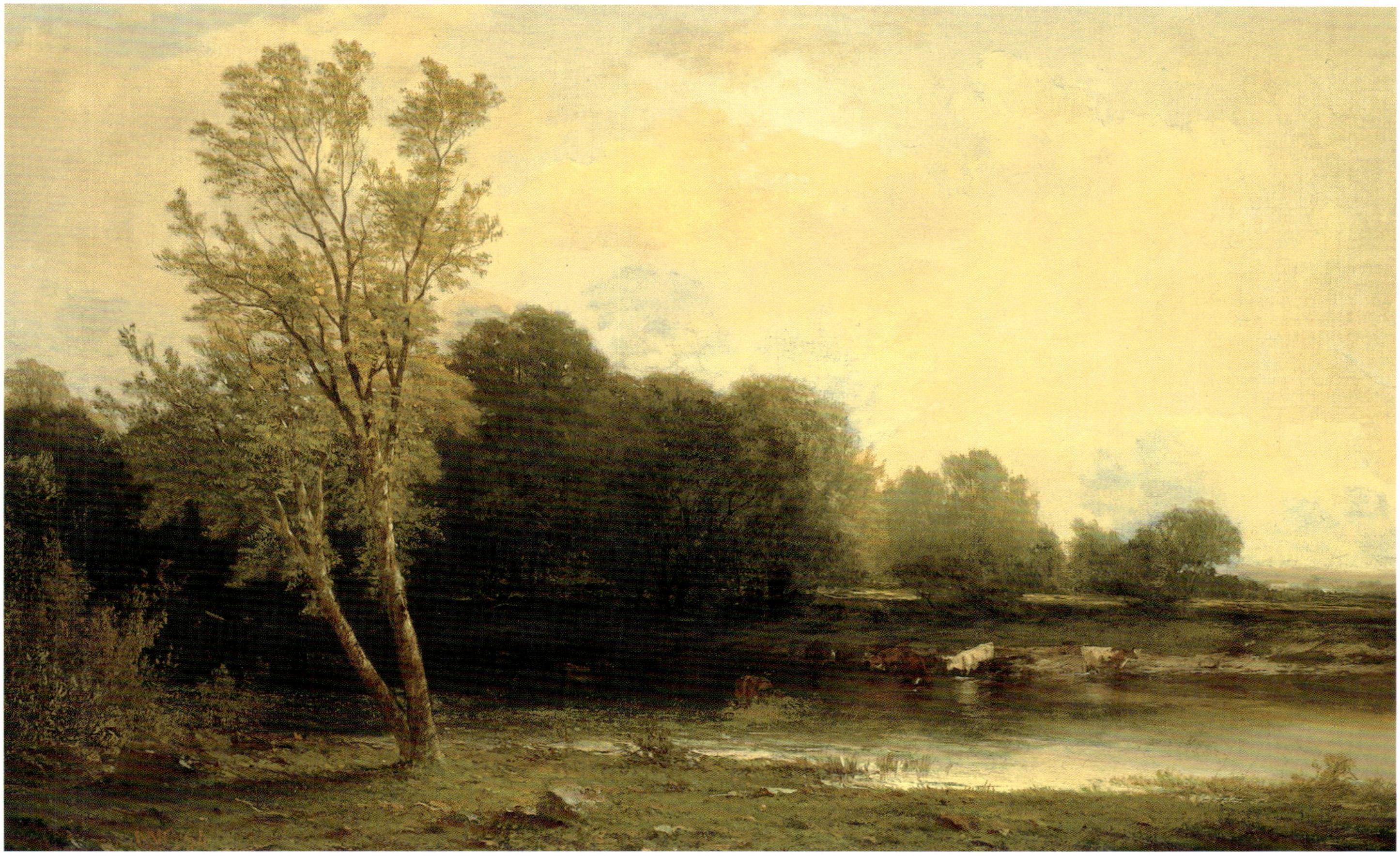

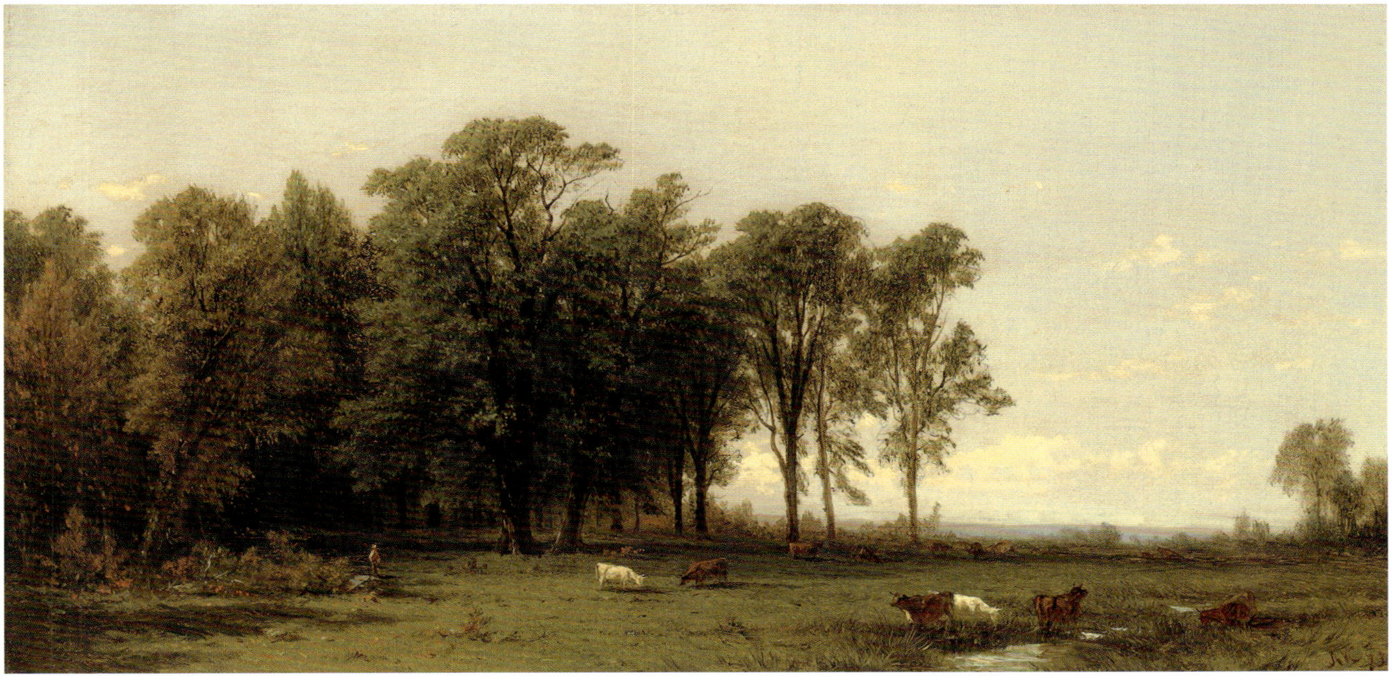

Educated at Yale University in New Haven, Connecticut, before studying painting in New York City, Richard William Hubbard also traveled in Europe, where he became an ardent proponent of the work of Claude Lorrain. After returning home to Connecticut, he developed into a prolific, highly respected member of the Hudson River School and was elected a full member of the National Academy of Design. The Claudian influence is evident in both paintings compared here, especially with respect to Hubbard's masterful use of subtle light effects and tonal coloring to evoke different moods. These two paintings exploit the same simple elements of trees, sky, and water to skillfully portray slightly different light and weather conditions.

In the earlier painting, a hint of autumn pervades the atmosphere. A soft gray overcast sky offers no ray of sunlight to bring warmth to the palette. Slightly foreboding, the mood is somber and still. Completed as a wedding gift to his niece,[7] Hubbard may have felt he had more artistic freedom in this family piece than if it had been intended for the public domain in that there is an unusual feathery lightness to his brush. He may also have wanted to imbue the painting with a specific symbolism, conveyed through the placement of two trees at the left of the composition, standing for husband and wife, surrounded by the younger growth, perhaps a reference to future offspring of their union. The trees sprout from an outcropping of bedrock, which could refer both to the solid foundation of marriage and to the emblem of Christ. One tree is green with summer foliage, the other has turned gold and red with seasonal change. The trees lean into the sky toward the valley below, crossed with fields and meadows that lead up to the blue haze of mountains. The taller tree reaches into the sky, aspiring to great heights, whereas the

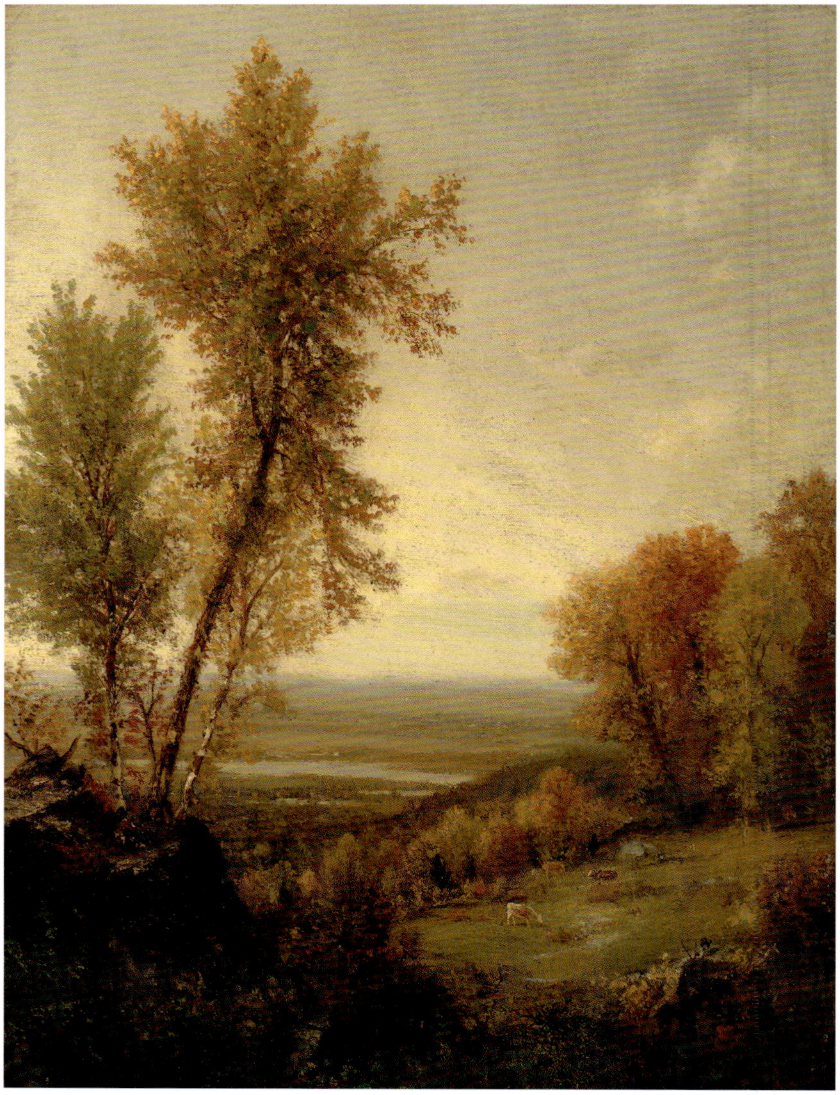

other stands in its shelter. Three cows graze in a meadow, a further allusion to family and domesticity. The style of this small painting, its lyrical poetry, and its layered symbolism make it a classic example of Hudson River School painting.

The second painting by Hubbard depicts a similarly bucolic valley, the composition divided in half by earth and sky, united by a tall Claudian tree on the left. Gentle clouds, lit on their underside by softening rays from a late afternoon sun, are benign and weightless in a pale blue sky. Cows graze in a meadow by a stream; two figures converse behind a stone wall. Multiple contrasts are created by adjacent areas of light and shadow juxtaposed throughout the composition, leading the eye to a distant V formation at the intersection of tree line and mountain. The atmosphere is more crisp; details more carefully articulated. The mood is uncomplicated, airy, and calm, differing from the more serious mood conveyed by the earlier canvas.

Richard William Hubbard (1816–1888)
Mount Holyoke Looking toward Connecticut River, 1877
Oil on artist's board, 15 x 12 1/2 inches

Richard William Hubbard (1816–1888)
Landscape with Cows, 1879
Oil on canvas, 13 x 12 1/4 inches

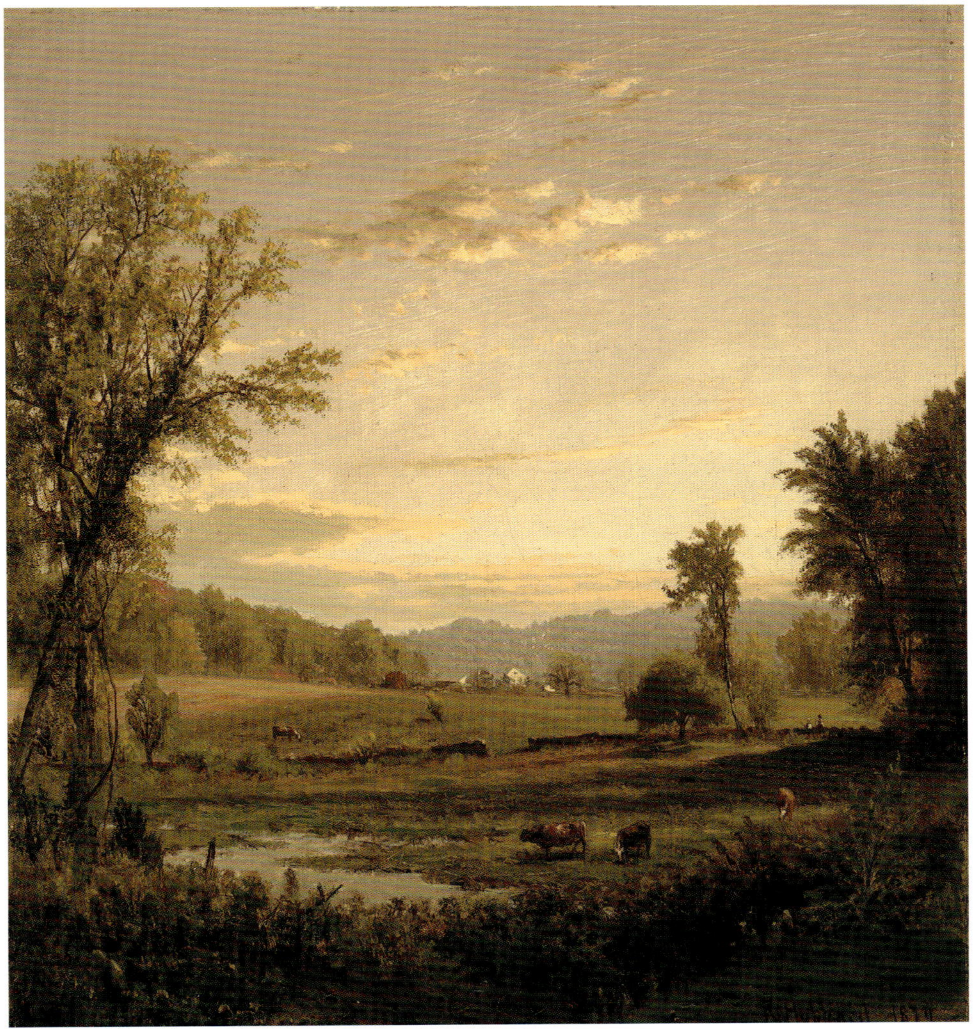

IV. Seasons

Our seasons are all poetical; the phenomena of our heavens are full of sublimity and beauty. Winter with us has none of its proverbial gloom. It may have its howling winds, and thrilling frosts, and whirling snow-storms; but it has also its long intervals of cloudless sunshine, when the snow-clad earth gives redoubled brightness to the day; when at night the stars beam with intensest lustre, or the moon floods the whole landscape with her most limpid radiance—and then the joyous outbreak of our spring bursting at once into leaf and blossom, redundant with vegetation, and vociferous with life!—and the splendors of our summer; its morning voluptuousness and evening glory; its airy palaces of sun-gilt clouds piled up in a deep azure sky; and its gust of tempest of almost tropical grandeur, when the forked lightning and the bellowing thunder volley from the battlements of heaven and shake the sultry atmosphere—and the sublime melancholy of our autumn, magnificent in its decay, withering down the pomp and pride of a woodland country, yet reflecting back from its yellow forests the golden serenity of the sky.

—Washington Irving, "The Catskill Mountains,"
A Landscape Book, 1868

IN THIS SECTION, WE SHOW SEVEN INTENDED PAIRS OF paintings and one sampler by six different artists who have focused on seasonal, comparisons and contrasts. Each artist has compared and contrasted changing effects of the seasons on landscape along with the particular symbolism of different times of the year. Spring reveals the hopeful optimism of youth with pure, clear atmospheric conditions; summer is painted with mature foliage in a heavier, more dense, and languid atmosphere; autumn's brilliant colors and more complicated, changeable weather and atmosphere presage the end of nature's cycle and the quiet dormancy of winter. When consciously creating pairs, the Hudson River School artist most frequently chose the opposing seasons of spring and autumn—the months during which contrasts can be either dramatic or subtle, depending on the stage within the seasonal transitional cycle. Therefore, even within the four individual seasons, there can be many marked differences in color, mood, and so on. Both spring and autumn are seasons of poignant change: the nascence of spring quickly evolving to summer's lethargic ripeness, whereas autumn's transient brilliance soon gives way to winter's barren slumber. While summer, with its scenes of recreation and harvest, was a favorite subject of single canvases, winter was the specialty and interest of only a few artists. In contrasting the seasons, Hudson River School artists frequently incorporated various subthemes—land versus water, cultivation versus wilderness—to underscore the interrelatedness of iconographical elements, adding philosophical meaning and depth to their landscape subjects.

Using a sampler-like format, Thomas Birch has created within one frame four identically sized horizontal ovals depicting the seasons, with contrasting weather conditions appropriate to each particular time of year. These small paintings demonstrate the artist's skill in rendering light effects and creating mood. In the center of the four ovals, Birch has placed a tiny roundel showing a moonlit night scene. Summer and winter are contrasted on the left half of the series, spring and autumn on the right. The heat and drama of a thunderstorm are represented in summer, as lightning flashes across a dramatic sky and Native Americans hunt and fish in the landscape. Winter shows no sign of life, as snowflakes fall on trees, meadow, and stream in a motionless countryside. Spring bounds with energy, as water rushes over rocks and spills into a foreground pool. Trees burst with new growth, bending their branches in the stormy clouds overhead. Autumn is dressed in the rich colors of that season, as a hunter works his way through a cold, driving rain. Birch has chosen to depict each season under stormy weather conditions but manages to express different emotions, ranging from excitement to stillness.

Thomas Birch (1779–1851)
Five Landscape Vignettes, n.d.
Oil on board, 9 7/16 x 13 inches

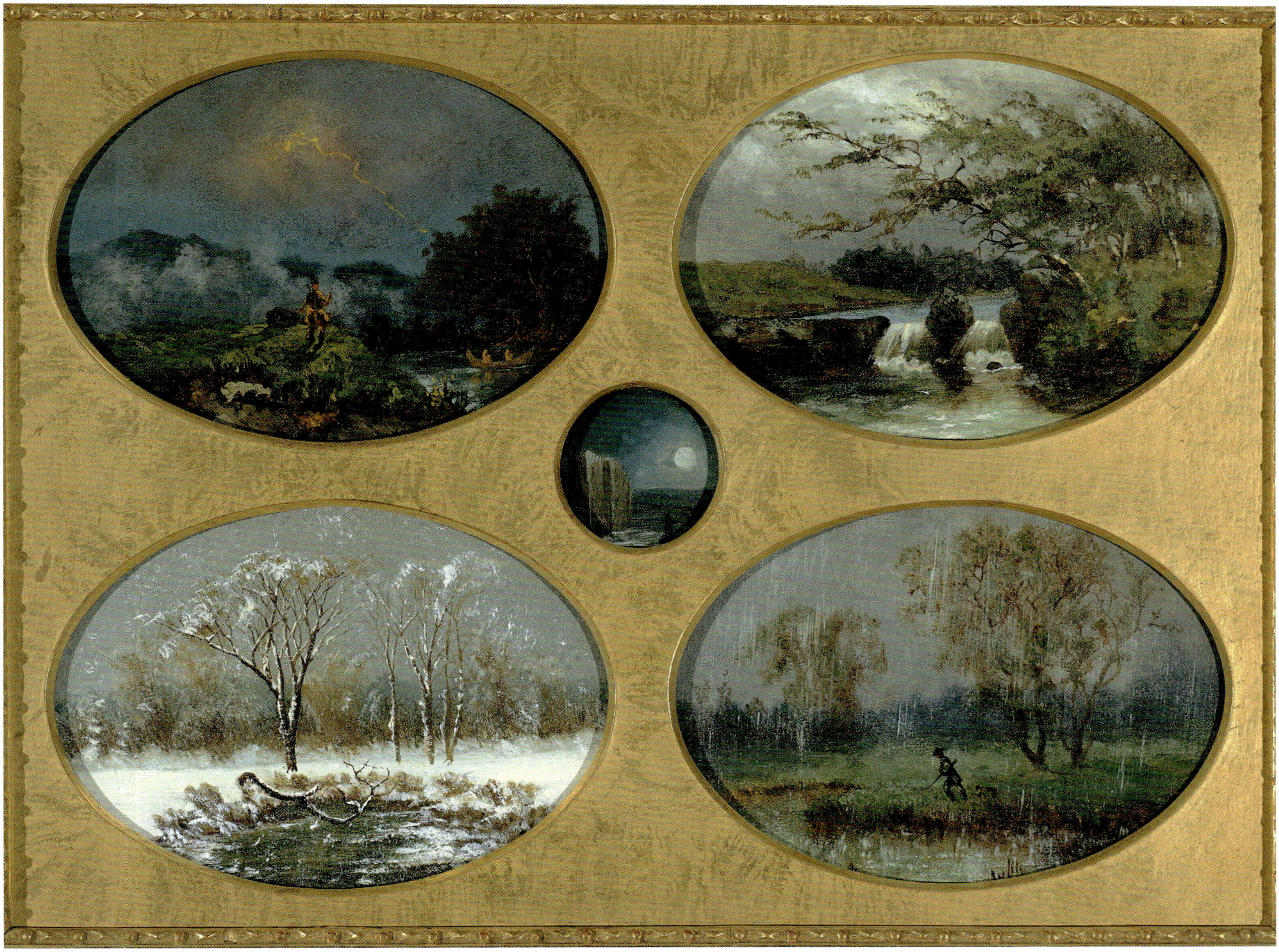

Clinton Loveridge is represented by three pairs of compact, horizontal paintings, each revealing his mastery of spare, simple compositions that create, on an intimate scale, the vast expansiveness of land, water, and sky. Modest in size, his scenes of the seasons are consistent but not formulaic. Autumn is contemplative, somewhat brooding, whereas spring is clear, scintillating, vibrant, and new.

In the first pair, *Autumn Landscape* and *Spring Landscape*, Loveridge uses groups of trees as brackets to unite the paintings, intended to be hung side by side. Trees colored in fall foliage on the far left of one painting bend toward and contrast with those bright with the green of spring on the far right of the other. Dense with moisture, autumnal clouds are gray and yellow compared to weightless, white cloud puffs of spring. Contrasting and intersecting

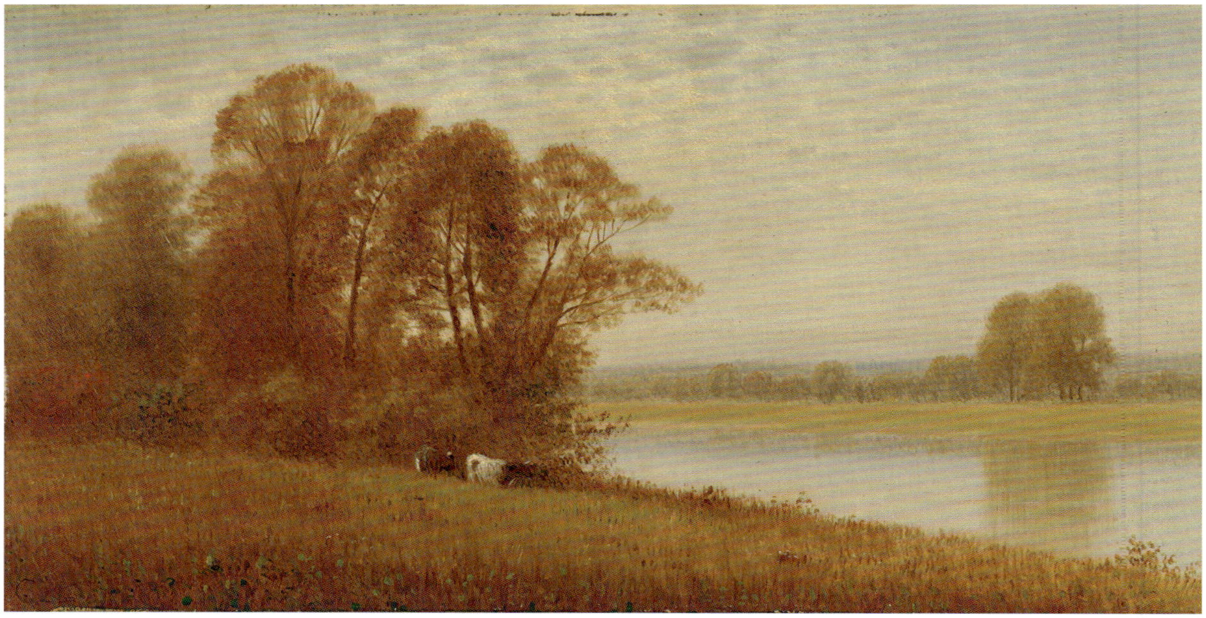

Clinton Loveridge (1824–1902)
Autumn Landscape, n.d.
Oil on artist's board, 7¾ x 13¾ inches

Clinton Loveridge (1824–1902)
Spring Landscape, n.d.
Oil on artist's board, 7¾ x 13¾ inches

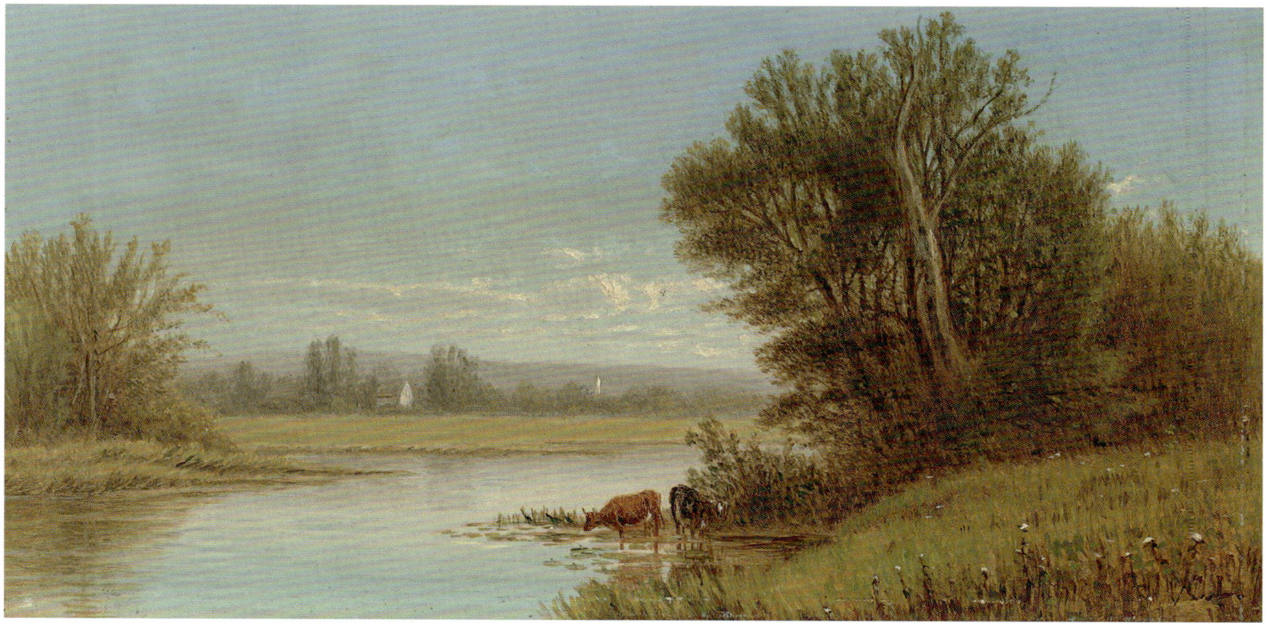

diagonals also unite the two canvases, the shape of the field in autumn sloping downward to meet the upward rise of a stream in spring.

In the next pair, autumn is more brilliant in color. The atmosphere is crisp and clear rather than weighed down with weather. The cool blue sky contrasts dramatically with the hot colors of fall foliage. A man pushes a sailboat with two people on board into the placid waters of the lake. The only other activity consists of mists rising from the water's surface to shroud the brightly colored trees along the shore. In springtime, storm clouds move across a cultivated New England farm scene, enlivened by a band of fruit trees dressed in the pale pink blossoms of the season. Cows grazing in an indolent green meadow seem to forecast the sleepy calm of summer.

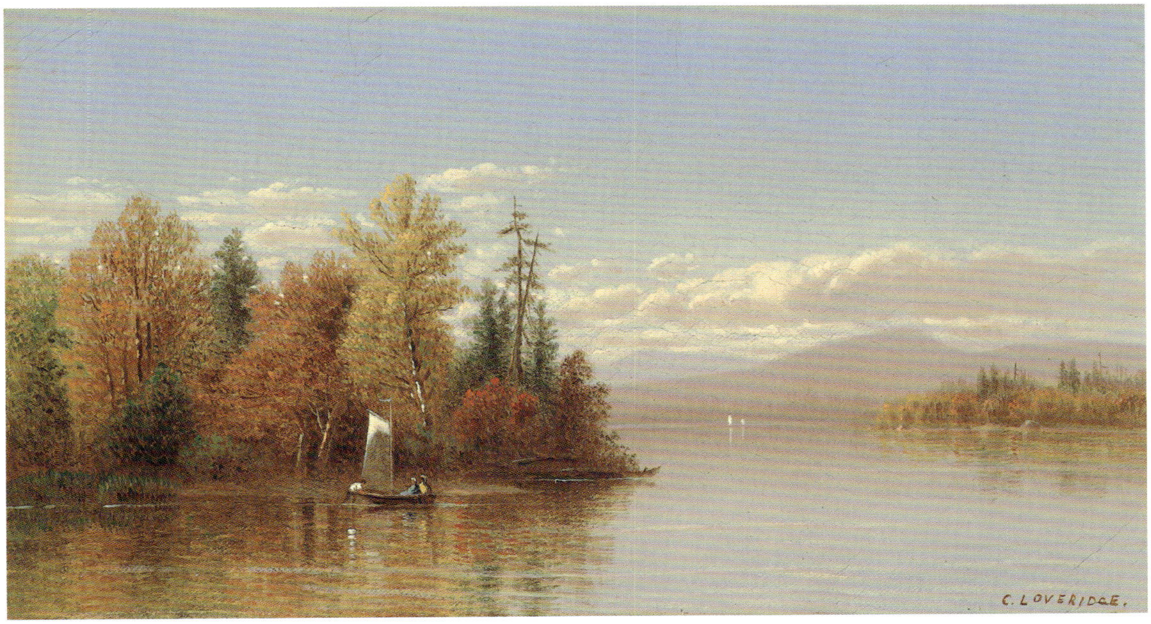

Clinton Loveridge (1824–1902)
Fall on a Lake in New England, c. 1870
Oil on canvas, 6 1/2 x 12 1/2 inches

Clinton Loveridge (1824–1902)
Farm Scene with Cows, c. 1870
Oil on canvas, 6 1/2 x 12 1/2 inches

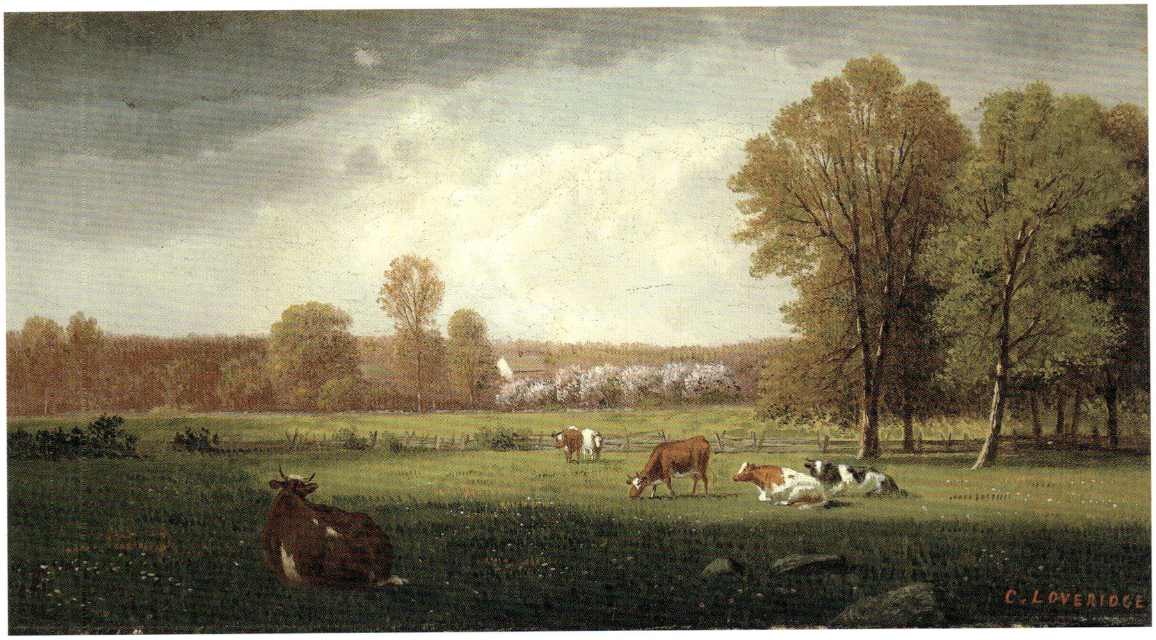

In the third pair, spring is colored in a combination of greens and darker, autumnal colors, illustrating that even within a single season, a whole range of palette becomes possible, based on the beginning, middle, and ending of a specific month. Loveridge uses a motif frequently employed by Sanford Gifford: a bar of land extending far out into the water upon which cows loll in the calm of day. The artist's creation of contrasting bands of light and shadow falling horizontally across the scene adds drama to the picture, simultaneously reinforcing the panoramic scale. A sense of perspective is created by the large framing tree on the right compared to the diminutive row of trees on the left. In the companion piece, autumn is again dressed in brilliant color made more vivid by dramatic light. Detail in the stream and rocks of the foreground is sharply observed. A visual crescendo is formed by the arabesque shape of bushes rising to trees and, in turn, to clouds. With the addition of birds flying, this autumn scene is active and dramatic rather than moody and introspective.

Clinton Loveridge (1824–1902)
Spring Landscape with Cows, n.d.
Oil on canvas, 9 x 14 inches

Clinton Loveridge (1824–1902)
Autumn Landscape with Cows, n.d.
Oil on canvas, 9 x 14 inches

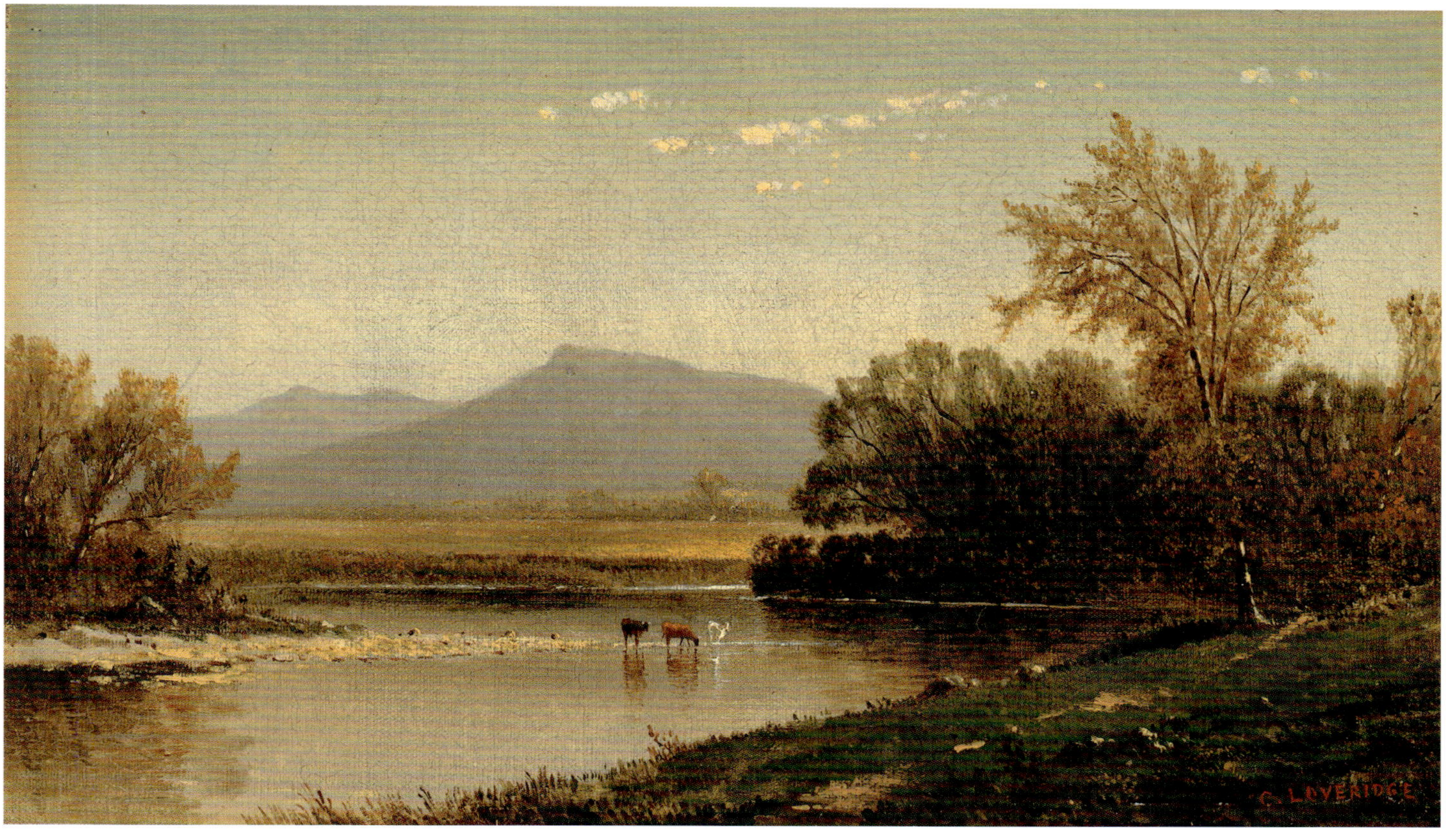
C. LEVERIDGE

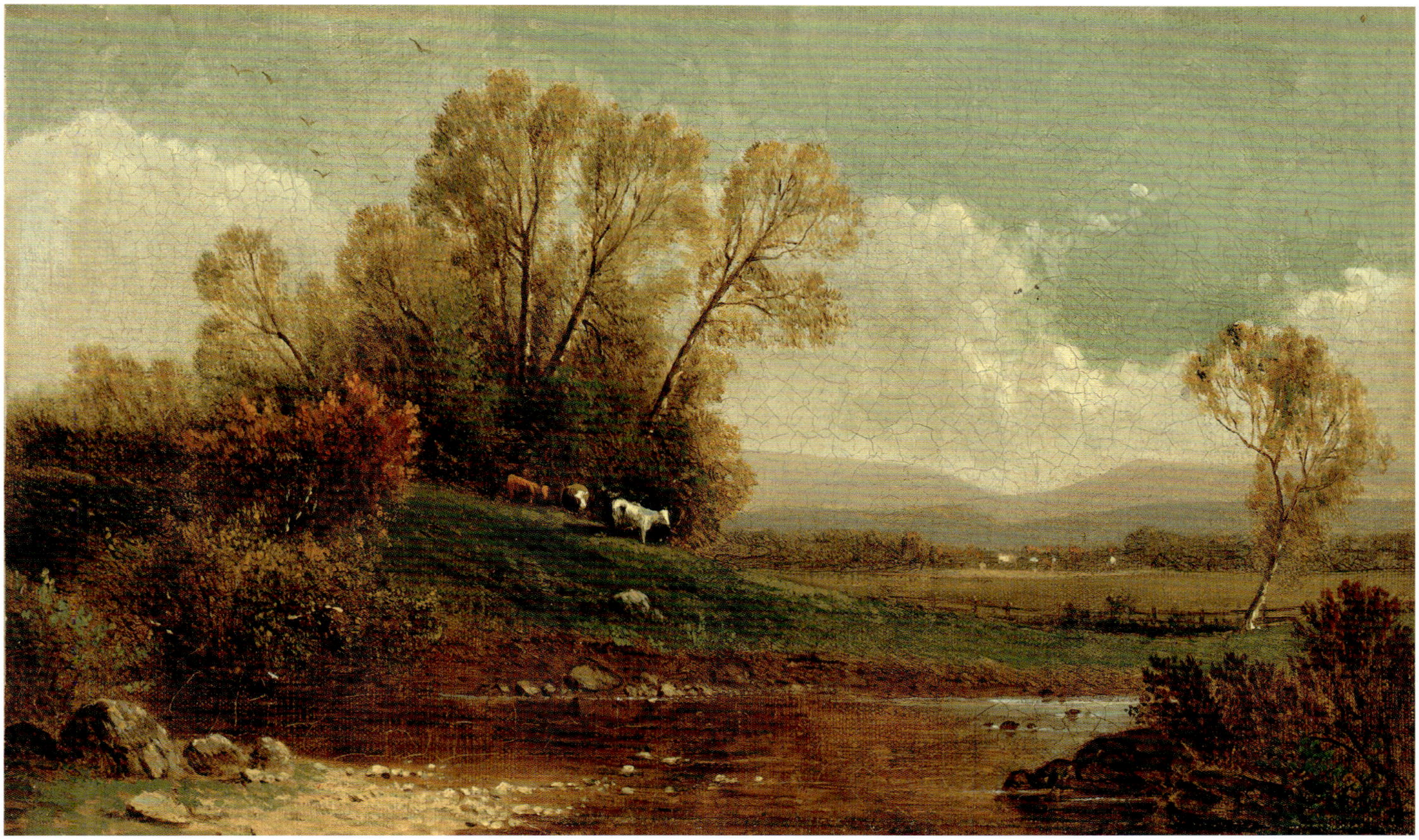

A pair of views of Newburgh on the Hudson by Henry Boese shows autumn and spring. The pair is united thematically, not only through the seasons but also through the life cycles that connect nature and man. Boese's fall scene shows a gray sky over the Hudson with the town of Newburgh on the distant shore. The shoreline is enlivened by crisp detail and rich color typical of the clear, penetrating light of this penultimate, changeable season. By contrast, the river and sky, their forms inherently less suited to distinct rendering, are further softened by mists and clouds in tones of pale blue. Two sailboats glide far off in the distance, and a rowboat sets off from a spear of land at the shore, showing man's various uses of water. A fallen trunk on the right of the composition and its living counterparts on land refer to life's cycles—those of both man and nature. The imminence of winter is suggested only by our own knowledge of the changing seasons.

Pastel shades of pink and yellow tint the sky in Boese's spring view, mimicking the clear pale hues of dawn and suggesting the parallel newness of the season. Young, fresh trees growing amid fallen tree stumps also refer to renewal and the regeneration of spring. Sailboats again appear on the blue waters of the Hudson, while along the shore path, a single person makes his way. A cottage deep in the woods reflects the comfort of home and echoes other signs of man's intrusion, including carriage ruts in the road, which indicate the passage of carts of industry, man's ultimate imposition on nature, and perhaps also the birth of progress.

Henry Boese (1824–1863)
Autumn View of Newburgh on the Hudson, n.d.
Oil on canvas, 6 1/2 x 11 inches

Henry Boese (1824–1863)
Spring View of Newburgh on the Hudson, n.d.
Oil on canvas, 6 1/2 x 11 inches

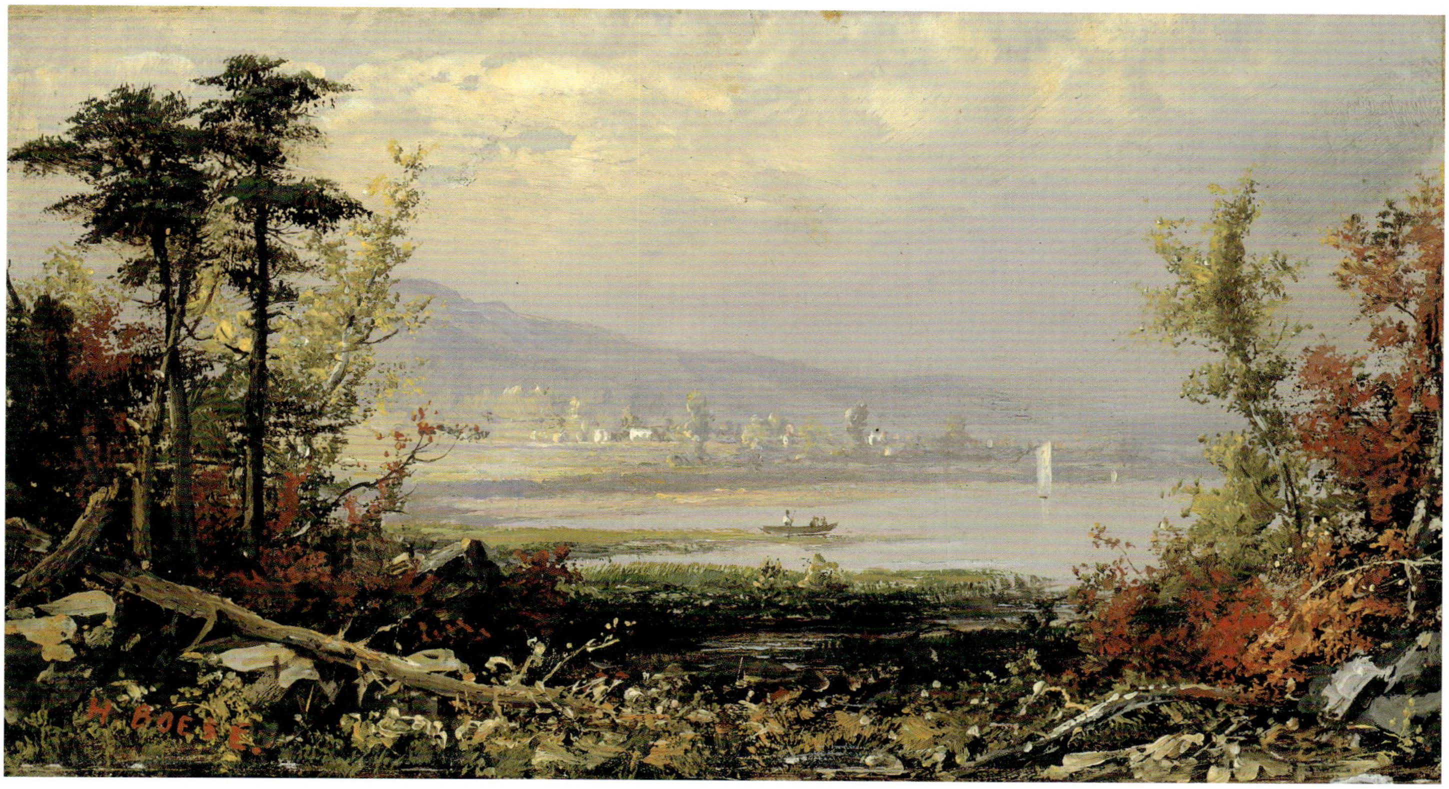
H. BOESE.

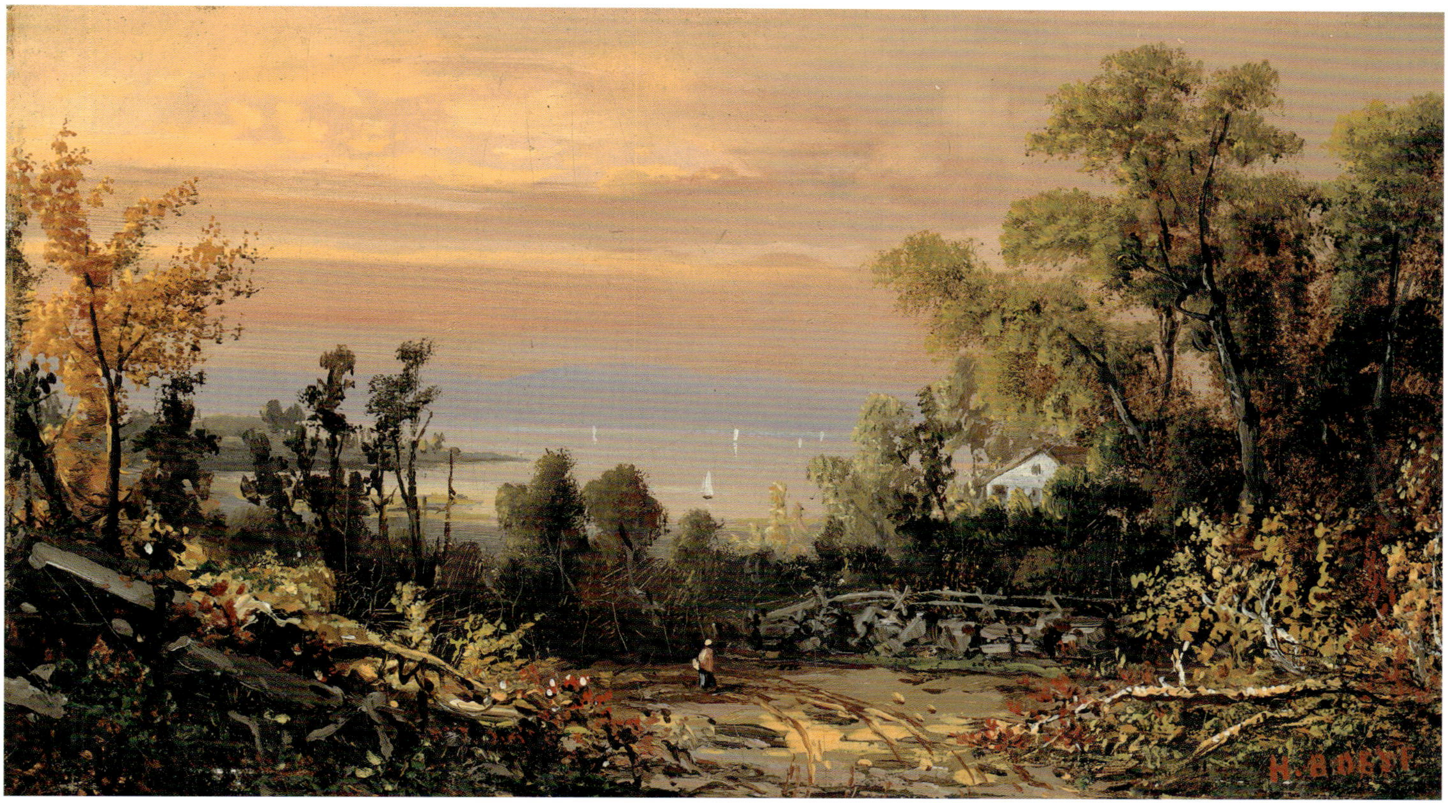

Early autumn is depicted by fall colors appearing throughout this landscape by William McDougal Hart. Cool grays and blues serve as foils to deep russets and reds of leaves in the harsh light of the season. There is a sense of benign acceptance in the bright afternoon air as both the day and the seasons enter their final stage. A single tree bends majestically over Esopus Creek in a gesture of benediction toward nature while cows water peacefully at the distant shoreline. Hart and his brother, James, had a studio on Esopus Creek, a pictuesque area that drew many artists. In the companion piece, Esopus Creek is now seen in springtime, fresh from a passing shower. Combining the effects of weather and light, clouds produce a curtain of rain that moves across the scene, revealing a clean blue sky with bright sunlight casting shadows on an emerald green meadow. Cows languish in the grass, waiting for the eventual passing of the storm. In everything, there prevails the sense of future promise and possibility that comes with this season, in stark comparison to the resigned but fiery conclusiveness of autumn.

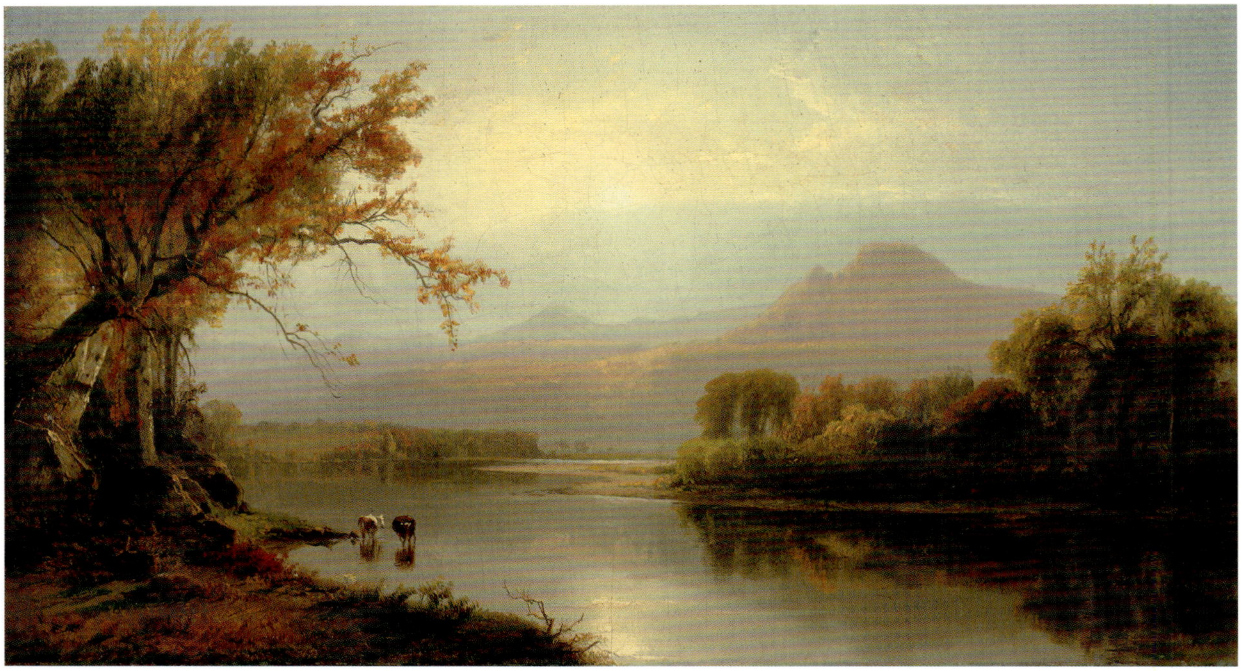

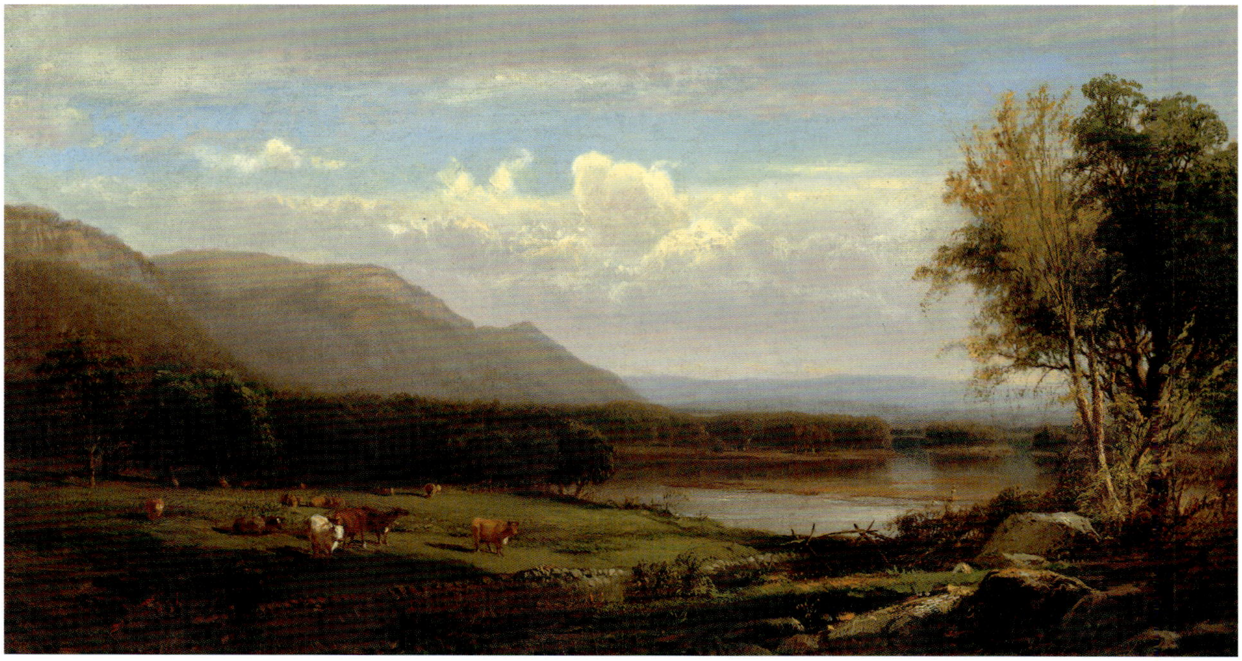

Daniel Charles Grose, a Canadian-born artist about whom little is known, depicted the effects of autumn and spring in a pair of carefully rendered, highly detailed paintings of the scenic Whissahickon Creek in Pennsylvania—a popular haunt for artists and poets (including Edgar Allan Poe) since the 1830s. The unusual vertical format is replete with foliage around a central chasm and stream. Autumn is bright with fall colors; spring is dense with green to set off the red shirt of a fisherman along the banks of the stream. The compositions are virtually mirror images of one another. Both use the convention of a large, framing tree on one side of the composition and a distant vista on the other. When hung together, spring on the left and autumn on the right, the framing trees come together in the center, joining the paintings and creating a sense of movement from spring to autumn as if within the same image.

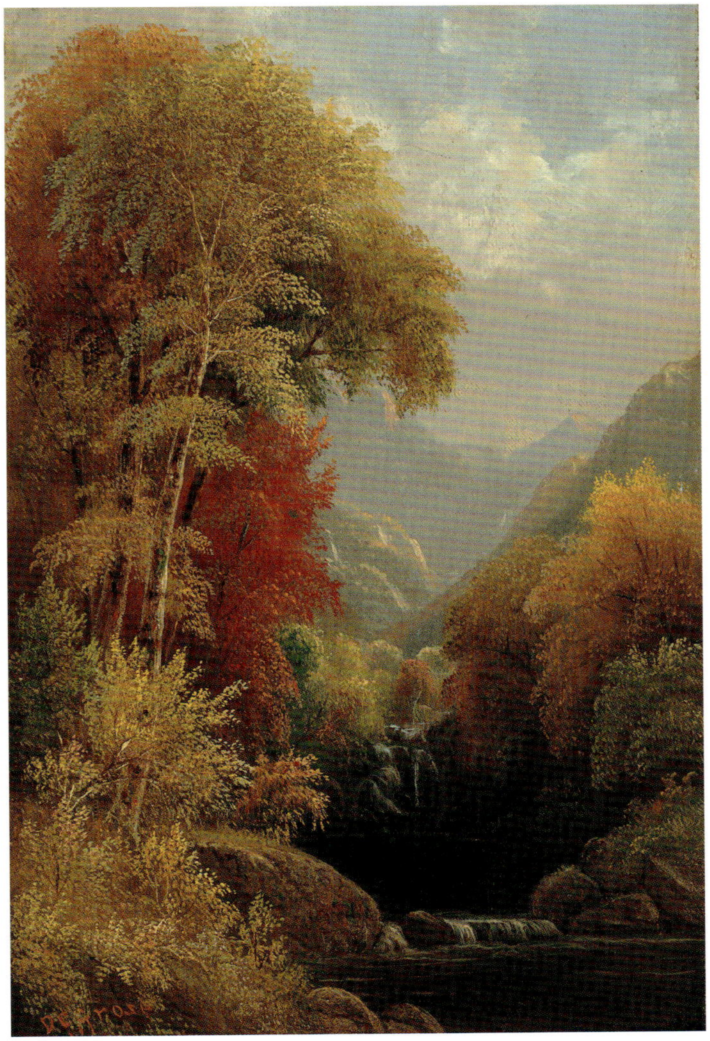

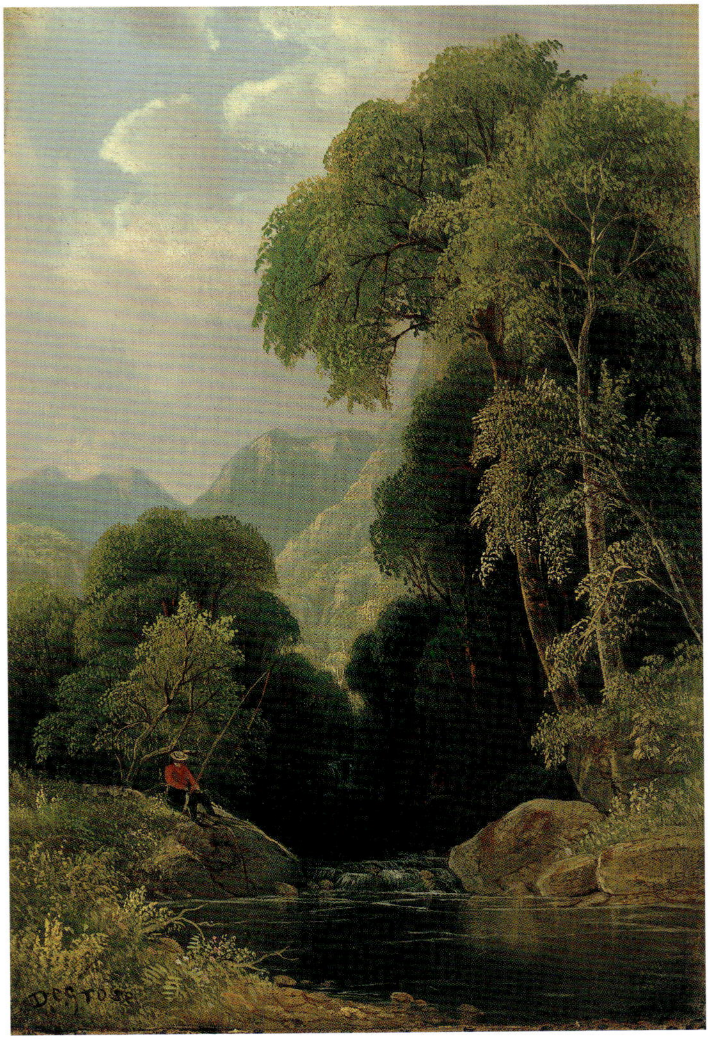

William McDougal Hart (1823–1894)
A View of the Esopus Creek in Autumn, 1864
Oil on canvas, 9 x 17 inches

William McDougal Hart (1823–1894)
A View of the Esopus Creek in Spring, n.d.
Oil on canvas, 9 x 17 inches

Daniel Charles Grose (active c. 1865–1890)
Autumn on the Whissahickon, n.d.
Oil on canvas, 18 x 12 inches

Daniel Charles Grose (active c. 1865–1890)
Spring on the Whissahickon, n.d.
Oil on canvas, 18 x 12 inches

Two landscapes employing water and mountains by Joseph Antonio Hekking compare and contrast summer and autumn. Summer, depicted in cool blues and greens, is the scene of domestication by man, whereas autumn, hot with russet and gold against gray, is wild and inhabited only by ducks and deer. Fenced meadows afford grazing land for cows in summer. The prominent placement of a sawed tree trunk reinforces the presence of man, indicated also by the farmhouse. In autumn, the thick, tangle of forested shoreline descends to crystalline water, where three ducks are shown. Two deer have emerged from the trees to drink. One deer stands on alert, head raised and ears drawn back—a symbol of primeval nature, presumably sensing danger in man's imminent arrival.

Joseph Antonio Hekking (1830–1903)
Summer Landscape with Cows Watering, n.d.
Oil on canvas, 9 x 15 inches

Joseph Antonio Hekking (1830–1903)
Autumn Landscape with Deer and Ducks on River, n.d.
Oil on canvas, 9 x 15 inches

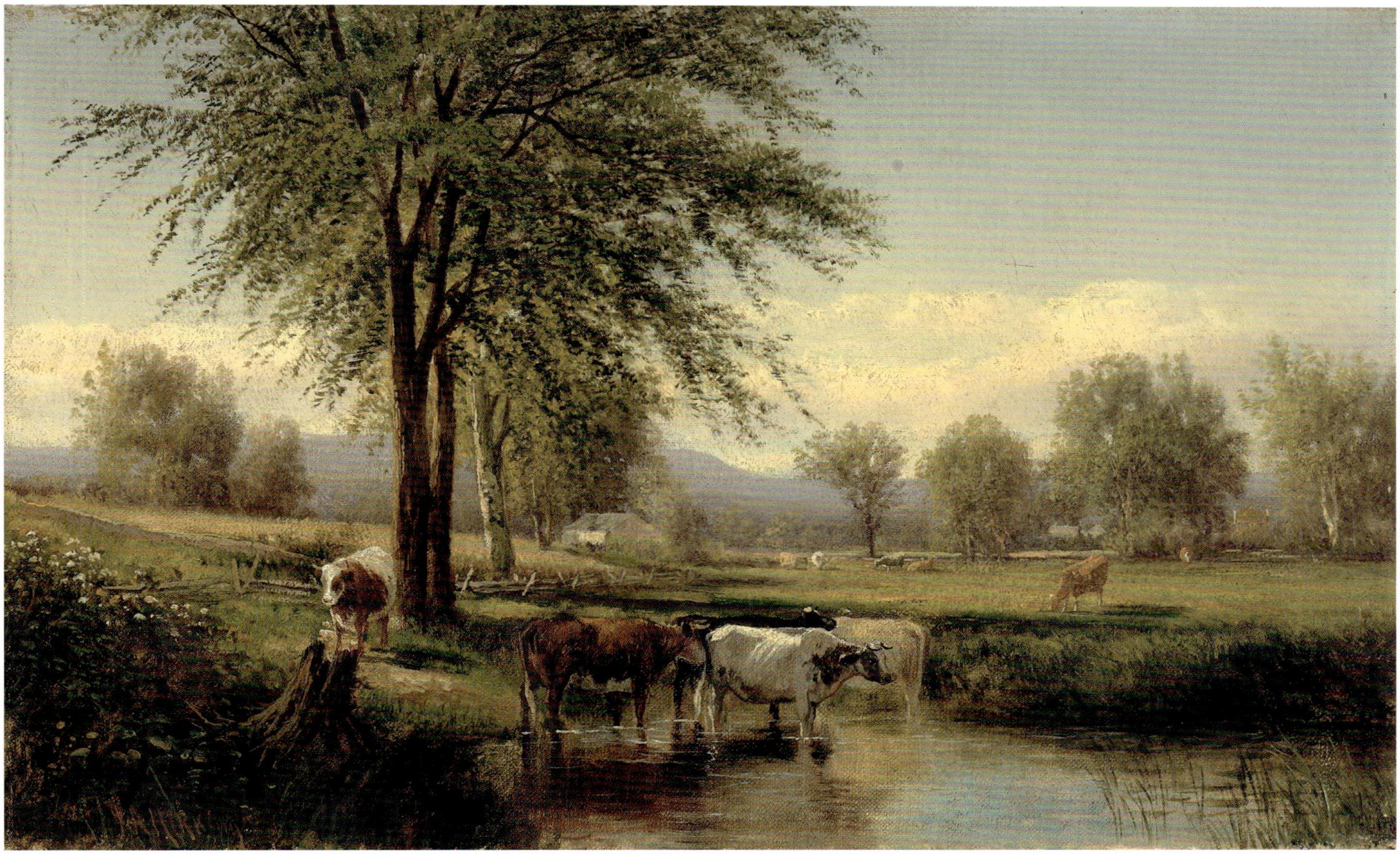

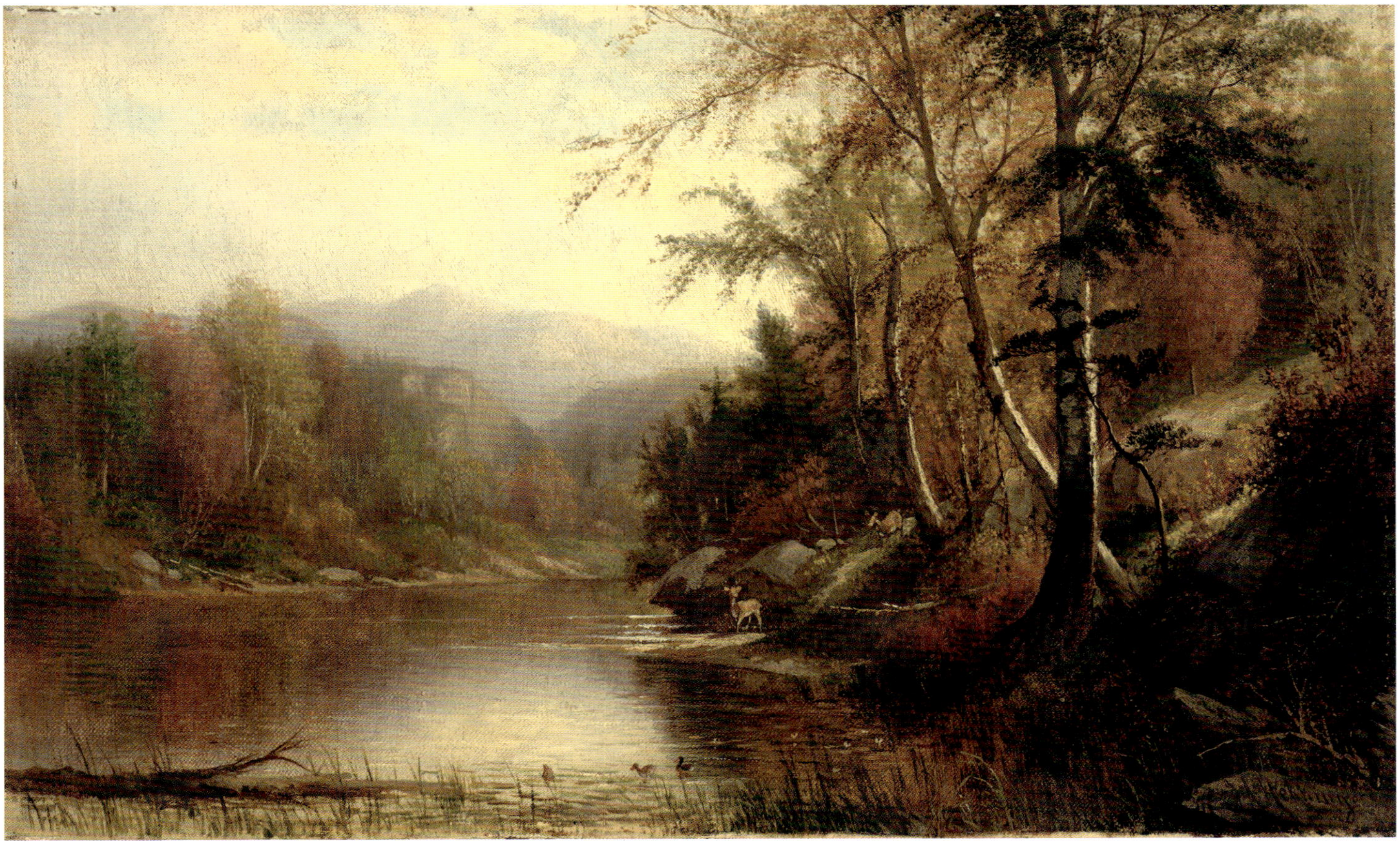

V. Nature without Man

The groves were God's first temples. Ere man learned
To hew the shaft, and lay the architrave,
And spread the roof above them—ere he framed
The lofty vault, to gather and roll back
The sound of anthems; in the darkling wood,
Amidst the cool and silence, he knelt down,
And offered to the Mightiest solemn thanks
And supplication.

—William Cullen Bryant, "A Forest Hymn," 1825

. . . there is a little valley, or rather lap of land, among high hills, which is one of the quietest places in the whole world. A small brook glides through it, with just murmur enough to lull one to repose; and the occasional whistle of a quail, or tapping of a woodpecker, is almost the only sound that ever breaks in upon the uniform tranquillity.

—Washington Irving, "The Legend of Sleepy Hollow,"
from *The Sketch Book*, 1819–1820

Hudson River School paintings are occasionally misconceived by critics, writers, and the public as being oversized and excessively detailed panoramic views. Individually, such isolated productions could appear labored and unfeeling, and after 1875, their popularity declined. These warhorses, exemplified by some of Albert Bierstadt's and Thomas Moran's paintings of western scenes, were, indeed, intended to impart the immense, majestic beauty of the American topography as well as to impress viewers with the awesome scope, sheer size, and power of America's natural resources. But these canvases by no means constitute a fair, complete overview of works by the Hudson River School. Critical assessments require much more balance by including other dimensions and qualities of the Hudson River School oeuvre. For example, collections such as this one reveal many different facets and aspects of the school, thereby providing a fresh insight into the remarkable depth and range of interpretations of the principal precept: inspired celebration of nature's richness and variety. Thomas Cole's initial travels into the Catskills beginning in 1825, as well as Asher B. Durand's oft-repeated call for Hudson River School artists to go out into the wilderness and paint from direct observation, caused many painters to become attuned to the "still small voice" and to appreciate on an intimate scale the fresh, genuine hush of nature. In these views of mountains, meadows, and forest interiors, artists more directly communed with nature by experiencing the true, untouched quality of the New World—God's new Eden.

Born in the Netherlands and trained at The Hague, Frerichs, after moving to the United States, first settled in New York City and later took a teaching post in Greensboro, North Carolina. While exploring the Blue Ridge Mountains, he became enamored of the rugged wildness of its terrain, so fresh to his European eyes. He painted many views in the wilderness, including a number of pairs celebrating various aspects of the untouched purity of the American landscape. A tragic fire that destroyed many of his works, along with the instability of life in the South during the Civil War, drove him back in 1865 to New York, where he continued to paint landscape subjects. Each painting in this pair represents a wilderness scene, a landscape virtually without sign of man's incursion. The pieces evoke different temperaments—one peaceful, the other turbulent—as well as different times of day.

Wilderness Scene with Falls (North Carolina), captures the light of early morning breaking across treacherous rock formations. Trees are shown in various states of their life cycle; twisted forms of branches have fallen to the ground. Daylight strongly delineated in the foreground is contrasted with the overwhelming darkness of the scene. A torrential waterfall cuts a diagonal path through rough, inhospitable terrain.

The primitivism and writhing movement of the wilderness in the first are contrasted to the calm, serene, magisterial aspect of nature in the second. Turbulent water is replaced by the still surface of a mountain lake. White Face Mountain rises like a pale apparition, colored in ethereal pink and lavender against the dark earthy colors of the forest. An iconic view in North Carolina and a symbol of the state's natural bounty, this mountain is awe inspiring, imbued by the artist with a religiosity almost demanding homage. Evocative of the dawn of civilization, only a single human figure huddles in a boat in the foreground, witness to nature's magnificence. Birds fly above the raw, untamed landscape, as if no earthly creature could navigate it. Autumn is beginning to show itself in the foliage as well as in the crispness of the atmosphere. The penultimate season suggests the close of man's own life cycle, symbolized by the truncated tree stump on the far right as well as by the depiction of day's end. Red, white, and blue tints of sunset, representing the flag of the United States, are reflected from the sky into the water.

Because Frerich's life was so disrupted by the Civil War and the events leading up to it, one may speculate about the impact this might have had on his art. His interest in celebrating various aspects of the American wilderness must have certainly been tinged with national pride. The contrasting moods in this pair of paintings could reflect the distraught state of mind of many new Americans at the threat to their union and their yearning for a more stable, harmonious political climate.

William Charles Anthony Frerichs (1829–1905)
Wilderness Scene with Falls (North Carolina), c. 1855–1860
Oil on canvas, 11 x 21½ inches

William Charles Anthony Frerichs (1829–1905)
White Face Mountain, North Carolina, c. 1855–1860
Oil on canvas, 11 x 21½ inches

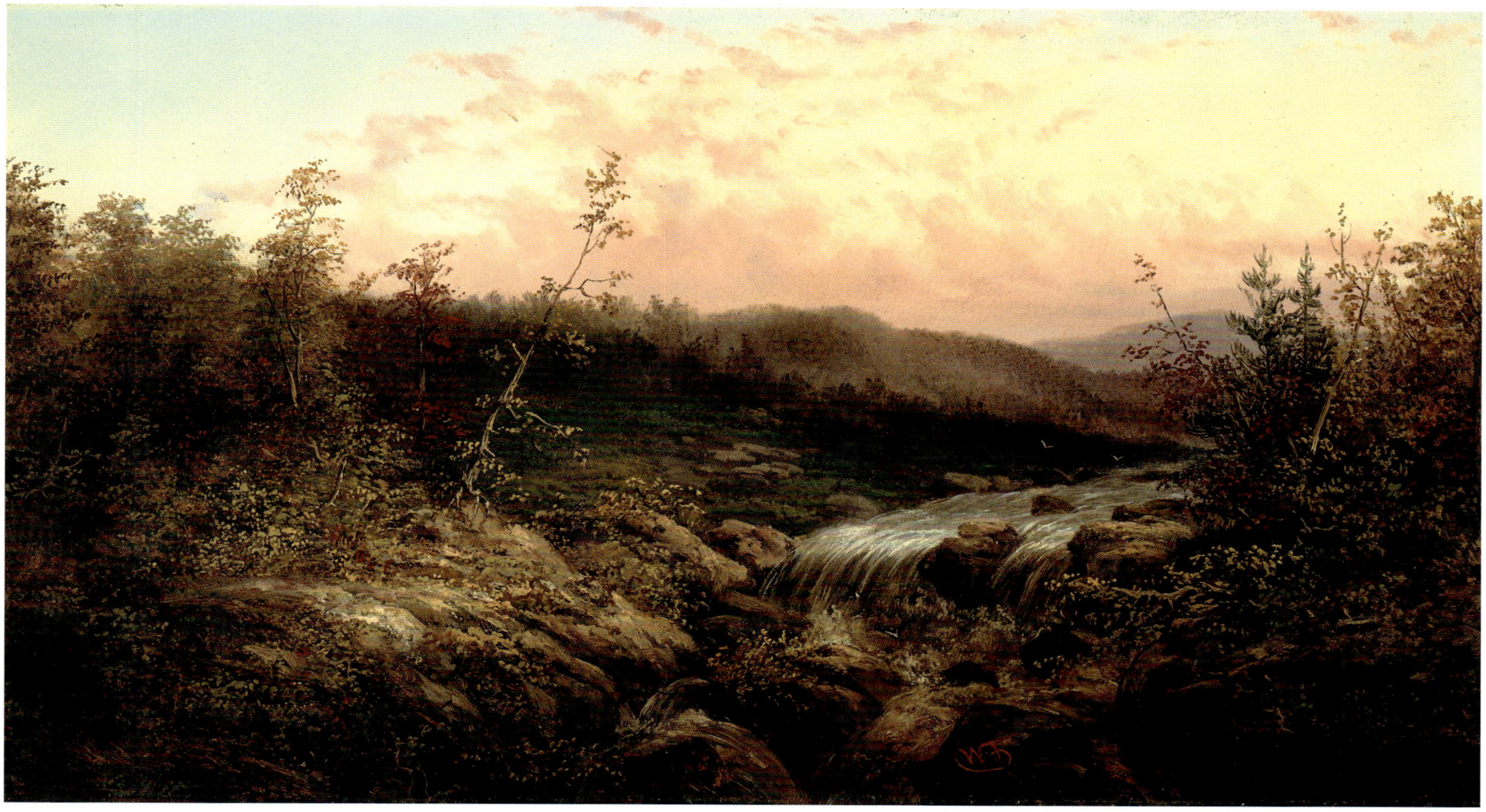

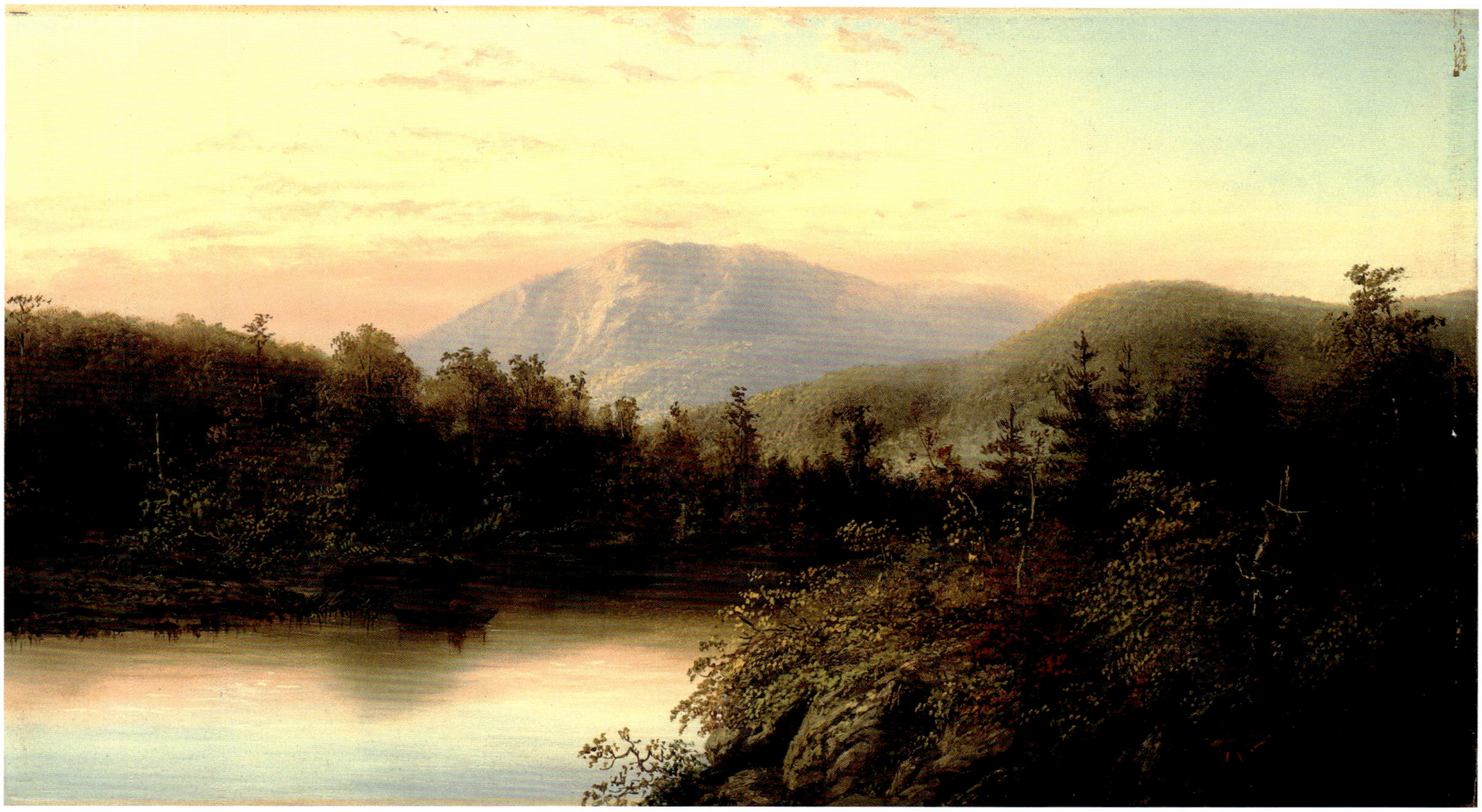

Forest Interiors

After the death in 1848 of his good friend and close associate Thomas Cole, Asher Brown Durand became the acknowledged leader of the Hudson River School. His nine "Letters on Landscape Painting," written in 1855 for the Crayon, influenced contemporaries as well as subsequent generations of Hudson River School artists and continue to inspire landscape painters to this day. Durand's famous *Kindred Spirits* (1849, oil on canvas, 46 x 36 inches, formerly collection of the New York Public Library, New York City) was commissioned as a visual eulogy to Thomas Cole. It shows Cole and his friend—the poet William Cullen Bryant—standing above Cole's beloved Kaaterskill Clove. Although the painting has remarkable depth of perspective, it is not a broad panorama but rather an intimate, enclosed view into the wilderness, revealing Durand's preference for compositions evoking "the still, small voice." Durand's training as an engraver, initially under the tutelage of his father, is apparent in his work. He attached great importance to the direct, close observation and transcription of detail, including the continuing variety and contrast of light effects and atmosphere. In his advice to other artists, Durand implored them to "go first into Nature to learn to paint landscape, and when you shall have learnt to imitate her, you may then study the pictures of great artists with benefit."[8] By this he meant that artists must train their eye first through direct experience in nature and later by studying the techniques of other artists. Durand also cautioned that mere imitation of nature was insufficient, writing that "such knowledge never can create the feeling, which overrules all principles, and gives the impress of great art."[9] Therefore we can understand that expressions of emotion, mood, and feeling are necessary components of great art and underlying core principles in Hudson River School paintings.

In *Woodland Interior*, Durand reveals a glimpse into virgin forest, without signs of man's presence or even of wildlife. Twin trunks of a large, gnarled tree are devoid of branches until their uppermost reaches, where twisted limbs strain out of the shadowy forest to touch slivers of sunlit blue sky. Other pairs of entwined trees also appear in the background as a kind of thematic amplification. Light falls along the torn bark of the trunks in the foreground to spill gently on to a small patch of earth. The forest floor is rich with plant life, including ferns and mosses touched only occasionally by sunlight. A small brook bringing nourishment courses through pebbles and branches, the debris of nature. A decayed tree trunk and fallen branches reach out like human appendages from the streambed. Life cycles seem continuous, accepted, natural. To Durand, Cole, Church, Kensett, Casilear, David Johnson, and others, trees were fascinating living objects of nature, imbued with individual character demanding close study. In the late 1840s and early 1850s, Durand produced numerous forest interiors resembling this one. He often paired his trees, as here, so that he could more readily compare and contrast their features and the different shades of green in their leaves. He delighted in showing their rough surfaces covered with lichen and moss. Their inherent nobility and grandeur were eloquently conveyed through his artistic mastery. The feeling of being in the wilderness is so realistically conveyed here that the viewer can almost smell the peat moss, the decaying trees, and other odors associated with the forest interior.

Asher Brown Durand (1796–1886)
Woodland Interior, c. 1855
Oil on canvas, 20 x 16 inches

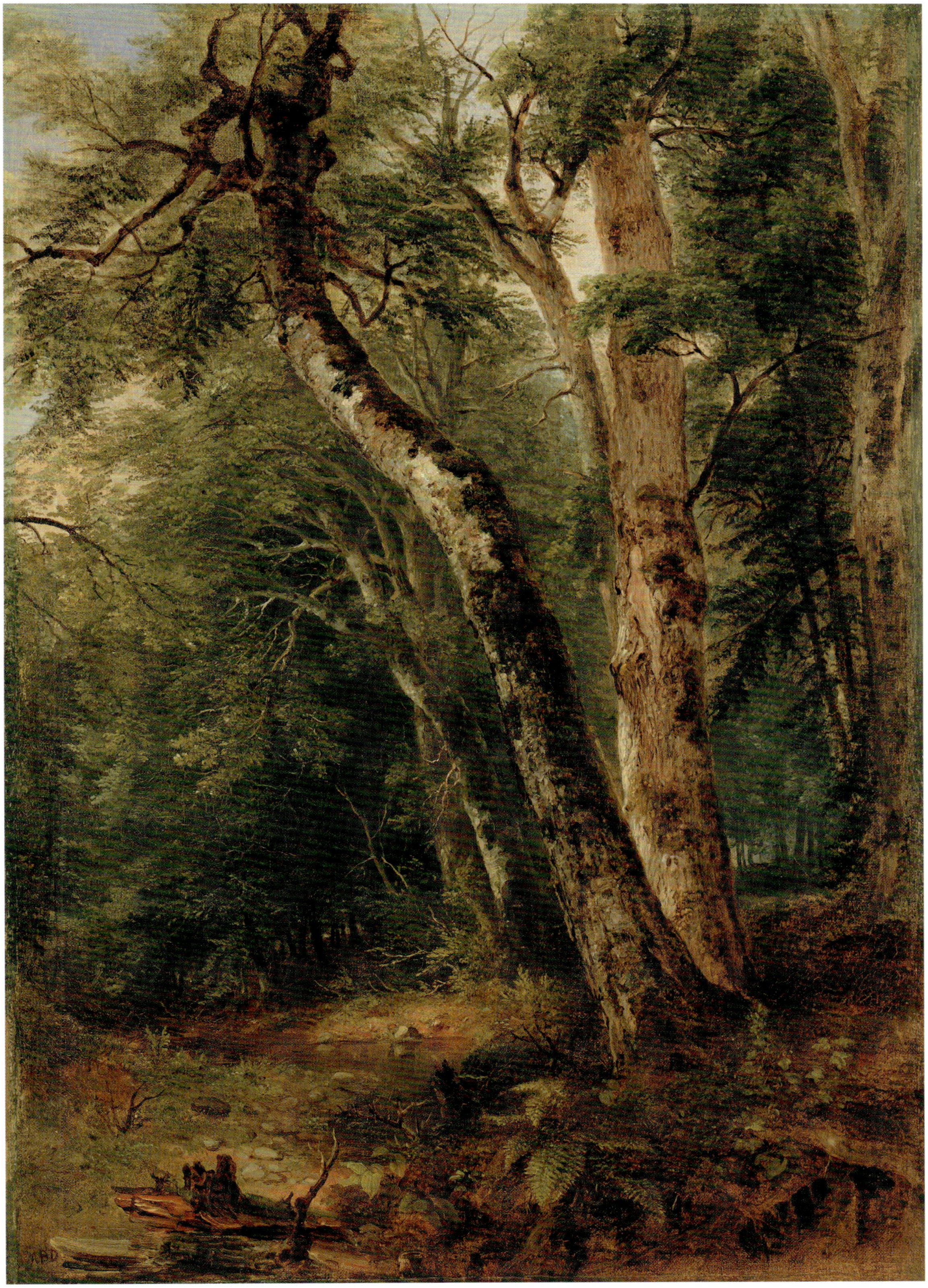

Once acclaimed for painting panoramas, Benjamin Champney spent his later years exploring and transcribing on a smaller scale his beloved countryside around the Saco River in North Conway, New Hampshire. He became recognized as the founder of the White Mountain School of landscape painting, located in New Hampshire near the Conway Valley and Saco River.[10] In this canvas, we are invited into a lovely forest for an intimate vision along a sun-dappled path, which bends and winds its way through the trunks of heavily foliated trees. We have the comforting sense that the path has been well traveled, despite the chaste freshness of the woods. We are made to feel as though we are accompanying the artist in a long midsummer's ramble along a favorite natural byway. Multiple light-dark contrasts enliven this very fresh yet clearly Durand-inspired evocation—a typical production of the Hudson River School principle to go directly into nature to study its smaller but no less intrinsic workings and manifestations.

Born in Pittsburgh, Pennsylvania, Linford was a member of the Scalp Level School, led by Düsseldorf-trained painter George Hetzel (1826–1899). Linford was the first of that

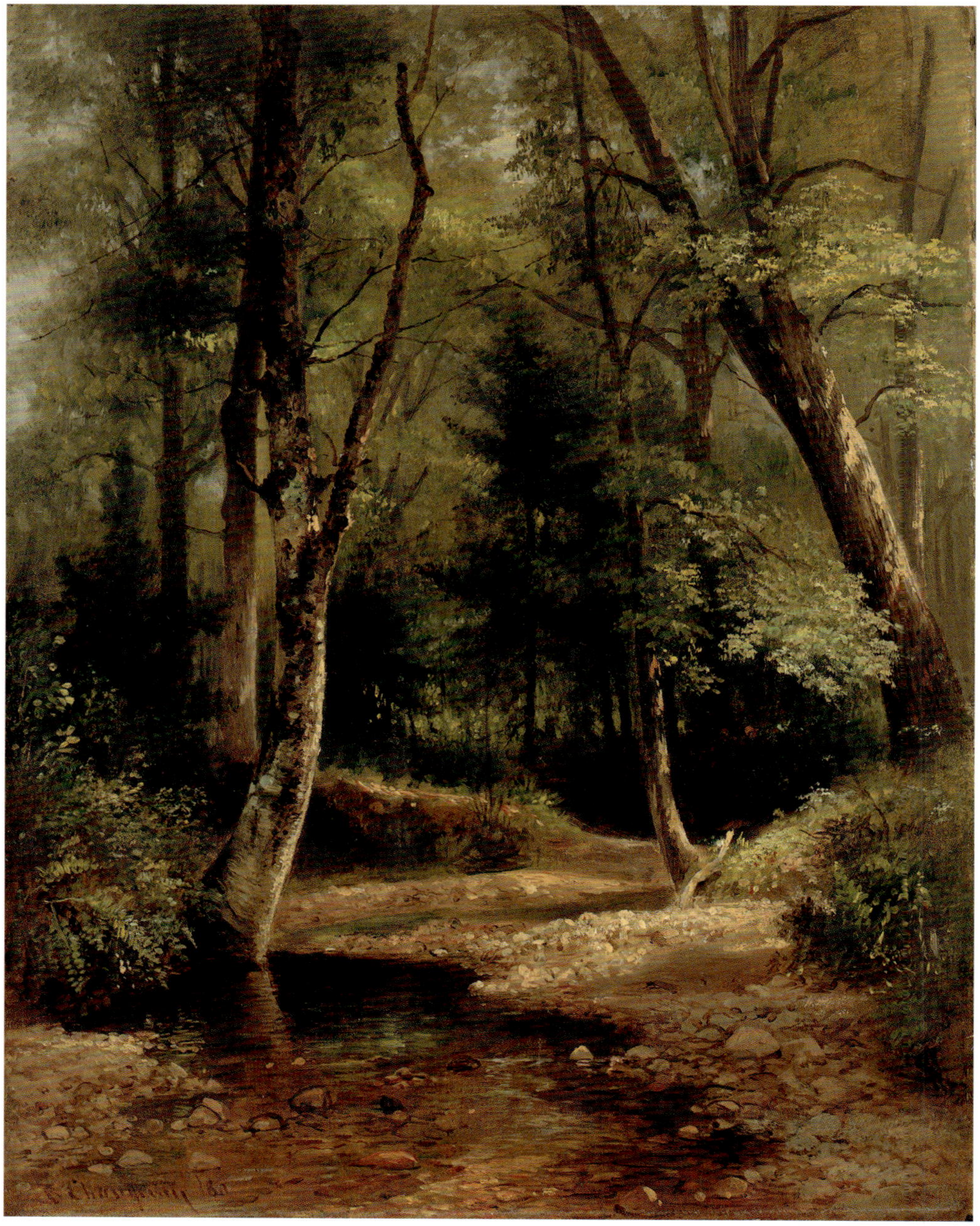

Benjamin Champney (1817–1907)
Woodland Interior, 1880
Oil on canvas, 20 x 16 inches

group to have discovered the bucolic landscape scenery near the small town of Scalp Level outside Johnstown, Pennsylvania. Hetzel introduced his followers to painting methods of the French Barbizon School. Like that group, they left industrial environs of the city to paint directly from nature, thereby creating more faithful depictions of it. In Linford's beautiful forest interior, a meandering stream cuts through woodlands fresh with the many shades of green in springtime. Two tall trees on either side of the water establish strong verticals to contrast with the diagonal path of the stream. Sunlight released from a small line of very light blue sky at the top of the painting plays from one place to another in the middle distance, turning the rapids bright white. The clarity of the mountain stream suffices to reveal the texture of its bed. However, light cannot penetrate the shadowy foreground, where tree trunks are dark against the distant sunlight, and ferns and plant life flourish by the stream's edge. By repeatedly contrasting light and dark areas along with vertical and diagonal forms, Linford enlivens his canvas with movement and rhythm akin to music.

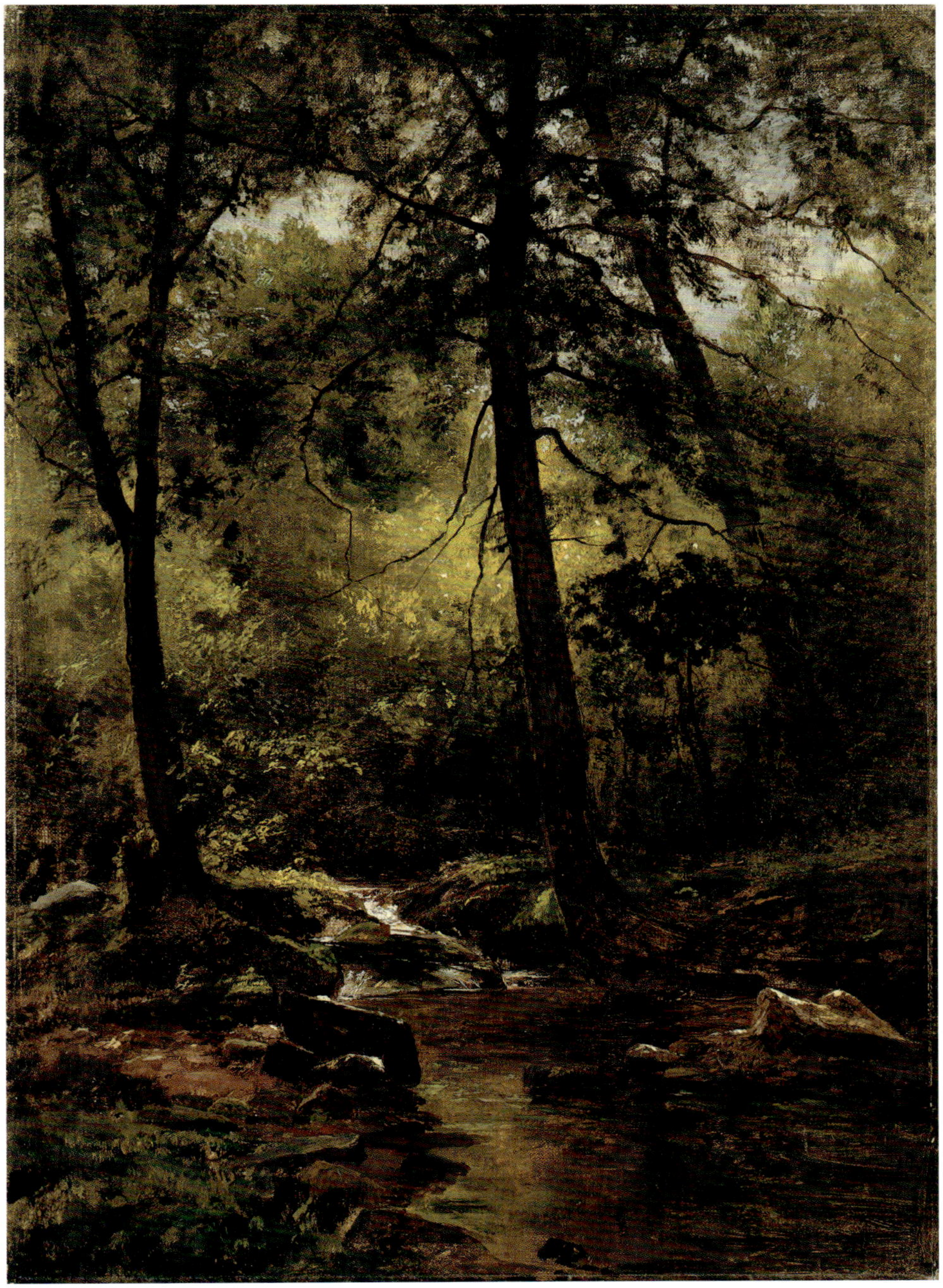

Charles Linford (1846–1897)
Woodland Interior with Stream, n.d.
Oil on canvas, 22 x 16 inches

STRONG AND RESONANT WITH RICH SHADES OF AUTUMN, William McDougal Hart's *A Forest Stream* is surrounded on both banks by golden woodlands. The bright foliage is contrasted with cool, white light that spills from a gray autumnal sky. Substantial boulders line the streambed, their gray masses softened by green moss. In the foreground, a tall, slender birch tree stretches its lofty branches across the top of the composition from right to left, creating a natural arch both protecting the scene and rendering it more intimate. The forested stillness is broken only by rapids in the middle ground and by a bird—the sole sign of wildlife—lighting the water's surface.

William McDougal Hart (1823–1894)
A Forest Stream, 1875
Oil on canvas, 17 1/4 x 15 inches

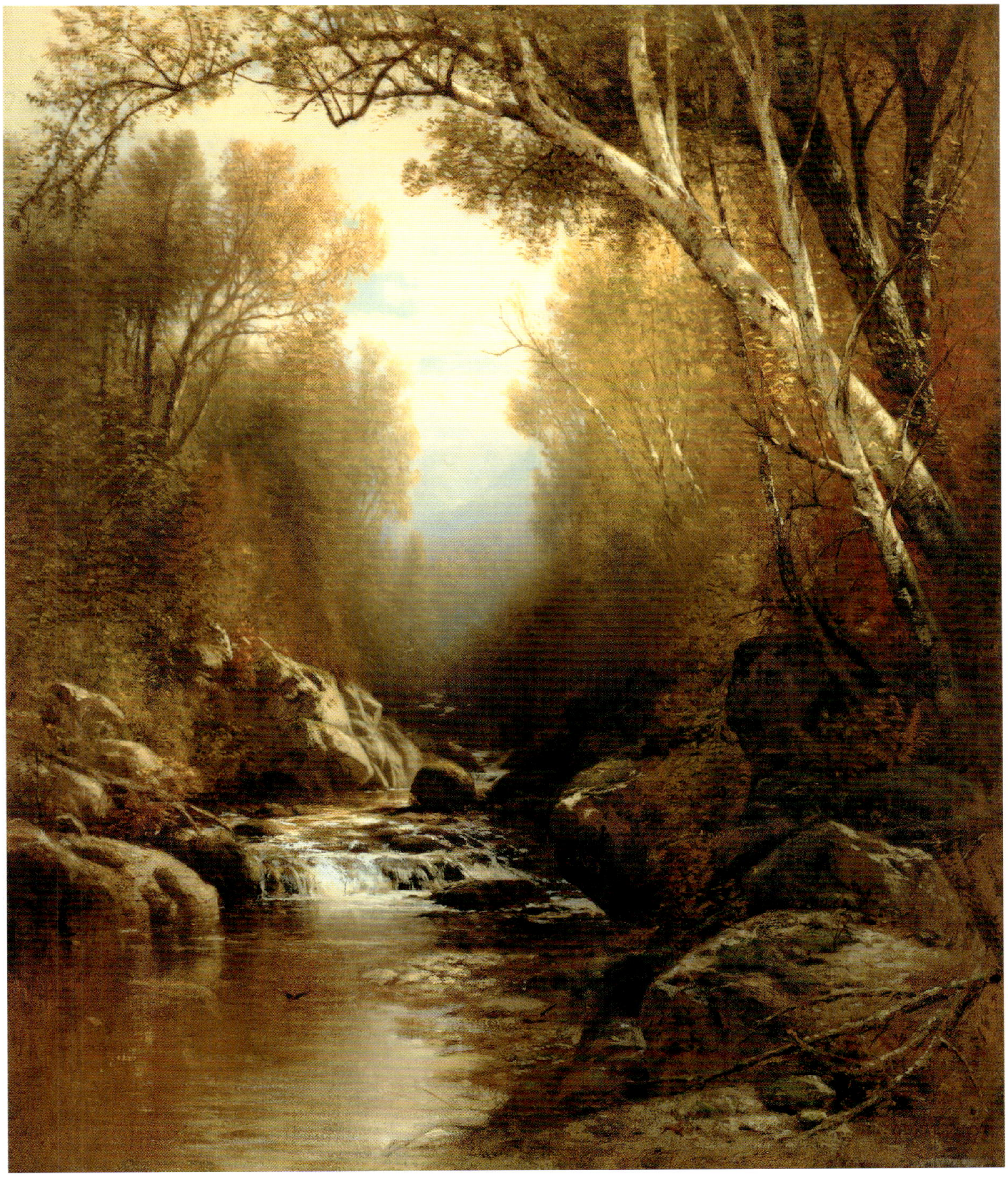

Landscapes with Deer

THOMAS COLE USED THE IMAGE OF DEER TO SYMBOLIZE the American wilderness and the harmonious coexistence of wild animals in nature. Later Hudson River School painters adopted this iconography and expanded it to depict man's disruption of and encroachment on nature as the march of civilization expelled wildlife from American forests.

A Lake Twilight is a notable work by Sanford Robinson Gifford, an acknowledged master in the evocation on canvas of light effects and a leading figure among second generation Hudson River School painters. Having grown up in Hudson, New York, amid the natural beauty of the Catskill Mountains and the Hudson River, he was a lifelong observer of the varying light effects on water, earth, and sky caused by changing seasons, times of day, and weather conditions. Gifford painted this canvas in 1861—the first year of the Civil War, which so violently disrupted the peace and optimism of the New World. Just one year earlier, Frederic Church created his tour de force *Twilight in the Wilderness.* In that context, this painting probably represents Gifford's response to the earlier work. Though less bloodthirsty in its dramatic use of color and light than Church's painting, *A Lake Twilight* still smolders with tension and hostility. Light and dark are contrasted throughout the composition: in the maple trees' bright red foliage against the dark green of pines; in the orange and blue bands of cloud and sky; in the bright white shirt of a hunter against the dark surface of the water. The pioneer struggles to remove a deer carcass from his boat, emphasizing the conflict between man and nature. Furthering this tension, the setting sun pulls in the opposite direction from the hunter, lighting the underside of clouds that skirt the uppermost part of the canvas. A third direction is established by the looming mountain, whose lofty peak pierces the clear blue sky. Below, the shoreline is littered with symbols of desecration: blasted trees, trunks demolished by the ax, writhing branches, hard outcroppings of rock. Powerful, emotive, and celebratory of the awesome beauty of nature, Gifford's *A Lake Twilight* is a sublime acknowledgment of man's inevitable, relentless struggles against one another, against nature, and against the cycles of life over which man has little control. Yet, as in many masterpieces of American luminism, a nearly palpable stillness and hush pervade the wilderness scene.

Sanford Robinson Gifford (1823–1880)
A Lake Twilight, 1861
Oil on canvas, 16 x 28 inches

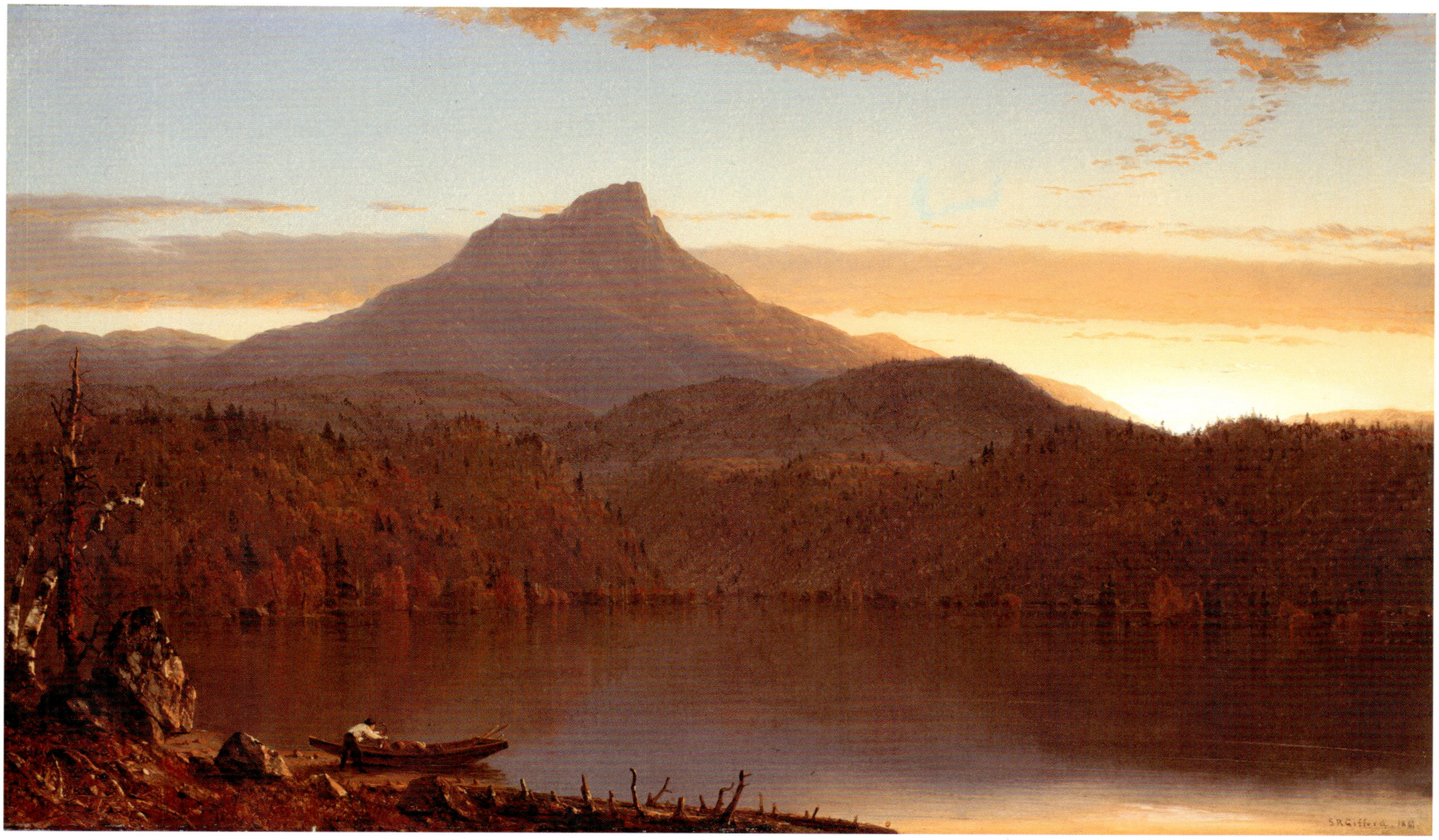

Two small paintings by two artists using different styles share common themes involving deer in the forest, including their utter compatibility with nature, birth cycles of animals in the wild blending harmoniously within seasonal cycles, and threats from man.

Deer in the Morning Mist by Ernest Lotichius, a wilderness scene evocative in its use of light and atmosphere, exemplifies the style of artists trained in the Düsseldorf School. Details in the foreground, especially the ferns, reveal the artist's skill as a close, accurate observer. Prominent use of rich earth tones further discloses his Germanic background. The artist shows several groupings of deer, almost as if the same animal were posed in different positions throughout its day. Such an arrangement refers to the manner of many medieval painters who depicted entire stories in a single work—as, for example, several significant events spanning the lifetime of a particular saint. This painting also has a narrative replete with suspense and potential drama, as read through the positions of the deer, made more intense by the heavy atmosphere. Deer are shown first on their way to a forest stream, then resting by it, and finally drinking from it. Two males watch over the others, the older one prominent on the upper slopes, the younger one, a bit further along, looking back and upward to the buck, as if waiting for affirmation. Three deer are seated, a mother doe and two fawns, as if in quiet conversation, protected by the males and suspecting no threat. A tree lends central focus to the painting, giving shelter to the deer and sounding a friendly note in an otherwise ominous, foreboding setting, typical of Düsseldorf landscapes.

Arthur Fitzwilliam Tait's canvas of 1869 shows a close-in view of the forest with a mother deer and two fawns. Every leaf is clearly represented in the dense cover of foliage that barely permits the pale blue sky to peek through. Tait emphasizes the deer rather than using them as accoutrements to nature. The sensitive and appealing face of the doe, her graceful legs, and the dappled backs of the fawns are centrally placed, carefully observed, and true to nature. The fur of the animals appears soft, their noses hard, and the glint in their eyes moist. Even though at home in the forest, the doe has her ears back, listening for possible danger, the clear insinuation being the presence of man, the observer. The promise of spring in the bright, young undergrowth, contrasted to the presence of dying trees, echoes once again the theme of nature's cycles: one generation supplanting another with the birth of the fawn to its parent.

Ernest Lotichius (1840–1874)
Deer in the Morning Mist, 1858
Oil on canvas, 10½ x 14 inches

Arthur Fitzwilliam Tait (1819–1905)
Deer in Nature, 1869
Oil on canvas, 8 x 10 inches

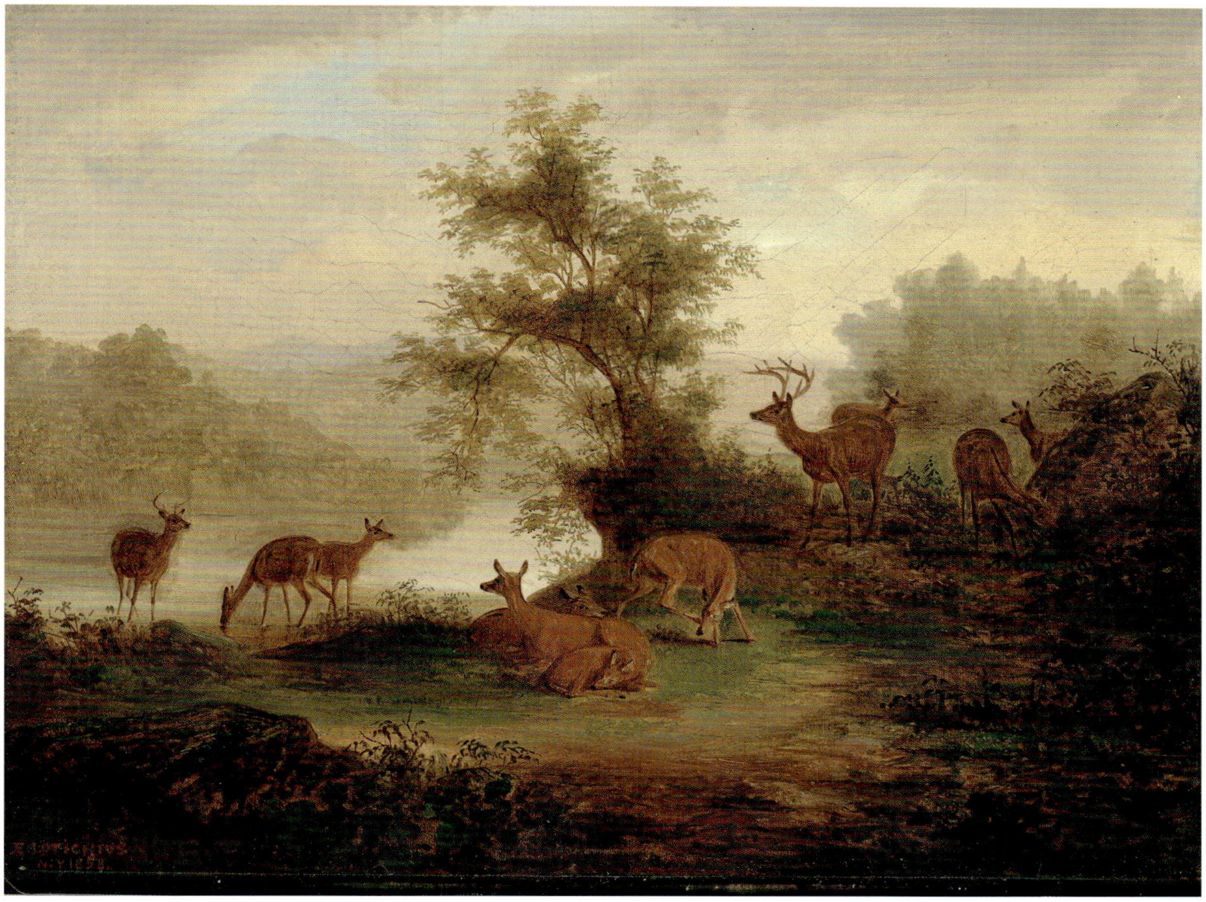

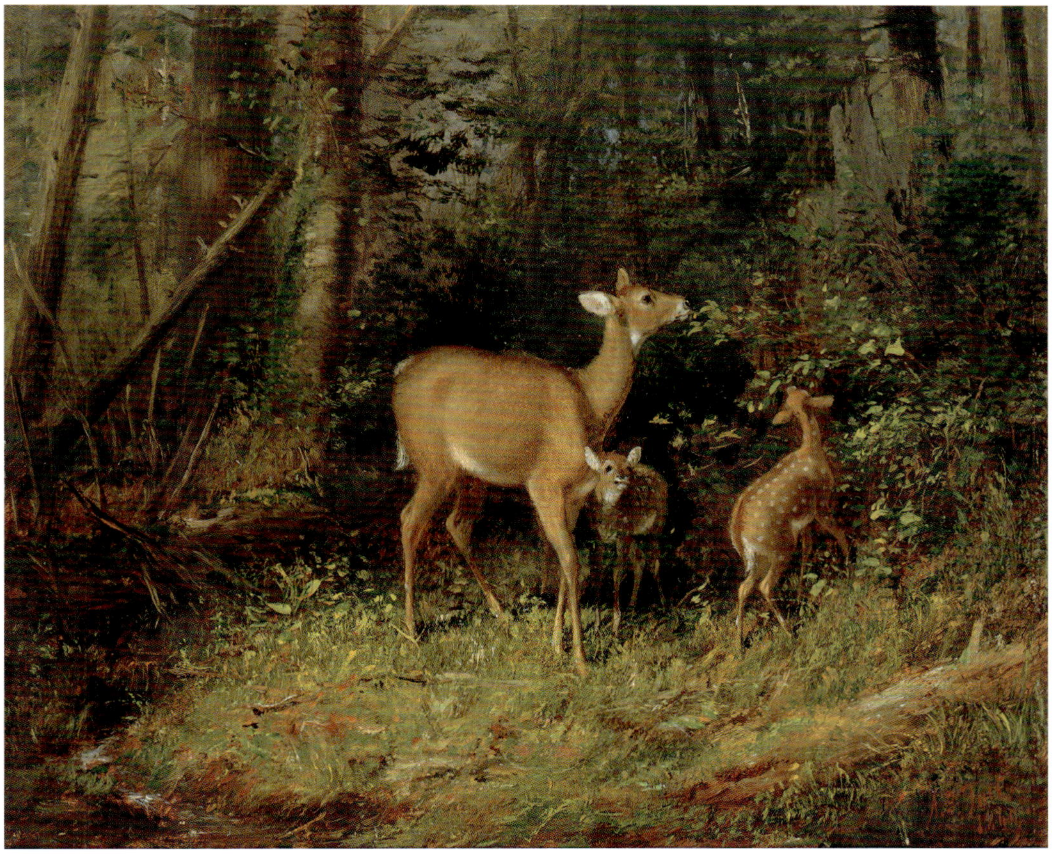

In 1876, the year of the American centennial, Rondel posed a single deer at the shore of a blue mountain lake in his compact but eloquent *Adirondack Landscape.* Surrounded by trees lit with autumn color reflecting in the water, the deer, an emblem of nature, appears in harmony with its surroundings. But the season is indicative of change: the coming winter will be followed by spring, when man will threaten the safe harbor of the wilderness. Bright bands of yellow, red, and blue flame across the sky, suggesting the colors of the American flag and symbolizing the burgeoning civilization of the new land in a composition otherwise devoid of man's presence. Light and color are used by the artist to create drama, in contrast to the stillness of his subject. Rondel's painterly style leaves detail to the viewer's eye and imagination, suggesting rather than completely describing each form, thereby further enhancing the theatricality of his image.

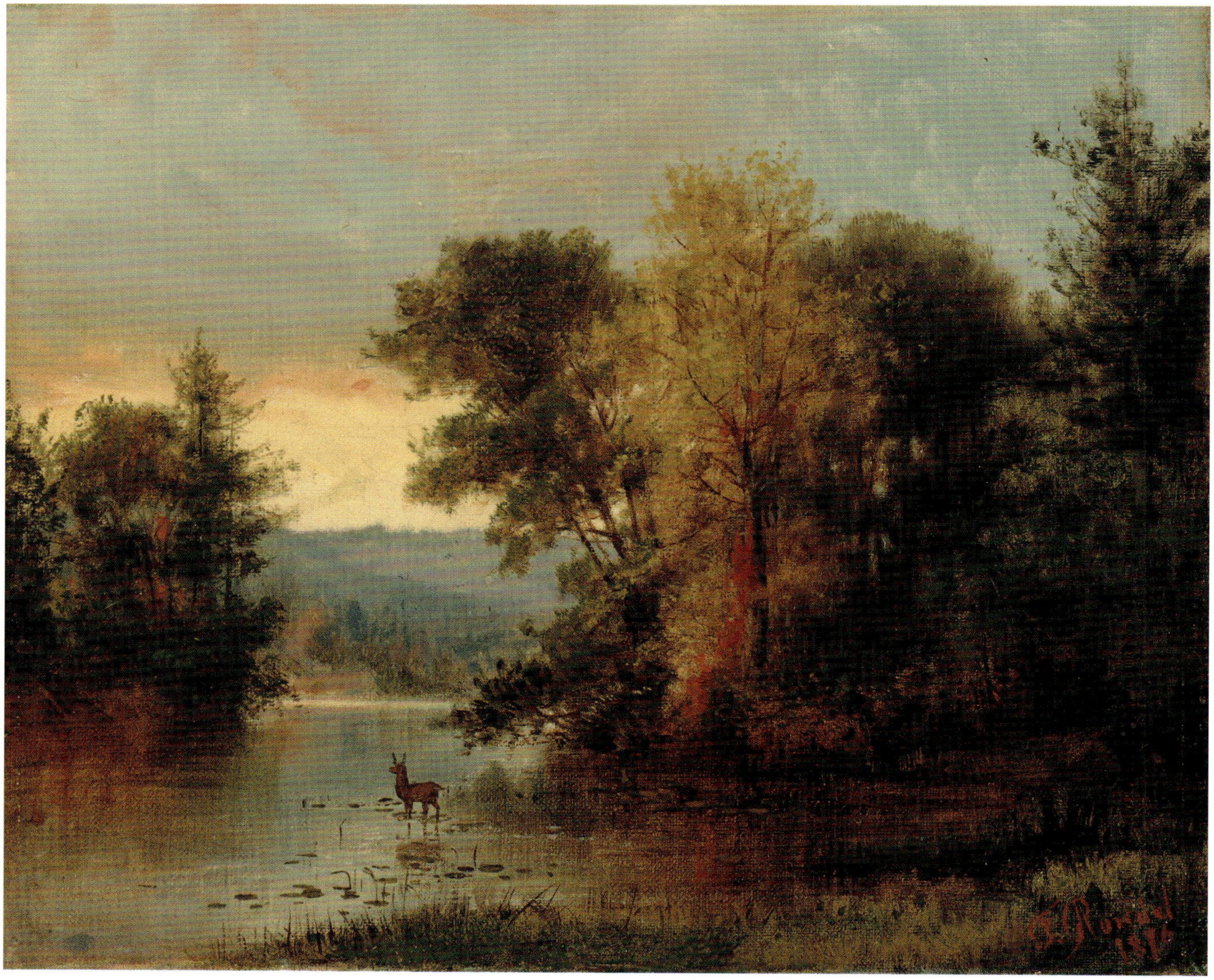

Frederick Rondel (1826–1892)
Adirondack Landscape, c. 1876
Oil on canvas, 8 x 10 inches

In her painting, Laura Woodward shows a forest interior with summer's filtered light streaming down on the left bank of a stream; the right bank is placed in the cool shade of trees bending toward the water. This contrast helps to create drama in the composition. Two deer—a buck and a doe—stand in the shade at the point where the stream curves away, hidden in the distance by a rocky outcropping. Having just come into sight of the observer, the pair has stopped, heads raised expectantly, ears pricked for sound. Though dwarfed by their surroundings, they form the point of tension with us, the viewer. We seem to be standing downstream—part of the painting and the source of the disruption to the forest's stillness. Although using a different technique, the artist develops the same theme as Rondel: man's imminent encroachment on nature.

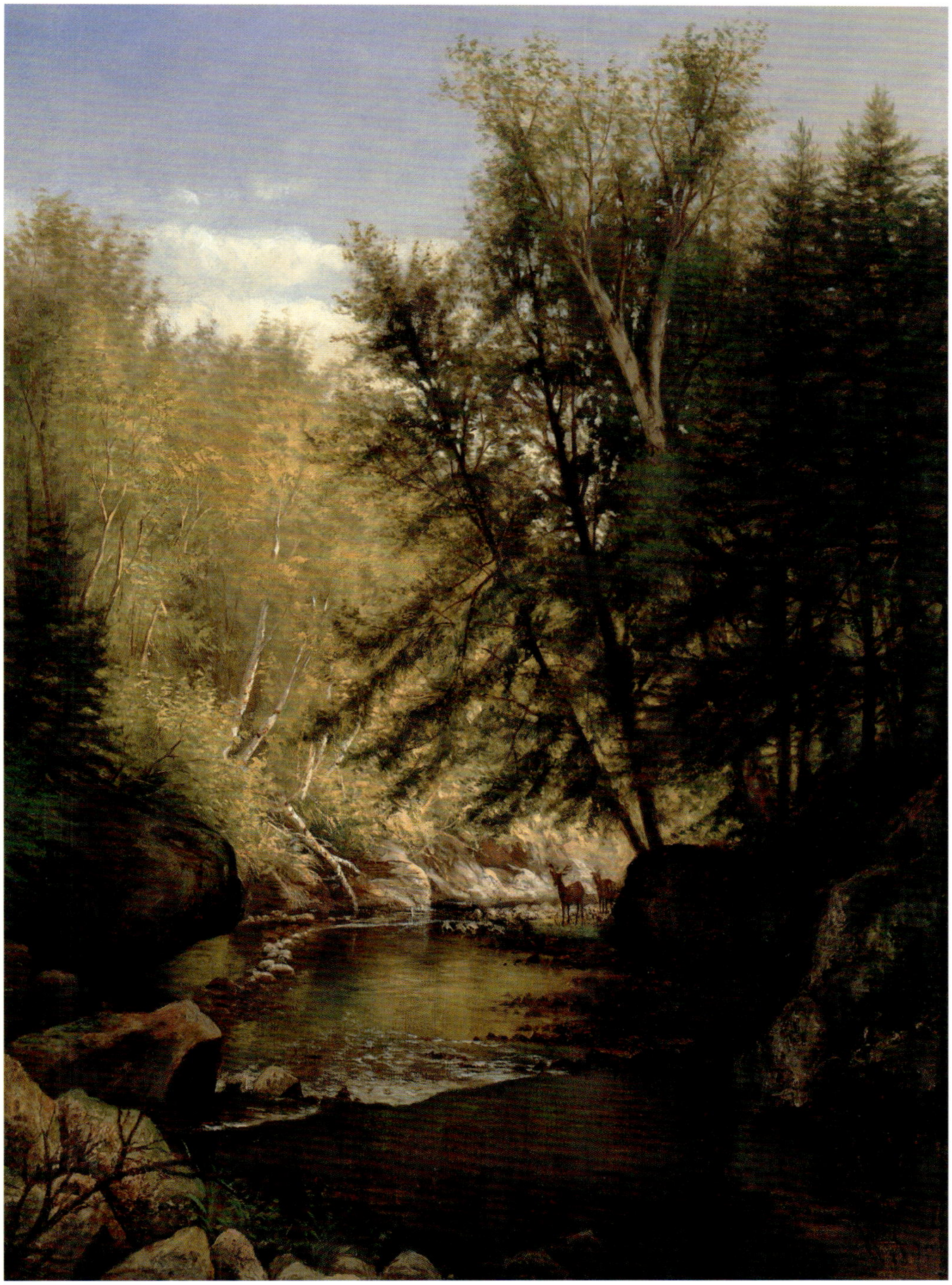

Laura Woodward (active 1872–1889)
By the Stream, 1876
Oil on canvas, 24 x 18 inches

HERMANN FUECHSEL CONJURED UP A WORLD OF INNOCENCE and mystery in this eloquent canvas, in which two deer pose by a mountain stream, calm and serene in a raw, wild environment. Majestic in its progression from dark to light, solid to ephemeral, the composition is divided into three parts. In the lower third, the solid forms of rock cliffs and promontories, separated by Kaaterskill Creek, are painted in rich, dark earth tones. In the middle third, contrasting trees on either side of the creek—a deciduous tree devoid of most of its foliage and a tall evergreen lush with color—frame the rushing torrent of Haines Falls, softened and subdued in color by diffused early morning sunlight. The upper third is devoted to the steep, forested slopes surrounding Kaaterskill Falls, from whose waters diaphanous mists rise to shroud the mountainside. A small fragment of blue sky crowns the scene, giving perspective but maintaining intimacy. Deer stand in the center of this deep cathedral-like interior, completely at one with nature and nature's stillness. One deer drinks from the pure waters of Kaaterskill Creek, the other lifts its head, pricking its ears to some sound that might have pierced the peace and quiet of this American Eden.

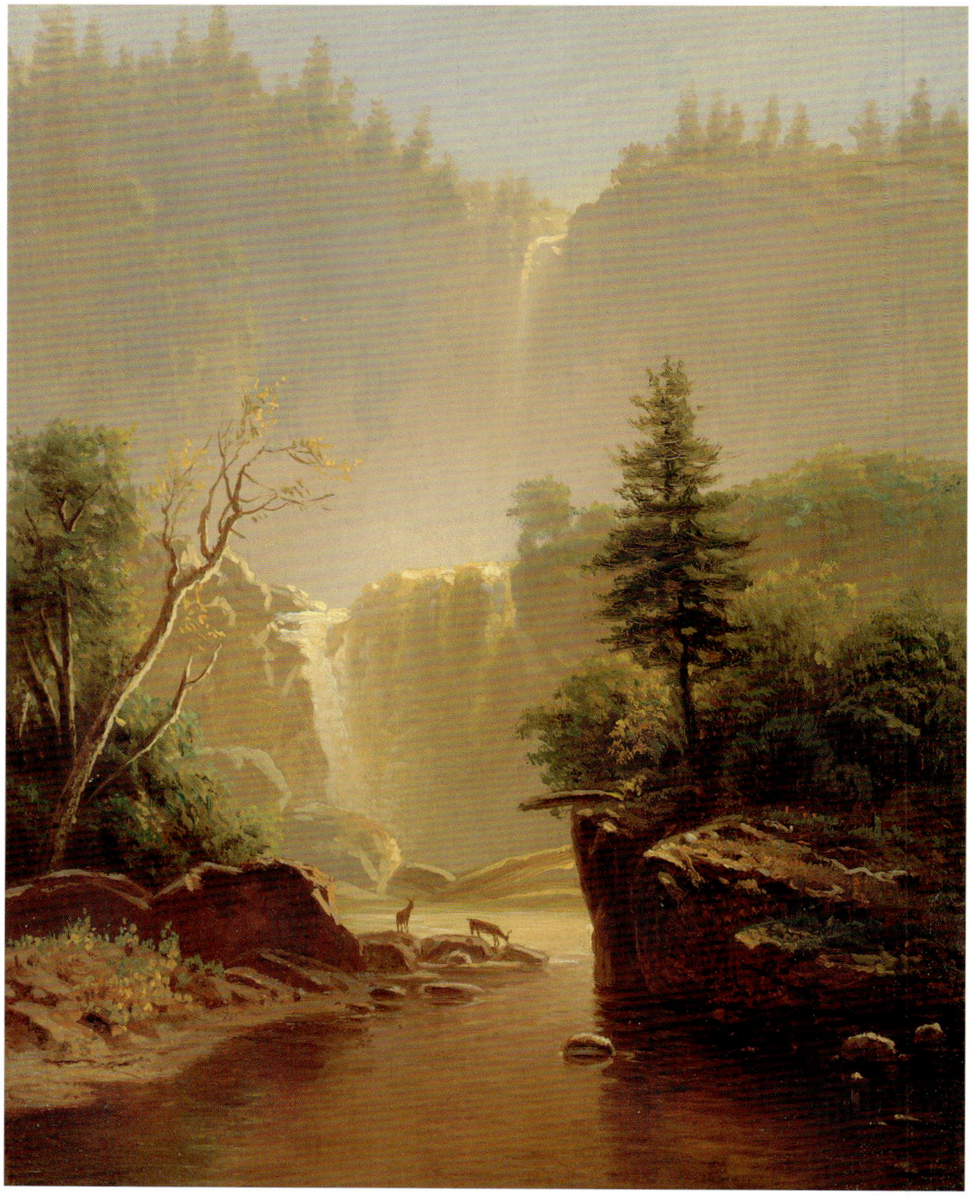

Hermann Fuechsel (1833–1915)
Kaaterskill and Haines Falls, c. 1865–1875
Oil on canvas, 14 3/4 x 12 inches

Thomas Worthington Whittredge also poses his deer by a waterfall, but the mood in his painting is very different—typical again of the Düsseldorf School, where he was studying when he painted this work in 1850. Dark and dramatic, the weather is ominous and foreboding. Dangerous, unnavigable rocks are piled high atop one another, and the waterfall rages in full torrent—all themes favored by Düsseldorf-trained artists. The narrow, vertical composition is crowded and claustrophobic. Two deer, surrogates for nature itself, are separated by cascading water from a hunter dressed in buckskin. The buck is alert to the dangerous predator on the opposite bank; the doe seems unaware. In formidable surroundings, hunter and his prey are pitted against one another, just as the American wilderness was confronted by the threat of man's incursion.

Thomas Worthington Whittredge (1820–1910)
Deer by a Waterfall, 1850
Oil on canvas, 20½ x 16½ inches

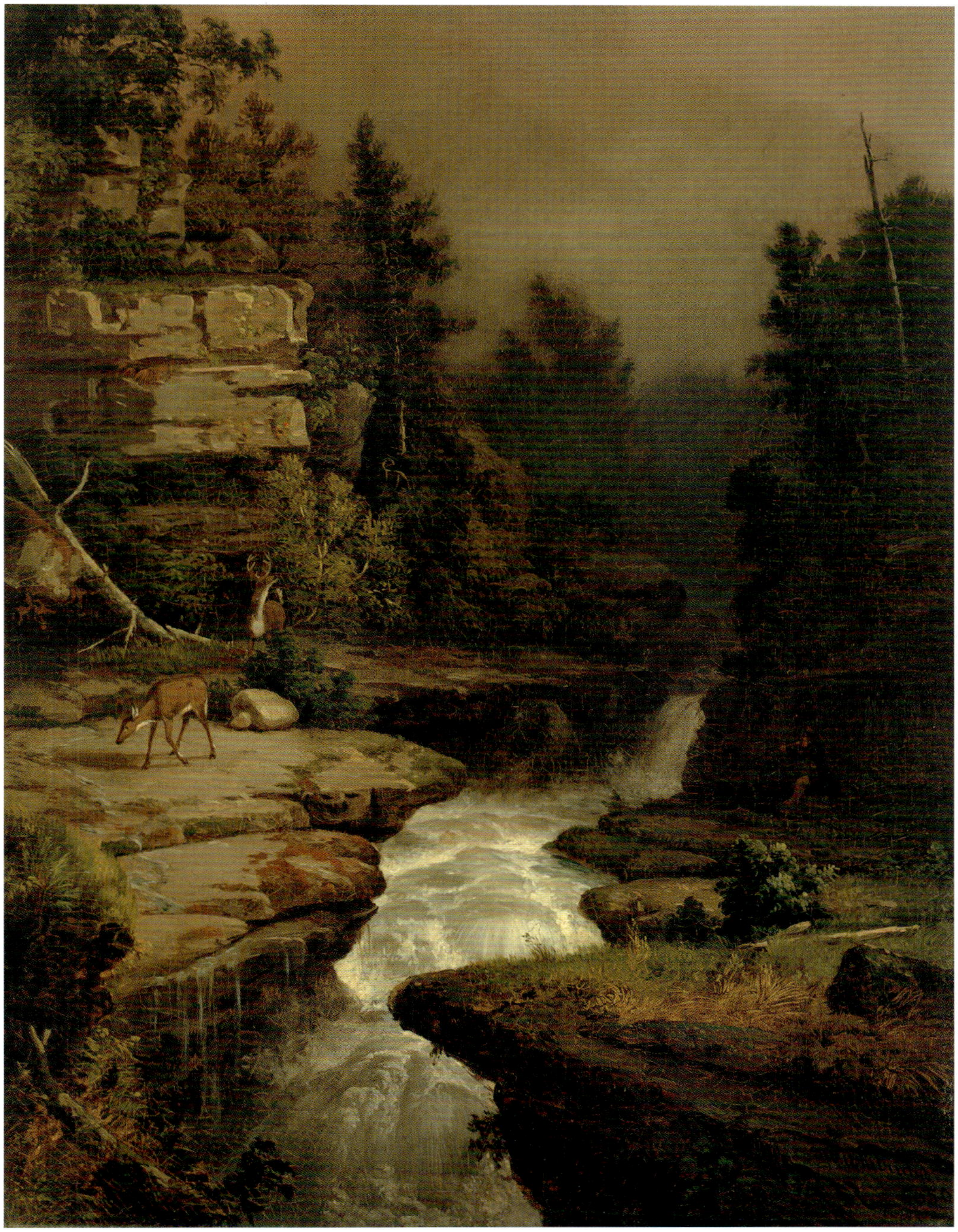

THE SINGLE DEER IN THE FOREGROUND OF CHARLES H. Chapin's scene is surrounded by the tranquil peace of a mountain lake. Alert to the sounds of nature, the deer is not confronted by any imminent threat, nor is there any disruptive sign of man. This deer seems to be communicating with three more deer, minutely depicted on the far shore of the lake. Red, yellow, and blue colors of sunset are reflected in the water, surrounded on both shores by dark lacy forms of trees that break the horizon line. Even so, the clear dark silhouette of the central deer, standing proudly against the bright light of sunset, can be interpreted as symbolizing a final moment in the natural harmony of the American wilderness and the subsequent, inevitable dawning of another stage in the cycle of civilization.

Charles H. Chapin (1830–1889)
Deer, 1870
Oil on canvas, 10¼ x 20 inches

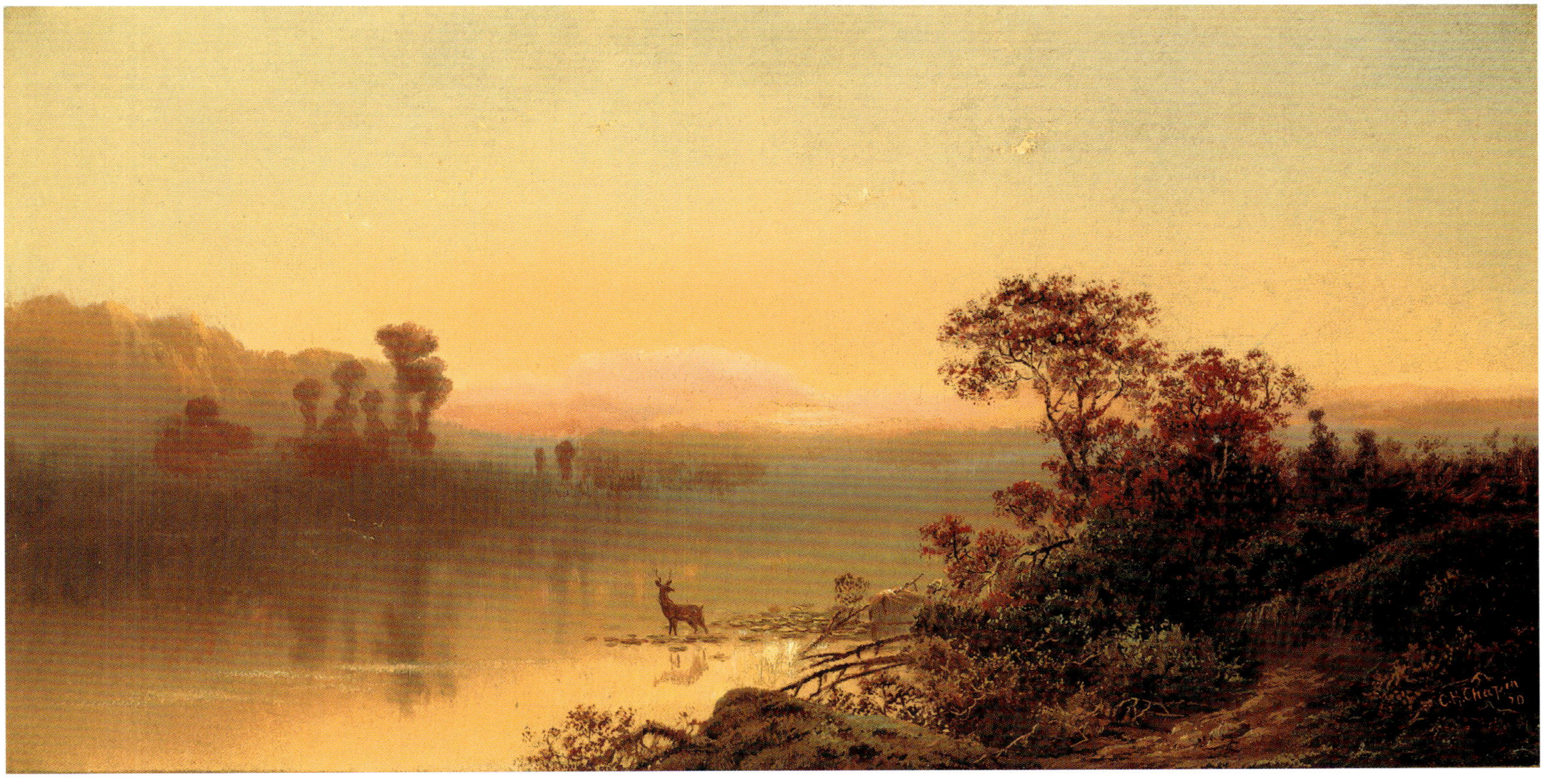

VI. Man's Activities in Nature: Pleasure

I hear America singing, the varied carols I hear,
Those of mechanics, each one singing his as it should be blithe and strong,
The carpenter singing his as he measures his plank or beam,
The mason singing his as he makes ready for work, or leaves off work,
The boatman singing what belongs to him in his boat, the deckhand
singing on the steamboat deck,
The shoemaker singing as he sits on his bench, the hatter singing as he stands,
The wood-cutter's song, the ploughboy's on his way in the morning, or
at noon intermission or at sundown . . . .
The delicious singing of the mother, or of the young wife at work, or of
the girl sewing or washing,
Each singing what belongs to him or her and to none else,
The day what belongs to the day—at night the party of young fellows,
robust, friendly,
Singing with open mouths their strong melodious songs.

—Walt Whitman, "I Hear America Singing," *Leaves of Grass*, 1860

IN ADDITION TO THE WIDELY RECOGNIZED ROLE OF Hudson River School painters as observers, their function as commentators on man's repeated encroachment on and potential desecration of nature has been only recently appreciated and described. Even through depictions of such gentle occupations as boating, fishing, hunting, and sketching, and such harmless accommodations for human travel as building bridges, the artists who recorded these scenes acted as ecologists and early environmentalists. With their belief in natural religion and the significance of a virgin state of wilderness to our national identity, these artists were troubled by the permanent mark that man was increasingly making on the American landscape.

Artists in Nature
Painting the Wilderness

A CUSTOMARY DEVICE OF THE PICTURESQUE MANNER OF composition was to place a single figure under a tree, contemplating the landscape. This metaphorical figure, generally idle and in repose, became a surrogate for the observer: our representative in witness to nature. In contrast to this unengaged figure in picturesque paintings, the following five works depict artists actively engaged in their profession, that is, keenly observing and transcribing nature *en plein air*. The artist's role is always that of the unseen observer, the creator of each painting; actual inclusion of the artist within his or her own composition, although uncommon, occurs occasionally and serves to reinforce this important function. The following unique grouping is the first to our knowledge, to compare Hudson River School paintings showing artists at work in their natural environment.

Charles W. Knapp's artist seems at home in his forested retreat, although he is perched slightly awkwardly on a boulder, a subtle reference to man's precarious position

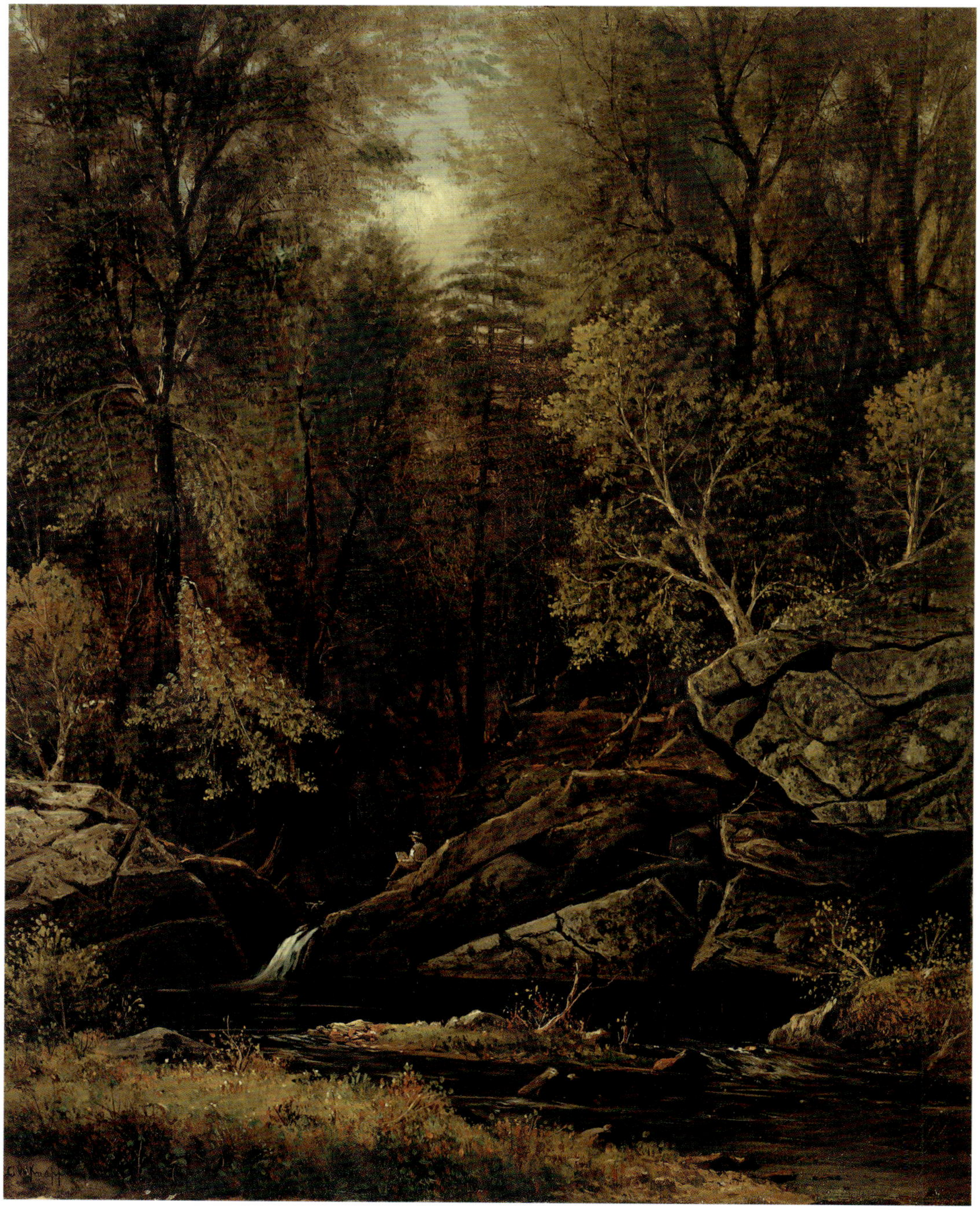

Charles W. Knapp (1823–1900)
Artist Sketching, n.d.
Oil on canvas, 29 x 24 inches

and general instability in nature. Following the solemn summons of Asher B. Durand and others, the artist has journeyed to nature's inner recesses in order to carefully observe and directly capture nature's beauty rather than, as had previously been the practice, rendering nature within the domestic surroundings and security of a studio. The deep, varied greens in this composition also resemble those of Durand's forest interiors. Situating his artist in deep, interior woodland intersected by a gentle waterfall, Knapp has included numerous iconographical elements traditionally associated with the sublime. References to the beautiful and picturesque are also present, such as the surrounding trees that bend gently inward in multiple gestures of protection. The bow of one tree on the left is particularly anthropomorphic, offering a specific sign of benediction. At the top of the composition, a small area of blue sky opens, shedding sunlight directly onto the artist's work, again a blessing. Nature, in this intimate and welcoming composition, becomes the font of artistic inspiration.

Catskill Clove, a charmed location for Hudson River School artists, was made so by the generations who painted there, beginning in 1825 with Thomas Cole, the father of the movement, and continuing with Frederic Church and Asher B. Durand. Carmiencke's view of 1863 is panoramic, encompassing the slopes of both North and South Mountains and the valley below. Outcroppings of rock refer to perils remaining in the hilly wilderness, whereas a cluster of small buildings contrasts this danger with the comfortable domesticity of home and hearth. A bridge traversing Catskill Creek provides a man-made transition from wilderness to civilization, indicating man's effort to control and alter his environment. The artist sits in shadow at the base of an outcropping on the left, observing but not readily observed. Resplendent autumn colors are touched by rays from a setting sun, sending reassuring warmth across the now peaceful countryside, contradicting signs of disruption that will come with man's future acts of encroachment. The serenity of this piece also denies the savagery taking place in the country at large, with the Civil War then being waged.

John Herman Carmiencke (1810–1867)
Catskill Clove, 1863
Oil on canvas, 16 x 24 inches

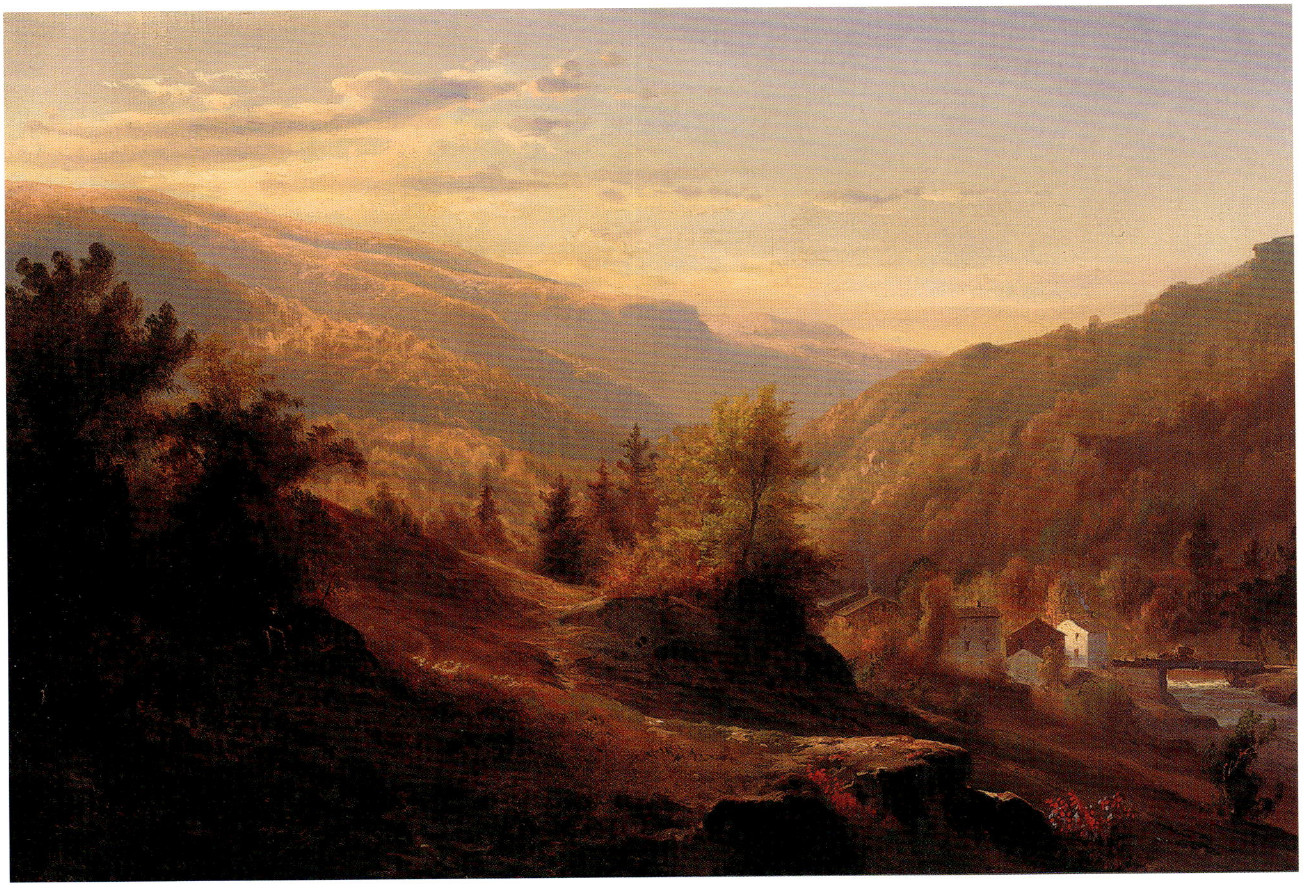

LOCATED ON THE EASTERN SHORE OF THE SUSQUEHANNA River, Columbia, Pennsylvania, is minutely detailed before us in this canvas by William Sanford Mason, who lived and painted in Lancaster County. Organized in horizontal bands, the composition moves in harmonious transition from wilderness to meadow, city to river, mountains to sky. The buildings of Columbia, including at least one prominent church spire, are nestled in greenery along the banks of the river, dotted by forested islands characteristic of the Susquehanna. A thunderstorm seems to be developing along mountain crests on the far shore, threatening the quiet domesticity of the scene. The artist sits apart, to the left of the canvas, in a relatively wild, elevated area on a dirt path, hidden by a large boulder. We observe him from a higher vantage point as he works at his easel. This positioning refers to Thomas Cole's influential and famous painting of Northampton, Massachusetts—*The Oxbow* (1836)—in which the artist also included himself painting in an elevated wilderness area in the left foreground of the composition just after a thunderstorm. In both paintings, there is marked separation between wild and cultivated areas. In each composition, the artist places himself in the wilder area, perhaps a sign of his alignment with nature and concern for the future desecration of the wilderness. Contrasts between clear and threatening weather conditions, along with varying states of wilderness and settlement, constitute principal themes here. In 1855, Mason was solicited by the citizens of Columbia to paint their prosperous town, since he had an excellent reputation for composing such views. The popularity of this painting with Mason's contemporaries is indicated by the fact that soon after its completion, it became widely available as a chromolithograph.

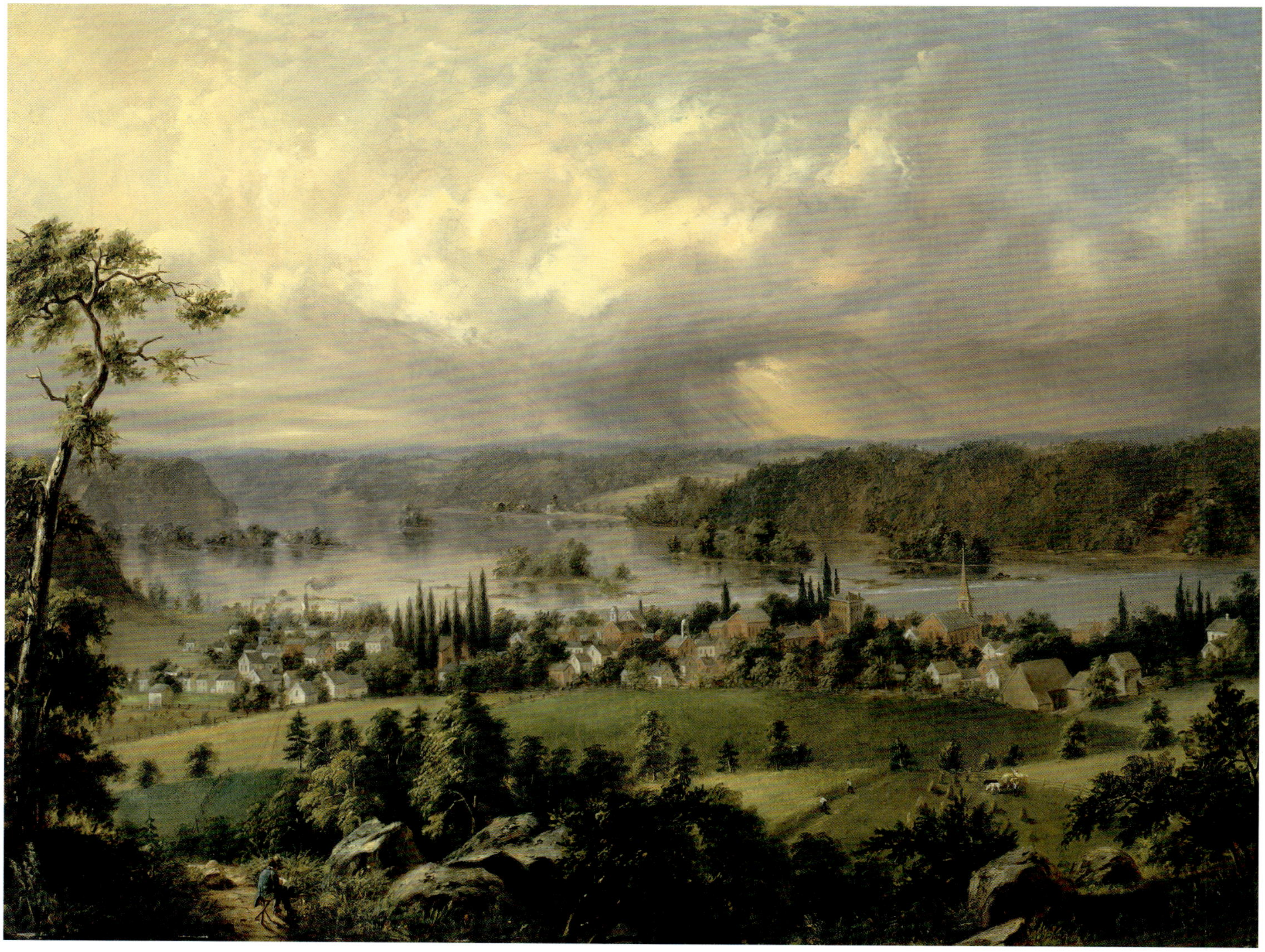

The circular shape of Boutelle's canvas adds to the beatific balance of its mood. Inspired by Cole and Durand, Boutelle was largely self-trained, learning his craft through direct observations made in nature. This picturesque view of an artist sketching contains numerous accurate transcriptions of fauna, especially the intricate designs of wildflowers and water plants in the foreground. Boutelle also succeeded in capturing the gentle stillness of a balmy late-spring afternoon. Under shelter created by large, generously foliated trees, the painter has set up an elaborate camp, complete with blanket, chairs, easel, shade umbrella, and picnic basket. A female companion and model is dressed in bright red. She, along with the red blanket and tip of the umbrella, contrasts with the surrounding earth colors. In the right half of the composition, trees form a strong vertical, reaching their feathery branches across to a horizontal intersecting band created by the far distant shoreline, its colors muted in the hazy atmosphere. Cows have come to the water's edge to drink. The harmonious relationship and peace prevailing between man and nature in this painting from 1862 again belie the horrific battles of the Civil War raging in other parts of the country that same year.

William Sanford Mason (1824–1864)
View of Columbia, 1855
Oil on canvas, 22 x 30 inches

DeWitt Clinton Boutelle (1820–1884)
Artist Sketching, 1862
Oil on canvas, 20 3/4 inches (tondo)

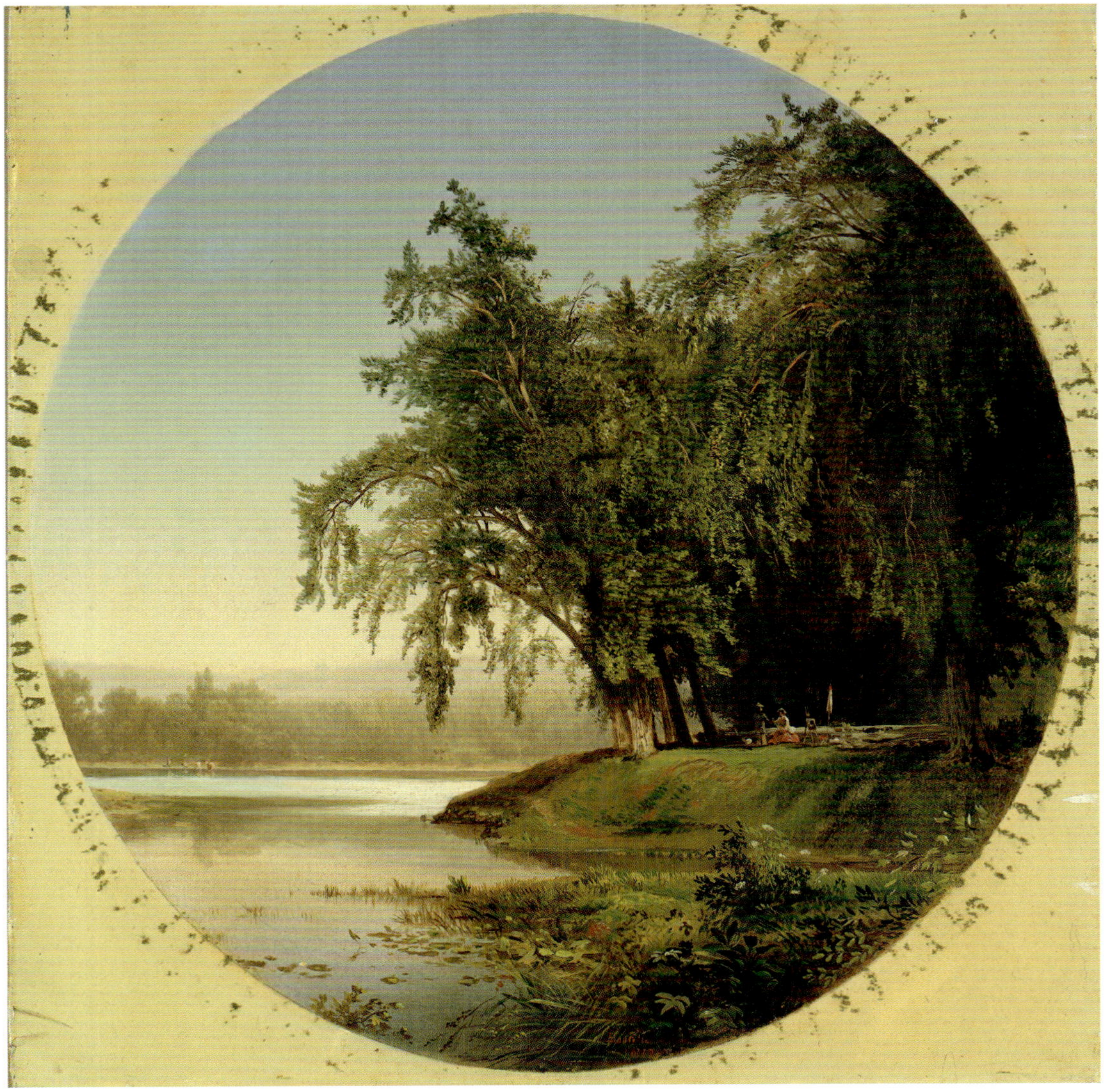

Born in 1800 in Paris, Joseph Morviller was to become a member of the White Mountain School of artists, who favored genre scenes and landscapes. His view of a serene, domesticated landscape shows a woman painter sitting slightly to the right of center along a river bank, sketch pad in hand. A male companion, possibly her instructor, stands behind her, observing both her progress and the expansive view laid out before them. A brightly colored tree in the lower foreground divides the canvas, separating the artist and her companion from a raft being pulled by two figures. Other signs of commerce and industry dot the river's edge. Cows have made their way down a dirt path to the water, indicating the presence of farming along with the development of industry. A small settlement of homes, punctuated by a tall church spire, is nestled in the middle distance. Calm and beautiful, the scene possesses a European quality. The suggestion of hard labor by the raftsmen adds to its picturesque nature rather than diminishing it, in a manner similar to workers depicted in paintings by Poussin and Millet. The active colonization of the New Land has not yet disturbed its natural balance.

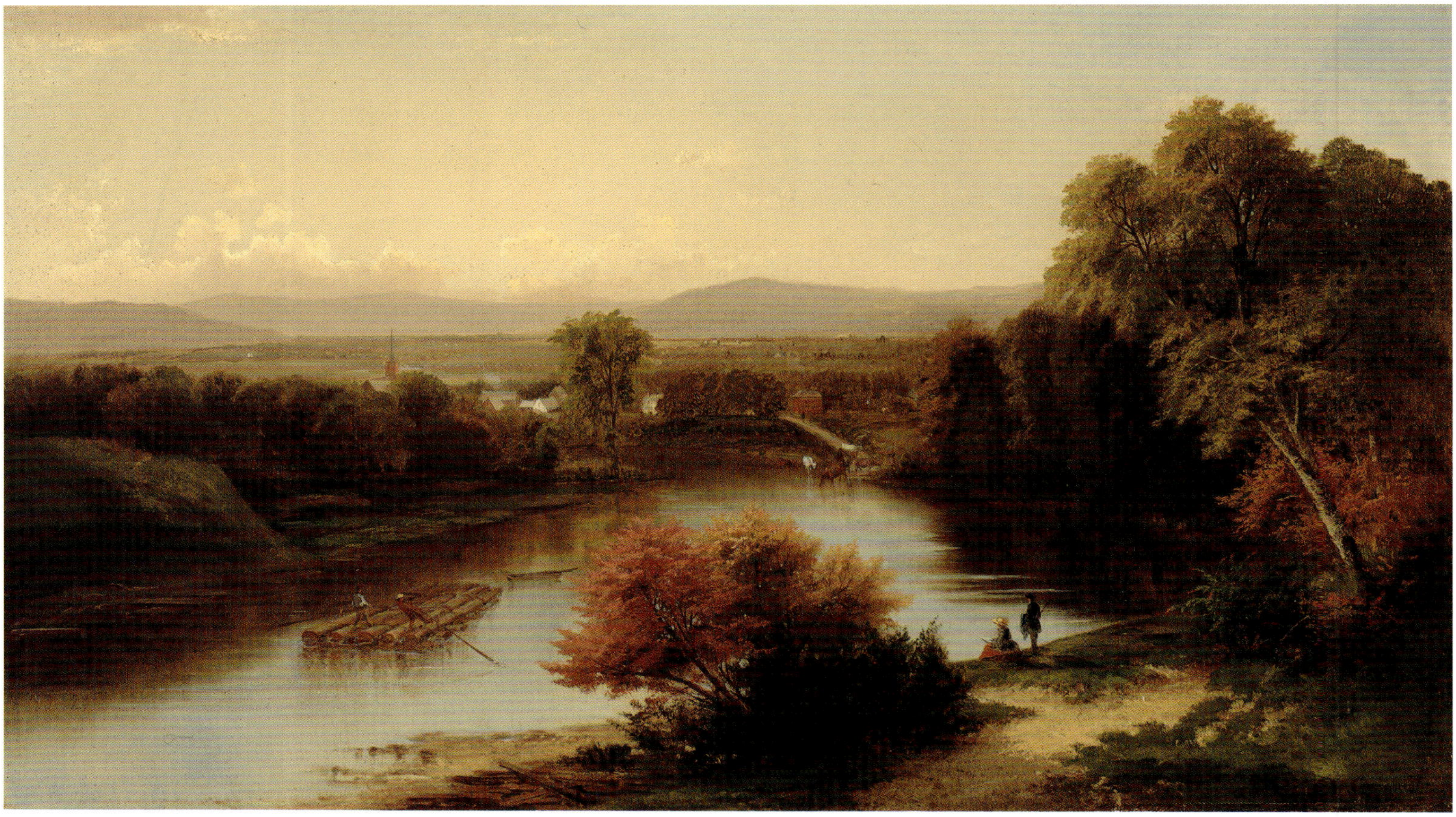

Joseph Morviller (1800–1870)
Autumn Landscape, 1860
Oil on canvas, 14 x 25 inches

Fishing

IN THIS QUINTESSENTIAL HUDSON RIVER SCHOOL SCENE, Casilear depicts a sunny, glowing late autumn afternoon in which most of the composition is devoted to the magnificent colors of the sky. The land below is smaller in comparison and much darker. The panoramic view discloses a deep river valley surrounded by densely forested slopes in brilliant autumn foliage, with water cascading over rocks in the left foreground. The artist's early training as an engraver is revealed in the detail with which he renders textures, color, and individualized features of the landscape and also in the marked contrast between alternating sunny and shadowed areas in the foreground. Yet details become hazy in the distant horizon where land merges with sky. A lone fisherman stands under a sheltering tree in the right foreground on the very perimeter of the composition, barely distinguishable from the tree against which he leans. Shown here is the least obtrusive and destructive of man's incursions into nature—in fact, one that is nearly imperceptible.

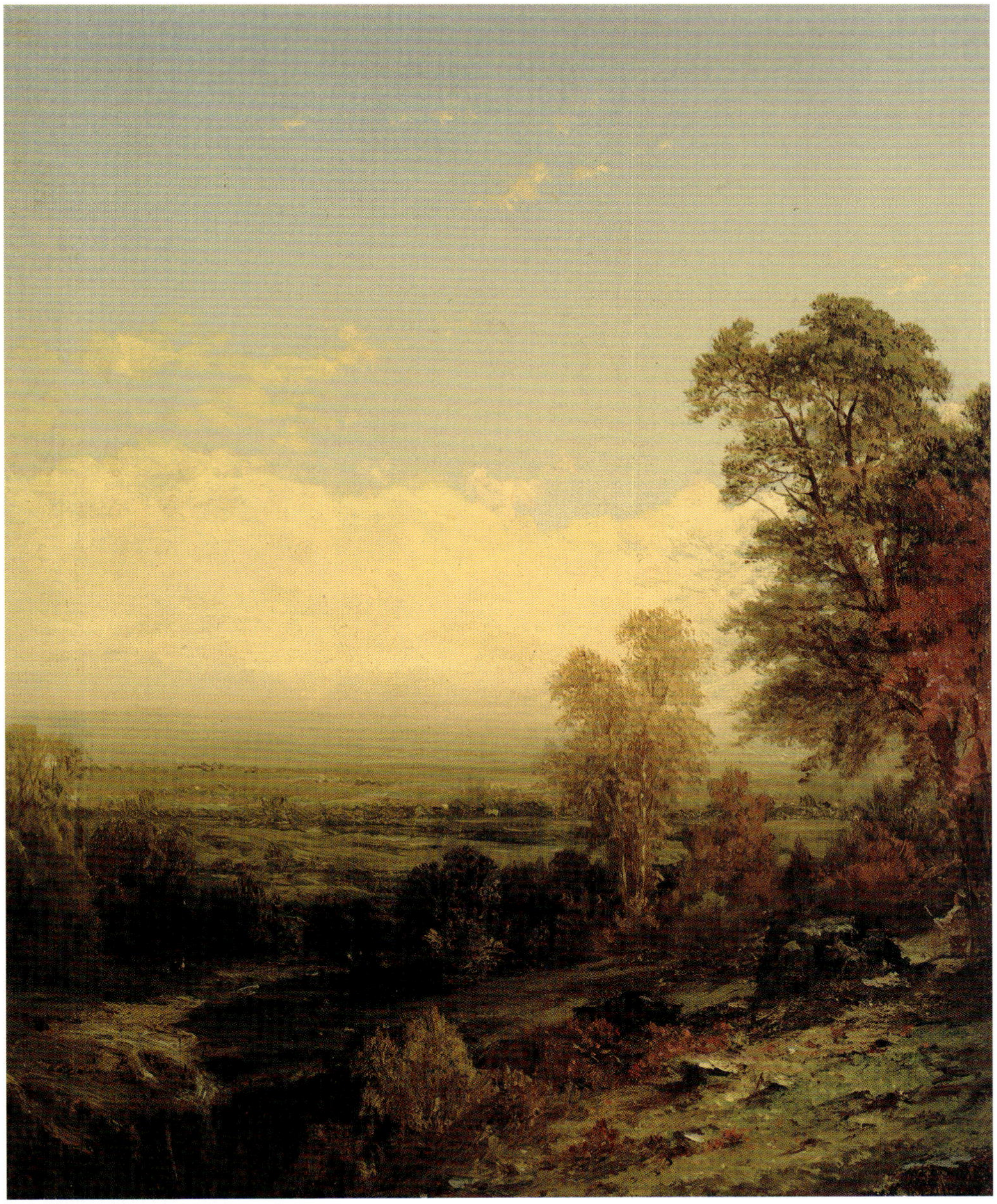

John William Casilear (1811–1893)
Autumn Landscape with Fisherman, c. 1865–1870
Oil on canvas, 12¼ x 10 inches

Boutelle evokes a tranquil late-summer afternoon. Two boys fish in a river running through a green meadow. Wild grasses and tiny bright flowers border the path along which the boys have walked. A bridge connects two sides of the meadow. One side has grazing cows; the other, boys fishing. This composition constitutes a serenely domesticated and appealing landscape. Pinkish gray clouds rise from behind the tree line on the right to mimic the shape of a large elm tree on the left. The standing boy holds his fishing rod straight up; it, in turn, echoes the line of the same tree. Earth and sky share equally in the composition, further creating a mood of balance and harmony. Not actively fishing, the boys appear instead to be engaged in contemplating the lovely view.

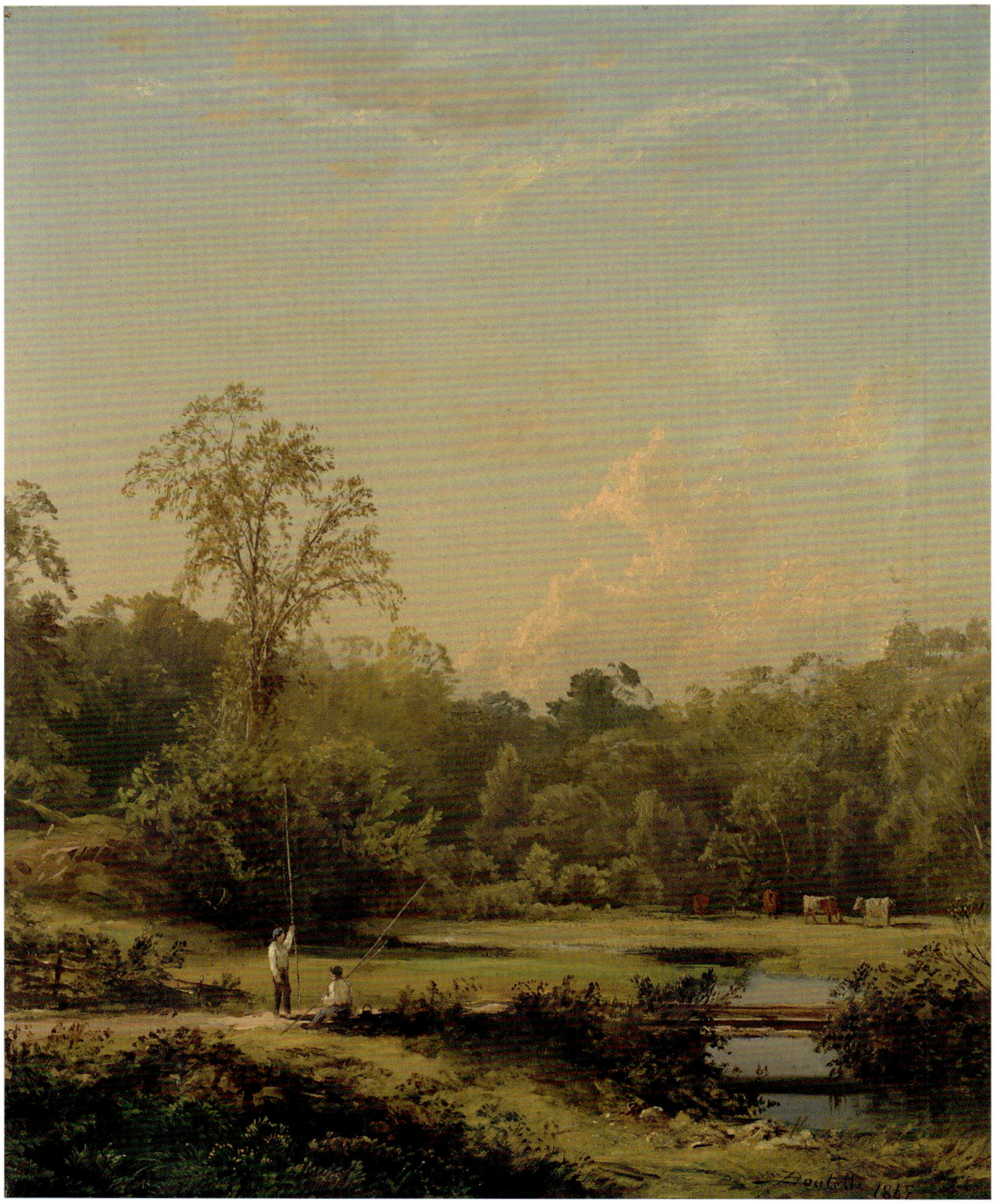

Like Boutelle and Casilear, Boese has created an ideal landscape in which to fish. Autumn colors on the shoreline surround and are in contrast with the blue shades of mountains and water. Pebbles on a sandy beach, the golden brown tumble of undergrowth, rough bark of tree trunks, and leafy foliage are described in abundant detail. Their intricate textures, like their earthen colors, are contrasted with the smooth glassy calmness of the blue water. Again, the boys do not seem to be fully engaged in fishing but are standing at the shoreline in conversation, one with his back to the water—a pole slung over his shoulder, echoing the curved line of the tree behind him. Horizontal bands of sun and shadow, trees, and mountain gradually lead the viewer's eye back through this pleasing painting to the distant shore.

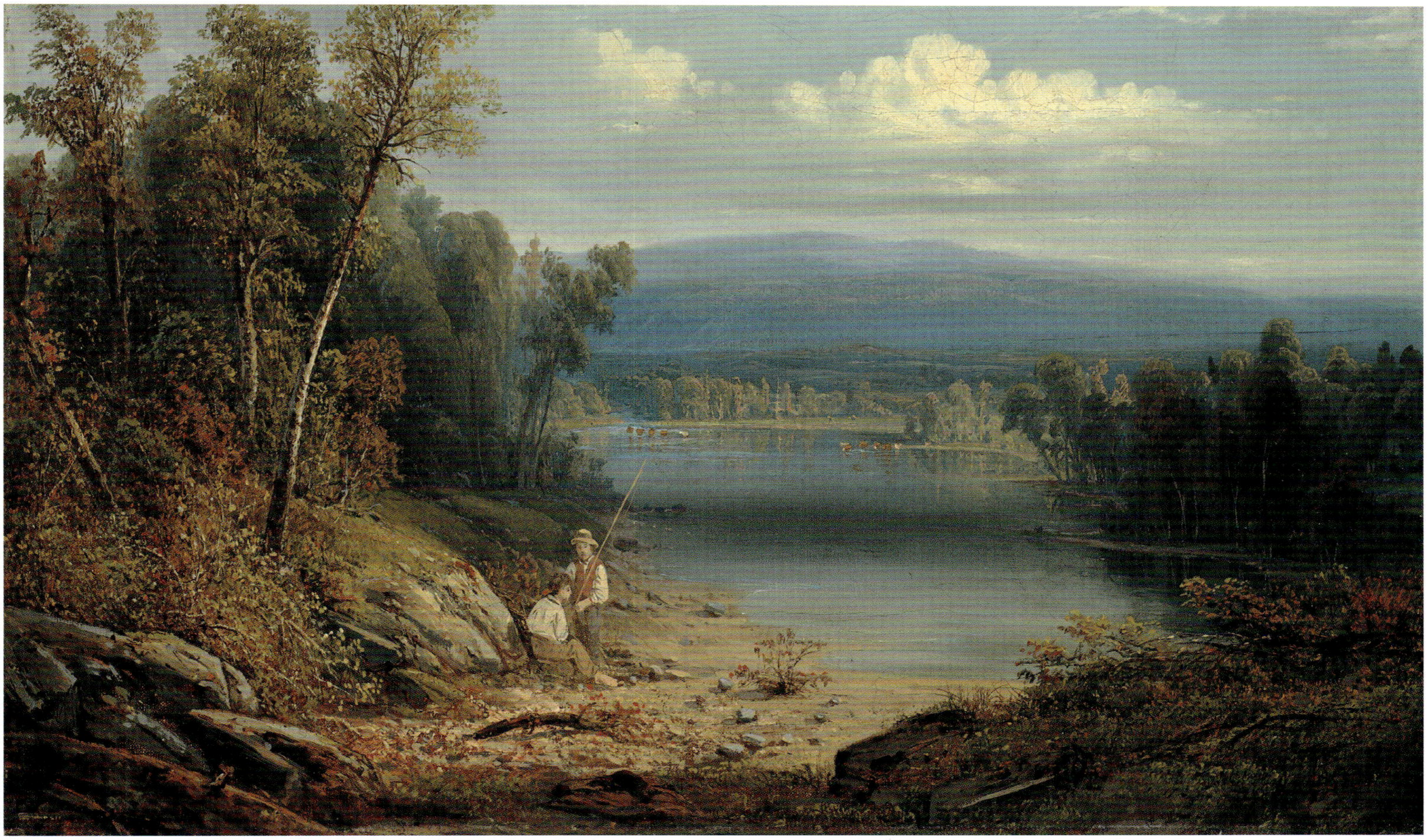

DeWitt Clinton Boutelle (1820–1884)
Two Boys Fishing, 1867
Oil on canvas, 12 x 10 1/4 inches

Henry Boese (1824–1863)
Autumn Landscape, n. d.
Oil on canvas, 13 1/4 x 23 1/2 inches

An early American landscapist and prolific genre painter, Alvan Fisher toured the eastern United States to discover bucolic scenes that became subjects of his brush. He found landscape painting a pleasant occupation, and this affinity becomes apparent in his art. Two fishermen stand at a river's bend, where a pool and short run of rapids have formed between two steep, rocky banks. Fisher's vertical compositional format emphasizes the steep diagonal rise of the far riverbank, which—along with the rocky outcropping of the near bank—serves to embrace the scene with a gentle intimacy, somewhat contradicting its solidity and scale. Diminutive in relationship to the natural formations that surround him, the dark figure of a fisherman stands erect against the red-orange sandstone just at the intersection of land and water. His companion, seated on a rock at the pool's lower edge, is less conspicuous, the line of his body parallel rather than perpendicular to nature, as it repeats the line of a tree trunk. These figures appear to be delineated as reverent observers or acolytes in the temple of nature.

This winter composition by Grunewald starkly contrasts with the warmer seasons usually depicted in fishing scenes. The cold clarity of winter's light seems to suit the artist,

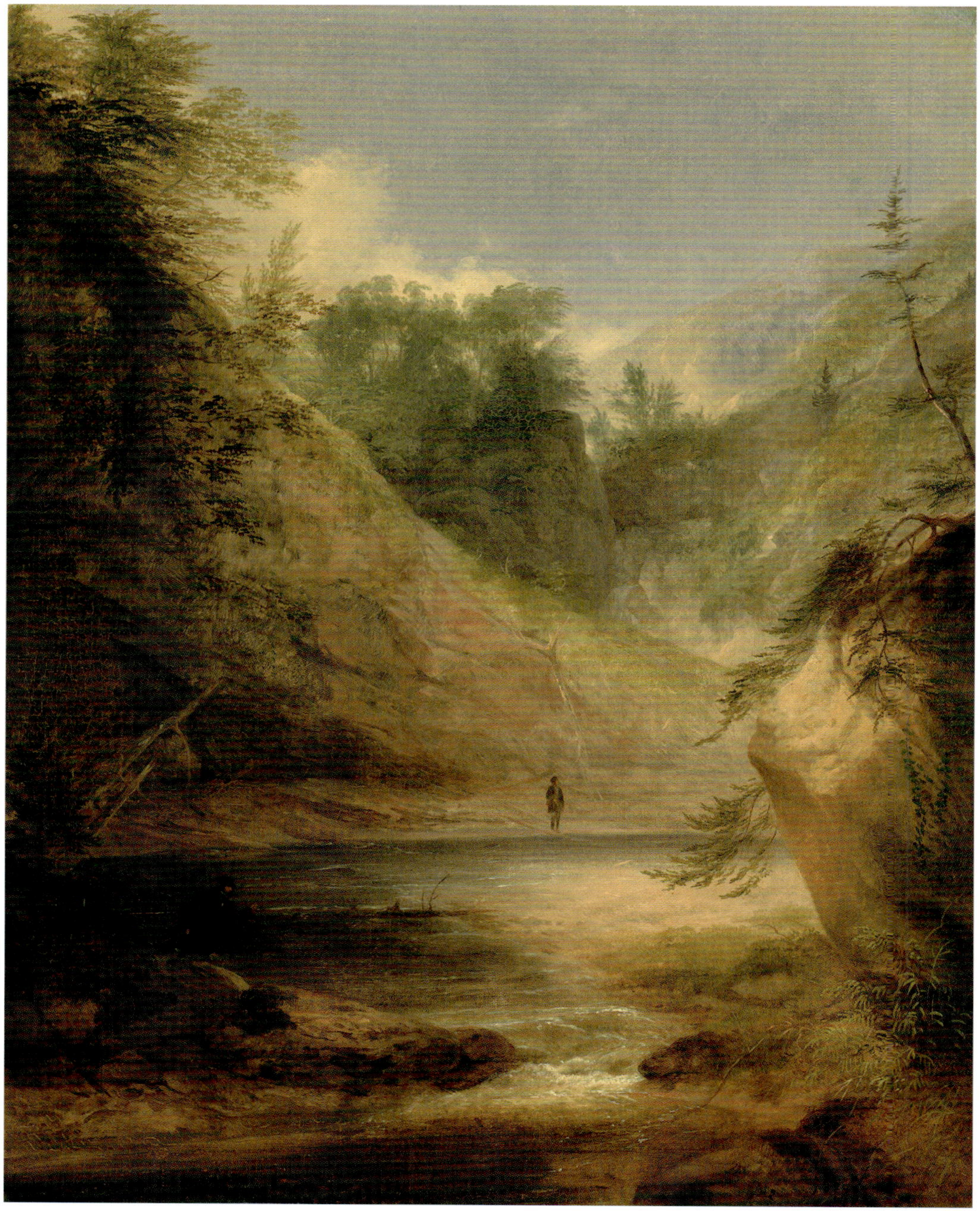

Alvan Fisher (1792–1863)
Fishing in New Hampshire, 1852
Oil on canvas, 27 1/4 x 22 1/4 inches

who studied under the great German Romantic painter Caspar David Friedrich (1774–1840). Jagged pieces of ice, one resembling a shark's fin, surround a hole in the lake's frozen surface, perhaps a reference to Friedrich's famous painting *Artic Shipwreck* (1823–1824). Friedrich's symbolism in that painting possibly applies here as well: the ice represents God's inaccessible kingdom and inscrutability; the shipwreck implies the futility of man's efforts to reach and understand the deity. In Grunewald's painting, a fishing hole cut into the lake's frozen surface in the foreground has been abandoned by two men who have moved on to fish at another, perhaps more promising spot. Majestic pines—some laden with snow, others stripped of branches—rise high into the cool, crisp azure winter sky. Birds, seemingly released from the top of one pine tree, soar into yellow-tinged clouds. They appear to be sounding an alarm that goes unnoticed by the men below, who concentrate on their own task. The rosy tints of sunset color the slopes of distant mountains, while long shadows have started to work their way across the ice. A sense of stillness and grandeur in the atmosphere is contrasted with man's smallness and with the mundane activities supporting his survival in the wilderness, as represented by the chore of fishing.

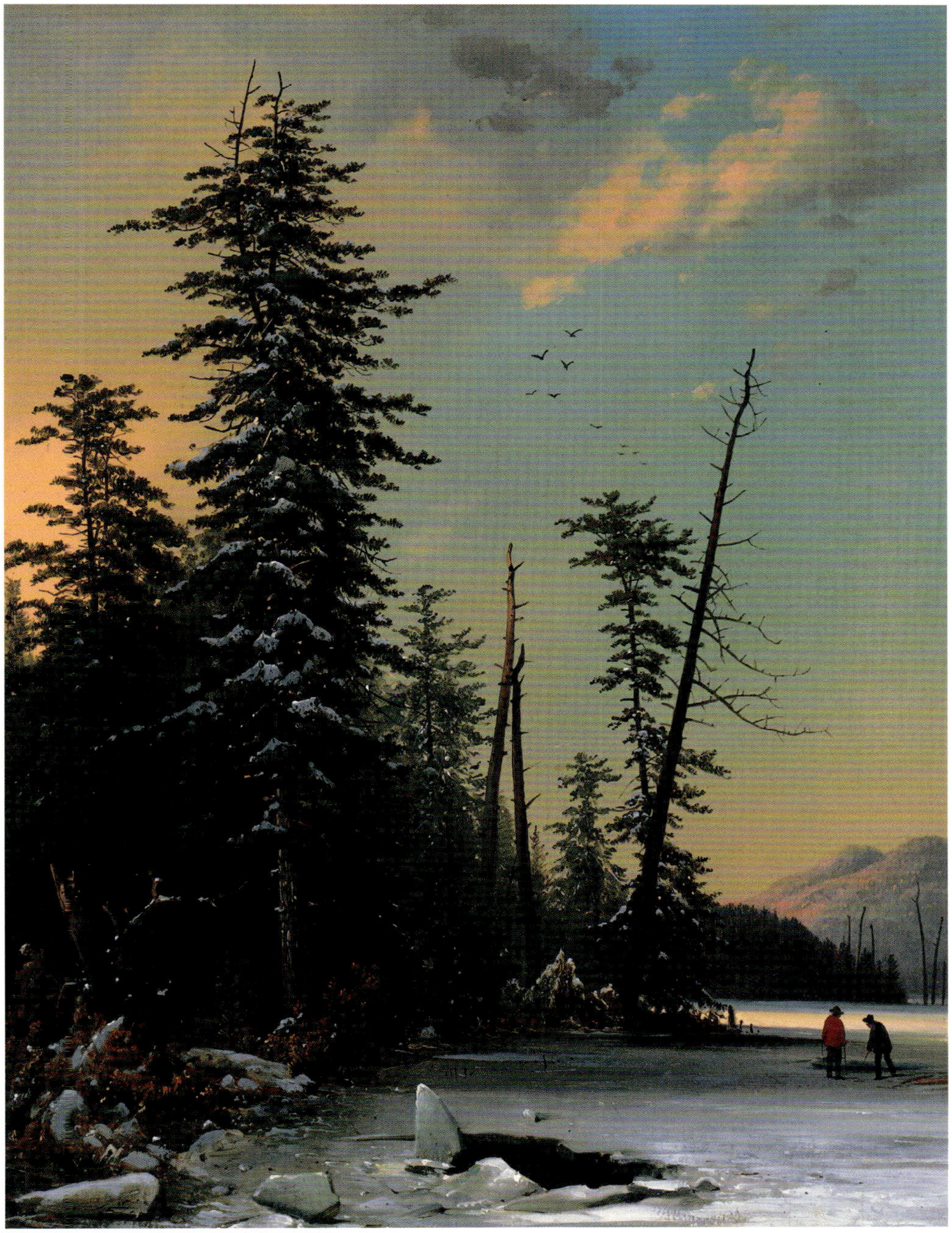

Gustavus Johann Grunewald (1805–1878)
Winter Fishing on a Lake at the Pine Swamp, 1856
Oil on panel, 20 x 15⁷/₈ inches

A scene made more intimate by the artist's choice of an arched canvas, *The Mill* conveys the lazy serenity of a summer day. The harmonious conjunction of man's work activities, as exemplified by the mill, with his leisure pastime—fishing—has been accomplished in a single view. The mill itself is engulfed in a wooded landscape, its wheel gently working the waters of a small stream. A church steeple in the background marks the town's closeness and reminds us of the presence of the spiritual in this earthly paradise. A fisherman, dressed in patriotic red, white, and blue, his pole laid alongside him on the ground, has stopped to rest on the hillside and to admire the summer afternoon under the protection of a large tree.

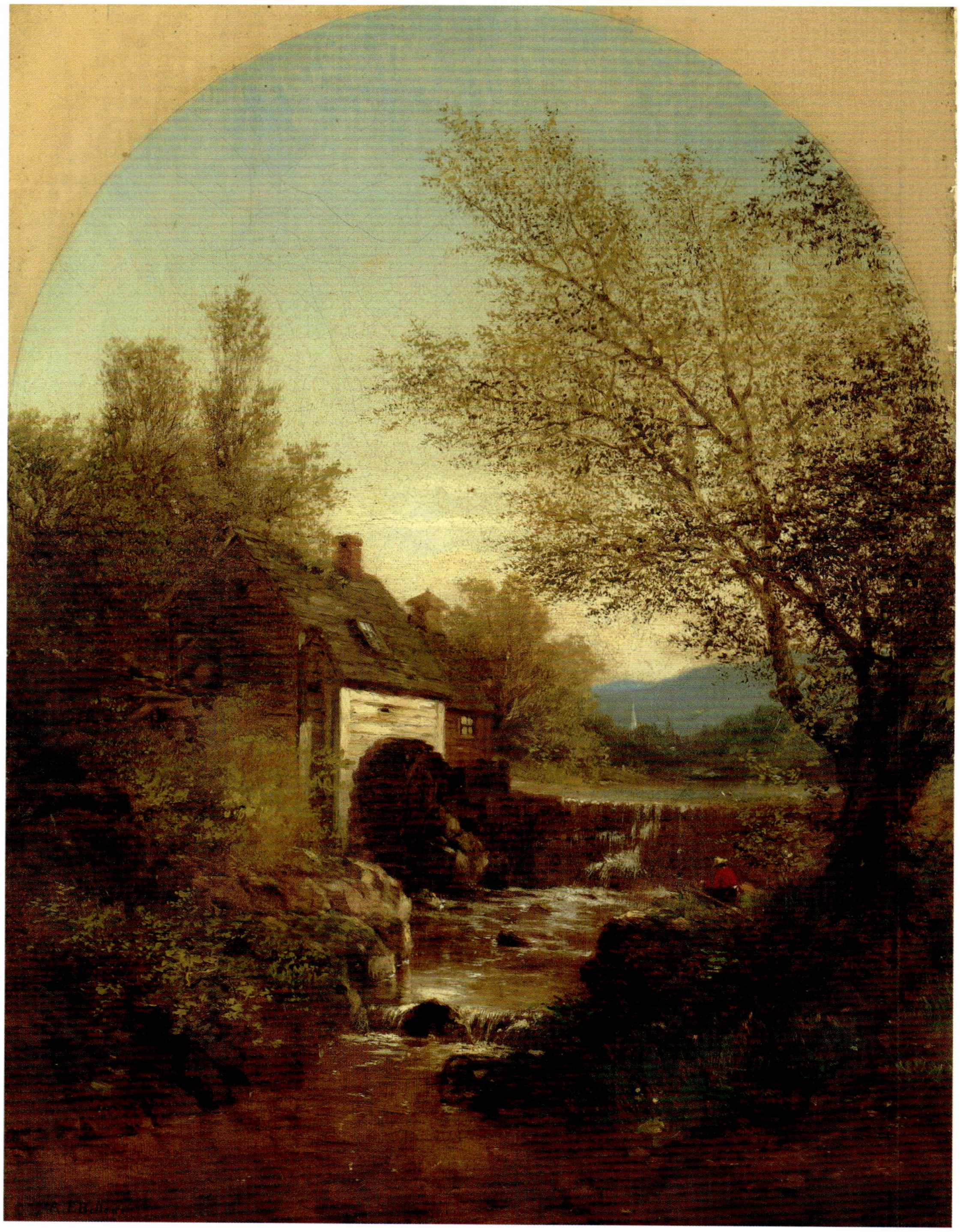

Luxuriant greens of varying intensity and hue blend harmoniously and subtly in this fertile, spring landscape, where water, earth, and sky are successfully integrated and unified. Even the buildings dotting the hillside seem at one with nature. Our fisherman, too, is completely incorporated into his surroundings, enmeshed in the vibrant greens of the season.

Albert Fitch Bellows (1829–1883)
The Mill, 1861
Oil on canvas, 14 1/4 x 11 inches (arched at the top)

Henry Pember Smith (1854–1907)
Man Fishing along a Stream, 1884
Oil on canvas, 15 1/4 x 12 1/4 inches

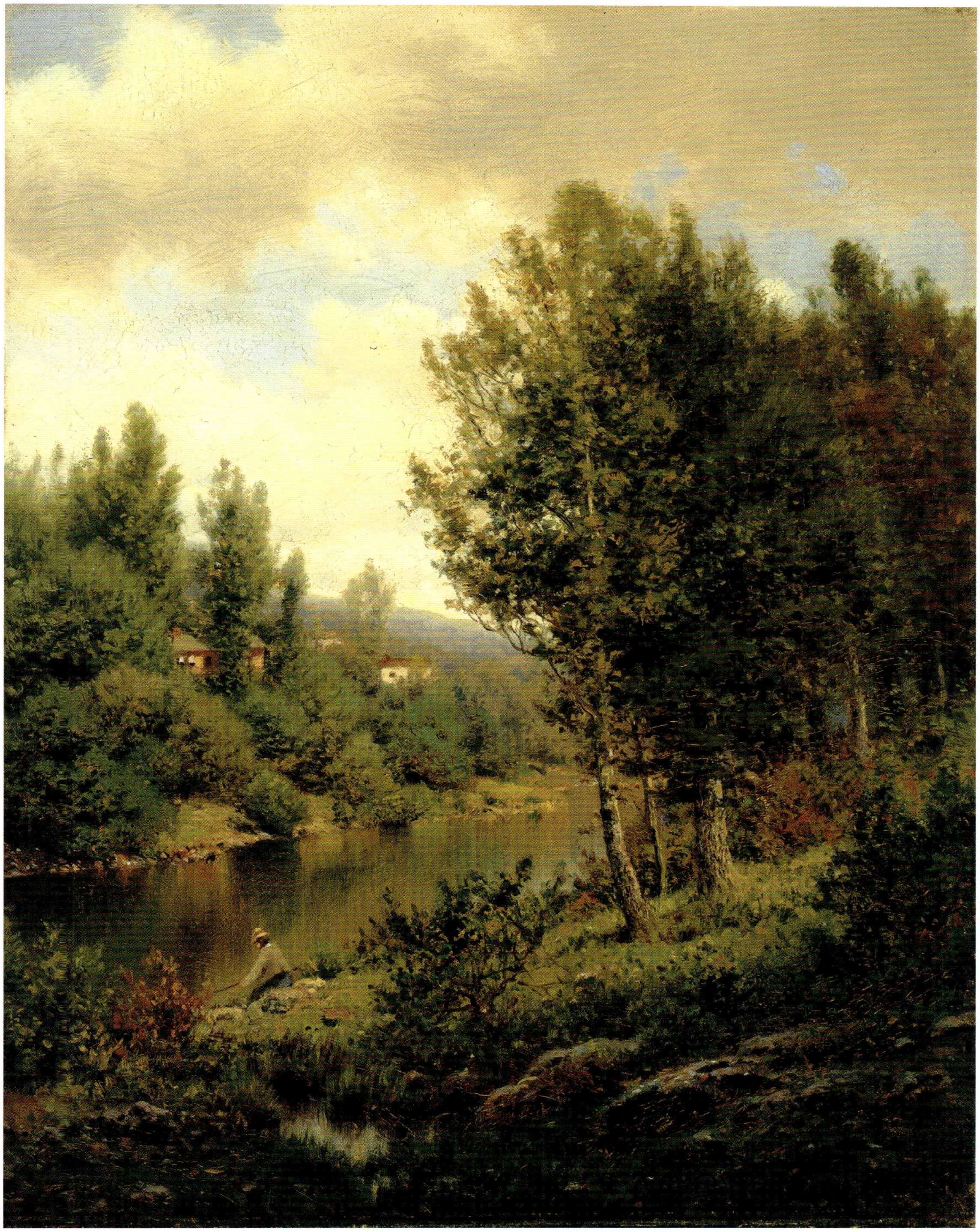

Barbara Novak describes contemplation of and meditation on nature in the American nineteenth century as "an avenue to the center of being" and "looking" as an "act of devotion."[11] Many fishing paintings evince this simultaneous need for solitary introspection and reverence toward nature, the activity of fishing seeming to serve as a mere contrivance, an excuse for being out-of-doors. In various scenes selected for this section, the figures are not directly engaged in fishing but absorbed in observing their natural surroundings. Influenced by Kensett, Casilear, Durand, and Cropsey, David Johnson has created just such a scene of quiet poetry and devotion to an all-subsuming landscape. In fact, this particular scene attracted him so much that he rendered several versions of it. A single figure sits central to the composition along the green banks of a river, half turned away from us, making us feel somewhat like intruders, somewhat welcome. We follow the fisherman's gaze into the colorful haze of a magnificent sunlit sky, purple clouds surrounding the yellow sun as it sinks into a blaze of red. Shadows are already cast across the land. We share the fisherman's gratitude and awe as witnesses to this daily spectacle of nature's splendors.

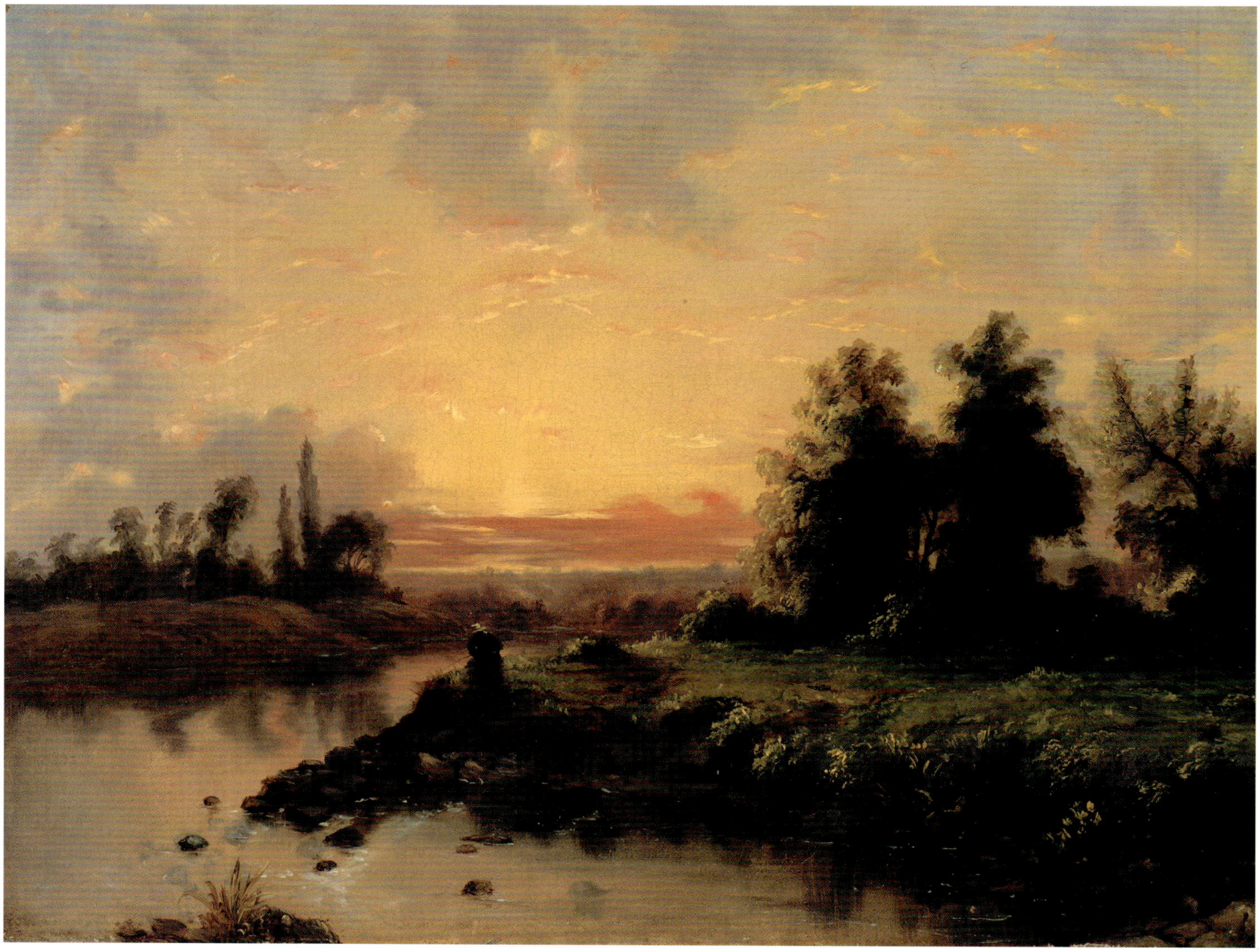

Boating

INDIAN SUMMER—A FAVORITE TIME OF YEAR FOR JERVIS McEntee, close friend of Sanford Gifford and Worthington Whittredge—offers especially dramatic and arresting colors and qualities of light that challenge an artist's evocative powers. Sanford Gifford's influence on McEntee is revealed in his ability to suffuse this composition in rich golden light. The sun's orb is only slightly visible in a sky sumptuous with color and thick with atmosphere. A boat is prominently and centrally placed on the water's edge. Figures on either side of the boat function as parentheses, emphasizing its emptiness and steadying it, perhaps, to invite the viewer to join them on their imminent outing. Receding promontories of land lead the eye back through the water to the horizon, creating a gentle sense of movement in this poetic picture. Light, time of day, season, and man's activity all join in this scene, blending harmoniously to induce a sense of morning's optimism and the promise of embarkation.

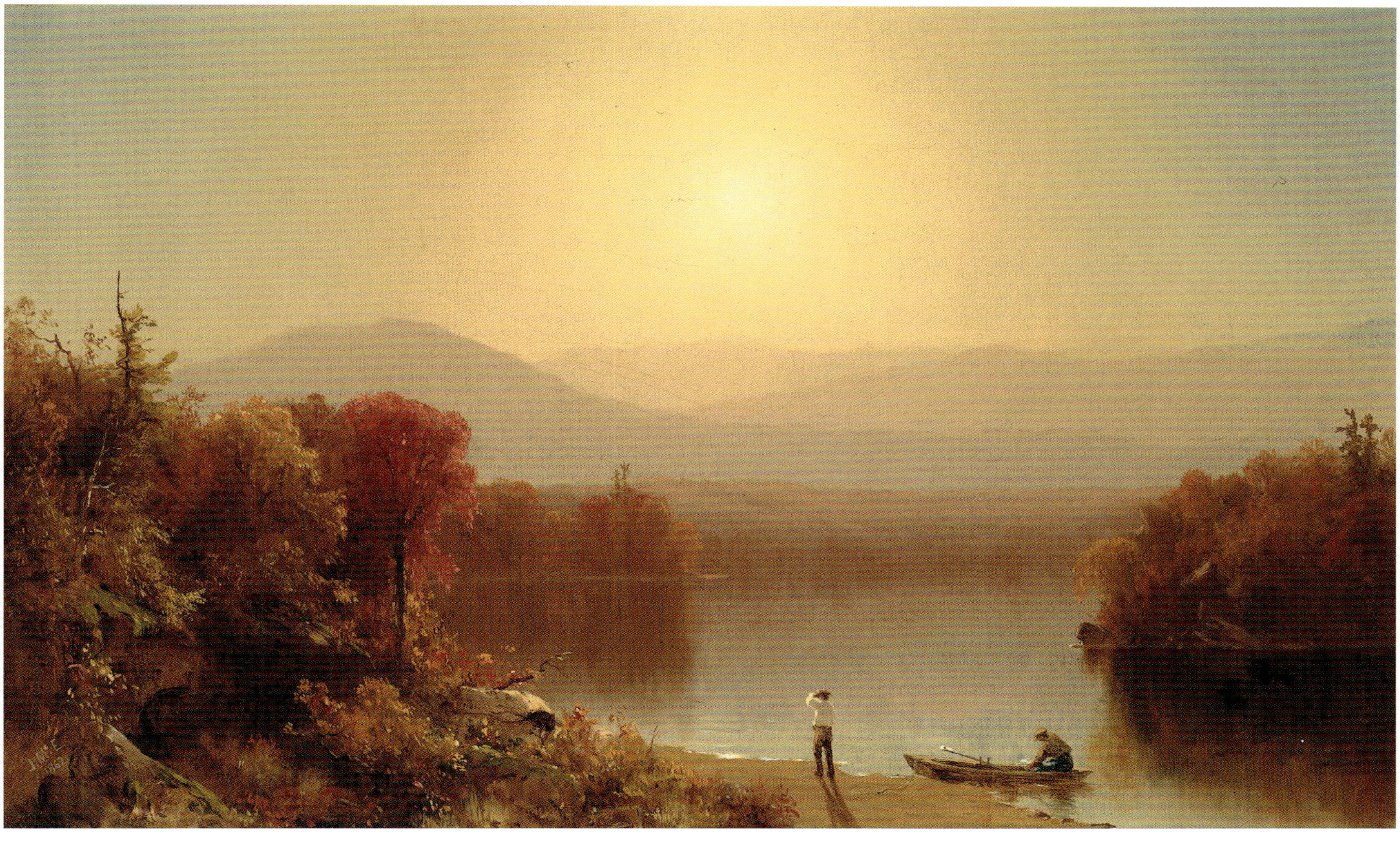

David Johnson (1827–1908)
Sunset in New Rochelle, n.d.
Oil on canvas, 12 x 16 inches

Jervis McEntee (1828–1891)
Indian Summer, 1862
Oil on canvas, 10 x 18 inches

Russell Smith's view of Pennypack Park (outside Philadelphia, where he lived) is permeated with soft silvery hues, conjuring up a mood of gentility and opulence. Two figures, one jacketed in bright red, the other wearing blue trousers, are embarking on a morning boating excursion. The benevolent, protective curve of a tree on the right cradles the scene, which is executed with delicate feathery brushwork and an elegant sense of compositional balance. The horizontals of water and sky in the center are framed to the right and left by strong verticals of rock. The pleasingly curved arches of the old stone bridge, built in 1697 and one of the oldest in the nation, invite us, the viewers, into the landscape with the boaters as we anticipate the adventures of a journey to unfold in the awaiting day.[12] This was a favorite location for Russell Smith, who painted it several times.

Edward Moran's scene of early evening contrasts dramatically with the mood and atmosphere of the Russell Smith painting. Moran shows a nearly empty boat beached on the shore at close of day, its contents only a few articles of clothing draped across the bow. Fishermen's nets indicate a utilitarian purpose for this vessel, the owner having retired for the night to the cottage nearly hidden by trees along the shore. The land and its tangle of undergrowth are cast in shadow. In brilliant contrast, the afterglow of sunset is ablaze in color. Long strands of pink and gray clouds reach evocatively across the sky, giving the painting its name. Two small sailboats glide through the still blue waters of the Hudson. The absence of human figures, emptiness of the boat, and urgency of evening as it draws the day quickly to a close create an intense and poignant mood of inevitability. The repetitive cycles of days, man's work, and life itself are palpable here in the context of a gentle, passing moment in nature's unfolding embrace.

Russell Smith (1812–1896)
Pennypack, 1880
Oil on canvas, 12 x 18 inches

Edward Moran (1829–1901)
Wings of the Evening, c. 1870
Oil on canvas, 10½ x 18 inches

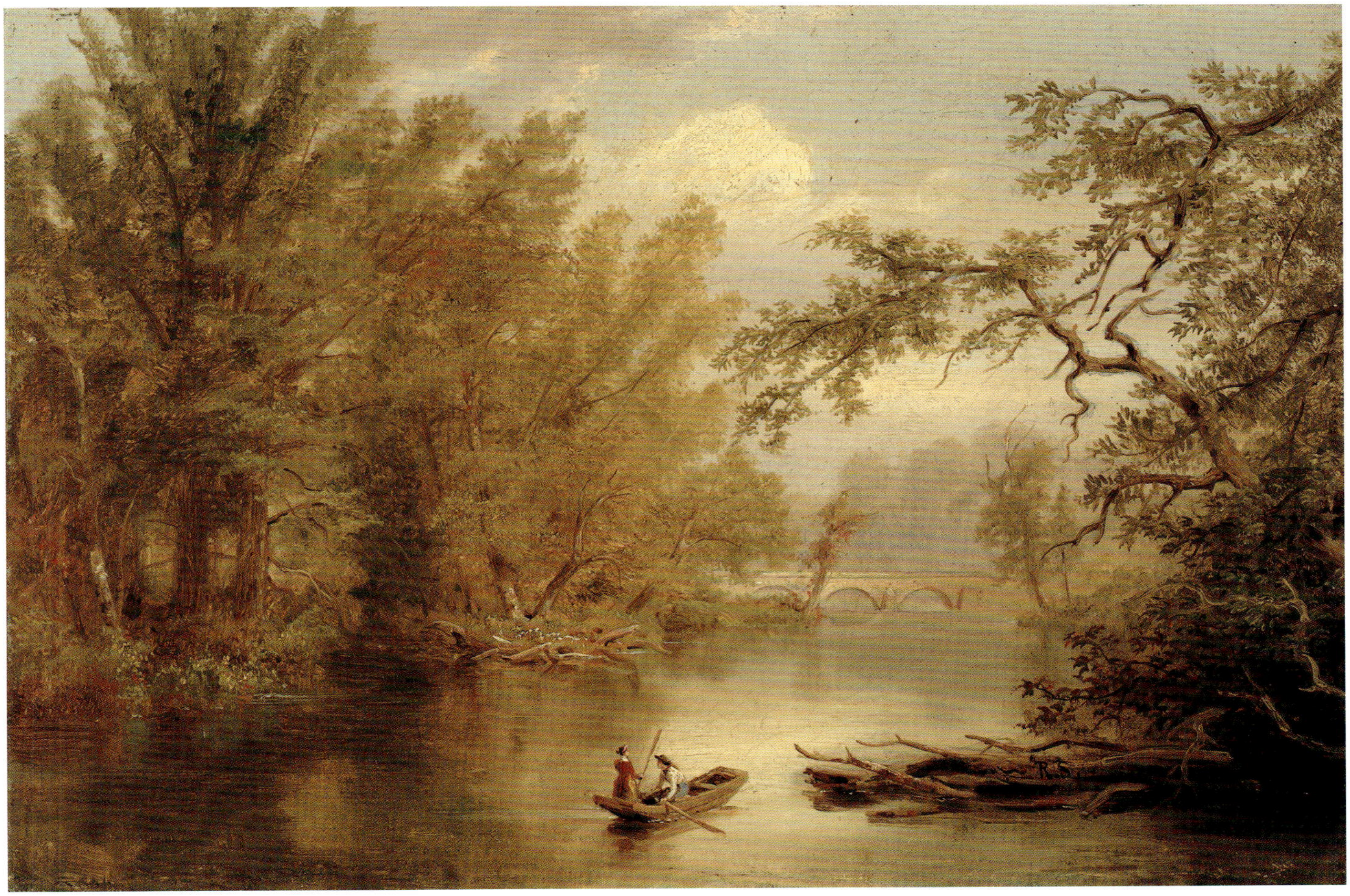

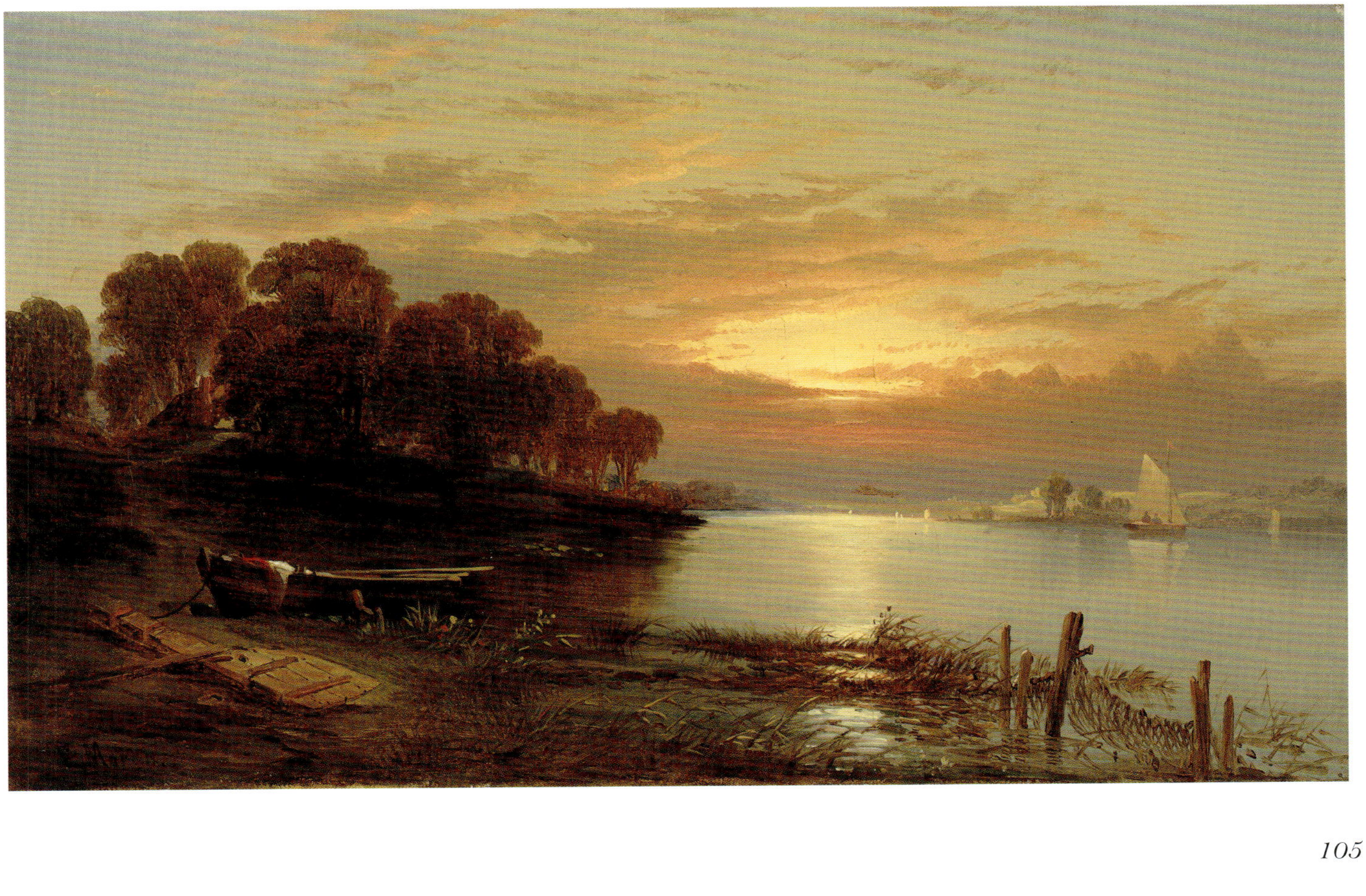

Light and the overwhelming vastness of an evening sky are the main subjects of James Hamilton's painting, which recalls a comment made in response to a sunset by Martin Johnson Heade, which could have been stimulated by Hamilton's canvas: "The rich hue in the sky of this sunset of Mr. Heade is a picture by itself, and only needed a foreground that would do it no harm."[13] In fact, in Hamilton's composition, land masses situated low on the horizon on either side of the marshes part, as would a theater's curtain, to reveal and draw the eye to the dramatic sunset. The elongated shape of the canvas emphasizes the sky's expansiveness, a sensation reinforced by zigzag patterns of clouds building upward into the atmosphere. Two witnesses to nature's twilight performance sit in stillness, fishing among the reeds in the foreground. They seem completely at peace and in harmony with nature, yet their bright red and blue shirts and the green of their boat distinguish them from their natural surroundings, setting them apart as beholders of rather than participants in the scene.

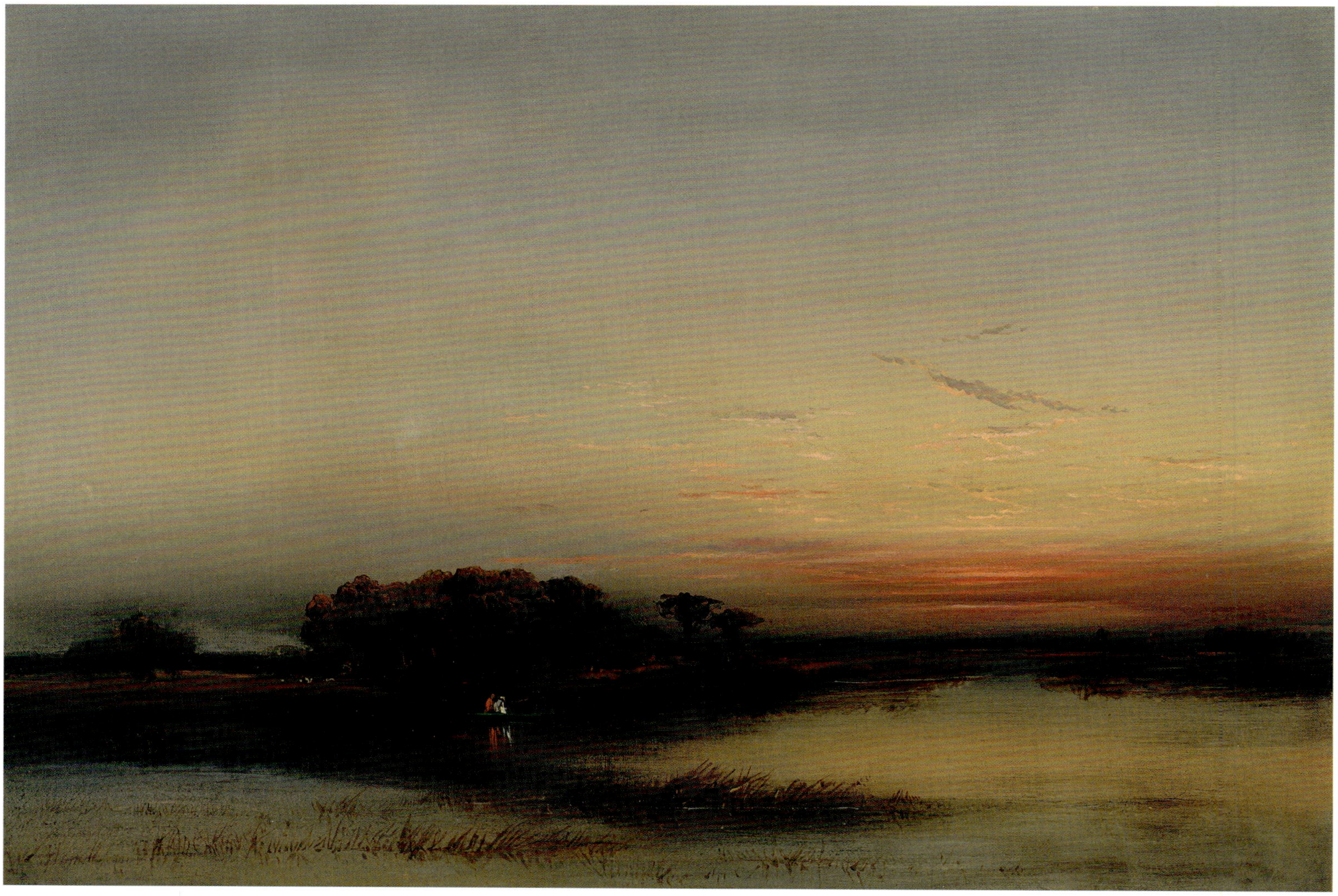

James Hamilton (1819–1878)
In the Salt Marshes of N.J., 1872
Oil on canvas, 20 x 29 1/2 inches

Positioned on a small outcropping of beach, a rowboat sits empty at the water's edge in this painting by Clinton Loveridge. The small craft points away from the viewer toward another shore rather than out into the water, thereby negating the expectations of a future voyage but suggesting, instead, that it has made its last voyage. Two tall trees to the right of center link earth to sky, stretching upward through brown and green shades of land to yellow, pink, and blue hues of a dramatic sunset. Beneath them, a fertile green slope meets the sandy beach, colored purple by the sun's dying light. Suggesting the completion of a voyage, the poignancy of the empty boat pulled to shore at sunset, painted nearly three decades after Cole's death, still evokes the memory of the premature departure of the beloved Hudson River School founder.

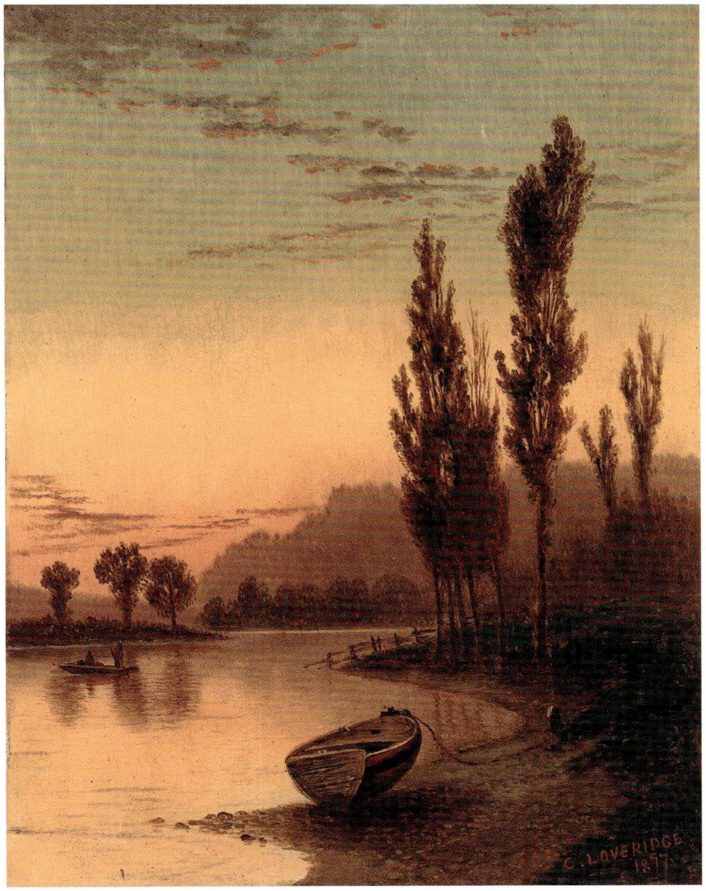

Clinton Loveridge (1824–1902)
Evening Sunset, 1877
Oil on wood panel, 9 x 7 inches

THE FORMIDABLE ROCK FORMATIONS OF AUSABLE CHASM in New York's Champlain Valley reveal a raw, dangerous side of nature. Champney has positioned a single boater, his back to us, paused in contemplation of the watery path opening before him, just as a young man would hesitate, weighing his options before proceeding in a rite of manhood or virgin voyage. The excitement of the American wilderness and the adventures to be provided by it lie before our voyager. Surprisingly inviting, the waters of the Ausable River flow gently past the hard, sunlit walls of the gorge, carved out over centuries by the river's persistent assault. In contrast, the walls rise menacingly above the diminutive figure in suspenders. The small boat and its passenger emerge into sunlight from deep shadow, furthering the analogy of youth passing from innocence into enlightenment. The river here is truly representative of the voyage of life as this young man embarks on its waters. Thomas Cole, whom Champney had met while Champney was still in his mid-twenties and whose work the younger artist much admired, made this symbolism popular through his series *The Voyage of Life* (1840–1841). Engravings of Cole's series were widely distributed and appeared on the walls of many American homes in the nineteenth century.

Benjamin Champney (1817–1907)
Ausable Chasm, n.d.
Oil on canvas, 21 x 17 inches

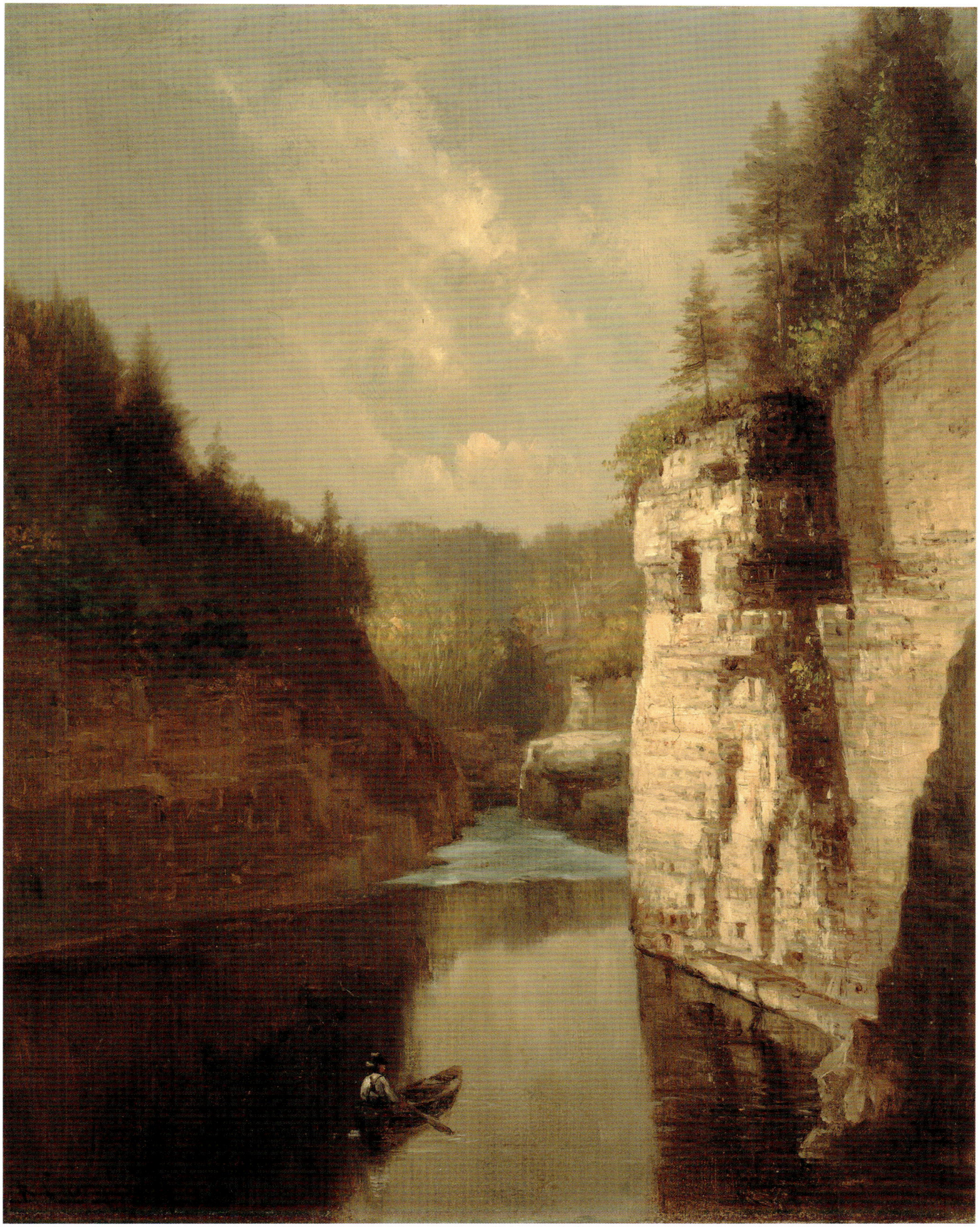

Hunting

This pair of paintings by Max Eglau, a German-born and Düsseldorf-trained artist, reveals a style rooted in realism, coupled with embellishments that add a touch of fantasy. In both works, Eglau uses color, light, and atmosphere, along with subject matter, to create different moods—the first benevolent, the second menacing. The influence of the Düsseldorf School is again apparent in the heightened sense of drama and urgency that pervades both paintings. The first depicts an American Eden, full of wildlife and exotic fauna. In the second, tension is introduced, as this paradise becomes threatened by the arrival of man in the form of a single hunter encroaching on nature.

The first, *Imaginary Landscape*, is a fanciful river scene with generic rather than specific mountains and trees, whose exaggerated shapes appear more typical of those surviving high on a mountainous slope rather than down in a peaceful valley. In the sky, bands of light blue are effectively juxtaposed to those of soft pink, peach, and light brown. These colors are then reflected in the water. A family of three deer and a group of heron picturesquely frame the scene on the right and left, respectively. At the center, along the horizon in the far distance, are diminutive forms of sailboats on the Hudson River: the nearly imperceptible, nonthreatening presence of man enjoying rather than disrupting or altering nature. The gentle quality of light, as well as the brilliant mixture of reality and fantasy, adds to the calmness and serenity of this vision.

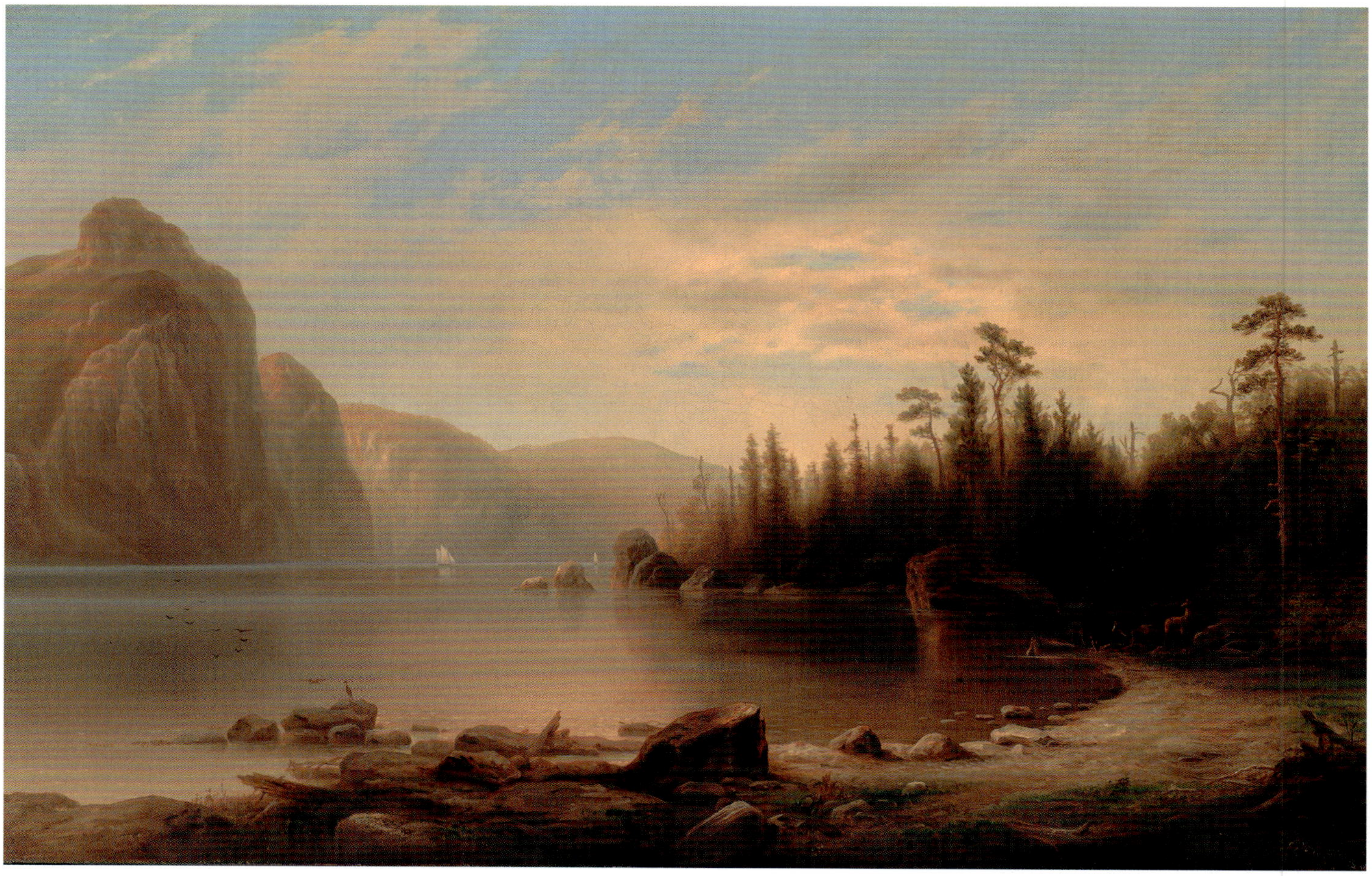

Max Eglau (1825–?)
Imaginary Landscape, n.d.
Oil on canvas, 20½ x 32½ inches

Hunter in a Landscape presents a contrasting scene from nature, dramatized by the use of specific motifs alluding to death in various guises. Dead trees are repeatedly juxtaposed to those still living. In one area, a dead tree appears to be falling from a stand of living ones; in another, an uprooted tree has dropped into the rapids. Across the water, expressive writhing forms of broken branches and twisted trees seem to cry out in agony. Birds, the only wildlife in evidence, flee into the clouds to escape the suffering on land, where the presence of a lone hunter is hardly needed to describe the threat to their existence. These birds, as well as their plight, are emphasized by their whiteness, silhouetted dramatically against the dark background. The atmosphere in this composition is thick and heavy. Eglau's use of light is hard and stark, revealing details with precise clarity, markedly different from the suffused sunlight of the previous painting.

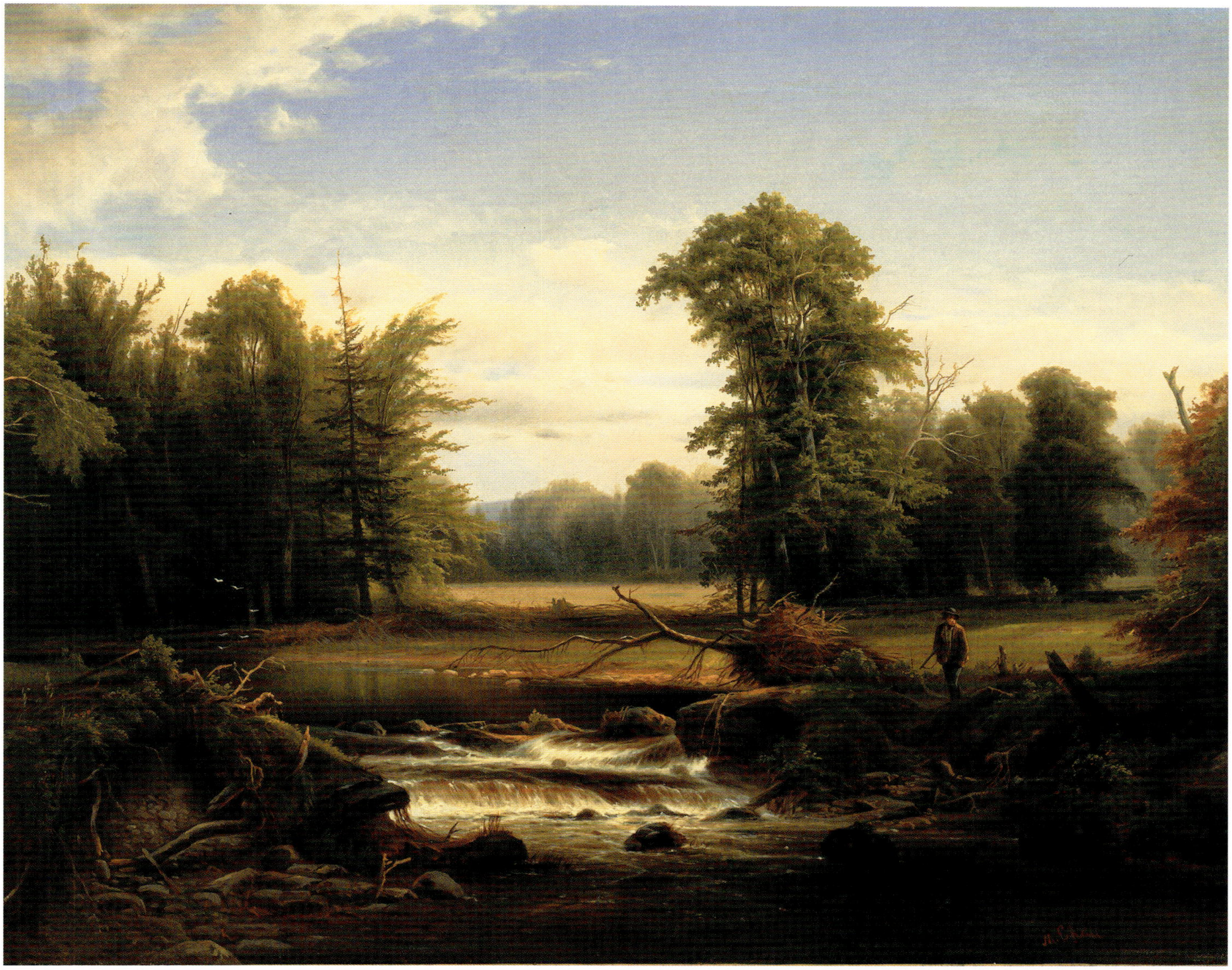

Max Eglau (1825–?)
Hunter in a Landscape, n.d.
Oil on canvas, 28 1/2 x 36 1/4 inches

One of the earliest of the nineteenth-century Hudson River School painters discussed here, Alvan Fisher traversed the East Coast painting genre scenes with animals and landscapes, often showing pioneers in vast wilderness settings. This pair of paintings by Fisher is particularly interesting in showing a progression through time of hunting parties as they move through hilly terrain. The vertical format of the pair accentuates the ruggedness of the landscape. In the first painting, hunters on horseback led by a black dog pick their way through a steep mountain path to reach a valley and stream below. The clear light of morning descends from the east to illuminate the underside of billowing clouds and the mountainside's rocky face. A slender tree, positioned across the water, bends its delicate branches toward the hunting party, as if protecting them on their journey across the streambed. The trunk of a large tree has fallen from the shore to a boulder, creating a natural bridge across the rippling rapids. Although the terrain is treacherous, nature has made some accommodations for the men traveling through it.

Alvan Fisher (1792–1863)
Hunters in a Stream with Dog, c. 1830
Oil on canvas, 24 x 20 inches

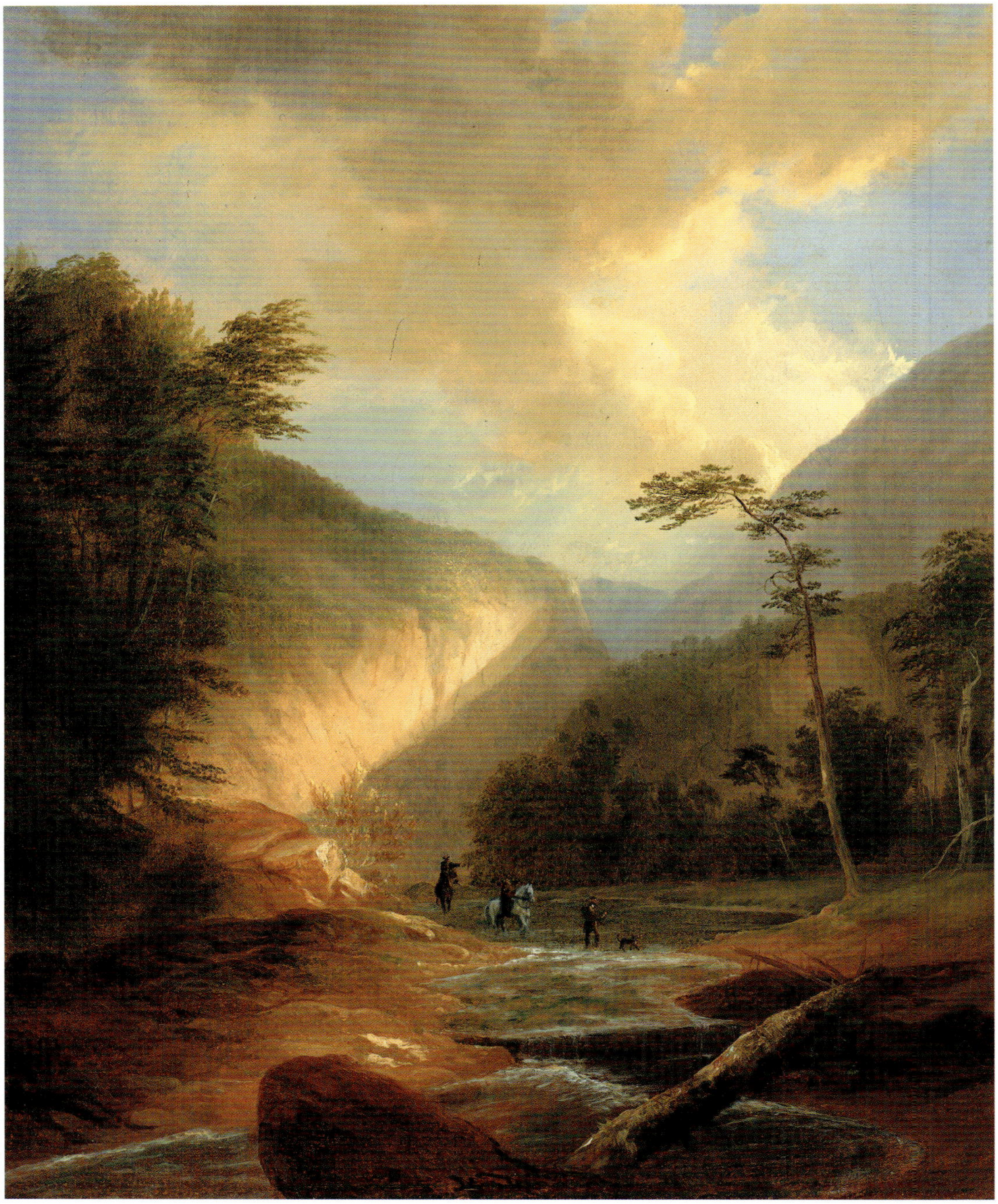

In the second painting of the pair, a larger hunting party has progressed farther down what appears to be the same valley, with the mountains now distant. This group appears to be dressed in uniform, with red belts or sashes around their waists. The time of day has changed to late afternoon. Clouds, similar to those in the companion piece, are now colored red and pink by the setting sun. A horseman with two dogs has separated himself from the other three members of his party to permit the animals to drink from a stream. One of the three is gesturing for the man to rejoin the group, pointing off to the right with some urgency. Again, a tree on the opposite bank of the water bends its branches toward the group, offering the same protection as in the other painting. However, the charged lighting of the clouds, along with the hunter's emphatic gesturing, serves to imbue this canvas with a sense of danger and alertness that is absent from its counterpart.

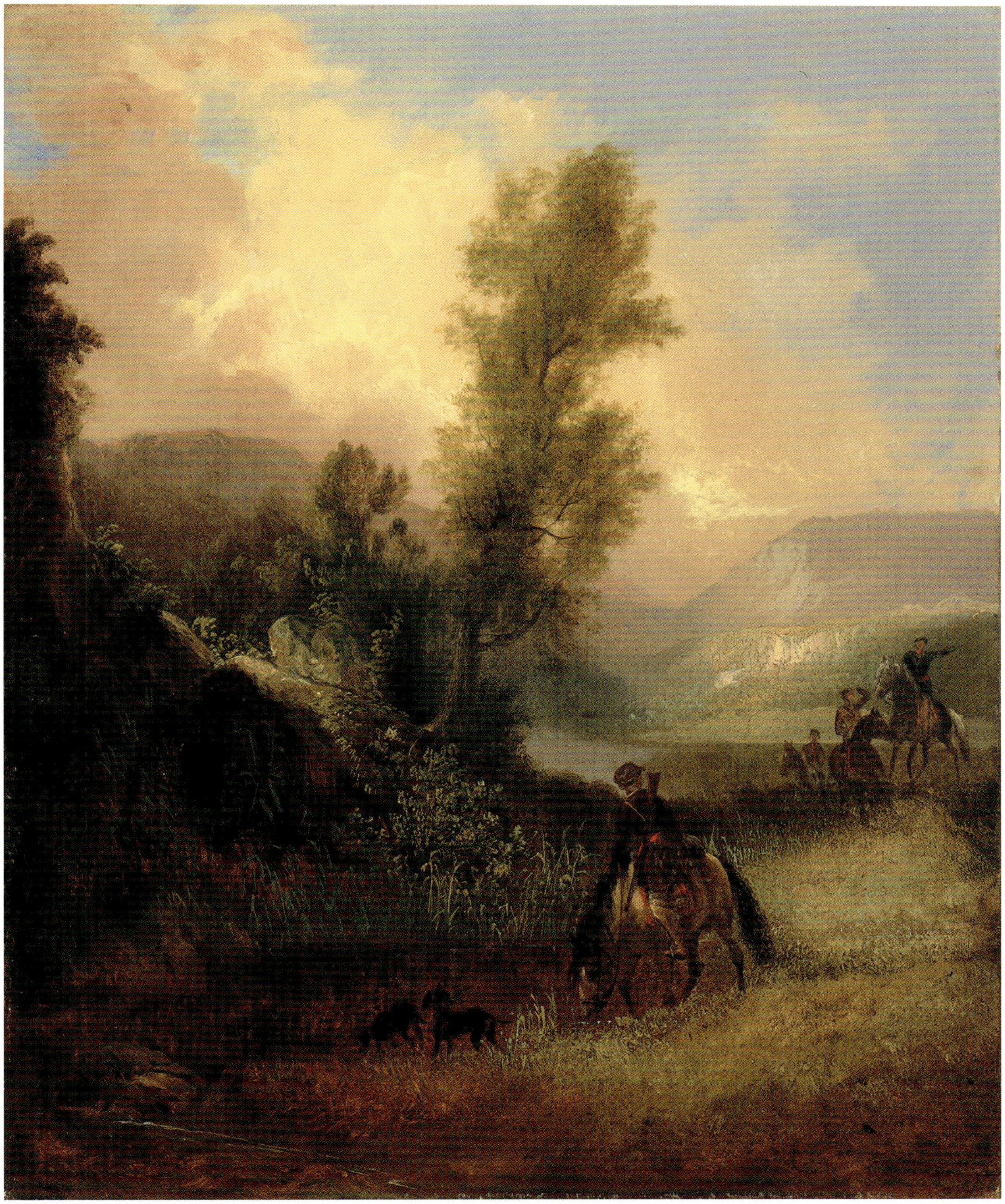

Alvan Fisher (1792–1863)
Hunters in a Landscape, c. 1830
Oil on canvas, 24 x 20 inches

VII. Man's Impact on Nature: The Machine in the Garden

[In Europe] the soul and centre of attraction in every picture is some ruin of the past. . . . He who journeys here [America] . . . must feed his imagination on the future. The American does so. His mind, as he tracks the broad rivers of his own country, is perpetually reaching forward. Instead of looking through a valley, which has presented the same aspect for hundreds of years—in which live lords and tenants, whose hearths have been surrounded by the same names through ages of tranquil descent, and whose fields have never changed landmark or mode of culture since the memory of man, he sees a valley laden down like a harvest wagon with a virgin vegetation, untrodden and luxuriant; and his first thought is of the villages that will soon sparkle on the hill-sides, the axes that will ring from the woodlands, and the mills, bridges, canals, and railroads, that will span and border the stream that now runs through sedge and wild-flowers.

—Nathaniel Parker Willis, *American Scenery*, 1840

The development of the railroad after midcentury as a safe, comfortable means of traveling from cities to the country enabled more than just the very wealthy classes to make excursions for pleasure. With increased tourism came the need for more accommodations to provide comfort for travelers. Even more dramatically, after midcentury, the Industrial Revolution began to change almost every aspect of the American way of life. Handworking made way for the machine age, and the country's vast natural resources came to be viewed not only as a visual treasure but also as a virtual economic storehouse set to fuel the rise of the United States as an international power. Many artists of the Hudson River School—including Thomas Cole, who envisioned impressive structures along the shore of his beloved Hudson River—were conflicted between their awe of the country's future potential and their fear that it would bring devastating changes to the unspoiled landscape that had served as both their inspiration and the source of their religious and artistic strength.

Two paintings by Herman Herzog relate different aspects of man's impact on nature: hunting and industrialization. The first shows man as an intruder in the woodlands, in direct confrontation with wildlife as a part of his basic survival—the need to eat. The second takes another step in showing man's effort to tame, or rather harness, nature in order to create the energy needed to make his existence more comfortable, thereby signaling the encroachment of civilization. Since Herzog was born and trained in Düsseldorf, and had a successful career there as a painter before coming to Philadelphia in his mid-thirties, these paintings reflect the intensity and realism of the German school.

Man Hunting (Western Landscape) is set within a hilly, forested terrain on the left, opening onto a lake and mountains expanding into the distance on the right. Storm clouds create a brooding, indecisive sky. Darkness falls across the foreground, while light breaks through along the shoreline to the left. The stark, bright light of the sun spotlights one section of the cloud cover, turning it from gray to brilliant white and forcing a burst of sunlight onto the water below. Also at the center and silhouetted against the hills, an eagle is majestically revealed in rays emanating from the sun. This theatrical lighting comes at the moment the hunter, alone against his prey, has raised his gun to his shoulder.

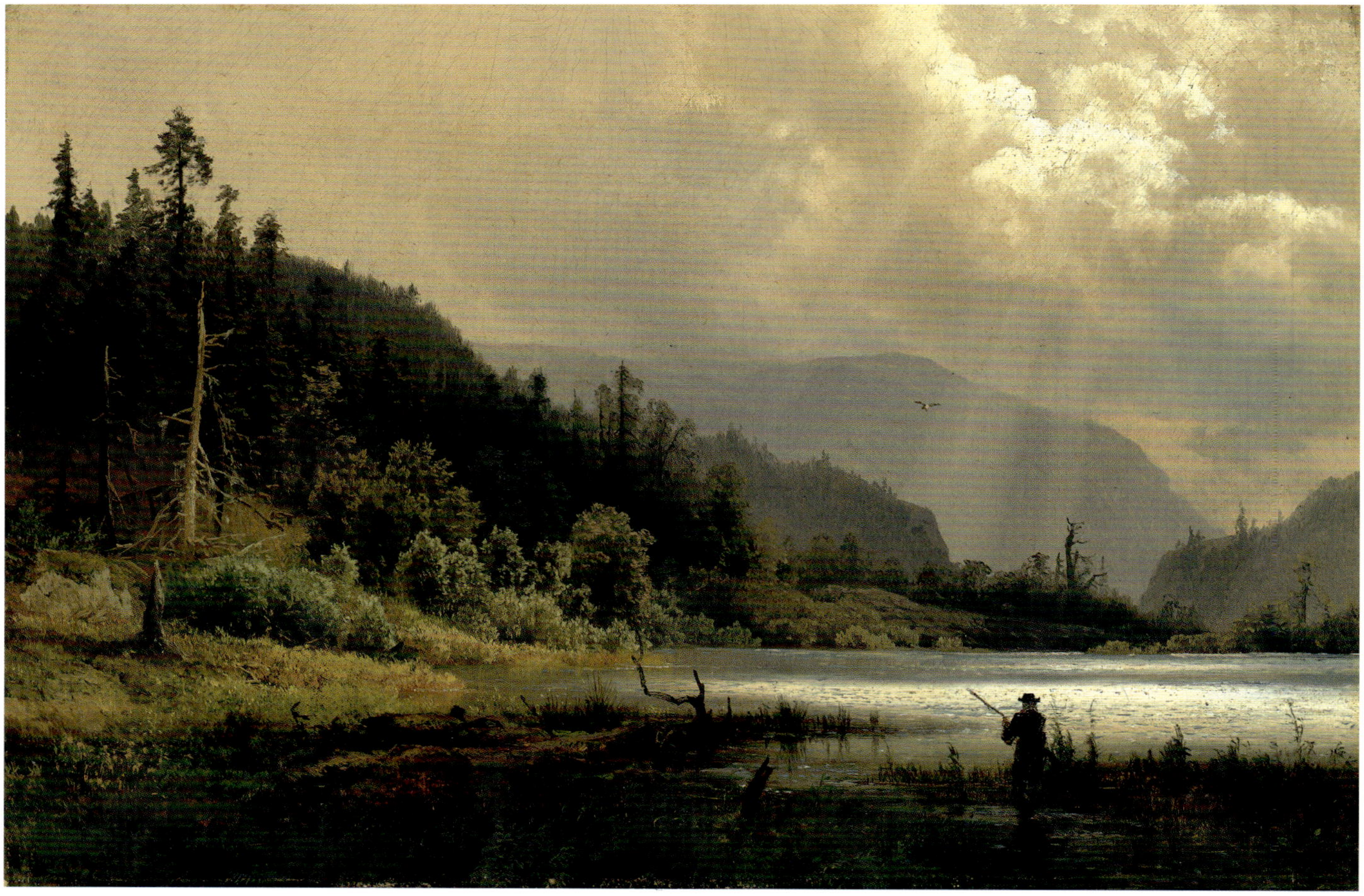

Herman Herzog (1832–1932)
Man Hunting (Western Landscape), 1871
Oil on board, 13 1/2 x 20 1/2 inches

Herman Herzog (1832–1932)
Mill with Raging Torrent [Sutter's Mill], c. 1870
Oil on canvas, 19 x 27 inches

The pictorial drama created by Herzog conveys more than just this single conflict of hunter against quarry: it points to the larger struggle of civilization's advance on the wilderness.

Mill with Raging Torrent [Sutter's Mill] is also charged with drama, manifested boldly in the form of a raging storm and torrent of water running through the center of the composition. The swiftly flowing mountain stream—a typical theme in Düsseldorf landscapes—provides power for the mill and symbolizes the raw force of nature, dividing the canvas from right to left between man's presence and the wild state of nature. A woman with her donkey moves along an overgrown path on the left, turning away from the industrialization symbolized by the mill and heading uphill toward a house. The dark palette and dramatic division of the canvas create a clash as vivid as the palpably angry release of water from the mountainside. The rigid geometry of the mill holds its own against the curvilinear forms of nature with which it is surrounded, but still appears potentially vulnerable to the force of nature.

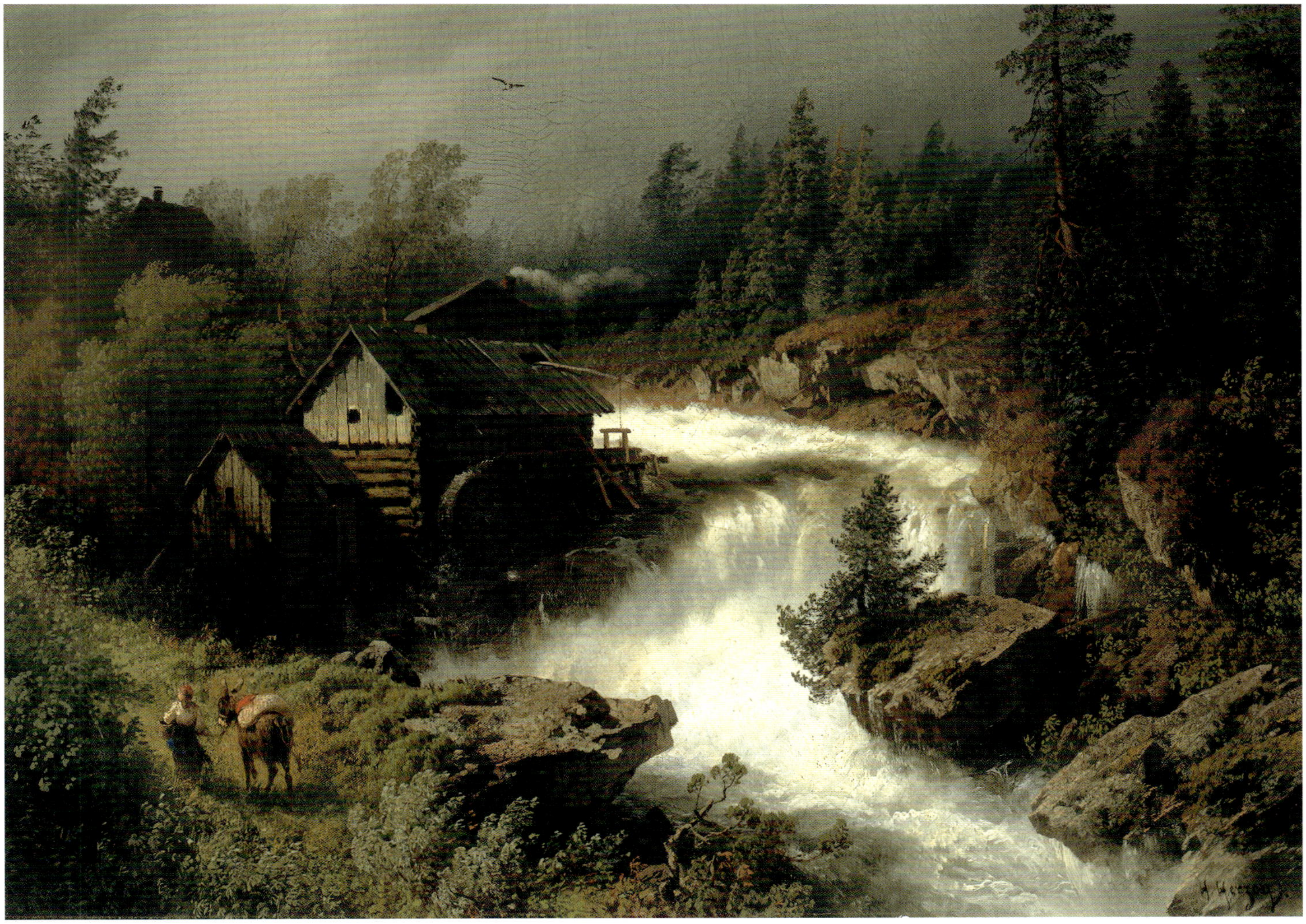

Haying Scenes

Haying scenes offered artists an opportunity to paint the countryside, celebrating nature's bounty while also demonstrating that those who cultivate the land live harmoniously on it. These scenes depict a balance between man and nature.

A magazine and book illustrator known for his watercolors, William Rickarby Miller was a keen observer with a gentle disposition. In his haying scene, he frames his composition with two graceful, inward-bending trees, which shelter a view of a distant farmhouse. A radiant blue sky creates an aura of lightness and warmth, contrasting with the dark, rich colors of autumn that, along with the harvest, identify the season. The field on the left is crisscrossed with neat bales of hay, and a hay wagon moves along a deeply rutted dirt road. Rounded mounds of hay are balanced against the shape of the barn; the house to the left of the road offers shelter and domesticity. Two distant mountains come together at the focal point where a stream converges with the road, offering two modes of transportation through the landscape. A sense of balance and harmony emanates from this painting, both in the pleasing comfort of the subject at hand and in the implied notion of acceptance and reassurance associated with seasonal cycles.

The earth is based very low in this composition by James Fairman—a painter, critic and musician who lived in the White Mountains. Most of the composition is devoted to a vast, cloud-filled sky which makes the fields of earth and the workers in them seem diminutive, almost inconsequential. The piece is further divided by the contrast between the shadowy colors of earth and the incandescent sky. Clouds effectively block direct sunlight except at the point where the hay, stacked high on the wagon in the foreground center, is dramatically backlit by a brightening of the sky, casting the animated figure atop the hay wagon into silhouette. A tree on the left reaches far up into the sky, well beyond the cloud line, in a grand, duplicitous gesture that both protects and diminishes the activity below. Absence of detail and emphasis on contrasting light and dark areas allow greater evocation of mood. Additionally, the pleasing simplicity of the composition, with just three elements—the cluster of trees in the far left background, the central hay wagon, and the tree on the right—adds to the exquisite combination of harmony and discord in this evocative little piece.

William Rickarby Miller (1818–1893)
Haying Scene, n.d.
Oil on canvas, 7½ x 9½ inches

James Fairman (1826–1904)
Haying Scene, n.d.
Oil on canvas, 6 x 10 inches

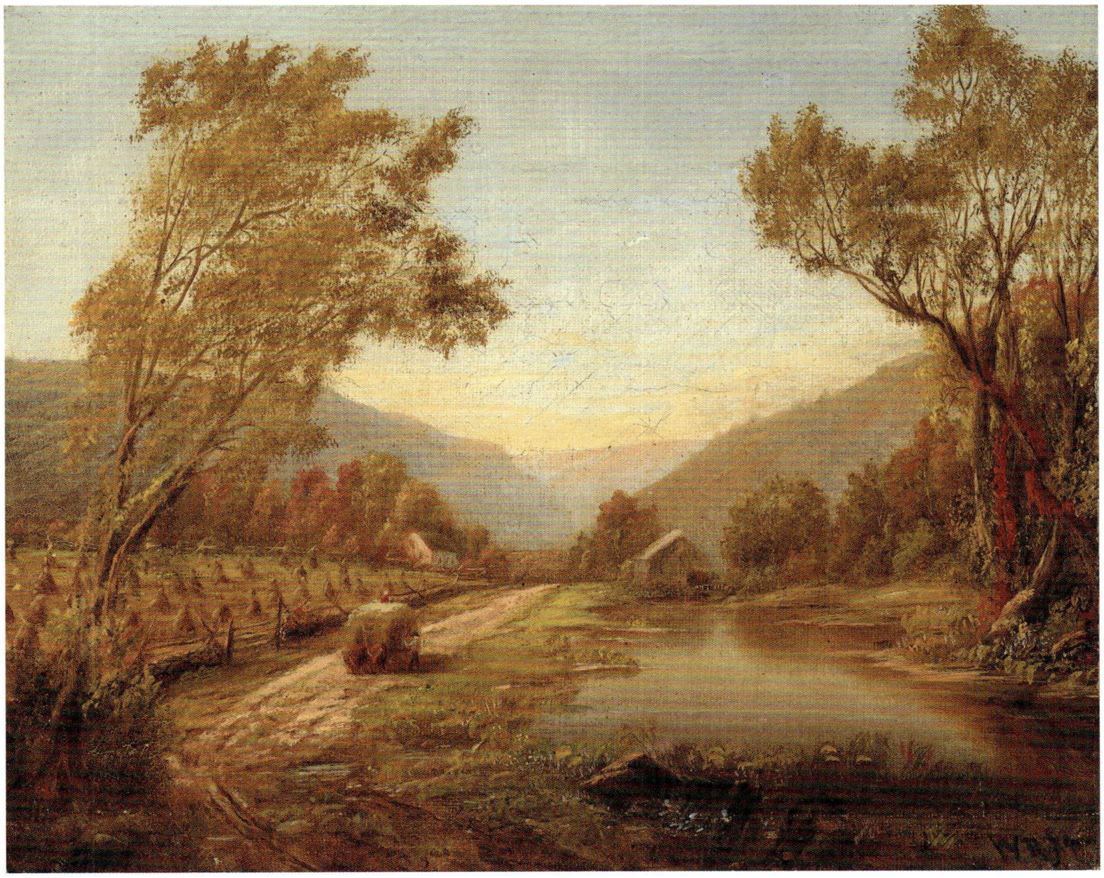

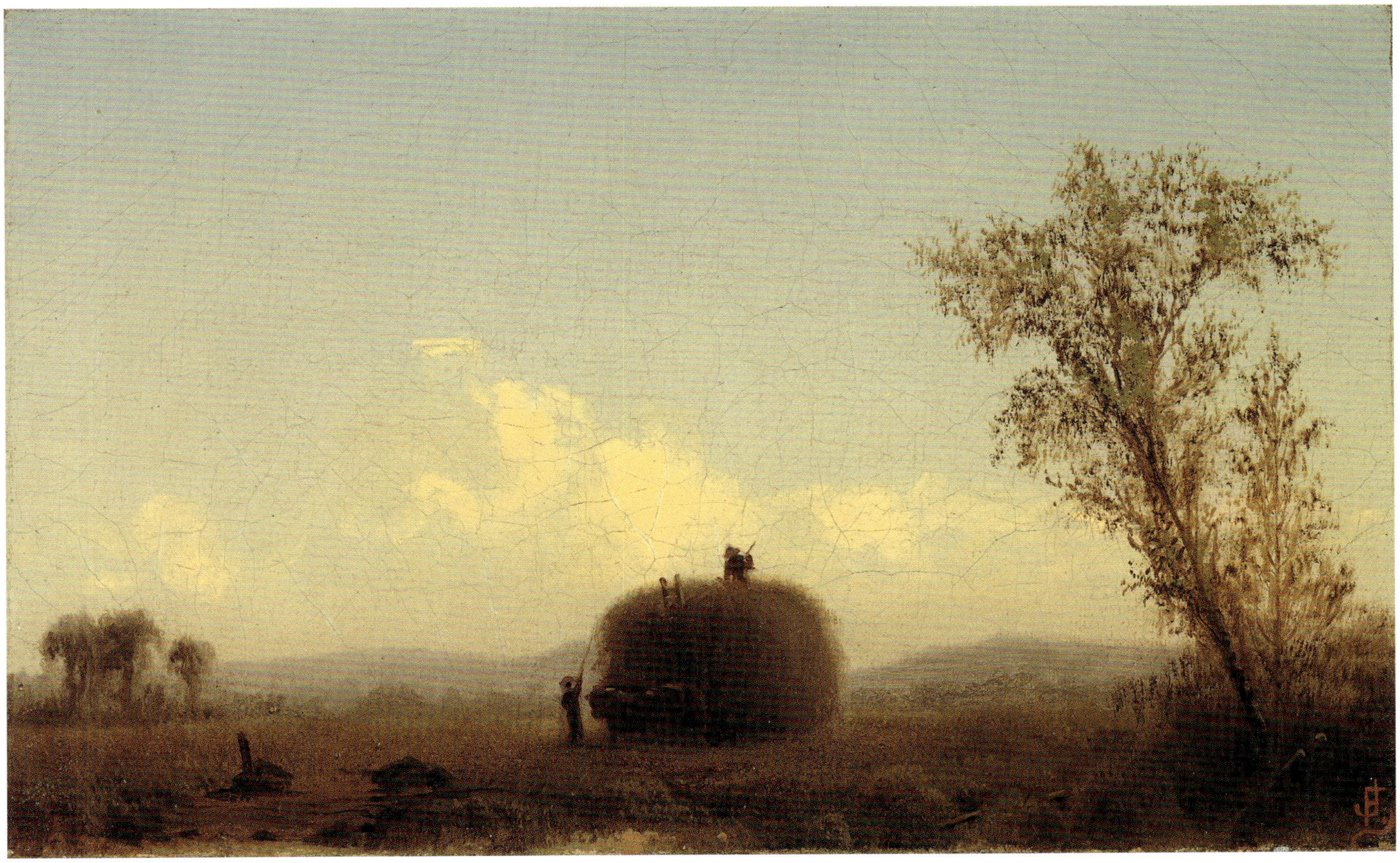

The main subject of Champney's view of the Conway Valley is the strong afternoon sunlight, which rakes across the scene from left to right, creating sharp contrasts of light and dark. Divergent bands of color in the landscape reinforce the pattern of light and dark, as do the trees on opposing shorelines—one sunlit, the other in shadow. A couple, man and woman, fishing along the shoreline serve to compare this recreational use of the land to the hard labor of the four field hands working the hay wagon in the middle distance. Many comparisons and contrasts appear within this painting, which became so popular that a chromolithograph was made of it.

Samuel Colman Jr.'s view of the Conway Valley is also based on contrasting horizontals, in this case lending stability to the composition rather than charging it with an uneasy mood. The artist's pastel palette is used to induce a dreamy atmosphere, suffused with the golden glow of late afternoon sunlight falling gently across the mountainsides. Shades of yellow and rose define the land; a soft blue tinges the mountains. The calm of the scene is undisturbed by the level of activity in it: two groups of workers and three hay wagons seem in accord with rather than intruders on their natural surroundings. The uniformity of light creates a balanced atmosphere—a painterly form of Colman's treatise *Nature's Harmonic Unity* written in 1912.

We see recreational use of the land contrasted simultaneously with workers toiling in the land in *Harvest Scene*, by Thomas Hiram Hotchkiss—an artist whose life was tragically cut short by illness. A small group of brightly dressed picnickers to the right of the composition enjoy the warmth of a sunlit meadow, set off by the contrasting band of dark trees. Farm hands are haying in the sunlight of the field, haystacks and meadows surrounding them. The evenness of light equalizes man and nature, apparently approving the dual activities of work and play in a picturesque manner. This rare scene of farming in the Catskill region is one of only a few extant by this gentle, talented artist who spent his last ten years in Italy, painting around Rome.

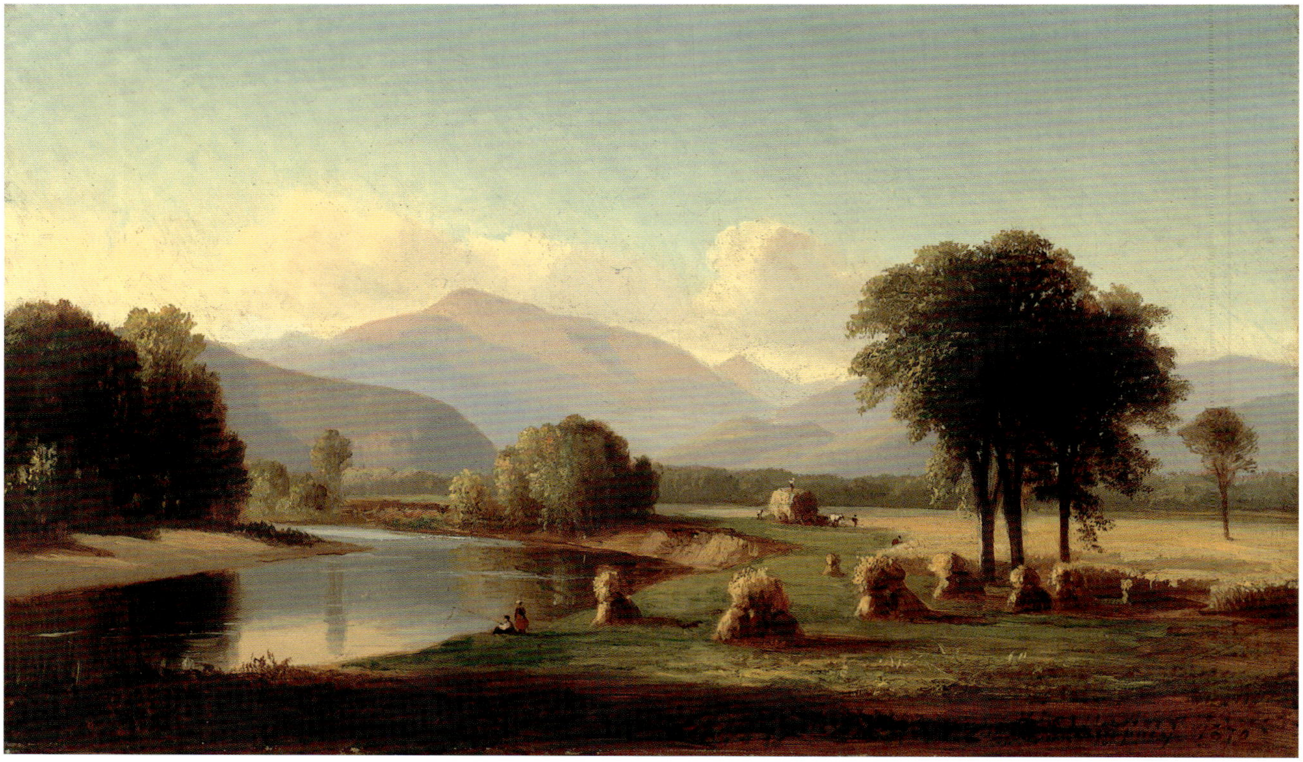

Benjamin Champney (1817–1907)
Harvest Scene, Conway Valley, 1870
Oil on canvas, 10½ x 18½ inches

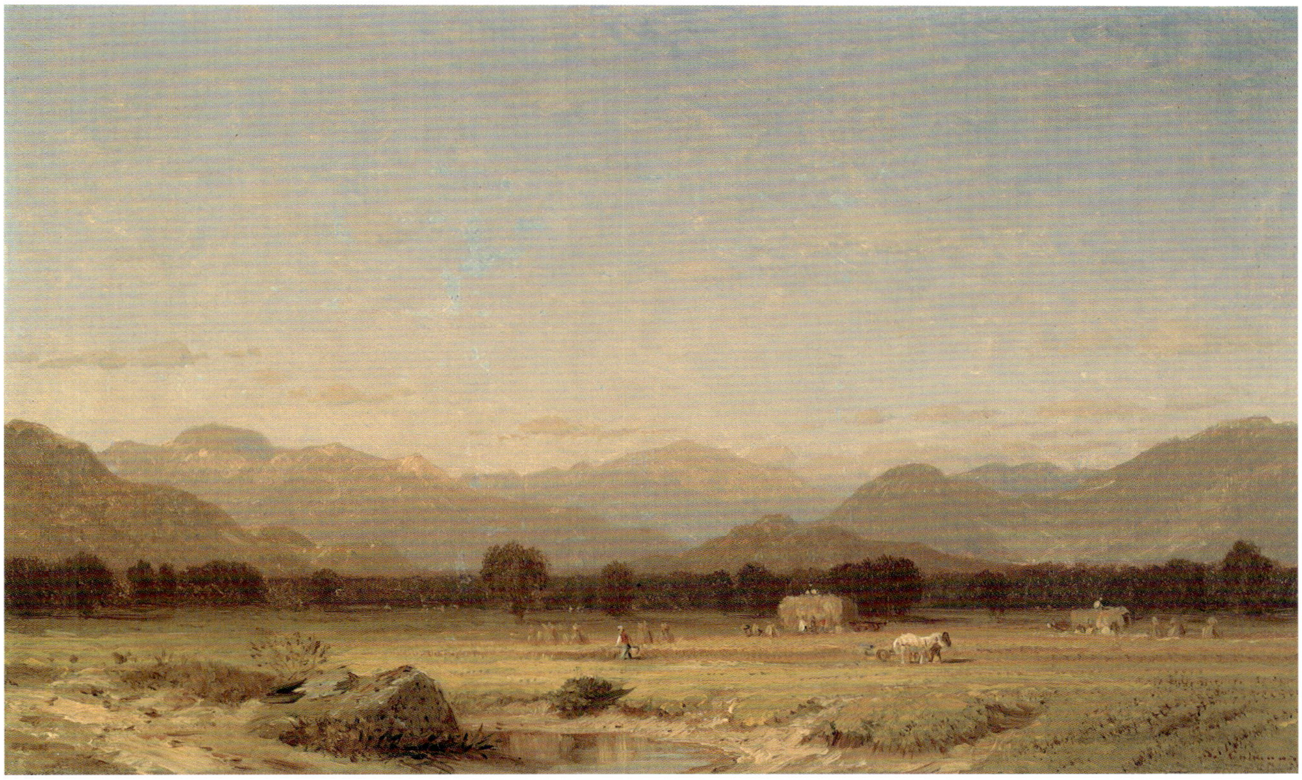

Samuel Colman Jr. (1832–1920)
Harvest Scene, n.d.
Oil on canvas, 10 x 17 inches

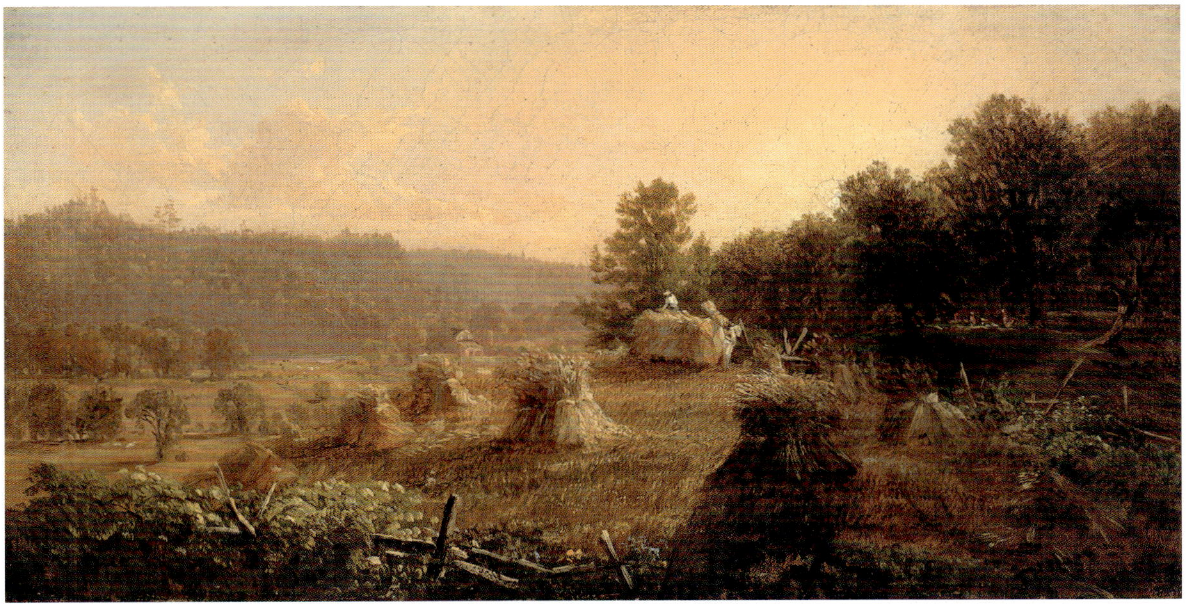

Thomas Hiram Hotchkiss (1834–1869)
Harvest Scene, 1858
Oil on canvas, 6 1/4 x 12 inches

Bridges

A MEMBER OF THE WHITE MOUNTAIN SCHOOL BASED IN New Hampshire, Samuel W. Griggs was trained as an architect and also studied painting with Albert Bierstadt. Made of wood, the bridge in this landscape is more rustic, less permanent, yet still establishes a clear transition from shore to shore. A pair of cows—one white, one brown—crosses the bridge, as if in companionable conversation during a midday stroll; another stands below in the water and drinks. The subject refers back to our section on Passages, with the motif of cows moving steadily and reliably through their daily routine, just as seasons, and other natural cycles, continually progress according to their own rhythms. On the right, trees dressed in bright autumn reds and yellows gently bend to protect the bridge and animals crossing it. The vertical emphasis of these sheltering trees—and of the compositional format itself—gently balances the horizontal statement made by the frail bridge.

Another member of the White Mountain School, Harrison Bird Brown was also known for his marine paintings of Maine. In his *Leaf Picnic*, he has created a wonderfully active, lyrical painting. The vertical format provides stunning contrasts in the vibrant colors of autumn foliage against the pale trunks of birch trees, through which distant mountains can be glimpsed. Movement throughout the composition reinforces the activity of seasonal change: clouds in the sky are in motion, water tumbles down the falls, and autumn leaves drop from branches into the stream. On one side of the water, two ladies have gathered colorful leaves as part of their benign excursion into nature. The ladies are diminutive and impart little impact on their surroundings. A simple log bridge, perhaps even a tree having fallen at the end of its life cycle, forms a connection between the side of the stream where the ladies stand and the opposite bank, where man seems not yet to have penetrated. The slight bridge itself does not constitute a permanent alteration to nature. One imagines that once the ladies have departed, the scene will revert to a near natural state. This brief visit to gather leaves can itself be considered an attempt to record a small cycle: a momentary occasion involving innocent interaction between humans and nature.

Like many other Hudson River School artists, William Mason Brown's early training was as an engraver. His charming composition, *The Bridge*, is finely painted, with attention given to individual textures, especially in the contrast between the hardness of stone and the feathery softness of trees. Color, too, plays a dramatic role here, with the bridge's stark whiteness in strong contrast to the varying dark greens of nature. Spring is resplendent in tender, young foliage and dainty flowers. A waterfall situated behind the bridge feeds the stream, contained by the solid arch of stone. Blue sky appears just above the central treetops, in line with the semicircular opening of the bridge. This permanent construction of man serves to harness the wilderness in order to accommodate human passage through it. A boy in white and his father in red have stopped along the bridge to gaze down into the water, as if searching for something. Aligned with the opening of the sky and the portal of the bridge, these figures appear to reveal and symbolize the human urge to traverse and organize nature.

Samuel W. Griggs (1827–1898)
Cows on a Bridge, Autumn, n.d.
Oil on canvas, 12 x 9 1/4 inches

Harrison Bird Brown (1831–1915)
Leaf Picnic, n.d.
Oil on canvas, 18 x 14 inches

William Mason Brown (1828–1898)
The Bridge, c. 1850–1860
Oil on canvas, 10 x 14 inches

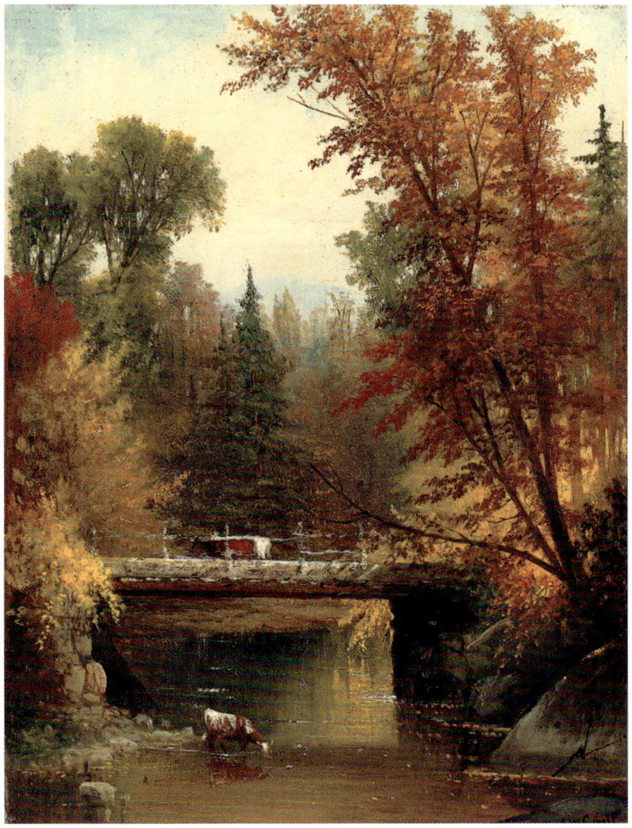

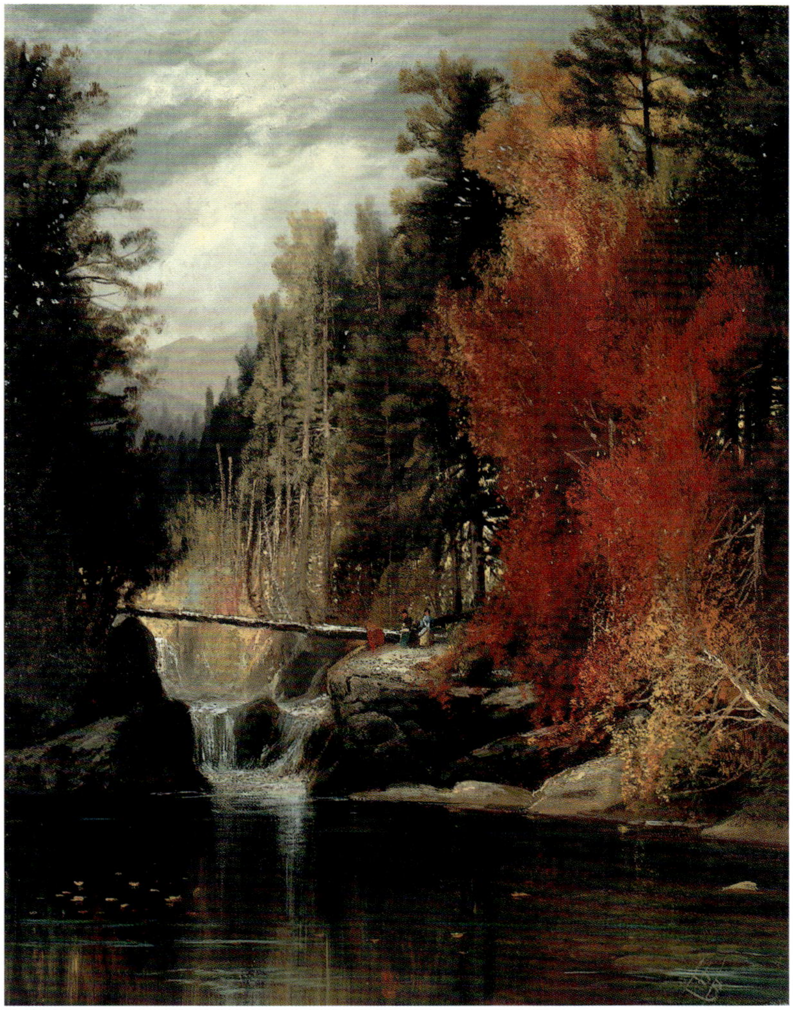

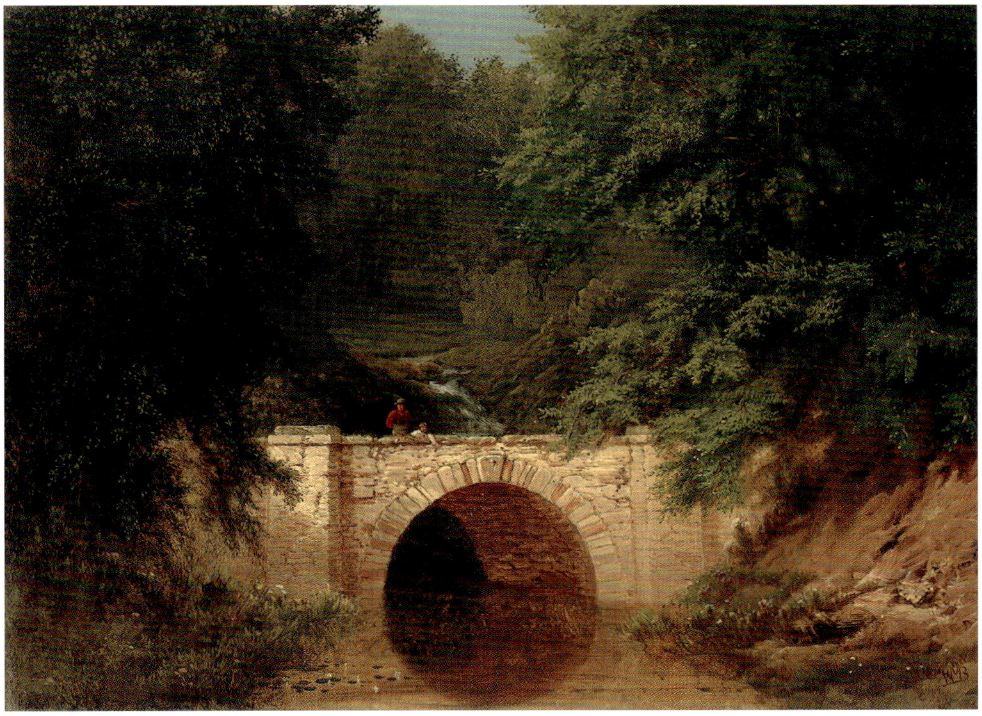

The Machine in the Garden

WHEN TREES WERE FELLED ALONG THE HUDSON, AND signs of man's encroachment on nature came close to his beloved Cedar Grove, Cole penned his poem *The Lament of the Forest* (1838). In it, man is described as "the enemy," and Cole becomes the voice of nature, imploring the artist who loved the wilderness to hear nature's lament. The penultimate stanza describes Cole's fears:

> A few short years!—these valleys, greenly clad,
> These slumbering mountains, resting in our arms.
> Shall naked glare beneath the scorching sun,
> And all their wimpling rivulets be dry.
> No more the deer shall haunt these bosky glens,
> Nor the pert squirrel chatter near his sore.
> A few short years!—our ancient race shall be,
> Like Israel's, scattered 'mong the tribes of men.

Perched high on an escarpment overlooking the Hudson River Valley, the Catskill Mountain House appears benign and even inconsequential, but symbolizes the beginning of tourism and all that would impact the natural environment in order to accommodate it. Constructed between 1820 and 1830, the Mountain House was a monumental feat of engineering, built to bring hundreds of admiring visitors into the Catskill Mountains. Cole, Durand, and Church, along with a multitude of other artists and writers, were among the many cultivated guests of this hotel. It became a favorite subject of Hudson River School artists, who painted it in different seasons and from various perspectives, including from Artist's Rock and other points along trails built to facilitate the outdoor pleasures of the hotel's guests. The Mountain House was the first to serve what became, and remains today, a thriving tourism business in the region. It would not be long before travel by railroad would permit easy access to remote and otherwise difficult-to-reach regions, where demands of the burgeoning tourism industry would have to be balanced against the need to preserve the natural beauty that the tourists came to witness.

Junius Sloan, an artist affiliated with Illinois, traveled to the Mountain House and painted this view encompassing the vast Catskill landscape. The hotel, situated high on the mountainside, is barely visible. The even light, pleasant autumn atmosphere, and rich colors, as well as the freshly flowing stream and cascades in the foreground, further reinforce the notion that man's encroachment on nature for pleasure has not yet seriously threatened the expansive wilderness. Contrasted with the striking autumn foliage of red maples on the right is the dark green of two entwined trees on the left. The latter serve to unite earth and sky, as well as to lead the observer's eye into the composition.

One of the relatively few successful women painters associated with the Hudson River School, Edith Wilkinson Cook exhibited regularly at the National Academy of Design in New York City and the Pennsylvania Academy of the Fine Arts in Philadelphia. She knew and worked alongside several famous members of the school, including the master of light, Sanford Robinson Gifford, in whose collection this painting by Cook once belonged and in whose family it descended. The elegant proportions of this small canvas, half as high as it is long, extend the broad horizontal reach of the landscape it depicts. Forlorn yet radiant, the scene unfolds before us. We scan across parallel bands formed first by a field laid barren of its trees, the jagged trunks still remaining; then by a meadow bordered in front by a split-rail fence and in back by a line of trees, deciduous and evergreen; and finally by a mountain ridge that rises to meet a luminous sky. Awash in a golden light reminiscent of Gifford's own canvases, the subtle palette is that of autumn, the penultimate season—the one most pregnant with melancholic change. The simultaneous close of both seasonal and daily cycles in this painting reinforces the suggestion of change and progression, just as the trees felled to provide lumber for a fence marking man-made boundaries suggest man's future—and more destructive—impact on nature.

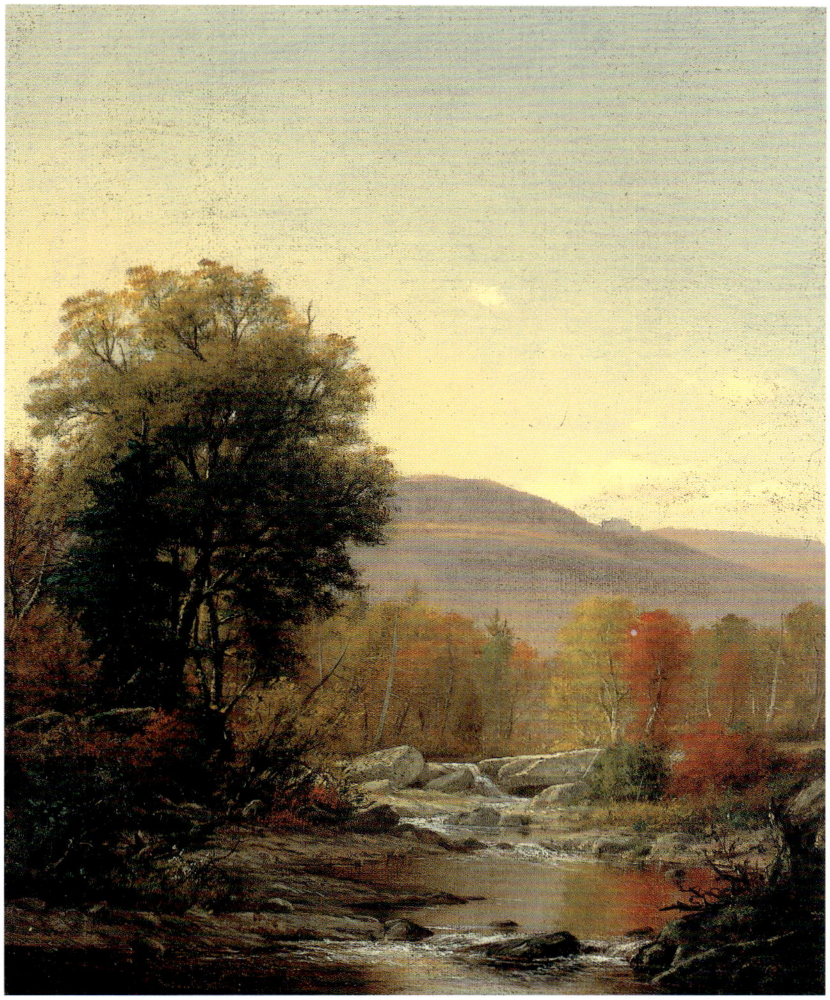

Junius R. Sloan (1827–1900)
Autumn Landscape (with view of Catskill Mountain House), c. 1866
Oil on canvas, $11^{3}/_{4}$ x 10 inches

Edith Wilkinson Cook (active 1851–1875)
Golden Landscape, 1867
Oil on canvas, $7^{1}/_{8}$ x $14^{1}/_{8}$ inches

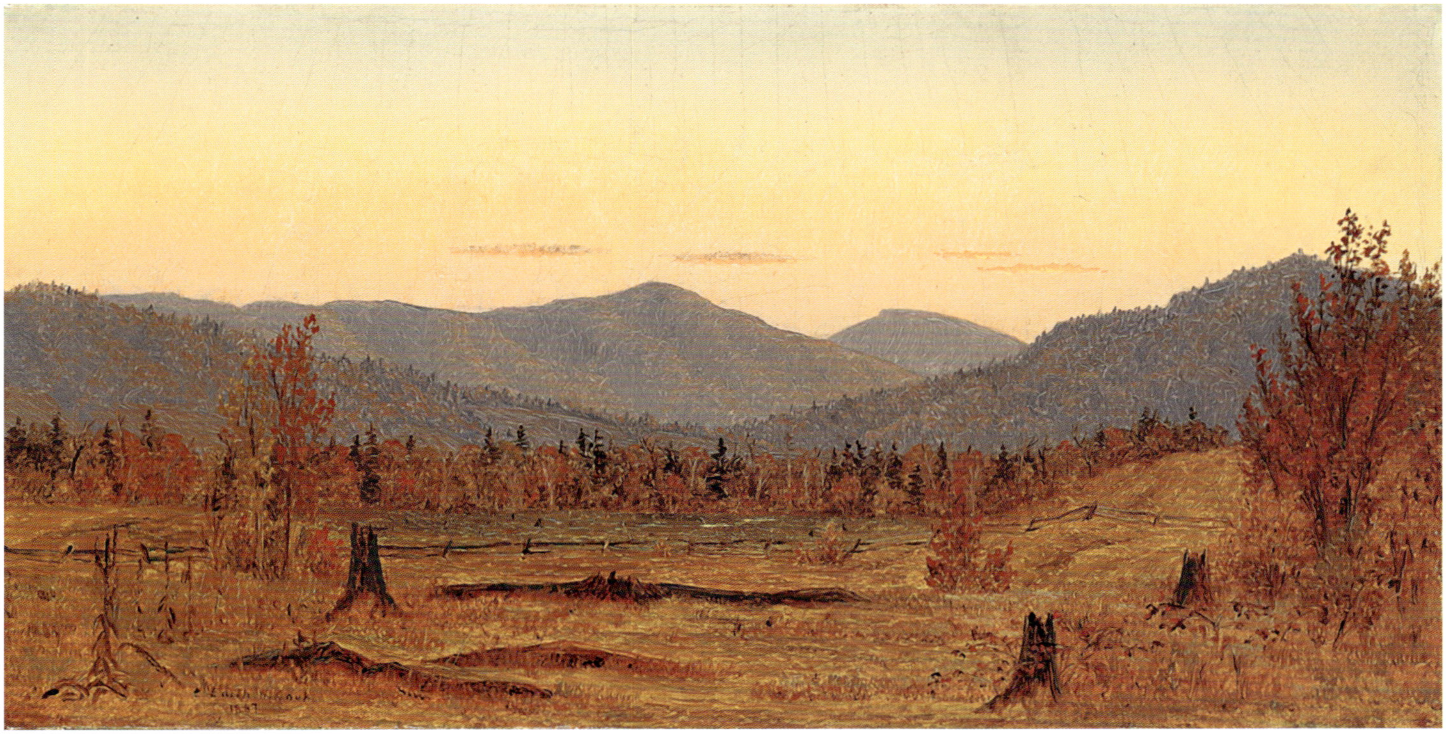

A PAIR OF HORIZONTAL OVAL PAINTINGS BY RUSSELL SMITH presents subtle differences in man's impact on nature, each in the context of a harmonious setting. Called a "romantic realist" by his biographer Virginia Lewis,[14] Smith has comfortably integrated man's presence within his natural environs. In each painting, the composition is divided nearly equally between earth and sky. A river flows diagonally through each, drawing the viewer's eye across the landscape toward distant mountains and the horizon beyond. Light, time of day, and weather conditions are all skillfully rendered and harmonized, creating a gentle, picturesque mood in each painting.

In the farming scene, a diaphanous sky illuminates distant mountains, which appear to pale in dawn's diffused light. The foreground meadow, woods, and farm are darker, more substantial. Farm animals gather near the homestead. Two figures, a man and a woman, converse on the back porch. Morning gently stirs activity. The whole vision is peaceful, tranquil, harmonious.

In *The Old Mill*, the day has progressed, and various activities transpire: cows water at the stream's edge, a shepherdess tends sheep in the meadow, a mill wheel churns. All of these activities are so small compared to the surrounding vastness of nature that they seem to exert little substantial effect. Even the mill, although rising above the distant mountain to be silhouetted against the sky, is balanced by a stand of tall trees across the river and does not seem to constitute an affront to nature. Clouds are well defined in a deeper blue sky. The colors of earth and sky appear more balanced than in the companion painting. Just as the day has progressed, man's activities have also advanced from farming to industry, paralleling the inevitable, ineluctable cycles of time and civilization. Even still, serenity and harmony appear to prevail.

Russell Smith (1812–1896)
Autumn on the Susquehanna, n.d.
Oil on canvas, 11 x 14 inches

Russell Smith (1812–1896)
The Old Mill, n.d.
Oil on canvas, 11 x 14 inches

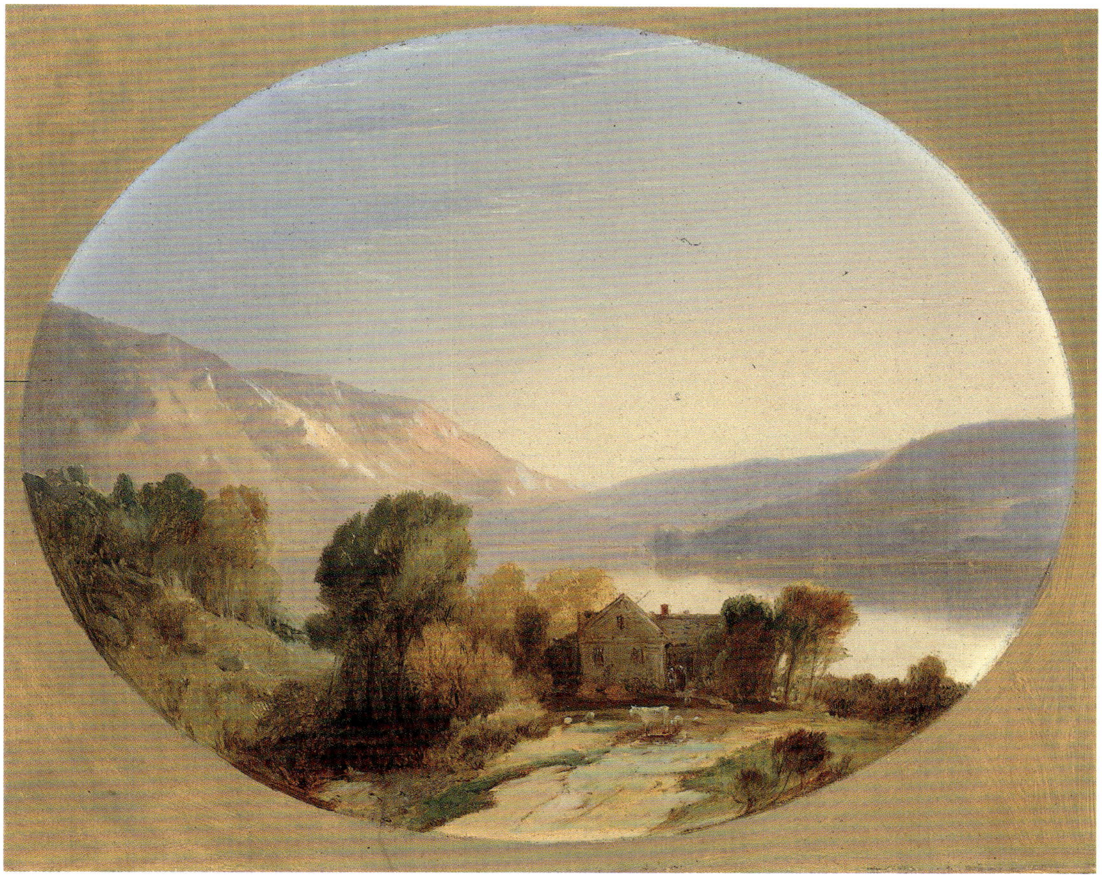

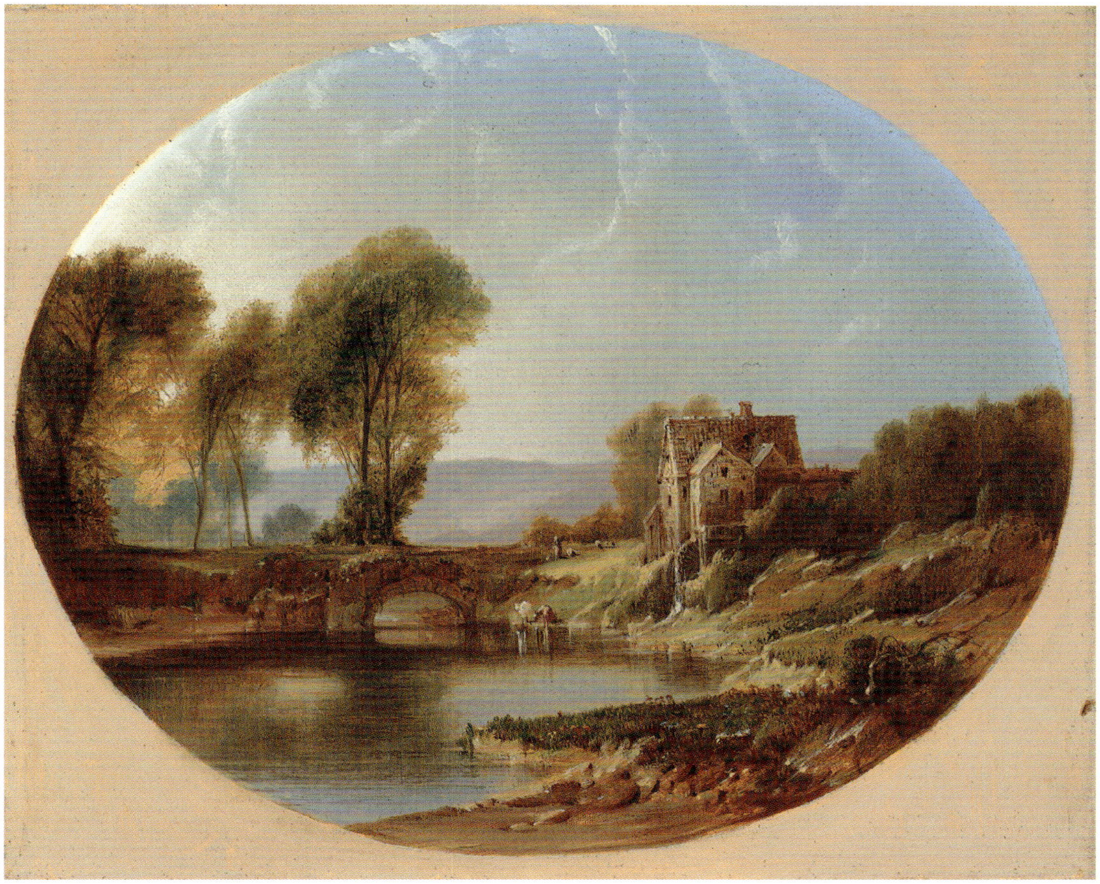

The Industrial Revolution posed the greatest, most potentially damaging threat to the natural environment. The village of Cold Spring, or Cold Spring-on-Hudson, provided artists with a view of spectacular nature as the river cut through the Catskill Mountains. The West Point Foundry was established there in 1817 as one of the first industrial sites in the Hudson River valley. Later in the century, it would manufacture ammunition to fuel the war that nearly divided the still young country.

In Loeffler's painting, the panoramic view unfolds to reveal the Hudson River valley and the Catskill Mountains under expansive skies. The pleasant, late-afternoon weather of summer draws children outside to play along the highlands of the Hudson, where the adjacent factory releases billowing smoke into the buoyant white clouds. Boats on the Hudson River echo the theme of man's recreational enjoyment of nature, as exemplified by the children. Although the foreground is dark, light falls evenly across the landscape, easing what tension might exist between nature, boaters, children and the factory. All seem to inhabit the picture harmoniously, each in its place, without adversely affecting one another. However, the sense of scale in the vast landscape clearly dwarfs man's activities, causing even the factory to appear transitory, perhaps only briefly tolerated. The permanence and majesty of nature remain paramount compared to the pleasures and industries of man, which are made to appear fleeting. One is reminded of Pieter Bruegel's (c.1525–1569) painting of Icarus falling into the sea. The figure of Icarus, as well as his tragedy, is barely perceptible within the large, panoramic composition, so small is his figure compared to the overwhelming expanse of ocean, sky, and landscape. A later painting by David Johnson (1827–1908) of the same foundry shows a harbor with a retaining wall not yet built in Loeffler's scene.[15]

A student of the great German Romantic painter Caspar David Friedrich, Grunewald closely adhered to the Germanic style, often using drama and contrast effectively in his work. Here he depicts an abandoned sawmill being reclaimed by nature, next to which stands a giant oak tree. This juxtaposition illustrates the theme of the machine in the garden, that is, the opposition of man's industrial power to the force and perseverance of nature. A sign of the early Industrial Revolution, the abandoned mill is America's equivalent of Europe's ruined castles and temples. The waterwheel has stopped turning; boards are scattered without order, some disintegrating in a slow return to nature, providing sod for a young bush sprouting up amid the stacks. The artist lights the mill with intense rays from the midday sun to reveal its hapless condition, no longer a threat to its environment. Surrounding the mill are verdant meadows in which a solitary horse grazes, no evidence of a rider present. Against the bright white of clouds, birds fly overhead, signaling the freedom of movement of wild creatures in nature. The bitter, underlying struggle between man and nature is obscured by the outward pleasantness of the day, just as the encroachments of man on nature are eventually subsumed by the cyclical rise and fall of civilizations.[16]

In this small, powerfully rendered painting, the old, abandoned smelter stands as an imposition on the wilderness. Hugh Bolton Jones accentuates this discord by capturing the way light continually changes—alternating with shadows, playing across a broad plain ringed by mountains. These contrasts between light and dark areas help create an impression of instability and imply the ominous power of nature to affect man's fate. While the smelter stands vacant and static, the landscape is active with changing light patterns. The sun, though not directly depicted, throws bands of light and shadow across the scene, demonstrating nature's awesome, unpredictable power. Mists steaming from a fold in the mountains and clouds passing threateningly overhead are charged with activity. The figure of a man walking along a road in the composition's center is diminutive, a miniscule and nearly insignificant human witness to the failed power of industry and the eternal, enduring magnificence and force of nature.[17]

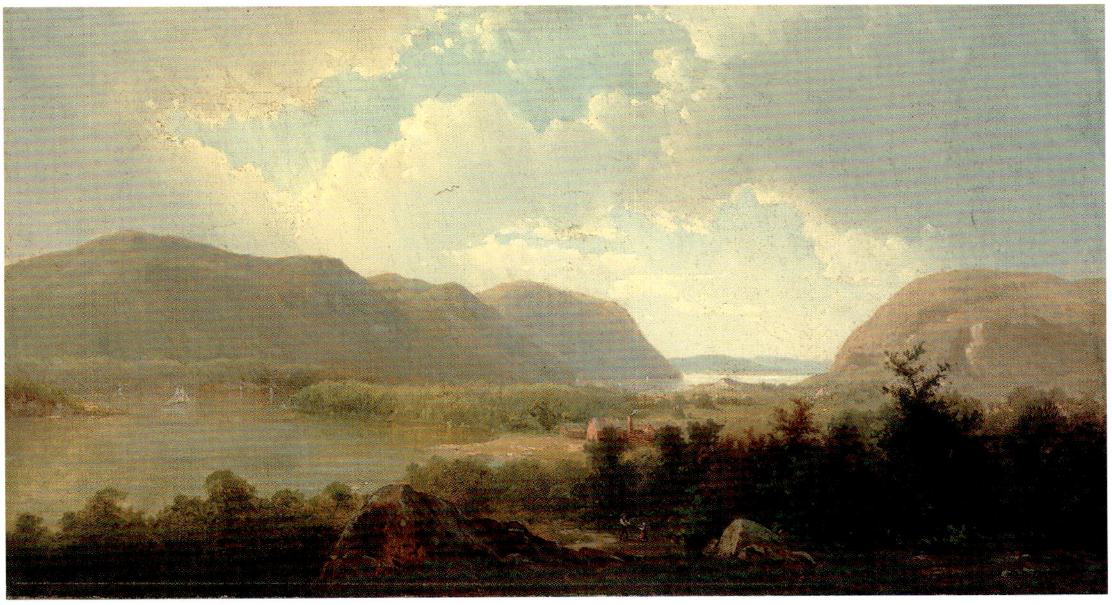

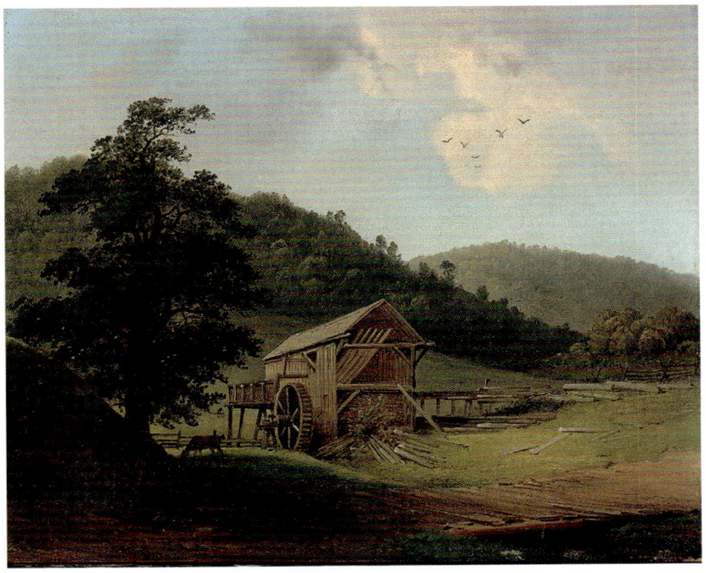

Charles Loeffler (active in New York, mid-1850s)
Foundry at Cold Spring, n.d.
Oil on canvas, 15 1/2 x 29 1/2 inches

Gustavus Johann Grunewald (1805–1878)
Pike County, Pennsylvania, Saw Mill, 1848
Oil on panel, 9 11/16 x 12 3/16

Hugh Bolton Jones (1848–1927)
Foundry [the Old Smelter], 1876
Oil on canvas, 8 x 14 1/4 inches

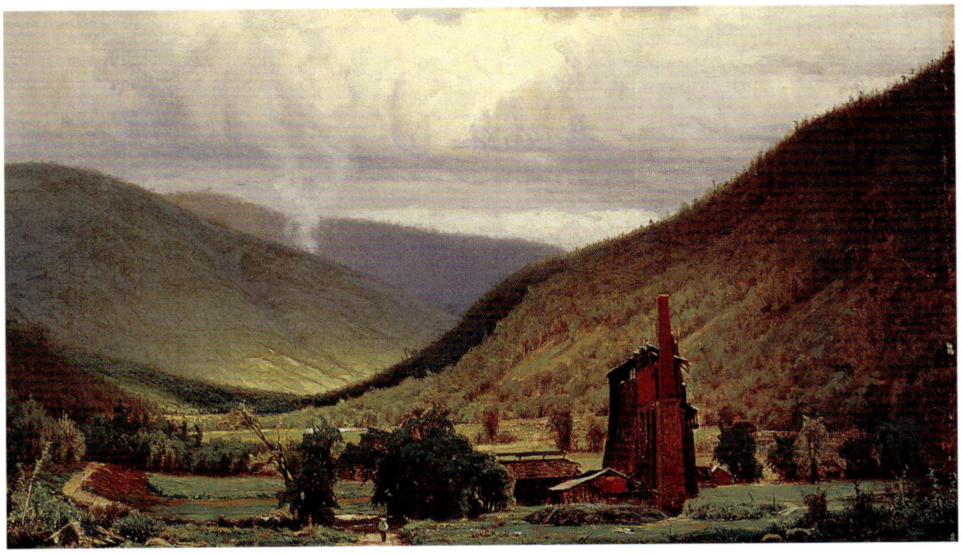

VIII. Interpretations of the Same Scene by Different Artists

How oft in visions of the night,
How oft in noonday dreaming,
I've seen, fair lake, thy forest wave—
Have seen thy waters gleaming;
Have heard the blowing of the winds
That sweep along thy highlands,
And the light laughter of the waves
That dance around thine islands.

—George S. Hillard, *Lake George*,
from *A Landscape Book*, 1868

OVER TIME, THERE DEVELOPED IN THE ARTIST'S mind a number of iconic locations—such as Thomas Cole's Kaaterskill Falls—that artists of the Hudson River School came to revere, visit, and paint. Subsequent generations traveled to these locations to pay homage to their predecessors and to create their own interpretations of these iconic sites. As America's strength grew, there arose certain national landmarks—including Niagara Falls, Lake George, and Mount Washington in the White Mountains—that drew tourists and artists alike and came to be closely associated with our national identity. Accordingly, the work of the Hudson River School artists helped to establish a firm link between these Edenic sites and our national identity.

Views of Lake George

Edmund Darch Lewis divided his canvas from left to right by color: cool blues and greens on the left, bright greens shot through with red on the right. In this manner, he has also represented two distinct seasons in a single small canvas. Mediated by the lake waters, summer and autumn begin to blend into one another. The artist has appropriately provided fewer details to the side of summer on the left, when the atmosphere is often hazy with warmth and moisture. By contrast, the autumnal shore is crisp with detail in every leaf and blade of grass, as revealed by the cooler, sharper light of that season. Lewis has created two atmospheric conditions combined in one painting. A solitary man in a rowboat moves from one shore to the other, as if sampling both seasons. Almost as a gesture of welcome, a tree breaks away from the woods on the left, its reflection on the water extending its reach further toward the man in the boat.

Alfred Thompson Bricher employs similar compositional and perspective devices to those of Edmund Darch Lewis but achieves a different effect through his handling of light both to ignite as well as to stabilize the scene. Bricher uses the same division, the left side of his composition dark and brightly colored, the right side pale and muted in palette. The detail described on the left in the tangle of undergrowth, brush, and rocks is defined by brilliant, effusive autumn light that creates bright yellow, red, and russet colors. On the right, the luminous sun of summer serves, instead, to diffuse color and obscure detail by uniting landscape elements as a soft lavender spills over the mountainside. A large tree on the left of the composition bows gracefully toward the sun in a gesture of benediction. No sign of man disturbs this glorious homage to nature.

Edmund Darch Lewis (1835–1910)
Lake George, n.d.
Oil on metal, 61/8 x 12 inches

Alfred Thompson Bricher (1837–1908)
Lake George, 1863
Oil on canvas, 7 x 12 inches

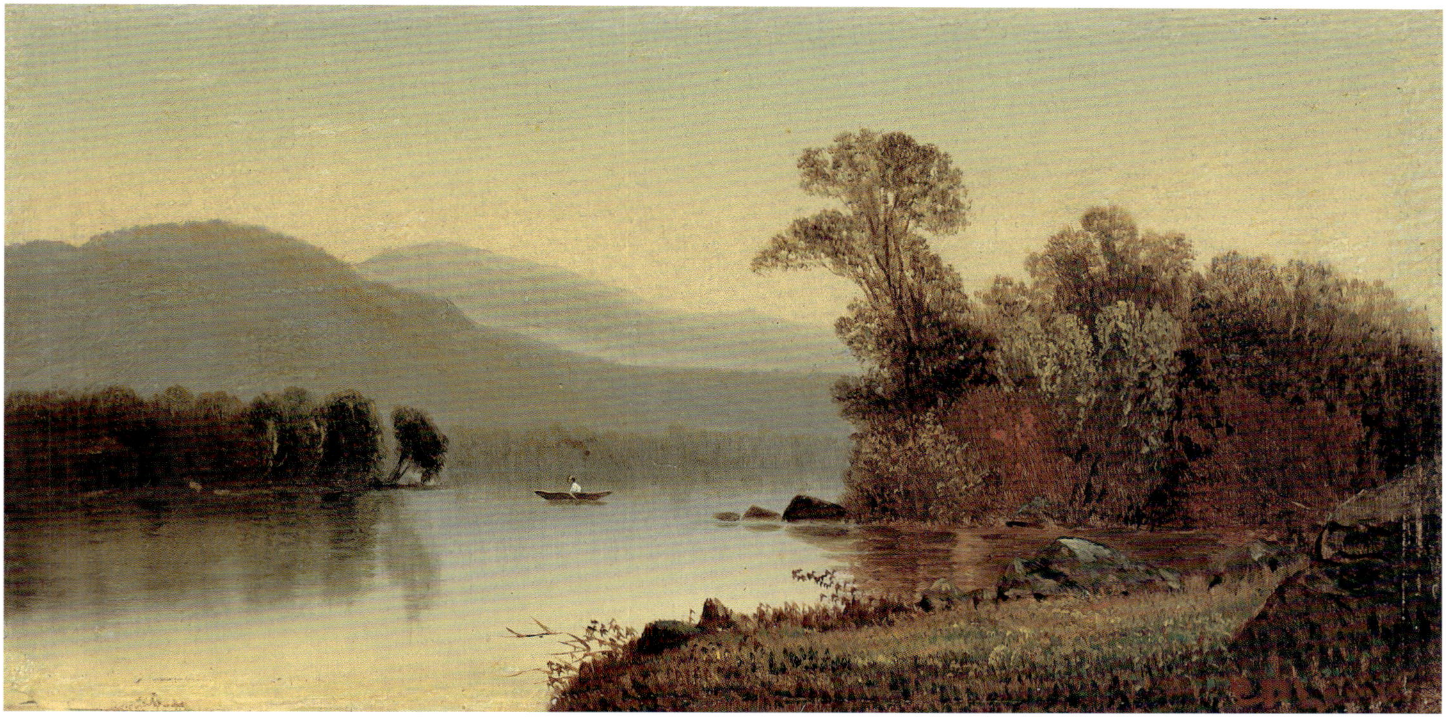

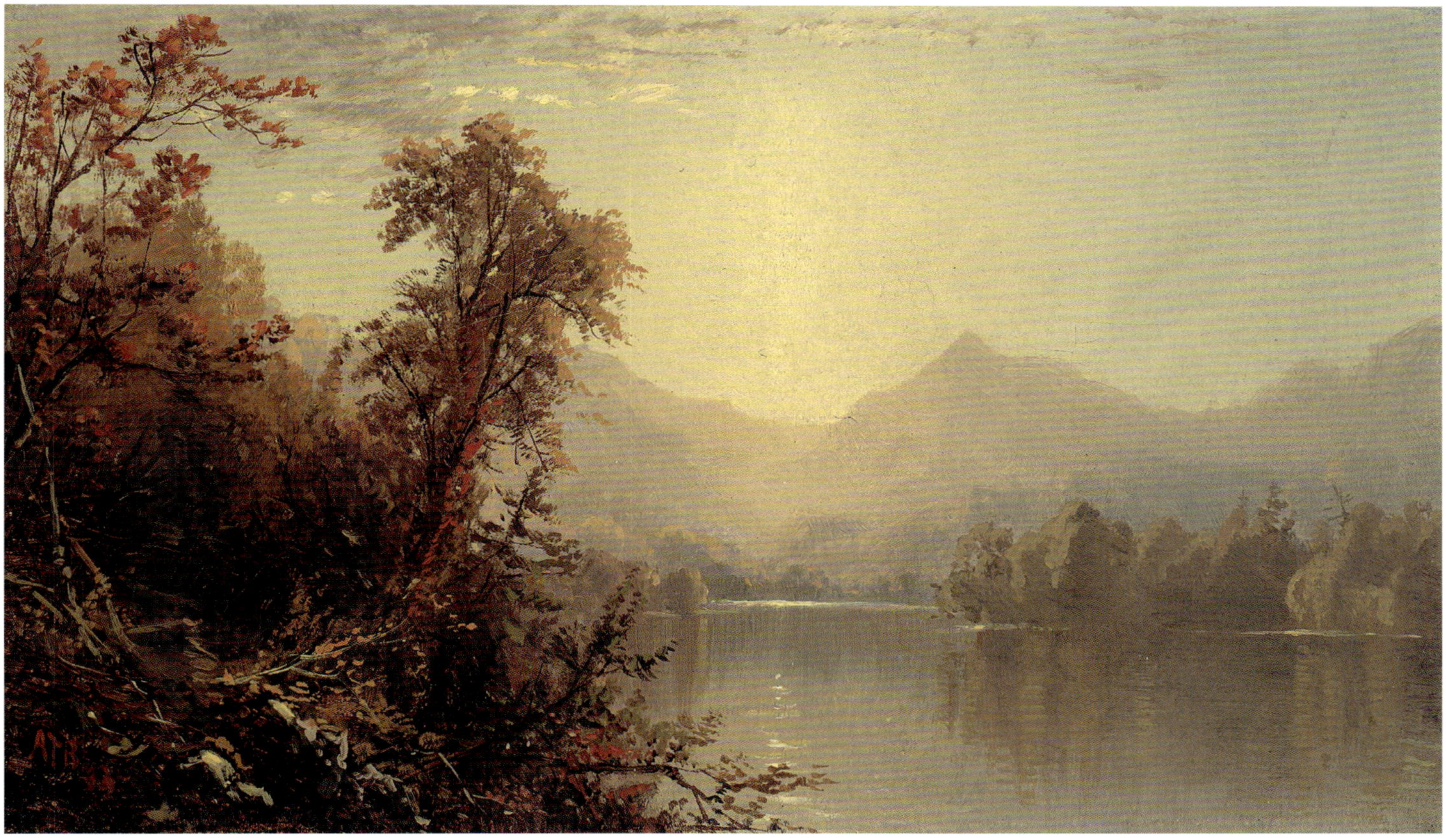

Nelson Augustus Moore divides his painting into horizontal bands of color, whereas previous artists used a vertical compositional divide. Blue sky at the top is blended into pink near the horizon, where it then meets the gray and pink slopes of the Catskills. Below the band of mountains, the line of pink sky is reflected in the lake. At the bottom, we come full circle to the reflection of the topmost section of blue sky. This symmetry in composition expresses the balance and harmony that can exist in nature. The geometry is broken imperceptibly by the green shapes of the lake's islands and by two foreground rowboats and a single, distant sailboat. These notations, signifying the presence of man, exert no disturbing impact on the peaceful scene, but coexist in silent accord with the natural surroundings.

Cropsey has captured a personal, intimate view of Lake George through both its diminutive physical scale and its content. By including himself and his wife as figures in a small boat on the water, Cropsey reasserts his position as painter, observer, and celebrant of nature. Cropsey was a master of the fiery, autumnal sunset, revealed with great surety in the spontaneous brushwork and radiant fall colors of this gem from 1877.

To the painter John William Casilear, Lake George was a siren to which he repeatedly returned, using its changeable character as a springboard for his paints and canvas. Light is the true subject of this composition, with its delicate subtleties playing across water, land, and sky. The unifying effect of light provides Casilear the means of achieving a refinement few other painters could attain. On the right, a tree rooted in the rocky shoreline at once lifts its leafy branches toward the sky and reaches yearningly toward the water. The air is pure, sweet, and crystalline. The privileged observer of this beatific morning in nature is moving slowly across the water in a boat that causes barely a ripple on its surface. The mood is one of hushed reverie. The artist's initial training and success as an engraver help explain the narrow range of color he employed, within which sensitive atmospheric effects of light and subtle gradations are brilliantly conveyed. Time seems to be suspended, as in other masterpieces of American luminism.

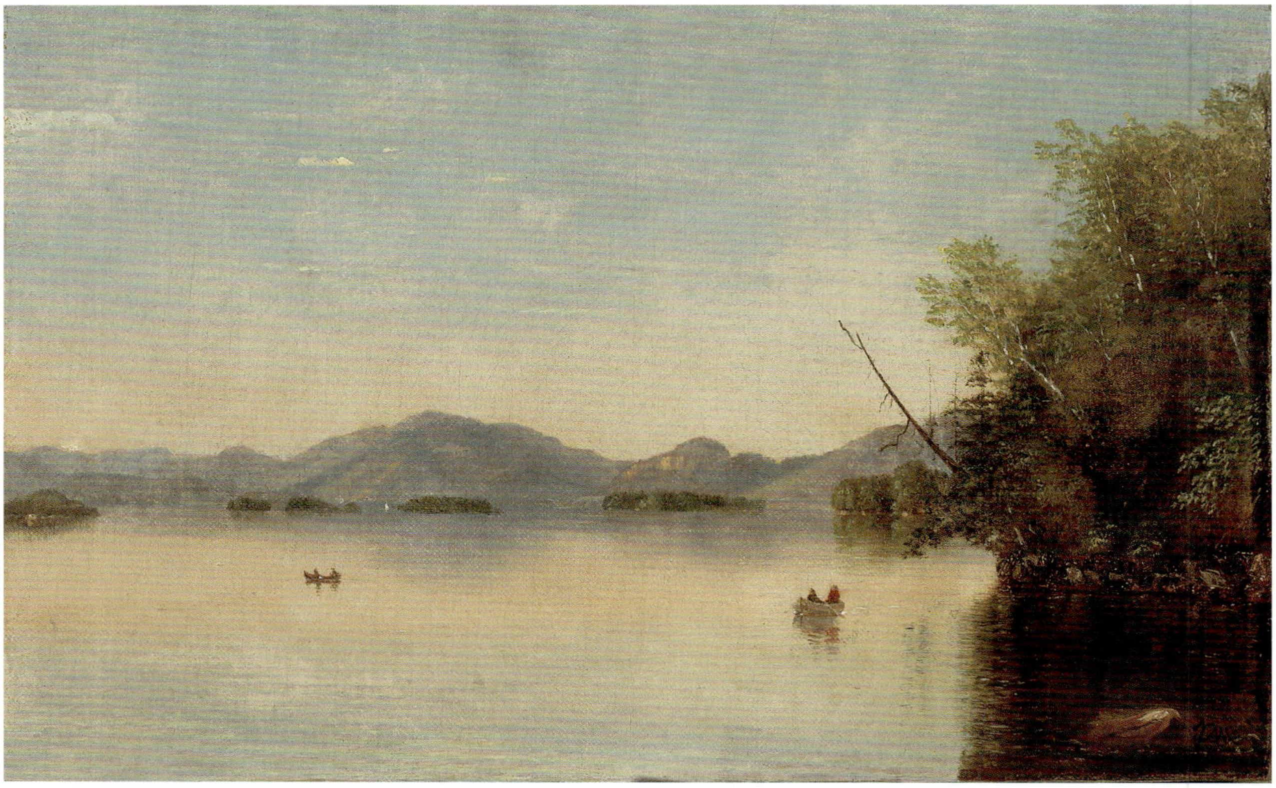

Nelson Augustus Moore (1824–1902)
Lake George, n.d.
Oil on canvas, 9 x 14 1/2 inches

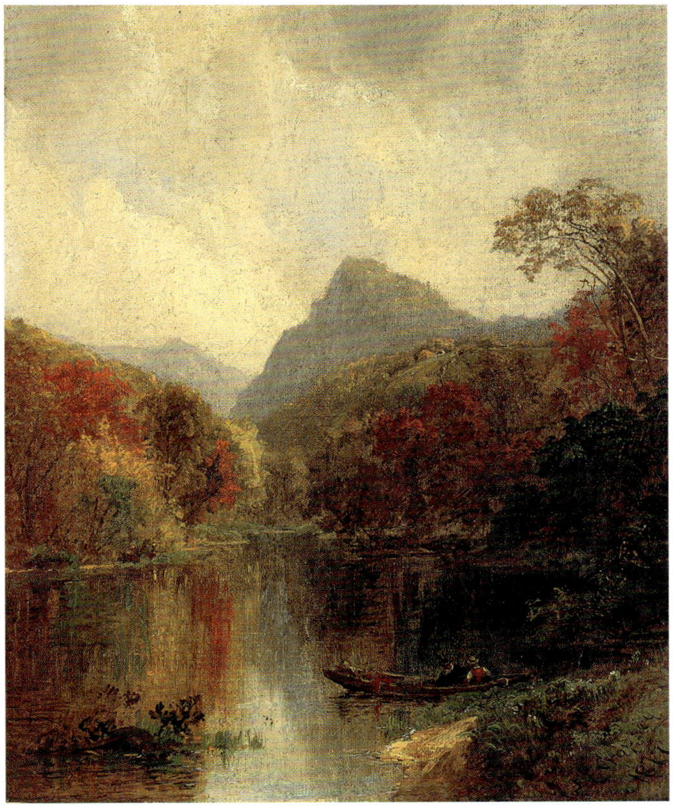

Jasper Francis Cropsey (1823–1900)
Lake George, 1877
Oil on canvas, 12¼ x 10 inches

John William Casilear (1811–1893)
Lake George, c. 1865
Oil on canvas, 15 x 25 inches

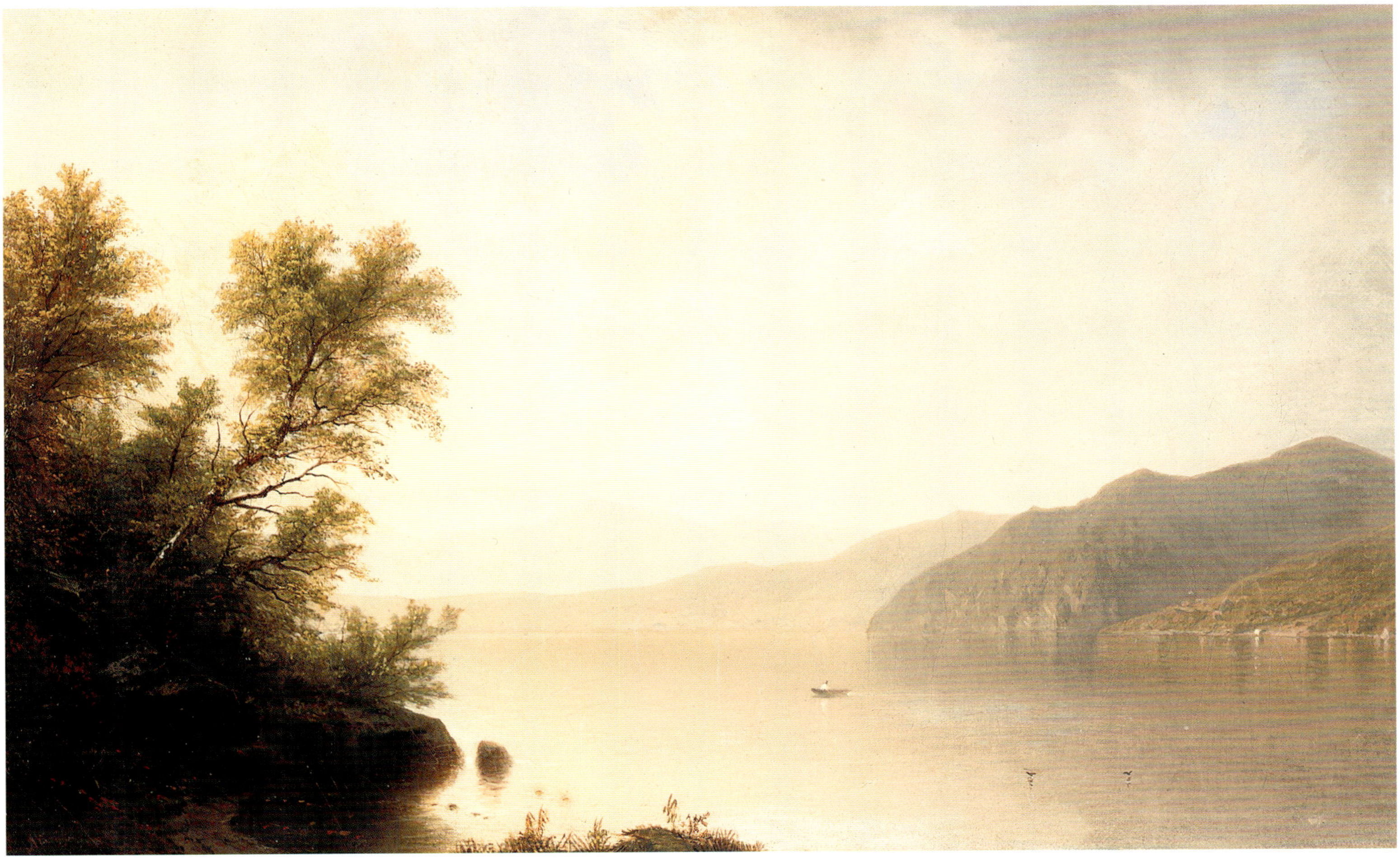

JAMES BRADE SWORD HAS CREATED A PAINTING RIPE WITH theme and variation: attention to realism yet evocation of the mystical; masterful light and dark contrasts; birth and death; heaven and earth; crisp detail opposed to diffusion of detail into atmosphere. Sword surrounded his view of Lake George with a realistic depiction of its forested banks, meticulously elaborating individual characteristics of specific flora and fauna through precise color and distinct forms. In the foreground, at a height above Lake George, a leaf-strewn path winds along a gurgling rivulet surrounded by mossy outcroppings of rock; rotting tree branches through which spring new growth; and tall birch trees, whose silver trunks shine with reflected morning sunlight. The tangle of primordial forest opens to reveal the serenity of the lake below, its islands, and the surrounding mountains, where filtered light, a muted palette, and less detail create a vision of freshness that must have been observed by those who first viewed this scene. On the left, a golden ash, too large for its apex to be included in the composition, extends one branch along the uppermost part of the canvas, gracefully gesturing to distant mountains and circling toward the lake in gentle acknowledgment of its mystery and attraction.

Although a frequent world traveler who produced views of South America, Europe, and Egypt, Henry Ferguson, a native of Glens Falls, New York, was especially dedicated to Hudson River and Adirondack subjects. Indeed, the first works Ferguson exhibited were views of Lake George,[18] painted as a young man in his twenties. In this scene, an exquisite evocation of light reveals an already accomplished artist, one who, like many of the later generation of Hudson River School painters, was keenly interested in capturing different qualities of light and in suggesting mood, while only secondarily concerned with rendering detail. A sandy beach with large rocks extends across the foreground, appearing and reappearing in concert with the lake's curving shoreline. Mountains in the distance shimmer through a mist created by means of layered glazes and varnishes—akin to those used by Martin Johnson Heade and others of the luminist movement. The surface of the painting is smooth, without a trace of brushwork, just as the lake's surface is unruffled by either wind or the passage of boats on the water. Contemplative and serene, the mood imparted by Ferguson describes nature at peace.

James Brade Sword (1839–1915)
Lake George, 1873
Oil on canvas, 18 x 30 inches

Henry Augustus Ferguson (1845–1911)
Sunset, Lake George, c. 1860
Oil on canvas, 10 x 18 inches

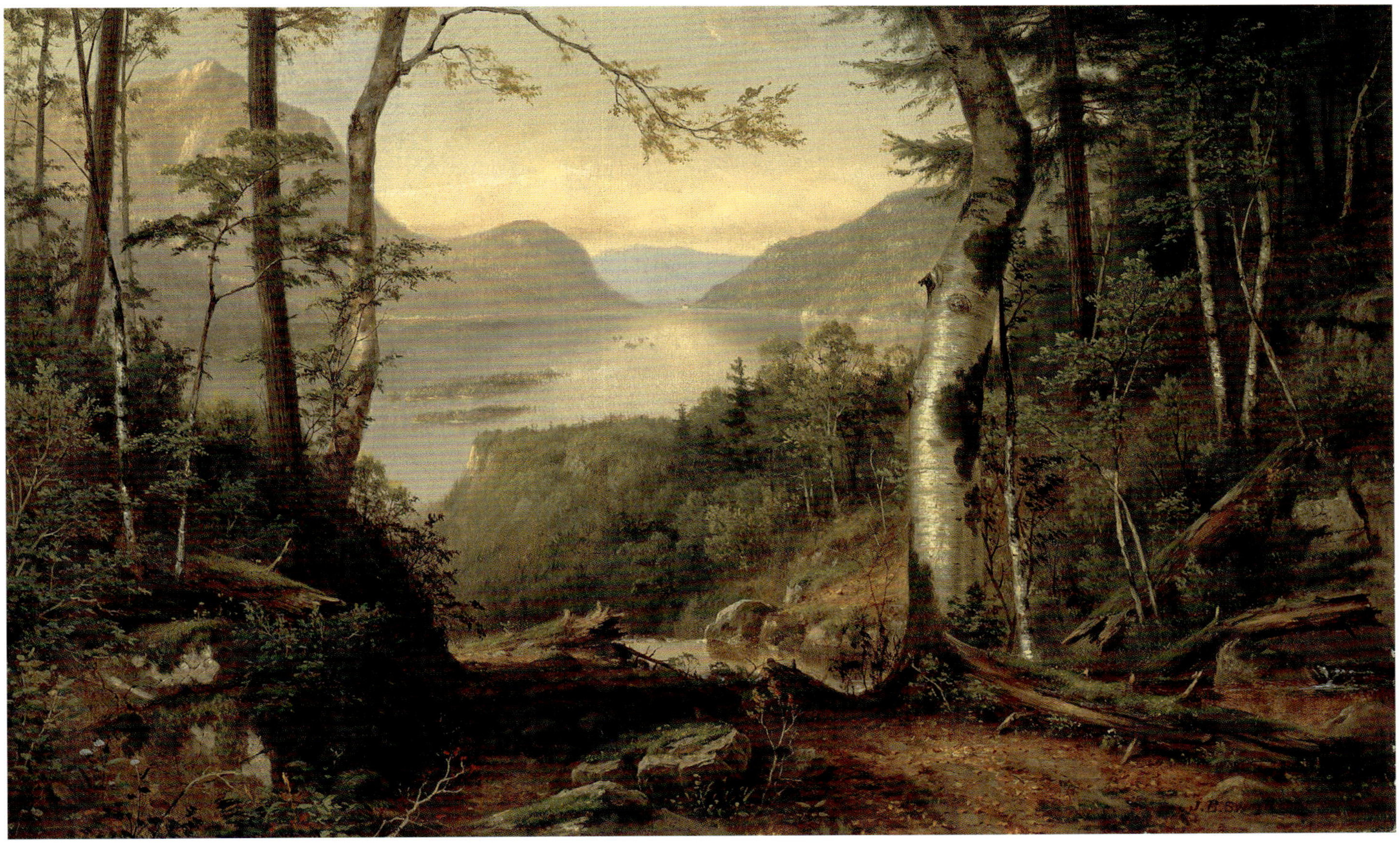

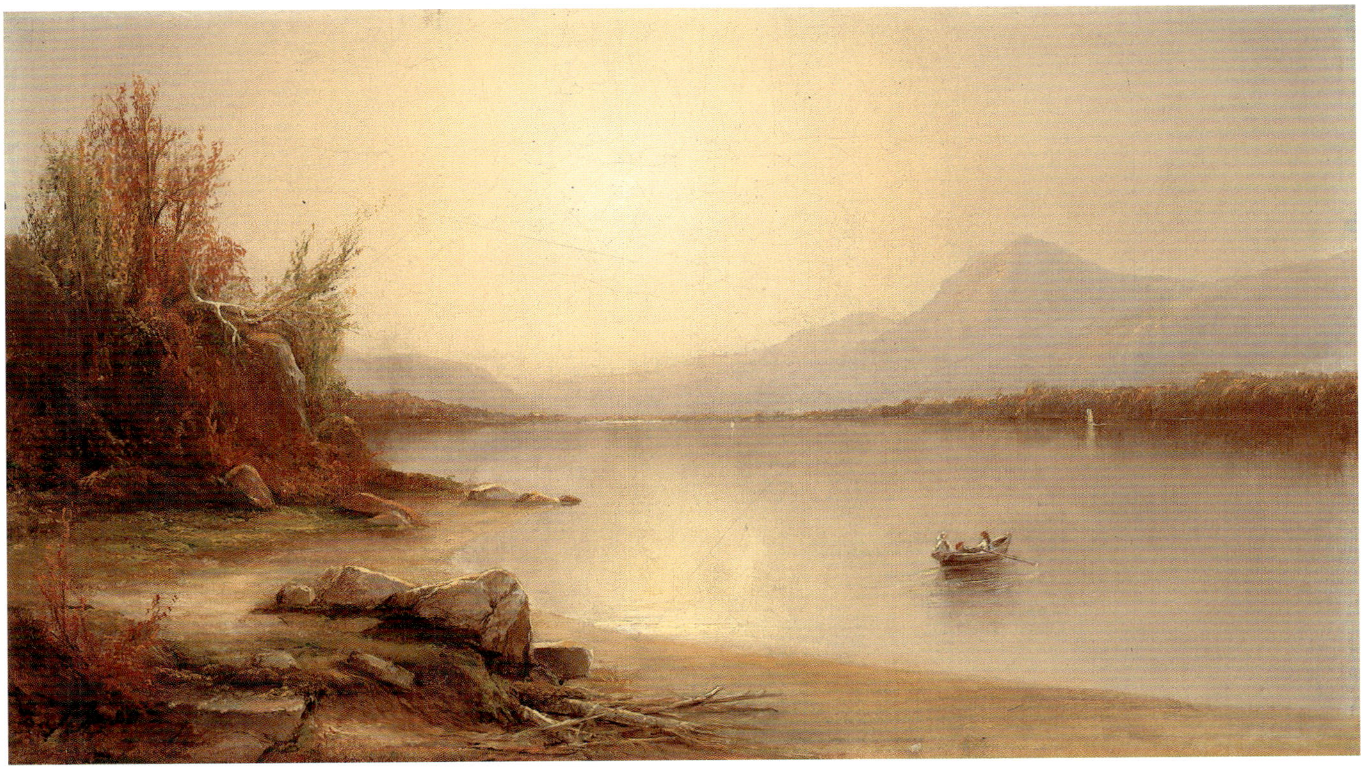

Views of Niagara Falls

John Vanderlyn (1775–1852) claimed to have been the first artist to paint Niagara Falls, one of the great natural wonders of the New World, in a work dated 1802 (*Nature and the American*). He was followed by many who attempted to capture various aspects of the magnificent, spellbinding falls—a hallmark of nature's sublime manifestations. Indeed, for the arriving landscape painter in America, these falls became a required pilgrimage and a true challenge to demonstrating ingenuity and originality. Each artist found his or her own way of representing the falls, approaching them from different perspectives—both physical and aesthetic—choosing or arranging the conditions of nature in order to guide the viewer to a unique representation.

Thomas Hill's view is observed freshly and startlingly from below the falls, with only a slip of clouds and sky above to help orient the viewer. The monumental, light-filled cascade of water in its rush of movement is starkly contrasted to the dark, immobile rock overhang, as precipitous as the water despite its solidity and the water's constant movement. Small outgrowths of vegetation cling almost hopelessly to the rock. A single robed Native American, leaning slightly against his bow with his back

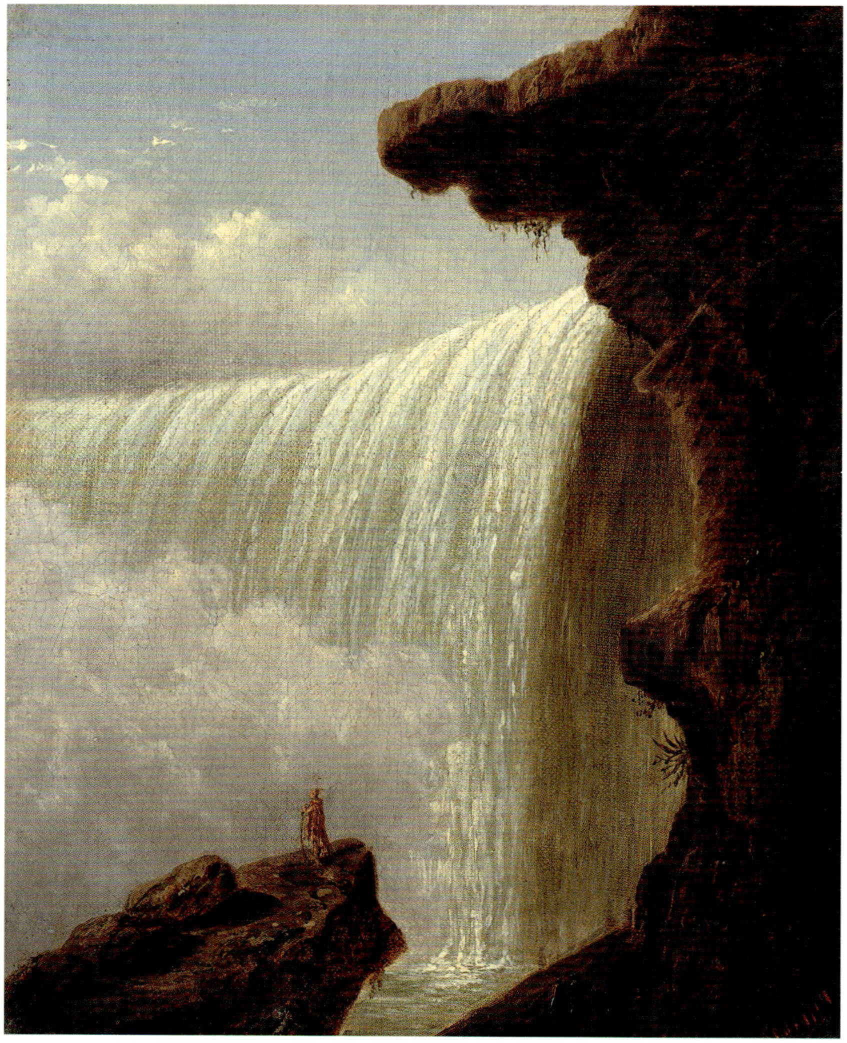

Thomas Hill (1829–1908)
Niagara Falls, c. 1860
Oil on canvas, 10½ x 8½ inches

DeWitt Clinton Boutelle (1820–1884)
Niagara Falls, 1861
Oil on canvas, 12½ x 16 inches

to us, is positioned on a boulder, itself atop and supported by a natural rock outcropping along the lower shoreline. He presumably gazes up into the falls through the billowing mist produced by its torrent. Two other figures walk away from the scene, as if leaving the foreground figure to his silent reverie. Measuring only 10½ x 8½ inches, Hill's image is one in which drama compacted is thereby intensified.

DeWitt Clinton Boutelle painted many versions of Niagara Falls, achieving wide recognition for his different views. In this painting of the dramatic falls on the Canadian side, Boutelle's subject is the torrent of water and the pastel-colored light effects it creates as it crashes over the curve of the falls. Water and foam are colored in greens and blues, the mist that rises from them a cotton-candy pink. The pleasure of the view is further sweetened by the appearance of a rainbow arching across the lower right corner of the composition, echoing the arc of water on the left. Perched atop the edge of the falls is a small dark-brown observation tower. The only indication of man's presence, it is set apart by its solidity amid the froth of bright water, the lone observer in this particular view.

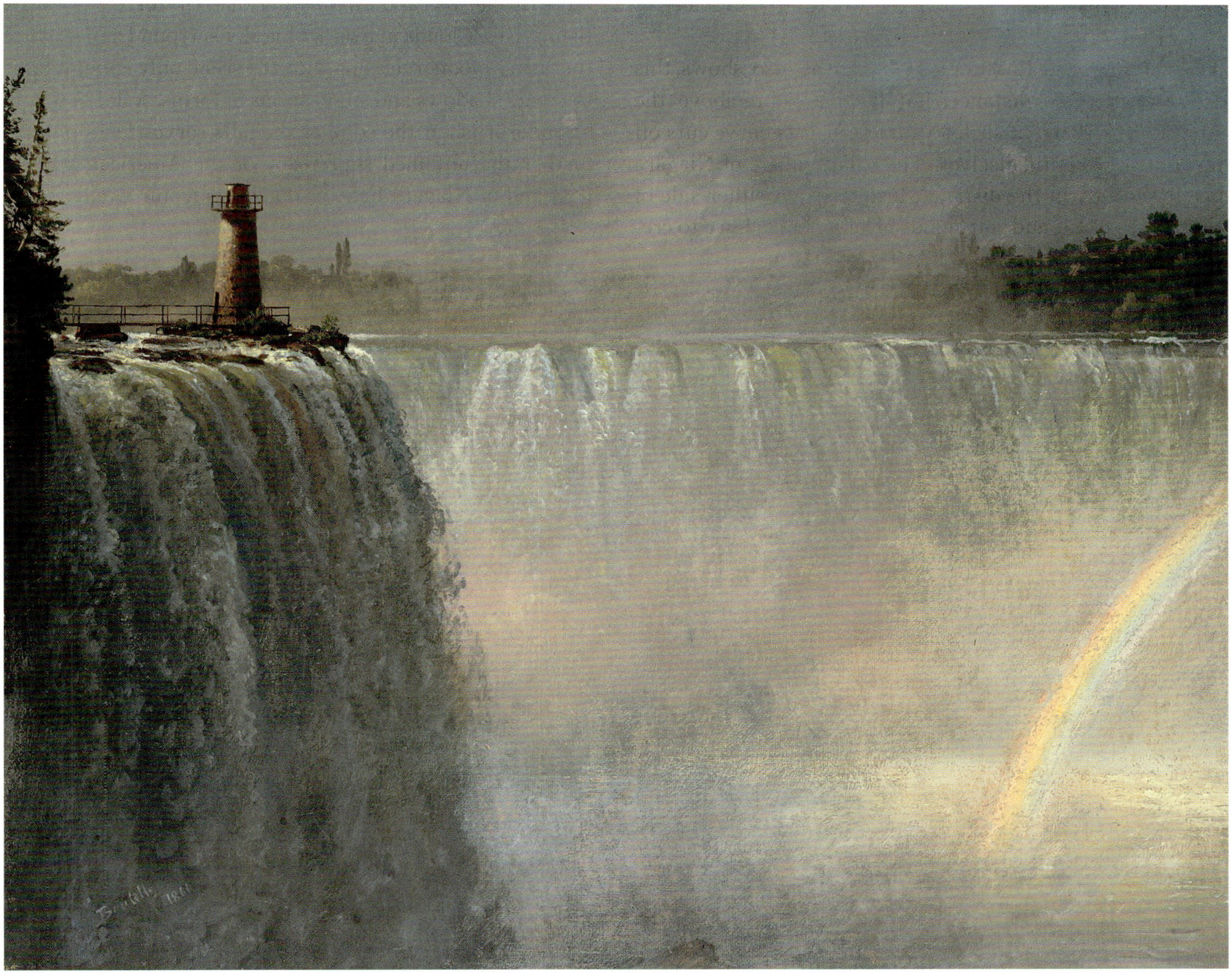

SUBLIME AND BEAUTIFUL EFFECTS OF THE FALLS ARE combined in John William Casilear's view from 1872. In the dark foreground, the observer—a single figure with a gun, who also represents the viewer—stands with his back to us at some distance from the water so that the awesome monumentality of the falls is minimized, and its forceful energy seems well contained and controlled within the picture plane. Soft blue skies and sunshine are reflected in the water as on a serene summer day. The Canadian curve of the falls stretches across the center of the canvas, occupying a third of the composition; the other two-thirds are taken by earth and sky, lending a serene balance to these three elements. The contrast between the dark triangle of land and the open lightness of the water and sky adds a welcome ingredient of tension in an otherwise tranquil, timeless vision. Once again, Casilear has demonstrated a mastery over the elusive and changeable qualities of light and atmosphere.

Thomas Prichard Rossiter's 1858 canvas also shows this scene from some distance, but from a point above the American falls and at such a vantage that its curve cuts off most of the falls themselves. The small village of Niagara nestled snugly in the distance, lush trees on either side of the picture plane, and soft clouds of summer coalesce to create an image of domestication rather than wilderness. The overwhelming use of green and pale blue reinforces the sense of calm. Interestingly, this painting is one of a pair by Rossiter, now separated by auction. The second painting of the pair depicted the opposite of domesticity, without a hint of civilization to suggest man's presence. In it, Rossiter revealed a completely wild view of the falls, its full torrent taking up most of the composition under just a sliver of darkened, menacing sky to further accentuate nature at her threatening best. Rossiter, an engraver as well as a painter, was a close friend of Durand, Kensett, and Casilear, with whom he traveled, painted, and shared ideas. He was also close to Cole, from whom he gained the impetus to imbue his landscapes with moral messages to edify his viewers.

An unusual night view of the famous falls, this dramatic painting masks the powerful waters in a veil of darkness more mysterious and threatening than the force of the falls themselves. Clouds in a dark blue sky surround and obscure the rising moon, releasing into the scene only enough light to create shadows and suggestions of forms. A dense tangle of underbrush at the edge of the falls serves to emphasize further the untamed supremacy of the American wilderness and of Niagara Falls as one of its iconic wonders.

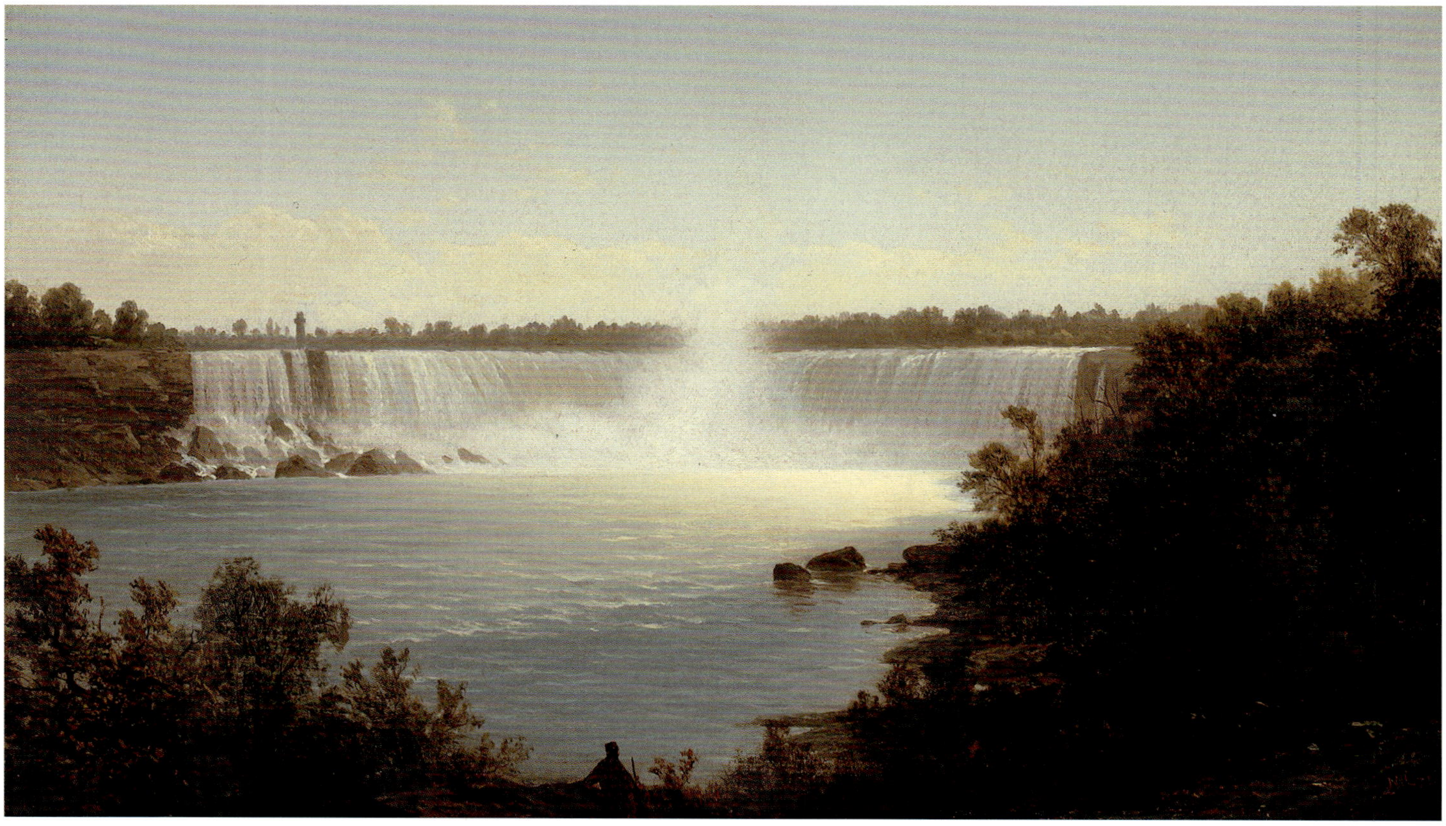

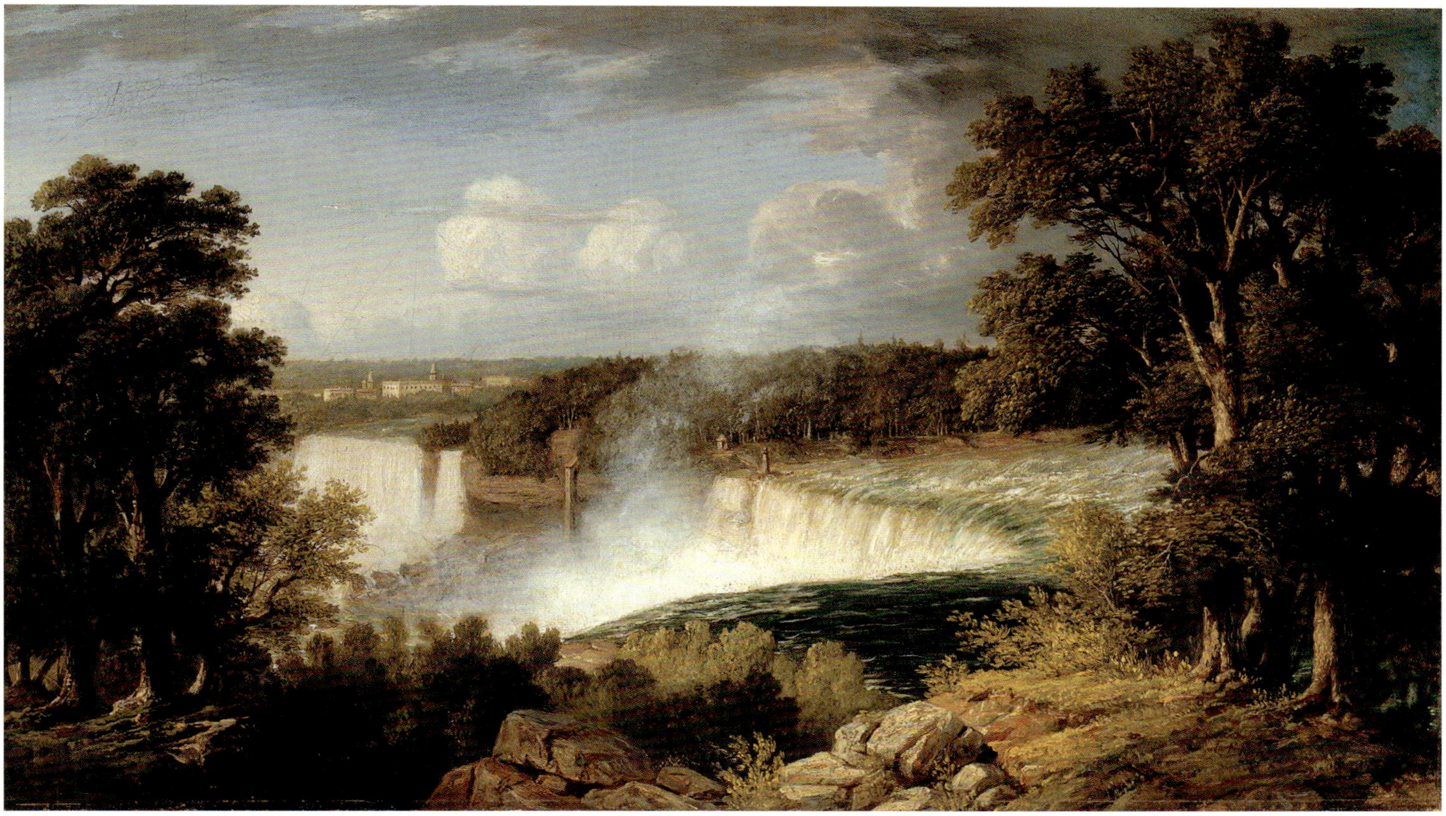

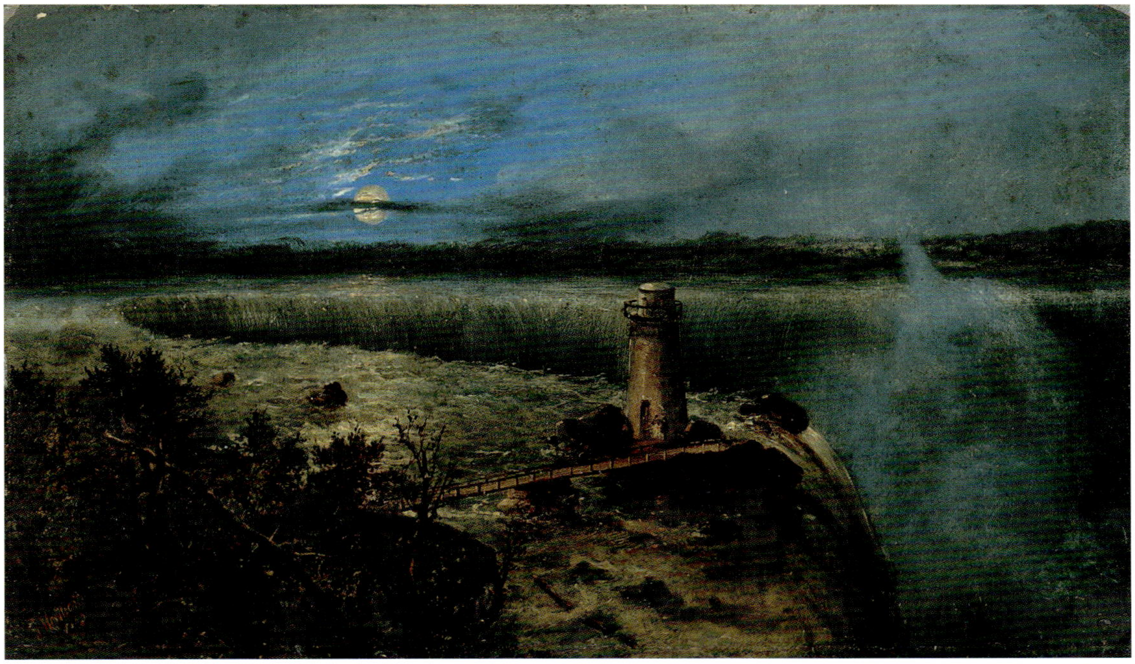

John William Casilear (1811–1893)
Niagara Falls, 1872
Oil on canvas, 13 x 23 inches

Thomas Prichard Rossiter (1818–1871)
Niagara Falls, 1858
Oil on canvas, 13½ x 24 inches

James Northcote (1822–1904)
Niagara Falls at Night, 1863
Oil on canvas, 8 x 14 inches

Views of Mt. Washington

Born in Darmstadt, Germany, and trained in Frankfurt, Paul Weber reflects in his style the Germanic penchant for precise draftsmanship, accurate rendition of detail, and a warm, earth-toned palette. Centrally placed in the composition, the peak of Mount Washington appears as a remote, snow-capped giant presiding over the rolling hills and valley below, set apart not only by its lofty height but by the coolness of its color and the icy blue of the sky, which it pierces. Warm, golden sunlight spills across the rest of the broad landscape, blocked only by two clusters of green, red, and yellow-tinged trees on either side of the Saco River, which meanders peacefully through the lower third of the composition. Tuckerman's Ravine, a deep gash in the eastern face of the mountain, is clearly recognizable. Cows water at the river's edge. A church spire, nearly hidden in the lower slopes of the White Mountains, glistens in the raking sunlight, a tiny representative of man's spiritual presence. The late summer afternoon scene is at once balanced, languid, magnificent. As John Driscoll observed describing this image of Mount Washington, Weber "paid homage to New England's greatest subject as a symbol of the new nation he had come to love."[19] In 1854, when this landscape was painted, the nation was still peaceful, unified, optimistic about its future, basking in the wonderful light that Weber captured here so effectively and eloquently. This masterpiece reveals why Weber was so highly regarded in Philadelphia, where he established his studio in 1848 and attracted such talented students as William Trost Richards and William Haseltine.

Paul Weber (1823–1916)
Mount Washington from the Saco, 1854
Oil on canvas, 25 1/2 x 37 inches

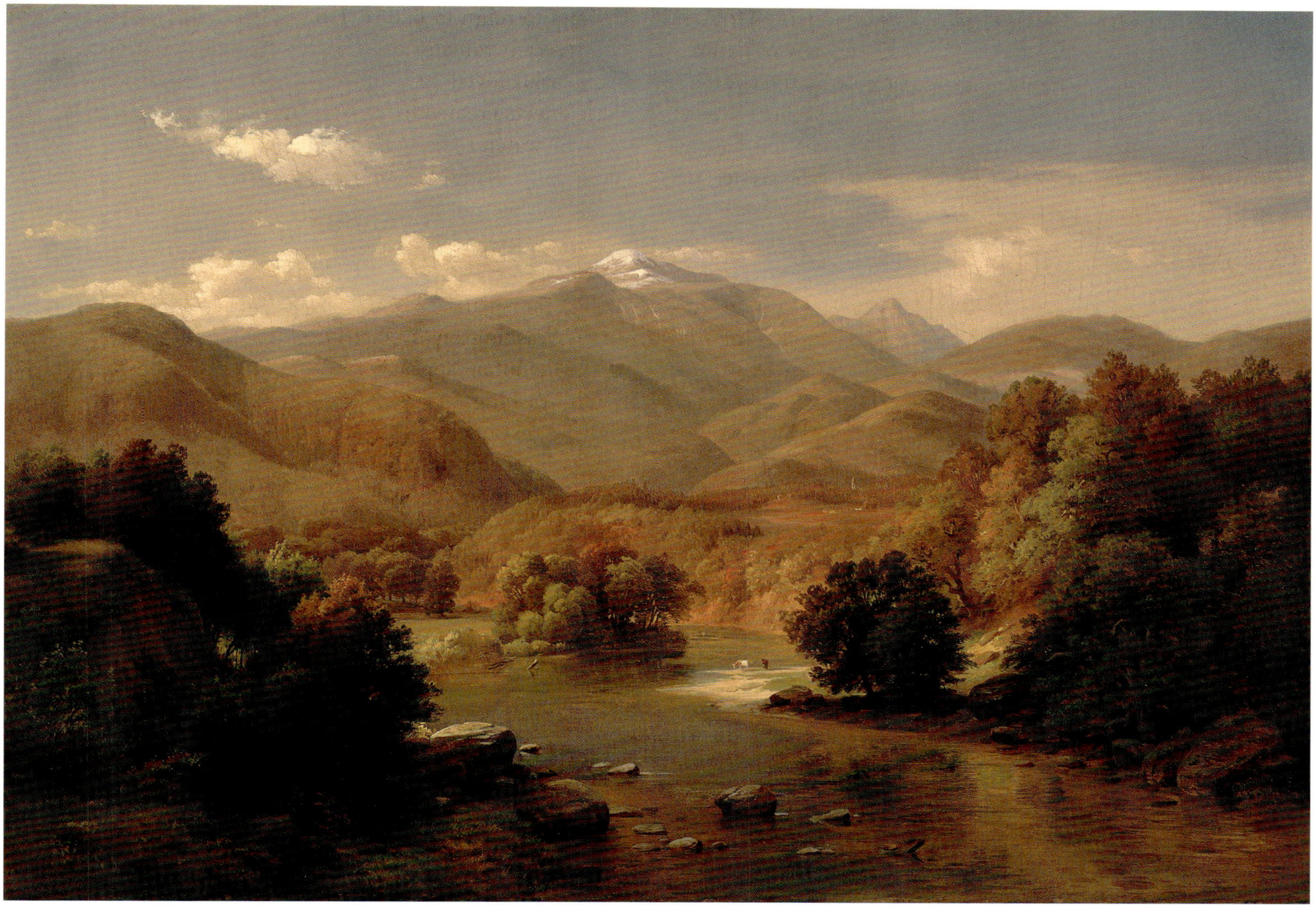

Martin Johnson Heade's 1871 evocation of Mount Washington is another peaceful, harmonic view of nature. The palette used by Heade, dictated largely by the weather conditions, differs greatly from that of Paul Weber. Rather than a pinnacle, the mountain here looms as a long, gray silhouette, acting as a recessive backdrop to the scene. An atmospheric apparition, it reaches horizontally across the canvas against a similarly colored blue-gray sky, dense with clouds. In contrast are the rich subtle colors of brown, green, and rust that Heade chose for the foreground. An additional contrast is the atmospheric ambiguity of the distant topography compared to the sparkling clarity of foreground detail. Cut through diagonally by a well-worn path, a meadow is punctuated horizontally by the progression of four trees across the composition's center, giving the painting both weight and balance. A rough-hewn fence, its angular shape softened by the overgrowth of tiny white roses on a vine, mimics the diagonal thrust of the path. This fence provides a subtle symbol of man's ineffectual attempts to reign in nature. Horses graze in fields humid from a recent rainstorm—a weather condition favored by Heade, who loved to capture on canvas delicate atmospheric effects created by passing storms. Light glistens in beads of water remaining on grasses in the foreground. The quality of light is uniform, diffused by cloud cover, giving the picture a sense of quietude and introspection despite the breadth of scenery it encompasses.

In this, the smallest and earliest of these three views of Mount Washington, William Hart has succeeded in making the mountain appear grand and imposing. The peak of Mount Washington rises high and white, once again set off from the rest of the landscape both spatially and through contrasting color. Rich vibrant hues of autumn warm the valley in the foreground. Like the previous views, there are no figures present, and the artist's interest focuses exclusively on nature itself.

Martin Johnson Heade (1819–1904)
White Mountain Landscape, Mount Washington, 1871
Oil on canvas, 9 x 15½ inches

William McDougal Hart (1823–1894)
Mount Washington, 1861
Oil on canvas, 6½ x 10¼ inches

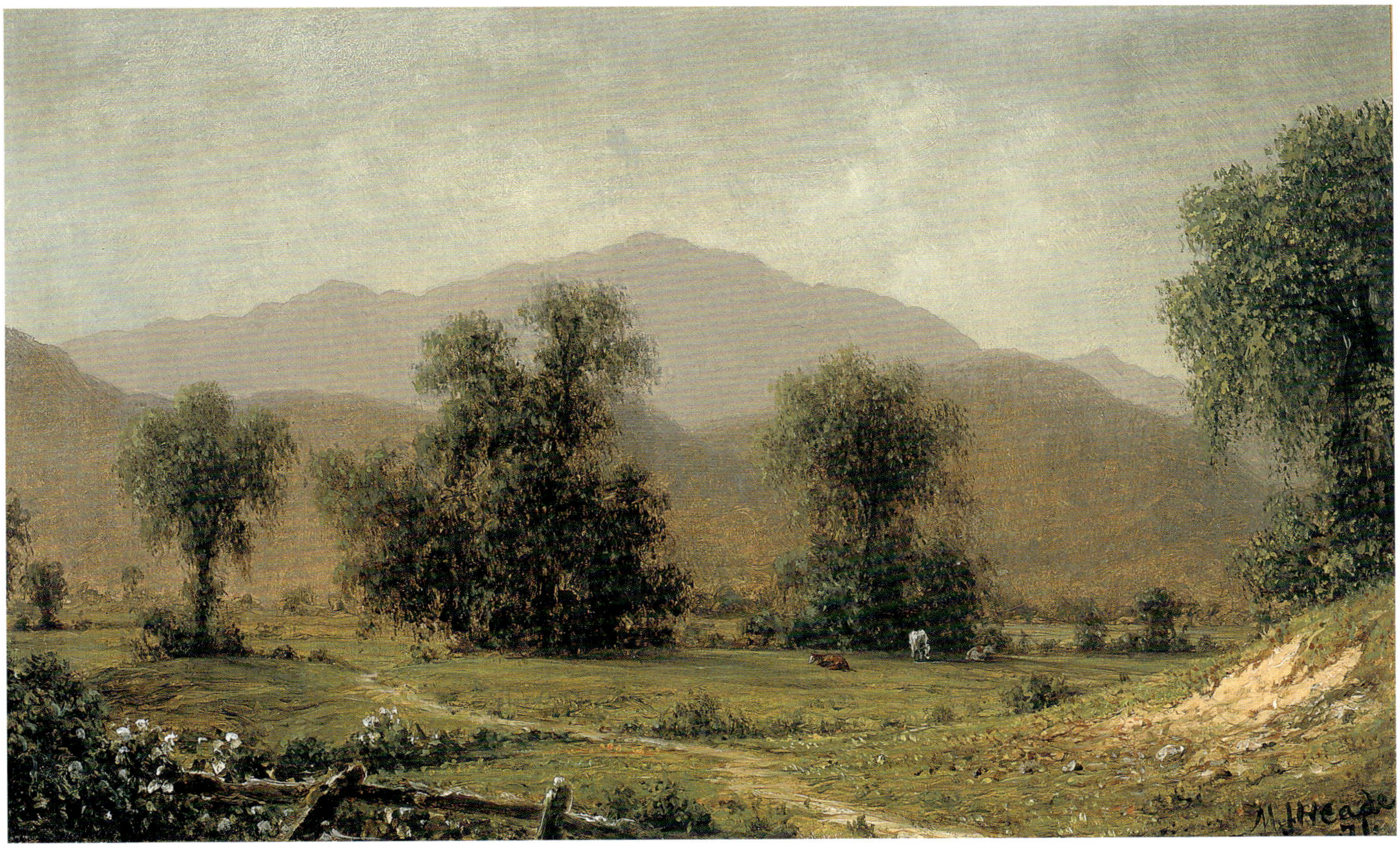

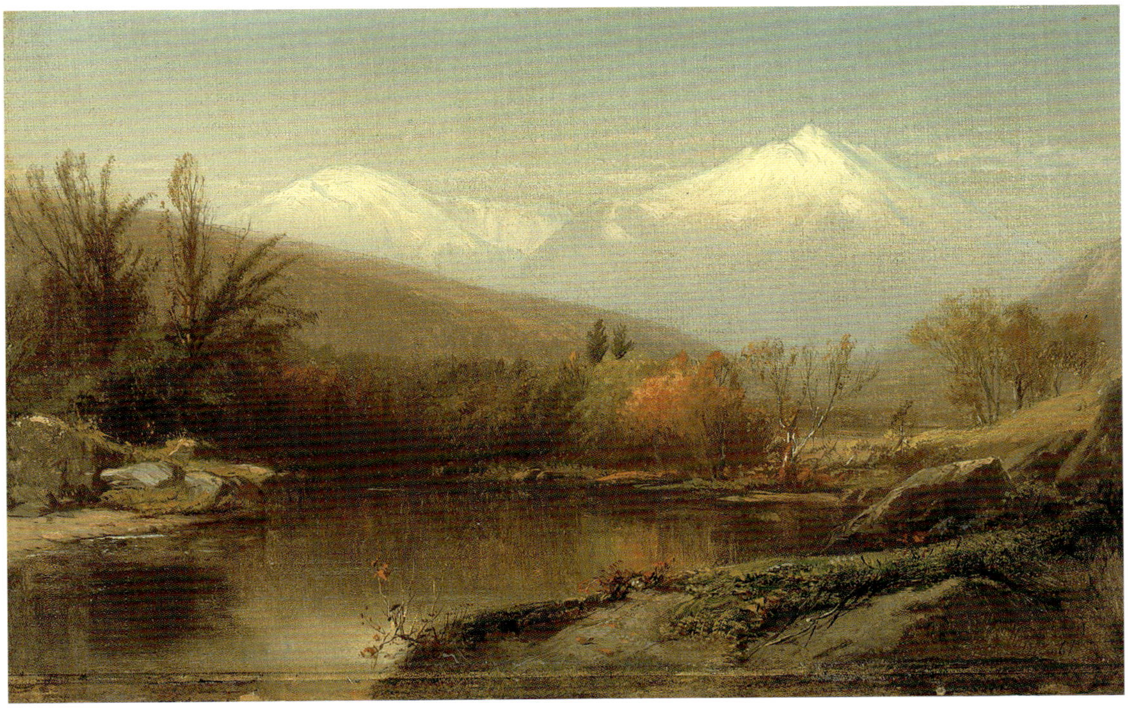

IX. Samplers

. . . when I consider with what mastery, yet with what reverence he [Cole] copied the forms of nature, and how he blended with them the profoundest human sympathies, and made them the vehicle, as God has made them, of great truths and great lessons, when I see how directly he learned his art from the creation around him, and how resolutely he took his own way to greatness, I say within myself, this man will be reverenced in future years as a great master in art. He has opened a way in which only men endued with rare strength of genius can follow him.

. . . the landscape painter is admitted to a closer familiarity with nature than the poet. He studies her aspect more minutely and watches with a more affectionate attention its varied expressions. Not one of her forms is lost upon him; not a gleam of sunshine penetrates her green recesses; not a cloud casts its shadow unobserved by him; every tint of the morning or the evening, of the gray or the golden noon, of the near or the remote object is noted by his eye and copied by his pencil. All her boundless variety of outlines and shades become almost a part of his being and are blended with his mind.

—William Cullen Bryant, *Funeral Ovation*, 1848

OUR FINAL GROUPING, LIKE OUR FIRST, CONTAINS just two works by two different artists. Yet because they are samplers, each contains more than one image—more than one painting in miniature. In essence, samplers provide the ultimate comparison and contrast in that they reveal to us each artist's interest in the diversity of subject matter provided by nature, and their individual ability to convey through these different landscapes various aspects of the sublime, beautiful, and picturesque. Sadly, these remarkable samplers functioned primarily as promotional pieces by artists and dealers wishing to interest a client in the range and diversity of a particular artist.[20] Their small scale provided a less cumbersome avenue for this demonstration than would displaying the same number of larger canvases. However, their diminutive size was the reason many have been overlooked, lost, or even discarded.

The two artists compared and contrasted here also have interesting differences in their biographies. Regis Francois Gignoux, a Frenchman trained at the academies in Lyons and Paris, came to America to find the landscape subjects in which he excelled bathed in the light and steeped in the atmosphere of the new country's dramatic seasonal change. Arriving in 1840, just eight years before the death of Thomas Cole, Gignoux placed himself in New York at the height of interest and activity in the Hudson River School, returning to France as the waning of the school began after the Civil War.

William Trost Richards, an American-born third-generation proponent of the Hudson River School, studied under Paul Weber in Philadelphia. An admirer of John Ruskin and the English Pre-Raphaelite movement, he was a keen observer and transcriber of detail. Most closely associated with water scenes later in his career, Richards achieved an ability to render light and atmosphere; his sensitive, barely visible brush seemed to be dipped in light rather than in paint. Characterized as a luminist—the name given to those of the last generation who specialized in capturing light effects—Richards lived to see the eclipse of the Hudson River School as it gave way to French Impressionism, Post impressionism, and Modernism.

The samplers themselves are very different. Gignoux's is lit by the fiery colors, animated brushwork, and complex compositions that characterized his style, often revealing comparisons and contrasts within a single image. The scenes are buoyant, exuding optimism. The drama of Niagara Falls, a spectacular natural wonder of the New World, is located centrally, demonstrating the awesome power of nature and implying the same strength as a descriptive of the new nation as a whole. Other individually recognizable scenes are the Natural Bridge (Virginia), Hudson River, Mohawk Valley (New York), and Dismal Swamp (North Carolina). Blue, gray, and green dominate in Richards's sampler. The centerpiece is not a spectacular landmark but rather a typical and charming Hudson River School subject. Day ends as the sun sets in a river landscape, while the coming of autumn, signaled by the changing color of leaves, signifies the parallel close of the seasonal cycle. A single figure, centrally positioned in a dirt road bearing ruts from wagon wheels, is aligned with the sun's path on the water and mountainside and, eventually, with

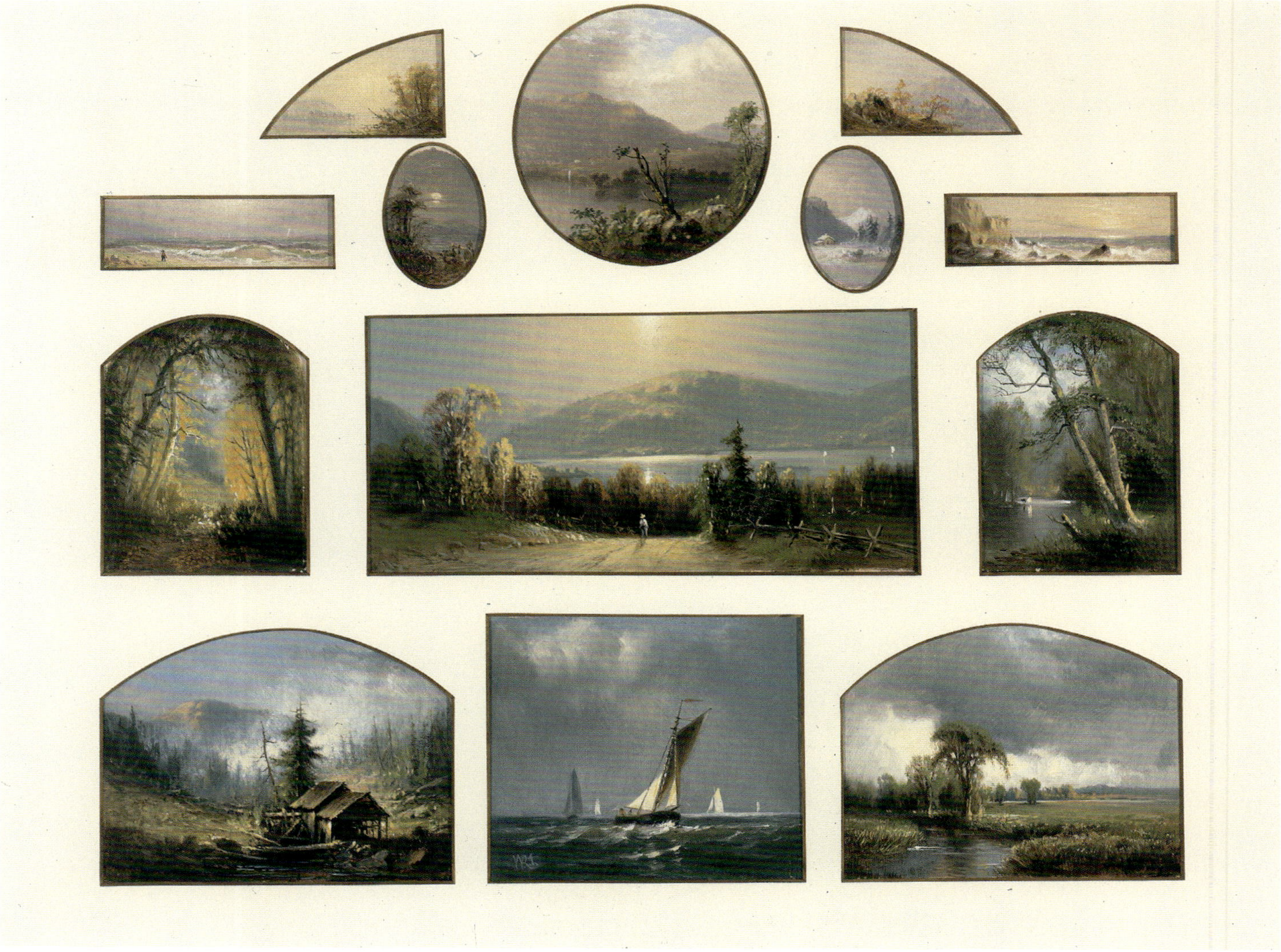

the source of light itself. The piece is contemplative and serene, indicating man's encroachment on nature as benign.

Indeed, these samplers represent a reprise of all that we have examined previously, containing diverse subjects, weather, light effects, seasons, times of day, and man's interactions with nature. United by one frame, the miniature paintings not only demonstrate the range of technique and subject matter of these two artists, but also encapsulate the fascination of all Hudson River School painters with landscape, as well as with the many factors that caused it to be ever-changing and illusive, appearing different at each new moment. To describe his sampler, Gignoux even borrowed the title, *American Scenery Sampler*, from Thomas Cole's article "Essay on American Scenery."[21]

Land, water, sky—observed faithfully, persistently, and skillfully by three generations of American painters throughout the nineteenth century. These landscape themes—tirelessly examined, studied, experimented with, and evoked by the artists—were avidly appreciated and consumed by the public until attention shifted from rural to urban subjects, and the new American image was sought and captured in its cities, industry, and cosmopolitan society.

Over the generations, Hudson River School paintings have had diminished voice and impact, as we have forgotten how to read their iconography. Hopefully what has been written here will reengage the American public with the language of landscape and the rich visual heritage left by the painters of the Hudson River School.

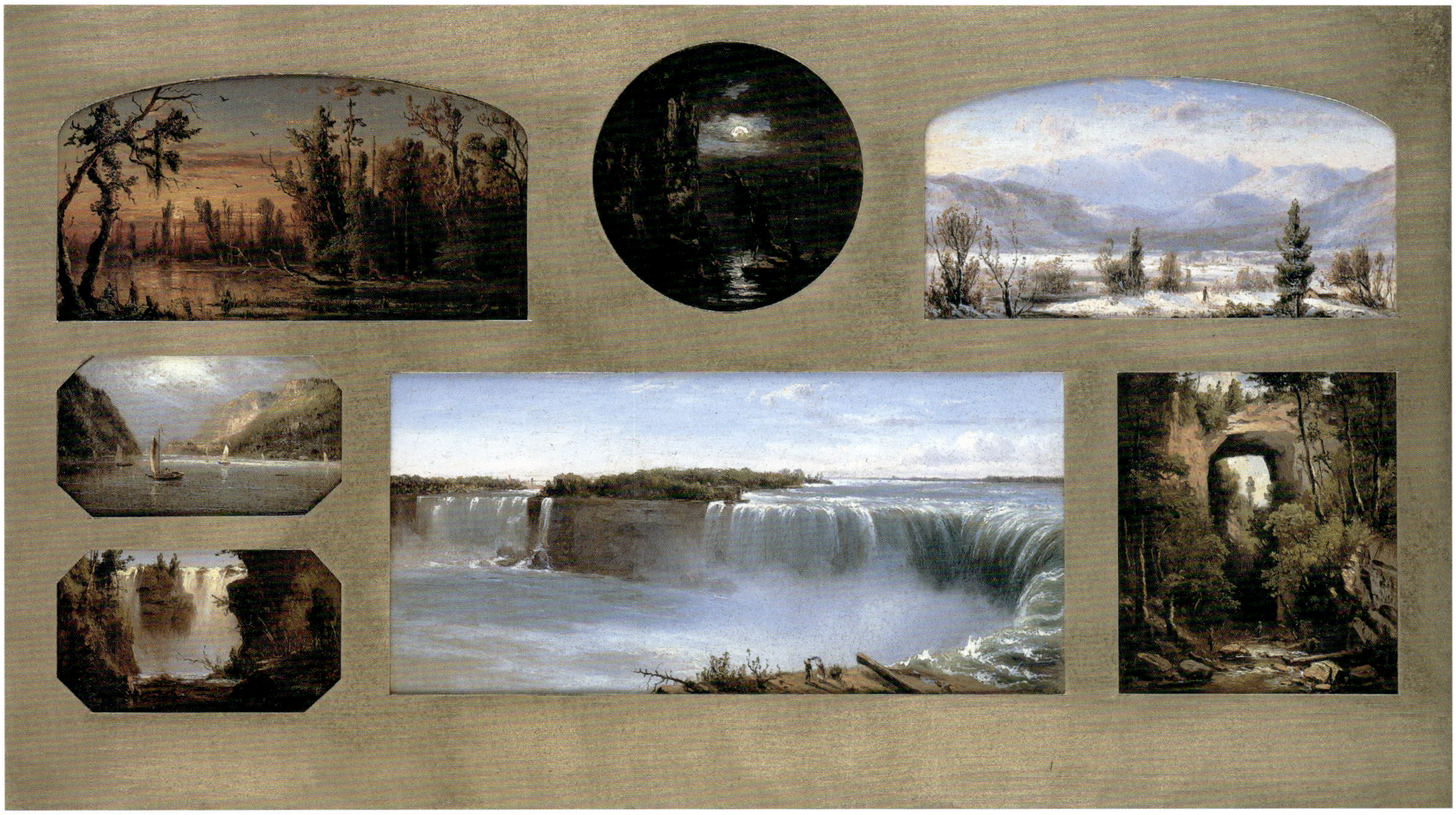

William Trost Richards (1833–1905)
Sampler, c. 1860
Oil on thirteen canvases mounted together

Regis Francis Gignoux (1816–1882)
American Scenery Sampler, c. 1861
Oil on canvas, 20 x 36 inches

NOTES

INTRODUCTION

1 Please refer to the list of Suggested Further Readings in this volume and, in particular, to the *New York Historical Society's Dictionary of Artists in America, 1564–1860*, by George C. Groce and David H. Wallace (Yale University Press, 1957), which is an excellent reference.

2 John Driscoll, *All That Is Glorious Around Us: Paintings from the Hudson River School* (Cornell University Press, 1997).

AMERICAN SCENERY

1 This exhibition is the second to be drawn from a single private collection and organized by the Westmoreland Museum of American Art. The first was John Driscoll, *All That Is Glorious Around Us: Paintings from the Hudson River School* (Ithaca, NY: Cornell University Press: 1997). That exhibition was in turn based on a much smaller one of the same name organized in 1978 by the Museum of Art, Pennsylvania State University (now the Palmer Museum of Art).

2 Barbara Novak's landmark book *Nature and Culture: American Landscape and Painting, 1825–1875* was an important contribution. In her preface to the first edition (New York: Oxford University Press, 1978), Novak wrote that in her volume, "I stress ideas, and attempt to show how the history of ideas flows freely through the membranes that compartmentalize the various disciplines comprising a culture. In the nineteenth century these compartments were less restrictive than they are now." In the following paragraph, she adds that her book "aspires through certain thematic identifications toward a form of cultural art history that probes for what, in Panofsky's terms, might be called *iconological* roots."

Throughout his study, *The Art of Thomas Cole: Ambition and Imagination* (Newark: University of Delaware Press, 1988), Ellwood C. Parry III discusses Cole's use of iconological language in his paintings, including linking changing seasons and times of day with the rise and fall of man, as well as the artist's use of series and pairs to communicate ideas. In particular, Parry wrote, "[I]t becomes clear that the perfectly overlapping time cycles—from dawn to dark, from early spring to late winter, from the advent of man to the fall of human civilization—were a fundamental part of Cole's thinking when it came to narrative pairs or sets of easel paintings, with each individual canvas intended to portray a different moment in time within the total continuum of the story-telling sequence. In large measure this was Cole's most original contribution to romantic art in America" (p. 148).

See footnote 4 for reference on Kelly.

3 In addition to the authors named above, see David Miller, ed., *American Iconology: New Approaches to Nineteenth Century American Art and Literature* (New Haven: Yale University Press, 1993). Especially note the contributions of Kenneth Myers. David Miller wrote the following about the underlying ideology that exists in paintings: "it transformed representation into a cognitive structure fraught with enormous ideological weight and it produced a 'textualized' version of reality as a series of semiotic codes that we are still living today."

4 Franklin Kelly, "American Landscape Pairs of the 1850's," *Antiques* (November 1994): 650–57. In this article, Kelly discussed pairs by Asher B. Durand, Sanford Robinson Gifford, John Frederick Kensett, William Mason Brown, and Federic Edwin Church, along with those of Thomas Cole.

5 Kelly has continued to allude to the occurrence of pairs in the Hudson River School and the debt to Cole—most recently in his essay "Nature Distilled," in which he discussed a pair by Sanford Gifford, *Morning in the Adirondacks and Sunset in the Shawangunk Mountains* (1854), stating, "The National Academy audience of 1854 would have recognized the dual homage to Cole: on the one hand, to his use of paired pictures to establish his narrative possibilities and, on the other, to his fondness for the mountain scenery of the upper Hudson River Valley." Franklin Kelly, "Nature Distilled: Gifford's Vision of Landscape," in *Hudson River School Visions: The Landscapes of Sanford R. Sanford*, ed. Kevin J. Avery et al. (New Haven and London: The Metropolitan Museum of Art and Yale University Press, 2003), 654.

6 Interestingly, several pairs of paintings by artists including William McDougal Hart and Frederick Rondel have recently come onto the market (Christie's American Paintings sale on September 27, 2004, included *Boating; and Fishing: A Pair of Works* by Rondel; and *Autumn Tints; and Summer Afternoon: A Pair of Works* by Hart). In addition, a series of ten oils framed together by Albert Bierstadt was sold at Sotheby's American Paintings sale on May 21, 2003. Although the lot description noted that there were other examples of similarly grouped paintings photographed in Bierstadt's studio, it did not discuss the practice by Hudson River School artists of working in series and groupings. This particular grouping appears to be related to a "painter's sampler," a concept developed in section 9 of the present volume. The fact there were other, similarly framed groupings in Bierstadt's studio indicates that he made a practice of creating these arrangements for the purpose of comparing and contrasting landscape views.

7 In 1822, Doughty exhibited two views along the Schuylkill, *View on the Schuylkill—Peter's Island* and *View of the Improvements on the River Schuylkill, at Fair Mount* (#373 and #376). His entries in 1823 list two views in watercolors of mills along the Brandywine River, *View of Gilpins Upper Mills on the Brandywine* and *McLane's Mill on the Brandywine* (#122 and #126). In 1824, he exhibited a single painting whose title indicates that it was one of a pair: *Landscape—Fairmount Water Works, Seen from Opposite Shore* (#96). Later, in 1827, he exhibited the former painting with its pair, *View of the Water Works on Schuylkill—Seen from the Top of Fair Mount* (#99).

8 Genre and history painters would have placed pairs and series in sequential order according to the linear progression of time, depicting the actual unfolding of events, one after the other, relating more to Cole's typical practice of creating multiple landscape pictures. The practice of still-life painters is closer to the generations of artists following Cole whose

messages were sustained through such devices as times of day (sunrise, sunset) and seasonal progressions, where any one painting in the series could be interpreted as either beginning or ending.

9 This is a general time frame. Many notable figures in the movement—including Frederic Church, Albert Bierstadt, William Trost Richards, and Jasper Cropsey—lived and worked into the early years of the twentieth century. For an excellent overview of the Hudson River School, see John K. Howat, *American Paradise: The World of the Hudson River School* (New York: Metropolitan Museum of Art, 1987), and, more recently, Elizabeth Mankin Kornhauser, *Hudson River School: Masterworks from the Wadsworth Atheneum Museum of Art* (New Haven and London: Yale University Press, 2003). Although this volume is based only on the collection at the Wadsworth Atheneum, it is an excellent source of information on the Hudson River School.

10 Many writers, painters, and travelers wrote about the sharp differences between European and American landscapes, noting in particular the "wildness" of the American landscape and the fact that the vistas of Europe showed the presence of man. See as an example J. Fenimore Cooper, *A Landscape Book, by American Artists and American Authors* (New York: G. P. Putnam & Son, 1868), chapter 1: "English and American Landscape Compared."

11 Thomas Cole, "Essay on American Scenery." *American Monthly* 1 (January 1936).

12 William Gilpin, *Three Essays: On Picturesque Beauty; on Picturesque Travel; and on Sketching Landscape* (London: 1792), 26.

13 J. Hector St. John Crèvecoeur, *Letters from an American Farmer: Describing Certain Provincial Situations, Manners, and Customs, Not Generally Known; and Conveying Some Idea of the Late and Present Interior Circumstances of the British Colonies of North America*, 1782. This collection of letters was written by Crèvecoeur in the guise of James, an American farmer, to inform a friend in England about the New World. His twelve letters included information on the scenery, customs, and conditions of the settlers and attempted, in letter 3, to describe the American identity. For an excellent discussion of Crèvecoeur and other European writers and artists on landscape painting, see Ellen Lawrence's introduction to *1800–1874, European and American Landscape: To Look at Nature* (Providence, RI: Brown University Department of Art, 1972).

14 "America generally is impressed with an air of freshness, youthfulness, and in many instances, to use a coarse but expressive term, rawness, that are seldom, if ever, met with in Europe." Cooper, A Landscape Book, 19.

15 Nathaniel Parker Willis, *American Scenery; or, Land, Lake, and River: Illustrations of Transatlantic Nature* (London: George Virtue, 1840).

16 Asher B. Durand, "Letters on Landscape Painting," *Crayon* 1, letter 1 (3 January 1855): 2.

17 For a thorough, now classical, discussion of American attitudes toward land, conservation, and development, see Hans Huth, *Nature and the American: Three Centuries of Changing Attitudes* (Lincoln: University of Nebraska Press, 1957).

18 From his home in Catskill, New York, Cole could witness the steady encroachment of man into nature, which, as he grew older, began to outrage him. Two paintings showing similar views of the Catskill River and—painted six years apart—depict the gradual yet inevitable changes in the landscape: *View on the Catskill—Early Autumn*, 1837, oil on canvas, The Metropolitan Museum of Art; and *River in the Catskills*, 1843, oil on canvas, Boston Museum of Fine Arts. The earlier composition reveals a near Arcadian paradise with people picnicking, rowing, and enjoying a landscape relatively unmarked by man, save a building or two nestled in the woods. The 1843 scene is of a pastoral valley; however, a railroad bridge, a train, buildings, and fewer trees have changed the landscape. In the later view, a single foreground figure observes the scene while leaning on his axe, surrounded by felled trees. A boater on the river and a small boy frolicking with his dog in a middle-ground meadow still indicate pleasurable use of the land, but signs of industry have clearly entered. See Barbara Novak, *Nature and Culture*, pp. 162–63, for a discussion of these. See also Allan Wallach's article "Thomas Cole's *River in the Catskills* as Antipastoral" (*Art Bulletin* 84, no. 2 [2002]: 343) for a discussion of the 1843 painting. Interestingly, Cole painted a second piece in 1837 that could have been conceived as a pair to *View on the Catskill—Early Autumn*. Whereas the American painting shows a beautiful pastoral, *View of Florence from San Miniato* (Cleveland Museum of Art) presents a view of that European city. Seen side-by-side, the canvases—identical in size—depict differences between American and European landscapes. The rivers running through them—the Catskill and the Arno—further unite these two paintings.

19 Thomas Cole, "Essay on American Scenery."

20 For a comprehensive study on Cole, see Ellwood C. Parry III, *The Art of Thomas Cole: Ambition and Imagination*. See also Louis Legrand Noble and Elliot S. Vesell, eds., *The Life and Works of Thomas Cole* (Hensonville, NY: Black Dome Press, 1997).

21 His home, which has become the Cedar Grove National Historic Site, is open to the public during certain months of the year (www.thomascole.org). It is located directly across the Hudson River from Olana, the much more sumptuous home of his only student, Frederic Church.

22 The full title is *View from Mount Holyoke, Northampton, Massachusetts, after a Thunder Storm* (1836, oil on canvas, 51 ? x 76 inches). Metropolitan Museum of Art, gift of Mrs. Russell Sage, 1908.

23 Cole had exhibited a small pair of paintings at the Pennsylvania Academy of the Fine Arts in 1822 titled *Sunrise* and *Sunset*. Peter H. Falk, *Annual Exhibition Record of the Pennsylvania Academy of the Fine Arts, 1876–1913* (Sound View Press, 1989), 62.

24 Cole's original notes for the painting *The Garden of Eden*, as transcribed by Franklin Kelly and Sarah Cash (Kelly, 21), called for inclusion of antelopes, sheep, dogs, and horses. His ultimate choice of portraying a single buck, prominently

placed in the composition and majestically posed, is significant. Deer populated the American forests, their strong upper bodies and agile legs well suited to the dense, uneven forest terrain. Their close association with Native Americans (see Cooper, *The Last of the Mohicans*, among other examples in literature) reinforced their function as a symbol of the American wilderness, which existed prior to the arrival of the Europeans. This is clearly illustrated in Cole's later painting *The Course of Empire: The Savage State*, 1834 (New York Historical Society), the first of five paintings in this epic series. In this painting, Cole depicted a sublimely wild landscape in which men dressed in skins hunt deer. A powerfully built deer in the lower foreground bounds away from the archer, despite carrying one of his arrows. Here, man is a true threat to the deer and to the wilderness in which they live.

25 The comparison of the American wilderness to Eden was a prominent theme in American literature throughout the nineteenth century, as was the theme of natural religion. William Cullen Bryant's first great published poem, *Thanatopsis*, equates communing in nature with prayer: "Go forth, under the open sky, and list / To Nature's teaching, while from all around— / Earth and her waters, and the depths of the air— / Comes a still voice."

26 Parry, *The Art of Thomas Cole*, 205.

27 See Parry, *The Art of Thomas Cole*, for the most complete discussion of these.

28 In his landmark book *Studies in Iconology*, first published in 1939 by Oxford University Press, Erwin Panofsky described three levels of viewing art. The first is simple recognition of the subject matter; the second, called iconography, is the identification of certain artistic motifs having particular connections to themes, concepts, and ideas; and the third, called iconology, is the apprehension of "underlying principles which reveal the basic attitude of a nation, a period, a class, a religious or philosophical persuasion" (p. 30) and are conveyed nearly unconsciously by the artist.

29 Christopher Wright, *Poussin Paintings: A Catalogue Raisonne* (London: Jupiter Books Limited, 1984). In this comprehensive study, Wright discusses this change in the way the artist approached landscape painting and further links it to Poussin's use of pairs of paintings (pp. 99–100). H. Diane Russel discussed a similar interest on the part of Claude Lorrain, especially in his use of contrasting different times of day—through the use of paired images—to refer to both the linear and cyclical passage of time (*Claude Lorrain, 1600–1682* [New York: George Braziller, 1982]).

30 H. Diane Russel, *Claude Lorrain*, 84. Her discussion on this topic continues through p. 93.

31 Ibid., 88.

32 Ibid., 84.

33 See especially Cole's poems #48, #67, and #85. Marshall B. Tymn, ed., *Thomas Cole's Poetry* (York, PA: Liberty Cap Books, 1972), 113, 140, and 178.

34 Durand, "Letters," 210.

35 Ibid.

36 For more detail, refer to Ellen Lawrence's introduction to *1800–1874, European and American Landscape: To Look at Nature* (Providence, RI: Brown University Department of Art, 1972).

37 Helmut Borsch-Suppan, *Caspar David Friedrich* (New York: George Braziller, 1974), 142.

38 Novak, *Nature and Culture*, 255.

39 Borsch-Suppan, *Caspar David Friedrich*, 7.

40 Ibid., 72.

41 Ibid., 15.

42 Herwig Guratzsch, *Dutch and Flemish Painting* (New York: Vilo, 1981), 253.

43 For example, artists including Cole, Church, Bierstadt, Kensett, Gifford, Whittredge, Heade, Shattuck, and Homer worked together in the Tenth Street Studio building. See Annette Blaugrund, *The Tenth Street Studio Building: Artist-Entrepreneurs from the Hudson River School to the American Impressionists* (Seattle: University of Washington Press, 1997) for an excellent discussion of this subject.

44 Durand wrote that artists may choose to take what he referred to as the "license of Art," giving permission to "exaggerate certain points in order to represent their real importance," enhance light effects, eliminate "subordinate objects," and so on without opposing "any of the great truths of Nature," rather doing this in order to create a "more complete expression of the sentiment of Nature, material and spiritual, wherein we discern the true mission of art." Durand, "Letters," 16.

45 Ralph Waldo Emerson expressed this in his essay *Nature* (1836), chapter 4, "Language." In section 2, entitled "Particular natural facts are symbols of particular spiritual facts," he wrote, "It is not words only that are emblematic; it is things which are emblematic. Every natural fact is a symbol of some spiritual fact. Every appearance in nature corresponds to some state of the mind, and that state of the mind can only be described by presenting that natural appearance as its picture. An enraged man is a lion, a cunning man is a fox, a firm man is a rock, a learned man is a torch. A lamb is innocence; a snake is subtle spite; flowers express to us the delicate affections. Light and darkness are our familiar expression for knowledge and ignorance; and heat for love. Visible distance behind and before us, is respectively our image of memory and hope."

46 Barbara Novak compared the "sublimely awesome" landscape that frightened man to the "bovinely pastoral" that depicted man's cultivation of the land for his own prosperity and sustenance. Novak, *Nature and Culture*, 191.

47 Vehicles including such journals as the *Crayon* helped foster this general understanding. The *Crayon* was established in 1855 to link audiences, "art lovers to artists to writers." *Crayon* 1, no.1 (3 January 1855): 2.

48 These are discussed and illustrated in Parry pp.147–48. Each card measures 8 ? x 3 ? inches. Published as *Panoramacopia* (London: T.T. Dales, 1824).

49 Alan Wallach discussed this in his article "Thomas Cole's *River in the Catskills* as Antipastoral," *Art Bulletin* 84, no. 2 (2002): 345.

DIFFERENT VIEWS

1 Louis Legrand Noble, *The Life and Works of Thomas Cole*, ed. Elliot S. Vesell (Hensonville, NY: Black Dome Press, 1997).

2 John Driscoll, *All That Is Glorious Around Us: Paintings from the Hudson River School* (Ithaca, NY: Cornell University Press, 1997). Driscoll noted that the subject of Church's painting must be other than Baalbek, as the title indicates, which is an inland city, and is rather most likely a site along the Aegean, Mediterranean, or Black Sea, visited during a trip in 1867 (see p. 46).

3 Helmut Borsch-Suppan, *Caspar David Friedrich* (New York: George Braziller, 1974), 72.

4 Barbara Novak, *Nature and Culture: American Landscape and Painting*, 1825–1875 (New York: Oxford University Press, 1978), 190–91.

5 Franklin Kelly, "American Landscape Pairs of the 1850's," *Antiques* (November 1994): 654.

6 Thomas Cole, "Essay on American Scenery," *American Monthly* 1 (January 1836).

7 Inscribed directly on verso are the words: "Painted for _ H. Hubbard by her uncle Richard W. Hubbard, NA wedding present Nov. 21st 1877 Brooklyn, Fifty Lexington Street."

8 Asher B. Durand, "Letters on Landscape Painting," *Crayon* 1, letter 1 (3 January 1855): 2.

9 Durand, "Letters," *Crayon* 1, letter 3 (31 January 1855): 66.

10 Benjamin Champney authored a charming memoir, *Sixty Years' Memories of Art and Artists* (*The Art Experience in Late Nineteenth-Century America*) (Woburn MA: Wallace & Andrews, 1900), in which he recalled his painting excursions and those of other artists, including Kensett and Casilear, around the vicinity of North Conway. See also John J. Henderson's exhibition catalog *Incomparable Scenery, Comparative Views in the White Mountains* (Laconia, NH: Glen-Bartlett, 1999) for information on Champney and the White Mountain painters.

11 Novak, *Nature and Culture*, 196.

12 Attached to verso of Smith's painting is this letter to the history painter Peter Frederick Rothermel (1817–1895):

> Weldon, Montgomery Co., Pa.
> Dec. 3rd 1883
>
> My Dear Mr. Rothermel,
> Being now old and a good deal used up with my neuralgia, I cannot hope to make much more use of my numerous sketches and studies from Nature; and I decided lately to give to each of the members of the Artists Fund Society a specimen as a token of my respect for my brother painters. The distribution came off on Thursday last: I have learned, however, that you, like myself, are no longer considered a member and as it would never do to leave you out in a token of respect, I hope you will accept the sketch I send with this as evidence of my long established esteem.
>
> With all good wishes appropriate to the season for you and all dear to you I am,
>
> Truly yours,
> Russell Smith

13 A critic from the *New York Daily Tribune* (1861) quoted by Theodore E. Stebbins Jr. in *The Life and Works of Martin Johnson Heade* (New Haven: Yale University Press, 1975), 69. Stebbins noted that Heade must have been familiar with Hamilton's work and interested in the artist's ability to paint "breaking waves, dark seas, and dramatic sunsets over flat horizons—all elements that had relevance for Heade at the time."

14 Virginia E. Lewis, *Russell Smith: Romantic Realist* (Pittsburgh: University of Pittsburgh Press, 1956).

15 *Foundry at Cold Spring*, oil on canvas, 19 _ x 27 _ inches, private collection, illustrated #42. John K. Howat, *The Hudson River School and Its Painters* (New York: American Legacy Press, 1983). Howat notes that Johnson's painting shows improvements to a small church near the foundry made in 1867, dating his painting after that year.

16 A note written in ink directly on verso of this painting describes the mill and states that it was no longer standing in 1868, twenty years after Grunewald painted it, but that the giant oak still survived. The author of the letter, the son of the former mill owner, had traveled with Grunewald on foot in 1848 from Bethlehem to his parents' sawmill in Pike County.

17 The art dealer, Patrick Orbe, notes that Hugh Bolton Jones painted a larger version of this subject (whereabouts unknown).

18 According to the records of the Albany Institute of Art, which once owned this painting, these were views of Lake George exhibited at the Young Men's Association in Troy, New York (1861), and at the Utica (New York) Mechanics' Association (1864). It is unclear whether either of these paintings was the current view.

19 Driscoll, *All That Is Glorious*, 130.

20 We know that Gignoux exhibited this sampler in 1861 at the Brooklyn Art Association, when he was president of the association. He also created a printed flyer entitled "American Scenery," which described each of the nine paintings then contained in the sampler, further enhancing its promotion.

21 Thomas Cole, "Essay on American Scenery." N. P. Willis used the same phrase for his book of landscape images by W. H. Bartlett entitled *American Scenery; or, Land, Lake, River: Illustrations of a Transatlantic Nature* (London: George Virtue, 1840).

SUGGESTED FURTHER READINGS

American Paintings from the Manoogian Collection. Washington, DC: National Gallery of Art; Detroit: Detroit Institute of Art, 1989.

American Paradise: The World of the Hudson River School. New York: The Metropolitan Museum of Art, 1988.

Appalachian Landscapes: With Naturalistic Eyes. Emil R. Weiss Center for the Arts, Dickinson College, Carlisle, PA, September 23–November 4, 1989.

Avery, Kevin J., et al. *Hudson River School Visions: The Landscapes of Sanford R. Sanford.* New York and New Haven: The Metropolitan Museum of Art and Yale University Press, 2003.

Belle, Adrienne. *George Inness and the Visionary Landscape.* New York: George Braziller, 2003.

Blaugrund, Annette. *The Tenth Street Studio Building: Artist-Entrepreneurs from the Hudson River School to the American Impressionists.* Seattle, WA: University of Washington Press, 1997.

Borsch-Suppan, Helmut. *Casper David Friedrich.* New York: George Braziller, 1974.

Carr, Gerald L. *In Search of the Promised Land: Paintings by Frederic Edwin Church.* Hanover, NH: University Press of New England, 2001.

Cole, Thomas. "Essay on American Scenery." *American Monthly,* 1 January 1836.

Cooper, J. Fenimore. *A Landscape Book, by American Artists and American Authors.* New York: G. P. Putnam & Son, 1868.

Davidson, Marshall. *The Artists' America.* New York: American Heritage, 1973.

Driscoll, John. *All That Is Glorious Around Us: Paintings from the Hudson River School.* Ithaca, NY: Cornell University Press, 1997.

Durand, Asher B. "Letters on Landscape Painting." *Crayon,* January 1855.

Guratzsch, Herwig. *Dutch and Flemish Painting.* NY: Vilo, 1981.

Huth, Hans. *Nature and the American: Three Centuries of Changing Attitudes.* Lincoln, NE: University of Nebraska Press, 1957.

Kelly, Franklin. "American Landscape Pairs of the 1850's." *Antiques,* November 1994.

Keyes, Donald. *The White Mountains: Place and Perceptions.* Durham: University Art Galleries, University of New Hampshire, 1980.

Kornhauser, Elizabeth Mankin, and Amy Ellis, with Maureen Miesmer. *Hudson River School: Masterworks from the Wadsworth Atheneum Museum of Art.* New Haven: Yale University Press, 2003.

Marx, Leo. *The Machine in the Garden.* New York: Oxford University Press, 1964.

Miller, Angela. *The Empire of the Eye: Landscape Representation and American Cultural Politics, 1825–1875.* Ithaca, NY: Cornell University Press, 1993.

Miller, David, ed. *American Iconology: New Approaches to Nineteenth Century American Art and Literature.* New Haven: Yale University Press, 1993.

Miller, Perry G. E. *The Life of the Mind in America: From the Revolution to the Civil War.* New York: Harcourt, Brace & World, 1965.

Myers, Kenneth. *The Catskills: Painters, Writers and Tourists in the Mountains.* Yonkers, NY: Hudson River Museum of Westchester, 1987.

Noble, Louis Legrand. *The Life and Works of Thomas Cole.* Ed. Elliot S. Vesell. Hensonville, NY: Black Dome Press, 1997.

Novak, Barbara. *Nature and Culture: American Landscape and Painting, 1825–1875.* New York: Oxford University Press, 1978.

Nygren, Edward, and Bruce Robertson. *Views and Visions: American Landscape before 1830.* Washington, DC: The Corcoran Gallery of Art, 1986.

Panofsky, Irwin. *Meaning in the Visual Arts.* Garden City, NJ: Doubleday, 1955.

Parry, Ellwood C., III. *The Art of Thomas Cole: Ambition and Imagination.* Newark: University of Delaware Press, 1988.

Russell, Diane. *Claude Lorrain, 1600–1682.* George Braziller, 1982.

Stebbins, Theodore E., Jr. *The Life and Works of Martin Johnson Heade.* New Haven: Yale University Press, 1975.

The Susquehanna: Visions of Solitude. Lancaster, PA: Heritage Center Museum of Lancaster County, 1995.

Sweet, Frederick A. *The Hudson River School and the Early American Landscape Tradition.* New York: Whitney Museum of American Art, 1945.

Truettner, William, and Allan Wallach. *Thomas Cole: Landscape into History.* New Haven: Yale University Press, 1994.

Tuckerman, Henry. *Book of Artists.* New York: James F. Carr, 1996.

Tymn, Marshall. *Thomas Cole's Poetry.* York, PA: Liberty Cap Books, 1972.

Van Zandt, Roland. *The Catskill Mountain House.* New Brunswick, NJ: Rutgers University Press, 1966.

Wallach, Alan. "Thomas Cole's *River in the Catskills* as Antipastoral." *Art Bulletin* 84, no. 2 (2002).

Weinberg, Barbara H. *The Art Experience in Late Nineteenth-Century America.* New York and London: Garland Publishing, 1976.

Willis, Nathaniel Parker. *American Scenery; or Land, Lake, and River: Illustrations of Transatlantic Nature.* London: George Virtue, 1840.

Wilton, Andrew, and Tim Barringer. *American Sublime: Landscape Painting in the United States, 1820–1880.* London: Tate Publishing, 2002.

Wright, Christopher. *Poussin Paintings: A Catalogue Raisonne.* London: Jupiter Books Limited, 1984.

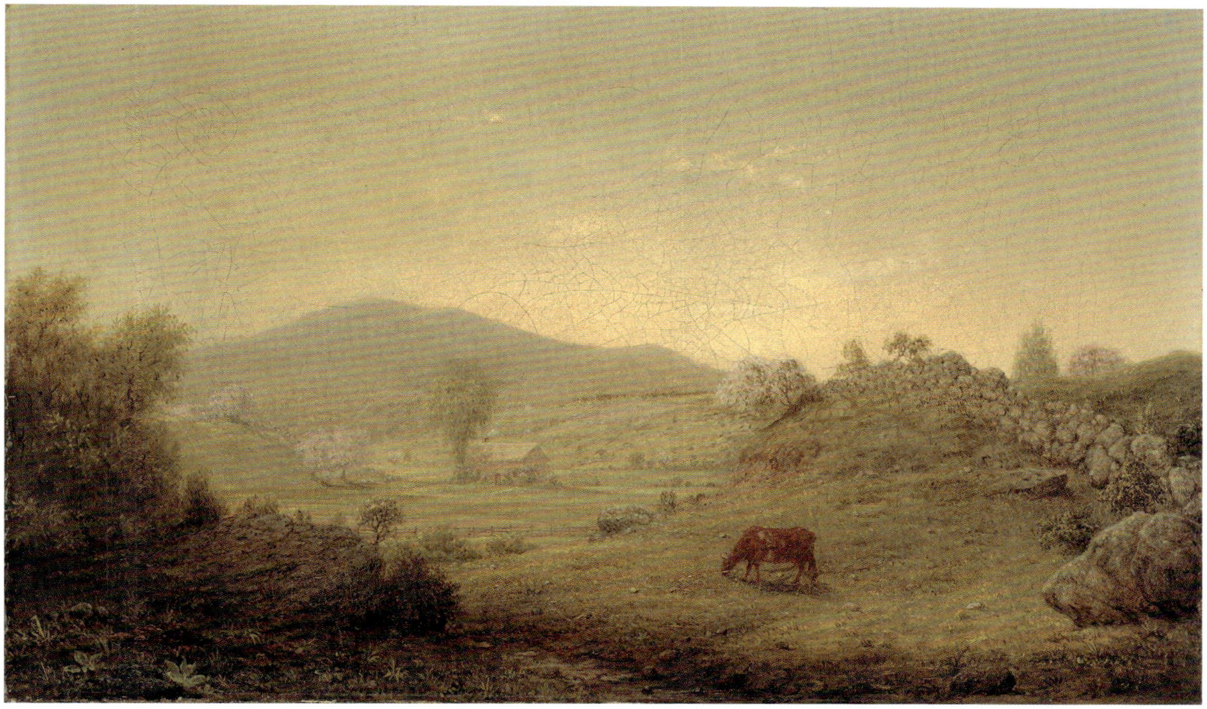

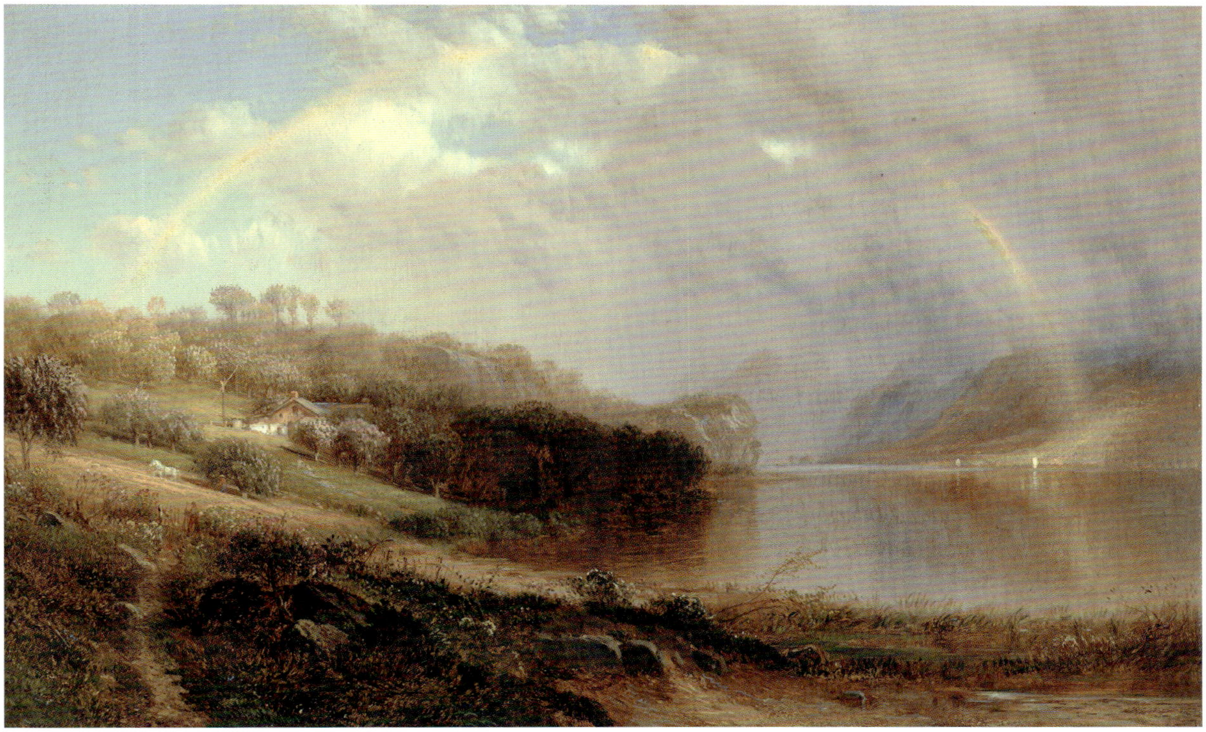

Martin Johnson Heade (1819–1904)
Springtime in Connecticut, 1867
Oil on canvas, 15 1/4 x 25 1/4 inches

Samuel Colman (1832–1920)
Rainbow on the Hudson, n.d.
Oil on canvas, 12 x 20 inches

PAINTINGS

Alfred Fitch Bellows (1829–1883)
Down to the Brook, 1863
Oil on canvas, 28 x $47\frac{1}{2}$ inches
35

Albert Fitch Bellows
The Mill, 1861
Oil on canvas, $14\frac{1}{4}$ x 11 inches
(arched at the top)
100

Thomas Birch (1779–1851)
Five Landscape Vignettes, n.d.
Oil on board, $9\frac{7}{16}$ x 13 inches
57

Henry Boese (1824–1863)
Spring View of Newburgh on the Hudson, n.d.
Oil on canvas, $6\frac{1}{2}$ x 11 inches
63

Henry Boese
Autumn View of Newburgh on the Hudson, n.d.
Oil on canvas, $6\frac{1}{2}$ x 11 inches
63

Henry Boese
Autumn Landscape, n. d.
Oil on canvas, $13\frac{1}{4}$ x $23\frac{1}{2}$ inches
97

DeWitt Clinton Boutelle (1820–1884)
Sunset, n.d.
Oil on canvas board, 26 x 36 inches
43

DeWitt Clinton Boutelle
Artist Sketching, 1862
Oil on canvas, $20\frac{3}{4}$ inches (tondo)
93

DeWitt Clinton Boutelle
Two Boys Fishing, 1867
Oil on canvas, 12 x $10\frac{1}{4}$ inches
96

DeWitt Clinton Boutelle
Niagara Falls, 1861
Oil on canvas, $12\frac{1}{2}$ x 16 inches
139

Alfred Thompson Bricher (1837–1908)
Lake George, 1863
Oil on canvas, 7 x 12 inches
133

Harrison Bird Brown (1831–1915)
Leaf Picnic, n.d.
Oil on canvas, 18 x 14 inches
123

William Mason Brown (1828–1898)
The Bridge, c. 1850-60
Oil on canvas, 10 x 14 inches
123

John Herman Carmiencke (1810–1867)
Catskill Clove, 1863
Oil on canvas, 16 x 24 inches
91

John William Casilear (1811–1893)
Quiet River (Genesee), 1874
Oil on canvas, 14 x 23 inches
51

John William Casilear
Genesee River Scenery, 1873
Oil on canvas, $9\frac{1}{2}$ x 20 inches
51

John William Casilear
Autumn Landscape with Fisherman, c. 1865–1870
Oil on canvas, 10 x $12\frac{1}{4}$ inches
95

John William Casilear
Lake George, c. 1865
Oil on canvas, 15 x 25 inches
135

John William Casilear
Niagara Falls, 1872
Oil on canvas, 13 x 23 inches
140

Benjamin Champney (1817–1907)
Woodland Interior, 1880
Oil on canvas, 20 x 16 inches
74

Benjamin Champney
Ausable Chasm, n.d.
Oil on canvas, 21 x 17 inches
109

Benjamin Champney
Harvest Scene, Conway Valley, 1870
Oil on canvas, $10\frac{1}{2}$ x $18\frac{1}{2}$ inches
120

Charles H. Chapin (1830–1889)
Deer, 1870
Oil on canvas, $10\frac{1}{4}$ x 20 inches
87

Frederic Church (1826–1900)
Ruins at Baalbek, 1868
Oil on canvas, $21\frac{3}{4}$ x $36\frac{1}{4}$ inches
23

Thomas Cole (1801–1848)
Sunset on the Arno, 1837
Oil on canvas, 35 x $51\frac{1}{4}$ inches
23

Samuel Colman Jr. (1832–1920)
Harvest Scene, n.d.
Oil on canvas, 10 x 17 inches
121

Edith Wilkinson Cook (active 1851–1875)
Golden Landscape, 1867
Oil on canvas, $7\frac{1}{8}$ x $14\frac{1}{8}$ inches
125

Jasper Francis Cropsey (1823–1900)
On the Susquehanna, 1877
Oil on canvas, 12 x $17\frac{1}{2}$ inches
41

Jasper Francis Cropsey
Lake George, 1877
Oil on canvas, $12\frac{1}{4}$ x 10 inches
135

Asher Brown Durand (1796–1886)
Woodland Interior, c. 1855
Oil on canvas, 20 x 16 inches
73

Max Eglau (1825—?)
Imaginary Landscape, n.d.
Oil on canvas, $20\frac{1}{2}$ x $32\frac{1}{2}$ inches
110

Max Eglau
Hunter in a Landscape, n.d.
Oil on canvas, $28\frac{1}{2}$ x $36\frac{1}{4}$ inches
111

James Fairman (1826–1904)
Haying Scene, n.d.
Oil on canvas, 6 x 10 inches
119

Henry Augustus Ferguson (1845–1911)
Sunset, Lake George, c. 1860
Oil on canvas, 10 x 18 inches
137

Alvan Fisher (1792–1863)
Fishing in New Hampshire, 1852
Oil on canvas, $27^1/_4$ x $22^1/_4$ inches
98

Alvan Fisher
Hunters in a Landscape, c. 1830
Oil on canvas, 24 x 20 inches
113

Alvan Fisher
Hunters in a Stream with Dog, c. 1830
Oil on canvas, 24 x 20 inches
112

William Charles Anthony Frerichs
(1829–1905)
White Face Mountain, North Carolina
c. 1855–1860
Oil on canvas, 11 x $21^1/_2$ inches
71

William Charles Anthony Frerichs
Wilderness Scene with Falls (North Carolina)
c. 1855-60
Oil on canvas, 11 x $21^1/_2$ inches
71

Hermann Fuechsel (1833–1915)
Cows in the Hudson River, c. 1875
Oil on canvas, 10 x 20 inches
37

Hermann Fuechsel
Kaaterskill and Haines Falls, c. 1865–1875
Oil on canvas, $14^3/_4$ x 12 inches
84

Sanford Robinson Gifford (1823–1880)
A Lake Twilight, 1861
Oil on canvas, 16 x 28 inches
79

Regis Francois Gignoux (1816–1882)
Heading Home, n.d.
Oil on canvas, $24^1/_2$ x 35 inches
43

Regis Francis Gignoux
American Scenery Sampler, c. 1861
Oil on canvas, 20 x 36 inches
149

Eliza Greatorex (1820–1897)
Landscape Near Cragsmoor, NY, 1863
Oil on canvas, 15 x 25 inches
39

Samuel W. Griggs (1827–1898)
Cows on a Bridge, Autumn, n.d.
Oil on canvas, $12^1/_4$ x $9^1/_4$ inches
123

Daniel Charles Grose (active circa
1865–1890)
Autumn on the Whissahickon, n.d.
Oil on canvas, 18 x 12 inches
65

Daniel Charles Grose
Spring on the Whissahickon, n.d.
Oil on canvas, 18 x 12 inches
65

Gustavus Johann Grunewald (1805–1878)
Winter Fishing on a Lake at the
Pine Swamp, 1856
Oil on panel, 20 x $15^7/_8$ inches
99

Gustavus Johann Grunewald,
Pike County, Pennsylvania, Saw Mill, 1848
Oil on panel, $9^{11}/_{16}$ x $12^3/_{16}$ inches
129

James Hamilton (1819–1878)
In the Salt Marshes of N. J., 1872
Oil on canvas, 20 x $29^1/_2$ inches
106

James McDougal Hart (1828–1901)
Mountain Falls, n.d.
Oil on canvas, 15 x 10 inches
29

James McDougal Hart
Conversation by the River, n.d.
Oil on canvas, 15 x 10 inches
29

James McDougal Hart
On the Farmington River, 1862
Oil on canvas, 19 x 32 inches
39

William McDougal Hart (1823–1894)
Sunset in the Valley, 1870
Oil on canvas, 14 x $23^1/_2$ inches
41

William McDougal Hart
A View of the Esopus Creek in Autumn, 1864
Oil on canvas, 9 x 17 inches
64

William McDougal Hart
A View of the Esopus Creek in Spring, n.d.
Oil on canvas, 9 x 17 inches
64

William McDougal Hart (1823–1894)
A Forest Stream, 1875
Oil on canvas, $17^1/_4$ x 15 inches
77

William McDougal Hart
Mount Washington, 1861
Oil on canvas, $6^1/_2$ x $10^1/_4$ inches
145

Gunther Hartwick (active 1847-57)
Landscape with Farm, 1854
Oil on canvas, 25 x 30 inches
35

Martin Johnson Heade (1819–1904)
White Mountain Landscape,
Mount Washington, 1871
Oil on canvas, 9 x $15^1/_2$ inches
145

Joseph Antonio Hekking (1830–1903)
Cows Watering in a Summer Landscape, c.
1870
Oil on canvas, 20 x 36 inches
37

Joseph Antonio Hekking
Summer Landscape with Cows Watering, n.d.
Oil on canvas, 9 x 15 inches
67

Joseph Antonio Hekking
Autumn Landscape with Deer and Ducks
on River, n.d.
Oil on canvas, 9 x 15 inches
67

Herman Herzog (1832–1932)
Man Hunting (Western Landscape), 1871
Oil on canvas, $13^1/_2$ x $20^1/_2$ inches
116

Herman Herzog
Mill with Raging Torrent [Sutter's Mill]
c. 1870
Oil on canvas, 19 x 27 inches
117

Thomas Hill (1829–1908)
Niagara Falls, c. 1860
Oil on canvas, 10½ x 8½ inches
138

Thomas Hiram Hotchkiss (1834–1869)
Harvest Scene, 1858
Oil on canvas¼ x 12 inches
121

Richard William Hubbard (1816–1888)
Mount Holyoke Looking Toward Connecticut River, 1877
Oil on artist's board, 15 x 12½ inches
52

Richard William Hubbard
Landscape with Cows, 1879
Oil on canvas, 13 x 12¼ inches
53

David Johnson (1827–1908)
Sunset in New Rochelle, n.d.
Oil on canvas, 12 x 16 inches
102

Hugh Bolton Jones (1848–1927)
Foundry [the Old Smelter], 1876
Oil on canvas, 8 x 14¼ inches
129

John Frederick Kensett (1818–1872)
Mount Chocorua, 1857
Oil on canvas, 14½ x 24 inches
30

John Frederick Kensett
Reminiscences of the Catskill Mountains, 1853
Oil on canvas, 22½ x 18¼ inches
31

John Frederick Kensett
Sunset over the Catskills, 1855
Oil on canvas, 18 x 25 inches
32

Charles W. Knapp (1823–1900)
Artist Sketching, n.d.
Oil on canvas, 29 x 24 inches
90

Alexander Lawrie (1828–1917)
Cold Springs on Hudson, 1871
Oil on canvas, 10¼ x 20¼ inches
47

Edmund Darch Lewis (1835–1910)
Lake George, n.d.
Oil on metal, 6⅛ x 12 inches
133

Charles Linford (1846–1897)
Woodland Interior with Stream, n.d.
Oil on canvas, 22 x 16 inches
75

Charles Loeffler (active in New York, mid–1850s)
Foundry at Cold Spring, n. d.
Oil on canvas, 15½ x 29½ inches
129

Ernest Lotichius (1840–1874)
Deer in the Morning Mist, 1858
Oil on canvas, 10½ x 14 inches
81

Clinton Loveridge (1824–1902)
Spring Landscape, n.d
Oil on artist's board, 7¾ x 13¾ inches
58

Clinton Loveridge
Autumn Landscape, n.d
Oil on artist's board, 7¾ x 13¾ inches
58

Clinton Loveridge
Fall on a Lake in New England, c. 1870
Oil on canvas, 6½ x 12½ inches
59

Clinton Loveridge
Farm Scene with Cows, c. 1870
Oil on canvas, 6½ x 12½ inches
59

Clinton Loveridge
Spring Landscape with Cows, n.d.
Oil on canvas, 9 x 14 inches
61

Clinton Loveridge
Autumn Landscape with Cows, n.d.
Oil on canvas, 9 x 14 inches
61

Clinton Loveridge
Evening Sunset, 1877
Oil on wood panel, 9 x 7 inches
107

Homer Dodge Martin (1836–1897)
Saranac Lake [morning], 1857
Oil on canvas, 18 x 32 inches
27

Homer Dodge Martin
Saranac Lake [evening], 1857
Oil on canvas, 18 x 32 inches
27

William Sanford Mason (1824–1864)
View of Columbia, 1855
Oil on canvas, 22 x 30 inches
92

Jervis McEntee (1828–1891)
Indian Summer, 1862
Oil on canvas, 10 x 18 inches
103

William Rickarby Miller (1818–1893)
Haying Scene, n.d.
Oil on canvas, 7½ x 9½ inches
119

Nelson Augustus Moore (1824–1902)
Lake George, n.d.
Oil on canvas, 9 x 14½ inches
134

Edward Moran (1829–1901)
Wings of the Evening, c. 1870
Oil on canvas, 10½ x 18 inches
105

Joseph Morviller (1800–1870)
Autumn Landscape, 1860
Oil on canvas, 14 x 25 inches
94

James Northcote (1822–1904)
Niagara Falls at Night, 1863
Oil on canvas, 8 x 14 inches
141

Arthur Parton (1842–1914)
On the Hudson, 1879
Oil on canvas, 12¼ x 20 inches
47

William Trost Richards (1833–1905)
Sampler, c. 1860
Oil on thirteen canvases mounted together
148

Frederick Rondel (1826–1892)
Adirondack Landscape, c. 1876
Oil on canvas, 8 x 10 inches
82

Thomas Prichard Rossiter (1818–1871)
Niagara Falls, 1858
Oil on canvas, $13^1/_2$ x 24 inches
141

Junius R. Sloan (1827–1900)
Autumn Landscape (with view of Catskill Mountain House), c. 1866
Oil on canvas, $11^3/_4$ x 10 inches
125

Henry Pember Smith (1854–1907)
Man Fishing along a Stream, 1884
Oil on canvas, $15^1/_4$ x $12^1/_4$ inches
101

Russell Smith (1812–1896)
Pennypack, 1880
Oil on canvas, 12 x 18 inches
105

Russell Smith
Autumn on the Susquehanna, n.d.
Oil on canvas, 11 x 14 inches
127

Russell Smith
The Old Mill, n.d.
Oil on canvas, 11 x 14 inches
127

James Augustus Suydam (1819–1865)
Sunset Landscape, n.d.
Oil on canvas, $7^5/_8$ x $6^1/_4$ inches
26

James Brade Sword (1839–1915)
Lake George, 1873
Oil on canvas, 18 x 30 inches
137

Arthur Fitzwilliam Tait (1819–1905)
Deer in Nature, 1869
Oil on canvas, 8 x 10 inches
81

Gottlieb Daniel Paul Weber (1823–1916)
Summer Landscape, 1861
Oil on canvas, 14 x 19 inches
48

Gottlieb Daniel Paul Weber
Haying Scene, 1863
Oil on canvas, 14 x 20 inches
49

Paul Weber (1823–1916)
Mount Washington from the Saco, 1854
Oil on canvas, $25^1/_2$ x 37 inches
143

Thomas Worthington Whittredge (1820–1910)
Deer by a Waterfall, 1850
Oil on canvas, $20^1/_2$ x $16^1/_2$ inches
85

Laura Woodward (active 1872–1889)
Adirondack Woodland with Deer, 1876
Oil on canvas, 24 x 18 inches
83

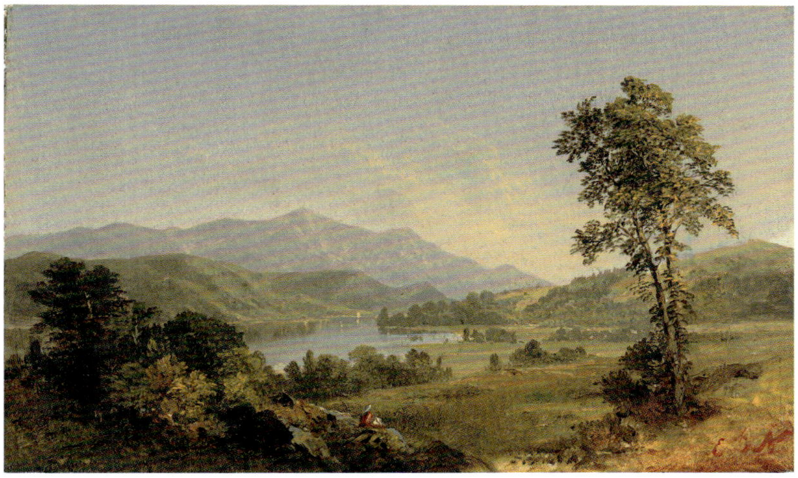

Edward Nichols (1819–1871)
Landscape, n.d.
Oil on canvas, $7^1/_2$ x 12 inches

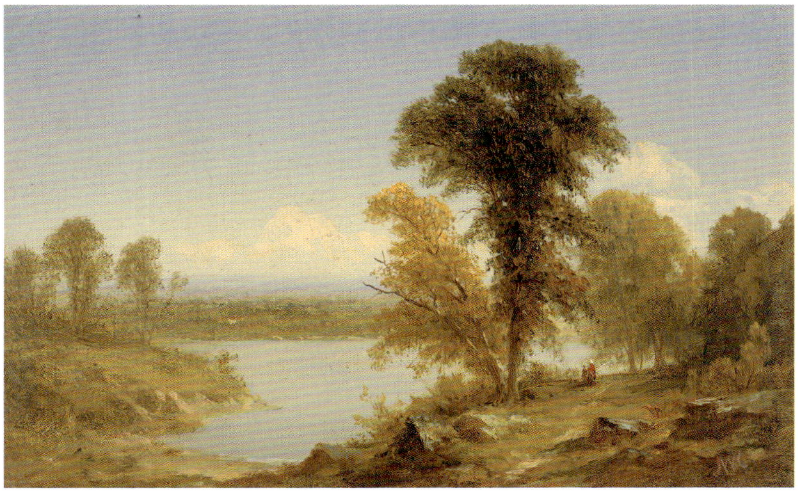

J. W. Casilear (1811–1893)
Landscape, n.d.
Oil on canvas, $6^1/_4$ x 10 inches

ACKNOWLEDGMENTS

There is no adequate means of conveying the profound generosity of the anonymous collector of these paintings, revealed to me and to many others—including scholars, collectors, curators, museum directors, dealers, and friends—with whom he sensed a common sensibility and passion for the artists of the Hudson River School. This text could not have been written without the benefit of his keen intuitive and deep scholarly knowledge. Having gathered these paintings by both the great names and the not-so-well-remembered ones of this nearly century-long movement, his greatest interest is in sharing them with as many individuals and as broad a public as can be reached. It is my very great privilege to have worked with such a learned and passionate gentleman.

John Driscoll, colleague and friend, first introduced me to the charms of the Hudson River School. His work on the first exhibition and two versions of the catalog *All That Is Glorious Around Us* provided the groundwork for this current work, to which he generously gave his blessing and encouragement.

I am indebted to many colleagues but would like to especially note the work of a few. Christine Oaklander, curator at the Allentown Art Museum, arranged *All That Is Glorious Around Us* according to common themes, when the exhibition was mounted at that museum. John Henderson's exhibition and catalog *Incomparable Scenery: Comparative Views in the White Mountains* (1999) paired paintings by artists of the White Mountain school. Franklin Kelly's article in *Antiques* entitled "American Landscape Pairs of the 1850's" (1994) served as an important precedent and model. Barbara Novak's landmark book *Nature and Culture: American Landscape and Painting, 1825–1875* (1995) has inspired many who study the Hudson River School, including me. Peter Bakal, director of Cedar Grove in 2003, was a generous guide during my visit to the Catskills and especially to Kaaterskill Falls.

An anonymous foundation in Pittsburgh afforded me the time and opportunity to do the research necessary for this project through a program supporting sabbatical leave for full-time senior administrators in the not-for-profit sector, similar to that extended to our colleagues in academe. I am immensely grateful to the foundation for recognizing the need for us to have the time to return to what first inspired us to enter our disciplines—in my case, looking at, reading, and writing about art and artists.

The board of trustees, led by Dr. Jack Smith, and staff of the Westmoreland Museum of American Art were unhesitatingly supportive of my sabbatical time and of myriad aspects of this project. Their investment in this endeavor is immeasurable. I am indebted to the collaboration of Barbara Jones, enthusiasm of Amy Baldonieri, and encouragement of Judy Ross. I also thank Janet Carns for her technical support, Doug Evans for his knowledge of this collection, and P. J. Zimmerlink for his keen interest in the project. Several interns—especially Gretchen Stickle, Jessica Golden, and Chad Gabersek—provided valuable assistance. While being grateful for the opportunity to return to the role of curator, I have reaffirmed my love for the multifaceted work I do as a museum director.

Seton Hill University gave me office space during the summer of 1993. Dear friends who listened to my theories and responded to my thoughts include Diane Samuels and Henry Reese. My father, Chadwick Hansen, patiently read and commented on many versions of the manuscript; he and my mother, Betty Jane, are a constant inspiration. Richard Stoner photographed all the paintings for this book with care. Arnold Skolnick of Chameleon Books was a passionate taskmaster who rose to the challenge of designing this book with remarkable results. Jamie Thaman was a patient and thorough editor.

This has been a labor of love that I dedicate to my husband, Kevin, and my daughters, Sarah and Rachel. And to Barbara, whose gift made this and so much else possible.

J. H. O'T

All paintings from a private collection.

All photography by Richard Stoner.